THE JEWS AND GERMANS
IN HAMBURG

Based on more than thirty years archival research, this history of the Jewish and German-Jewish community of Hamburg is a unique and vivid piece of work by one of the leading historians of the twentieth century. The history of the Holocaust here is fully integrated into the full history of the Jewish community in Hamburg from the late eighteenth century onwards. J. A. S. Grenville draws on a vast quantity of diaries, letters and records to provide a macro-level history of Hamburg interspersed with many personal stories that bring it vividly to life. In the concluding chapter the discussion is widened to talk about Hamburg as a case study in the wider world.

This book will be a key work in European history, charting and explaining the complexities of how a long-established and well-integrated German-Jewish community became, within the space of a generation, victims of the Nazi Holocaust.

J. A. S. Grenville was Professor of Modern History, Emeritus, at the University of Birmingham. He is the author of a number of books, including *Europe Reshaped, 1848–1878* (2000) and *The History of the World from the 20th to 21st Centuries* (Routledge, 2005), and co-editor of *The Major International Treaties of the Twentieth Century: A History and Guide with Texts* (Routledge, 2001).

THE JEWS AND GERMANS IN HAMBURG

The destruction of a civilization 1790–1945

J. A. S. Grenville

Routledge
Taylor & Francis Group

LONDON AND NEW YORK

First published 2012
by Routledge
2 Park Square, Milton Park, Abingdon, Oxon OX14 4RN

Simultaneously published in the USA and Canada
by Routledge
711 Third Avenue, New York, NY 10017

Routledge is an imprint of the Taylor & Francis Group, an informa business

British Library Cataloguing in Publication Data
A catalogue record for this book is available from the British Library

Library of Congress Cataloging in Publication Data
Grenville, J. A. S. (John Ashley Soames), 1928–
Jews and Germans in Hamburg: the destruction of a civilization
1790–1945 / J.A.S. Grenville.
   p. cm.
   Includes bibliographical references.
   1. Jews—Germany—Hamburg—History. 2. Jews—Germany—Hamburg—
   Social conditions—19th century. 3. Jews—Germany—Hamburg—Social
   conditions—20th century 4. Jews—Persecutions—Germany—Hamburg—
   History—20th century. 5. Holocaust, Jewish (1939–1945)—Germany—
   Hamburg. 6. Hamburg (Germany)—Ethnic relations. I.
   Title.
   DS134.34. G74 2011
   940.53′180943515—dc22   2011008331

ISBN: 978-0-415-66585-8 (hbk)
ISBN: 978-0-415-66586-5 (pbk)

Typeset in Times New Roman
by Book Now Ltd, London

MIX
Paper from
responsible sources
FSC® C004839
www.fsc.org

Printed and bound in Great Britain by
TJ International Ltd, Padstow, Cornwall

In memoriam Werner Jochmann

CONTENTS

PREFACE

'Be glad you are a German', was the essay set for the leaving class of Hamburg's orthodox *Talmud Tora Schule*, reflecting how the great majority of Jews felt before the First World War. So why exclude German in the title of the book? Were not the German Jews Germans too, as they passionately asserted? But that does not alter the feelings of the great majority of Germans who regarded them as 'other', as not part of the German *Volk* or fully integrated in a multicultural nation. Some scholars have tried to rectify this wrong, referring to 'Germans and their Fellow Citizens'. Yet the generations of German Jews living in the decades before the First World War had good reasons for looking to the future with confidence. Should we simply assert then with hindsight that their feelings were misguided? They had settled for centuries in the German lands and over generations had come a long way to integrate in society. Was there before 1914 anywhere in Europe which held out more promise for the Jews to better themselves?

When they looked back on the achievements of past generations they believed they could face the future with confidence that, over time, prejudices would diminish and that any lingering discrimination would disappear. They were a cultured, integrated and prosperous Jewish community, and nowhere more so than in Hamburg. They were aware of, and did not ignore, the latent antisemitism, but when they looked at the lives of Jews elsewhere they felt they were fortunate to be living in Germany, a land of refuge for the persecuted. Their advance in society had been attained by working in harmony with gentiles. Should then the Holocaust cast its shadow over the whole of the past? Yet it is as futile to place a wall around the Nazi years as to assert that they were predestined from the start.

To understand the times and to answer the question how a society can lapse into barbarism, we need to begin our account not with Hitler but a century earlier, before he dominated the lives of Jews and gentiles, when seemingly well-established traditions were destroyed. What has been lacking is a 'complete' history of German Jews and Germans from earlier times to the Holocaust.

It is possible to write a distinctive history of one Jewish community, actually the largest in Germany early in the century, during the century before the First World War. The lives of the Jews of Hamburg were determined by the Christian elites of the city-state. The senate, the government of Hamburg, elected by a narrow privileged franchise, took pride in offering good government for Jew and gentile, though giving in from time to time to the anti-Jewish pressure of the clergy and the ignorant mob. By the mid-nineteenth century Jews played a prominent and beneficent role in the culture, politics and commerce of the city-state.

The unification of Germany made a big impact on Hamburg's economy and social fabric but left the undemocratic political paternalistic structure in place. The decades of slow and hesitant political reforms were, paradoxically, also the most fortunate years for the Jews. They are recounted in the first chapter. The monarchy had allowed Jews to live in safety and growing prosperity; democracy proved to be the prelude to their destruction.

A deeply divided republic replaced the Wilhelmine Empire after the First World War. The existence of the monarchy had been a guarantee of the upholding of the *Rechtsstaat*, the Prussian tradition of the supremacy of the law safeguarding the liberties of all, including the Jews. The constitution of the Weimar Republic removed the remaining discrimination, but would it be strong enough to survive, and what would take its place if it succumbed?

Assaulted by extremist groups and under the shadow of the Nazis, the Republic fell into a state of paralysis during its closing years. The democrats and the Jews had fought an unequal struggle which they had already lost two years before Hitler came to power. Remarkable, nevertheless, was the strong resistance in Hamburg, Prussia and throughout Germany by a sizeable minority and their assertion of decent traditions. That too deserves to be recorded and not forgotten. But no region could hold out against Hitler's control of the *Reich*.

In 1933, the relationship between the city-state of Hamburg and the *Reich* changed fundamentally. Hamburg's democratic structures quickly vanished. New relationships were formed between Hamburg's masters, the bureaucracy, the people and the *Reich*. The Jews too had to adjust their own institutional relationships. The history of these times could therefore no longer focus on Hamburg alone. The lives and fate of the Jews of Hamburg were now determined to a diminishing degree by the new local Nazi rulers, though vestiges of local influences remained. Strong personalities in Hamburg, however, preserved a surprising degree of independence in Jewish affairs, though national Jewish institutions were established in 1933 to meet the Nazi challenge.

The question generations have grappled with is how a once civilized society could have descended to pitiless inhumanity in so short a time. Younger Germans are not concerned so much with the details of decision making as with trying to understand the lives of their parents and grandparents. How far had they adjusted to Nazi requirements of conformity? Did they not realise what was happening to the Jews? Jewish descendants also ask why their forbears were so blind and did not leave earlier while there was still time? We can address these questions and gain fresh insights by looking at contemporary lives, how individuals accommodated themselves to the turbulent times, rather than trying to generalise about *the* Germans, *the* Jews or even *the* Nazis. The people in this book lived in Hamburg, but their behaviour was not unique to one city. The focus on one place, and time, provides a truer reflection of attitudes than plucking illustrations from different regions to substantiate conclusions often already reached. Each region claims it was different during the Nazi years, and Hamburg is no exception in this regard. That is not to deny differences between regions or of life in a city or a small community, but civilisation collapsed everywhere in the end just the same.

This is not a monolithic story of one single *Volksgemeinschaft*. Jewish responses to changing times were just as diverse as those among the Nazi 'community of people'. The Jewish leadership during the Nazi years has been much maligned. Everyday Jewish life during the war years inside Germany, furthermore, has remained an almost wholly hidden story, while relations among the Nazi elite have benefited from intensive research and debate. Fortunately records in Hamburg ordered to be destroyed by the Gestapo have survived thanks to the caretaker of the finance building, who sensed they were important for posterity. I was given the key to the cellar of the building in the Magdalenenstraße where they were scattered in huge piles covered in dust. These records, which were later transferred to the State Archives, enable us to do justice to the courage and resilience of the last representatives of German Jewry.

Civilisation is too easily taken for granted when we enjoy its benefits; it is in reality fragile, not just as it was in Germany during the 1930s but everywhere at any time. Power when held by leaders with extreme ideologies is able to corrupt sufficient followers to achieve its ends. Hitler understood this, observing in one of his interminable monologues in the *Wolfsschanze* in August 1942, 'the broad mass of people are neither bad nor good. They possess neither the malign intent nor the courage to be absolutely bad or absolutely good. The extremes determine the outcome.' History has shown how true that proved to be, then and later. But evils can be reversed and ideologies discredited, enabling succeeding generations to follow a different path.

Holocaust histories omit the many subtle shades of grey between the 'blacks' and 'whites' which alone can make what occurred understandable to succeeding generations. What I have tried to reveal is how the Nazi years were experienced by German Jews and millions of other misguided Germans for whom they appeared to herald 'better times'. The discrimination of Jews and other minorities did not touch the majority, while the gradual escalation of persecution allowed people time to get used to it. The treatment of the Jews before the Holocaust did not appear so unreasonable. Of course some aberrations had occurred. A German proverb was popular at the time: 'you cannot plane wood smooth without making many shavings'. Nor did the majority of Jews attempt to leave before Crystal Night in November 1938. Times, after all, had not become bad all at once. Even then, few Germans or Jews could envisage a Holocaust.

What this account shows is that German-Jewish society was not wholly separate from German society, that 'Jews' could not be excised from what the Nazis defined as 'German' without the destruction of *German* civilization. That is why German-Jewish history and the Holocaust cannot be detached as a disconnected, distinctive part of German history. There are lessons for today as minority cultures become imbedded in the wider stream of national cultures.

I could not hope to cover everything in the archives in an academic life-time, so I have also drawn on the researches of others. But the printed page, collating the work of other historians, invaluable as their researches are, does not convey events with the immediacy of seeing with your own eyes an original piece of evidence, deciphering a scrawled comment on the margin of a document recording the instantaneous reaction of the official to whom it was addressed, the entry in a diary at the time not intended to be read by others, a letter to a friend, an appeal to higher authority. The seemingly trivial is often illuminating.

There are many influences that shape events. The challenge is to show how they interact – policies and individuals, Nazis and Jews, institutions and their members, people in high places and those in humble occupations, daily experiences, relations between Berlin and a region, to mention only some – and to bring this all together in a coherent narrative, or, in other words, to write an 'integrated history'.

There was no category in any archive which alone would illuminate the questions I had. This study is largely based on archival searches I began in 1980. Documents showing how Jews were dealt with during the Nazi years were scattered through practically every file, department and office of Hamburg's state administration. Tens of thousands of documents have to be examined to identify the small proportion dealing with Jews, and it was impossible to foretell what might turn up – like the files in the cellar of the Ministry of Finance building in the Magdalenenstraße. Undoubtedly there is more still to be unearthed. With unbelievable patience Dr Gabrielsson, the Deputy Director of the Hamburg State Archives, made everything available to me year after year. But even he finally queried why I should want to look at the cemetery administration listing everyone buried in Hamburg. This search too turned up unexpected information: handwritten lists entitled 'Ashes from Auschwitz', which had reached Hamburg during 1943 and 1944.

The Federal German Archives remain indispensable: they also now house personal party members' files, which I examined earlier in Berlin at the Document Centre. Records from the Ministry of Justice add to our understanding of the Wannsee meeting and enable us to examine David Irving's claims exonerating Hitler's role in their context. In New York, the Leo Baeck Institute Archive has the most extensive holdings of Jewish family records and other source materials. The late Dr Sybil Milton's extraordinary deep knowledge enabled me to locate valuable holdings in this archive. The Hoover Institute's Archive is also a valuable depository of documents for the years from 1933 to 1945.

Of the principal archives I have cited, I refer last to the Research Institute of Contemporary History in Hamburg. For Hamburg, and also Germany, this valuable collection was largely built up by the late Professor Werner Jochmann, its former director, which brings me to acknowledge the much more personal help which I have enjoyed during the course of my research. Werner and *Frau* Dr Jochmann offered hospitality and warm friendship in their small flat in the Rutschbahn, a former Jewish quarter, where we gathered weekly with visiting colleagues from all over the world for 'master classes' over a bottle of good wine and cheese. We intended to write the book together before his untimely death. His closest associate was Professor Ursula Büttner, whose knowledge of Hamburg history and the intricate and complex Hamburg state administration is second to none. She always found the time to help and guide me. Over the years academic counselling has turned into a close friendship. It was Professor Bernd-Jürgen Wendt who was responsible for bringing me to Hamburg in the first place as a guest professor at the university. Since then, the welcome of his whole family and their hospitality over the years have linked our two families.

Among the colleagues at Hamburg's Research Institute of Contemporary History I particularly wish to acknowledge how much I benefited not only in a culinary sense from spending time with Uwe Lohalm over frequent lunches exchanging views on the Nazi bureaucracy. I also had many helpful discussions with Frank Bajohr, Angelika Voss and other members of the staff.

No author can sparkle without stimulation; I have been blessed with generations of lively, intelligent students attending my seminars in Germany, France, Britain and the United States. A new generation brings fresh questions to historical enquiry. Maybe this book will be the last, certainly among the last, written by someone from the generation who as children lived through the Nazi years and were old enough then to be able to recall them now. My own recollections are not, however, of Hamburg, where my great uncle Emil Misch and my great aunt Olga lived until she too was deported in 1942. Olga Misch, a devout convert, was a member of the *Jerusalem Gemeinde*, about which I have written. I grew up in Berlin. Personal experiences can add life and colour to historical narrative but hopefully in this case not at the expense of scholarly distance and judgement.

I gratefully acknowledge the support of a number of foundations – the British Academy, the *Internationale Studentenfreunde*, the *Hamburg-Stiftung*, the *Friedrich-Ebert-Stiftung*, the *Deutscher Akademischer Austausch-Dienst* and my own university, the University of Birmingham.

I reserve a special word for my knowledgeable and supportive agent, Bruce Hunter, without whose advice the manuscript would not have been revised to its present form. The patience of my long-time personal private secretary and friend, Mrs Pauline Roberts, and her constant encouragement despite retyping repeated revisions sustained me, and this gives me an opportunity to express my thanks.

I am very much indebted to Michael A. Meyer, Jeremy Noakes, Raphael Gross, David Sorkin, Bernd-Jürgen Wendt, Bernard Wasserstein and Ursula Büttner for their perspicacious suggestions, hastening to add that they are not responsible for my interpretations or any errors. I have received indispensable technical support from Simon Baugh, and this gives me an opportunity to thank him.

The spouses of married authors who have not divorced them on grounds of neglect deserve very special gratitude. My obligation is not routine. For many weeks at a time over the years I left my wife at home to care for five children and hold it all together, and then when I returned it was to a well-ordered household that gave me space to write and work.

Four Oaks
June 2010

PROLOGUE

Last days in Hamburg

Early in the morning on one fine autumn day in October 1941, the trams, the underground and the overhead electric railway were full as usual as the people of Hamburg were going to work. Between the Sternschanze and the Dammtor stations a young woman, Gisela Solmitz, was travelling on the *U-Bahn* that day.[1] Casually looking out, she caught a glimpse of an unusual sight as the train passed the small triangular Moorweide park in front of a handsome classical building, once the Masonic Lodge of Lower Saxony. The small grassed area was usually quite empty. Today it was crowded. A thousand people – young, old, and families with babies – were all standing about holding bundles, waiting. What set them apart was the Yellow Star prominently sewn to their coats. Gisela recognised in an instant what was going on. That evening she told her mother, who wrote in her journal:

> Everyone knows that many Jews, who are said to be immigrants, are being deported to Poland, and apparently they are to be found work there. The weight of their luggage is prescribed and limited; everything else has to be left behind. It is said this will be distributed to the people who have suffered bomb damage.

Gisela was actually repeating the propaganda of the authorities – that these people were not Hamburg Jews but immigrants – to make their expulsion more acceptable. They need not have been so concerned: there was no show of public disquiet. Although it was only the first of the mass deportations of German Jews, news got around swiftly by word of mouth.

On that morning of 24 October a family group – Erwin Baehr, his wife and three children, the youngest only eighteen months old, and his parents-in-law with their three children – were all standing among the crush of people in the little park watching the departing train, whose passengers were living in another world, able to carry on with their daily lives.[2] All those crowded into the park had, overnight, become prisoners, had lost their possessions, were disoriented, and were dependent on the whims of the Gestapo. Four years later, Erwin Baehr would be the only survivor of his family. In the ghetto he had loaded his three children onto a lorry, never to see them again. Left behind, numb in utter desolation, husband and wife too were separated. He was selected with the able-bodied and taken to a forced labour camp in Poland and ended the war in the Buchenwald concentration camp. He could get no news of his wife or children. No news meant death. Not even a grave to visit.

Just the story of one family: about most of the other thousand people in the park we know little more than their names and ages, from the lists drawn up for their deportation. Fewer than twenty from that transport survived. There were babies and the very old. Not everyone had turned up. Additional names had been added to the list to compensate for the shortfall. The missing had not fled or hidden. They had committed suicide, unable to face the expected hardships and uncertainties; better to end it all among familiar surroundings and in the city that was their home. They despaired after all the changes that had turned their lives upside down in just a few short years.

Three weeks later Gisela Solmitz witnessed a similar scene.[3] Long lines were again waiting outside the entrance of the building. She recounted to her mother how 'people gaped out of the carriage windows as another deportation transport of "non-Aryans" was being assembled at the Masonic Lodge'. What went through their heads? Gisela, a *Mischling*, was the daughter of a so-called racially mixed marriage: her father was baptised but his parents were Jews; her mother was an 'Aryan'Christian. The whole family had already suffered years of discrimination since Hitler came to power. Gisela was filled with foreboding. But what were her fellow passengers without Jewish connections thinking? For most, it was an event, perhaps something to look at, akin to a traffic accident, soon overtaken by the concerns of the everyday.

Another family of four was waiting in the park that morning. Manfred Rosenberg, too, was to be the lone survivor of his family.[4] Here is his account.

> On 7 November 1941 we received the deportation order, 'The Jew Fritz Rosenberg and his family are to appear on 8th November 1941 at noon at the *Logenheim*-Dammtorstraße [the former Masonic Lodge]. The house keys have first to be handed to the police. The apartment and its contents must neither be sold nor damaged. Each member of the family can take with them luggage weighing no more than 50kg. As of today all your money and possessions are confiscated.
>
> When my parents informed my sister and myself at our place of work of what had happened, we immediately stopped work to return home to help with the packing. But we were no longer calm; we heard who else would be coming, and that many were committing suicide. Our neighbours came to see us, but by and large the people in general were indifferent …

We said goodbye to our relatives, friends and acquaintances, and then took just one last look. My father locked the front door and brought the key to the police, while we meantime waited on the staircase; we had been driven from house and home. We knew that we would never see our home again.

My friend Erika called and offered to accompany us when she heard that I and also her adopted parents were to be deported. She went with her foster family of her own free will, as did many women and children with their parents. We first made our way to the former Jewish school to check in with our suitcases, which we left there, then took our rucksacks and bags to the *Logenheim* [Masonic Lodge], which we reached about midday.

In front of the entrance stood many fellow sufferers thrown out of their own homes – men and women, children and the old, all in confusion, waiting for hours on end, as the SS, who were in control, only permitted them to go in slowly. At long last, about 3 o'clock in the afternoon, it was our turn. First of all we had to hand over all our money as well as the hundred *Reichsmark* we were supposed to be permitted to take with us. Then a statement had to be signed by everyone that said that we admitted to have been involved in anti-state and communist activities and in doing so had become state enemies number one. It was for that reason that we had forfeited our German citizenship. All our money and possessions were confiscated and we declared that we would make no claims against the German *Reich*. After we had all signed, we had to surrender our passports, identity and registration cards; only then at long last could we enter the Logenheim.

The Jewish community of Hamburg had placed old beds and straw in the empty halls so that our last night would be as comfortable as possible. Hot lentil soup, tea and bread were distributed, and in the evening we younger ones even began to dance. The general atmosphere was good, as no one foresaw what was to come. Everyone met friends and relatives and no one could sleep. Some were writing, others started to pack, and others cried. There was a lot of confusion. The next morning, at five o'clock, the chief of the Gestapo appeared and made a little speech telling us that any apprehension was unjustified, since we were to be employed in the 'reconstruction' of the conquered eastern territories. We were also informed that a cheque to the amount of 30,000 *RM* had been made out for the SS in Minsk; it would be paid out for our use in Minsk. Our luggage would be transported there in additional carriages. Also food and medicines were being sent with us.

At 5.30 on the morning of 8th November 1941, large blacked-out police coaches took us in turn to the Hamburg goods station, where a train of twenty carriages with five additional carriages for our luggage and a large police contingent was waiting for us. Fifty people were assigned to each carriage. Three lorries arrived, loaded with food and additional supplies from the Jewish community. Everything was distributed among the carriages.

The passengers in this normal *Reichsbahn* train had no idea what awaited them. As the train sped from the Hamburg goods station through the well-kept houses in the suburbs, they had the last sight of their city. Fewer than 600 Jews would return from the 5,898 deported to the East during the war.[5] Among those who did not come back was Heinrich Wohlwill.

The Wohlwills were a Hamburg family held in high esteem. Was their pride in being Germans and love for German culture an illusion? Were they living among uncaring people who were glad to see them gone? Had they really never belonged? How had it come to this, the death of a civilisation? But they did not doubt even now, on this cold November day, that they were Germans and that no one could deprive them of that.

1

EARLIER TIMES

Immanuel Wohlwill and the early reformers

A hundred years earlier, Heinrich Wohlwill's great-grandfather had settled in Hamburg on the Elbe, a jewel among the cities of Germany, with its canals and lakes, medieval streets and thriving port, looking back on more than a millennium of cultured tradition. Once famed as a prosperous member of the Hanseatic League, a republic ruled not by princes but by an elite of merchants, it was surely the last place on earth to descend to barbarity. Nowhere did Jews feel more at home.

They had reached Hamburg relatively late. The first, towards the close of the sixteenth century, were the Sephardic Jews from the Iberian peninsula, known in Hamburg as the Portuguese 'nation'.[1] Expelled from Spain and Portugal, they settled in Hamburg, London and Amsterdam. Superficially converted to Catholicism, they secretly practised Jewish worship. They were not poor refugees but brought with them money, skills, mercantile experience and commercial contacts elsewhere in Europe and overseas.

Among them, already settled in Hamburg in 1591, was Rodrigo de Castro, a doctor of great renown who had treated King Christian IV of Denmark and the nobility. When the Black Death threatened to decimate the people, the senate turned to him to master the outbreak. In gratitude, he was freed from the restrictions placed on Jews and lived in a fine house in the best quarter of the city, visited there by the good and the great. Hamburg's senate, dominated by the powerful merchants, were happy to admit the 'Catholics' and to close its eyes to their Jewish faith. In 1612, the senate listed 125 of them. They had to pay a substantial annual tax of 1,000 marks, doubled in 1617. For more than a century the senate protected them from the envy of the less successful and from the preaching of the clergy, who incited the people against them. The Sephardic Jews helped to develop Hamburg into a major trading port, until the senate in 1697 gave in to popular pressure and began to levy a punitive annual tax of 6,000 marks. The wealthier Jews emigrated to Amsterdam and London. A small community of Portuguese Jews with their own rites and synagogue survived.

The nineteenth century was dominated by the Ashkenazi, the 'German' Jews.[2] The largest and most important community was that of neighbouring Altona. The Altona Jews under Danish suzerainty enjoyed more freedom than the Sephardic Jews in Hamburg. They could worship openly, own houses, and engage in crafts, business and the professions. They built a large synagogue and had their own burial ground. To overcome religious restrictions, Hamburg Jews formed in 1669 with the Altona Jews a 'dual community', and two years later, when Prussian Wandsbek joined, the 'triple community', uniquely spanning three states. In 1812, at the time of the French occupation, the Hamburg Jewish community, with 6,299 Ashkenazi and 130 Portugese Jews, became independent, with their own synagogue in the Elbstraße hidden from public view behind residential houses.[3]

I

Early in the century, the majority of Jews earned a scant living as street traders or small shopkeepers. By dress and religious practice they were distinct. They observed a day of rest not on Sundays but the Sabbath, from sundown on Friday to sundown on Saturday. While following their own laws and ways, Jews were not isolated from German culture. They spoke the same language, though continuing to converse in Yiddish among themselves. The more educated were better acquainted with literature than the majority of Christians. The Enlightenment era had set in motion the process of emancipation and acculturation. The dramas of Friedrich Schiller, apostle of freedom, adorned their library shelves. But there were still barriers. They were excluded from the guilds and all positions related to the state. A wide range of careers was thus closed to them. The Jews were only able to enter the 'free professions', medicine and journalism and engage in commerce.

For a few, as craftsmen, administrators, architects, builders and teachers, the Jewish community provided opportunities.[4] Teaching Hebrew and arithmetic to poor Jewish boys, however, was neither highly regarded nor well rewarded. That was the profession of Joel Wolf. His son Immanuel grew up in this poor orthodox family. At the age of eight he was an orphan. By good fortune Immanuel was accepted as a 'free pupil' in the school in Seesen founded by Israel Jacobson, one of the remarkable early Jewish reformers, a member of the elite who helped to transform German-Jewish relationships.

Jacobson was a banker and court Jew to the Duke of Brunswick. In 1807 the duchy was incorporated into the kingdom of Westphalia. The Jews were granted equality as citizens. Jacobson was held in high regard, a knight of the royal order of Westphalia and a member of the Westphalian *Reichstag*. He was also appointed head of the Jewish Consistory. A *Maskilim* follower of *Haskalah*, the Jewish Enlightenment, Jacobson was determined to free Jews from external discrimination and from what he believed were their self-imposed shackles. Jews would be encouraged to abandon unnecessary differentiation from their Christian neighbours without having to stop being Jews. Synagogue services would be modernised, with sermons delivered in German, just as in Christian churches.

The best hope for change lay with the young. And so he founded the Jacobson School for poor Jewish children. In 1810 a 'temple', like a Christian chapel, was attached to the school, with an organ; bells summoned the boys to service. German as well as Hebrew was taught. The boys were to be brought up as Germans and Jews. The school shaped Immanuel's outlook in later life. Aged fifteen, he left Seesen for Berlin.

These were years of hope and excitement for educated Jews. The celebrated German dramatist Gotthold Ephraim Lessing, friend of Moses Mendelssohn, philosopher and leading light of *Haskalah*, preached toleration, and in 1779 his play *Nathan der Weise* was published. In it he proclaimed that true religion is love in the service of mankind and that, of the representatives of the three great religions of the world – Islam, Christianity and Judaism – only Nathan, the Jew, lived up to the full ideals of humanity. Such civilised attitudes were not common in the German lands or in Europe, but German society was not uniquely hostile to Jews or to their emancipation.

When Immanuel entered the University of Berlin, Hegel occupied the chair of philosophy. Hegel's philosophy appealed to Jewish reformers for its promise to end Jewish separateness in a state based on morality, in an idealised Prussian kingdom. Philosophy, the Jewish reformers believed, would destroy the myths and vicious lies about Jews and the falsehoods spread for centuries by the churches. Immanuel expressed his positive outlook by changing his name to Wohlwill, to indicate his faith in harmony.

Jewish reformers took heart from the revolution of thought among the educated elite. Enlightenment would spread from the top to the masses. But the reformers were not prepared just to wait. They were determined to play an active part. One new approach early in the century was 'scientific study'.[5] Scholarly Jews founded the *Wissenschaft des Judentums*, 'the scientific study of Judaism', among them Dr Leopold Zunz, who befriended the young Wohlwill and furthered his reforming zeal. The study of Judaism would show that Jewish ethical values were universal.

A fierce debate ensued among Jews about the future.[6] The Jewish reformers wanted to get rid of outworn traditions, of all 'otherness', abandon making claims for exclusive truth and become a part of German society. 'We are and want to be solely Germans!', declared Ludwig Philippson, the publisher of the progressive *Allgemeine Zeitung des Judentums* in 1848. 'We possess and desire no fatherland other than the German. Only in our faith are we Israelites; in every other respect, with our innermost feelings, we belong to the state in which we live.'[7] It will always be a minority who spearhead change. The liberal reformers believed that only by adapting to modern times and the wider society among whom they lived could the essence of their Jewish faith be preserved. Traditionalists feared that so-called reform would end with the abandonment of Jewish observance altogether, but accepted just as enthusiastically the mission of adoption of the German fatherland and immersion in German culture.

The Jewish community of Hamburg was the largest in Germany until the mid-century, when it was overtaken by the rapid growth of Berlin's Jewish population.[8] To signify its German loyalty, with the consent of the senate, the government of Hamburg, the community changed its name to *Deutsch-Israelitische Gemeinde* (German Israelite Community). The community, overseen by a board which derived its authority from the senate, was accorded a legal status and exercised delegated powers of taxation and supervision of welfare, Jewish schools and religious affairs, including the appointment of rabbis, but ultimate approval remained with the senate. Relationships between the Jewish board and the Christian senate were cordial and supportive for more than a hundred years, the board not infrequently turning to the senate for advice. This throws another light on Christian–Jewish relations deriving from accounts only emphasising the growth of anti-Judaistic animosities. These were, however, troublesome times of dispute among Jews, as communities adopted different ways of bringing worship closer in line with their changing status in German society. Hamburg played a leading role in these controversies surrounding reform.

On 18 October 1818, the anniversary of the battle of Leipzig freeing Germany from Napoleon's rule, a group of liberal Jews consecrated a new synagogue, the *Tempel*, and introduced a prayer book with prayers in Hebrew and German. This outraged Hamburg's orthodox rabbis and the majority of the board, who were just then looking for a leading reforming but orthodox rabbi. He should be learned in the Talmud while also benefiting from a German secular university education. For orthodox Jews, prayers in German and an organ, as in Christian churches, was anathema. The board's choice fell on Isaak Bernays, who vehemently opposed the changes of ritual made by the *Tempel*. The senate, meanwhile, mindful of Hamburg's interests, worked to maintain peace in the community. It did not escape their notice either that the *Tempel* congregation was composed of the more prosperous Jews whose commercial talents were valuable to the state. The senate now played a moderating role in setting out the terms of Bernays's appointment. He would, after all, not only be Hamburg's leading rabbi but at the same time occupy the position of a *geistlicher Beamter* (spiritual senior servant of the state), thus being subordinate both to the board and to the senate. Bernays's adoption of the Sephardic title of *chacham* (sage) rather than rabbi met with no objection, but a clause was inserted in his contract which forbade him to 'harass the *Tempel*'. Bernays nevertheless over the years frequently overstepped this injunction in his disputes with the *Tempel* congregation.

The confrontation once more came to a head in 1841, when the *Tempel* introduced a second edition of their prayer book and asked the senate for permission to construct a new *Tempel* building in the Poolstrassße. The board and Bernays were opposed. The Lutheran senate, however, adjudicated in the *Tempel*'s favour both on the issue of the prayer book and the building plans, meantime calling on the Jewish community to exercise tolerance. In 1844 the Poolstraße synagogue for the enlarged

800-strong congregation was consecrated. Bernays's death in 1849 and a succession of less belligerent chief rabbis reduced tensions. However, they resurfaced from time to time until Nazi persecution brought the community close together.

Bernays's influence and legacy extended beyond Hamburg. He belonged to the founders of 'modern orthodoxy' who believed that the rabbi should play a central role in worship and in the community. Religious services were to bring the congregation together in Hebrew prayer. A charismatic rabbi would also deliver a sermon in German. Modern orthodox rabbis, moreover, saw no conflict in following orthodox Judaism and embracing German culture.

Orthodox Jews sent their children to religious schools. One of these in Hamburg was the *Talmud Tora Schule*, founded in 1805. Apart from arithmetic, study was devoted to religious subjects. Under Bernays's influence in the 1820s and 1830s, despite some vehement opposition, history, German and the natural sciences were added to the curriculum. The combination of a strictly orthodox upbringing and a secular German education became the hallmark of this renowned school down the centuries.

Reformers, orthodox and liberal, in the nineteenth century urged that Jews should become 'normal' Germans. The children of the poor, of hawkers and street traders, should be taught skills and the German language to enable them to move up the social scale and be trained as craftsmen, even though membership of the craft guilds was closed to them, preventing their rise to the status of master-craftsmen. For gifted boys, the way to social progress might eventually be opened by higher education. Jews also began to attend Christian schools. The most elitist was the *Johanneum*, with close ties to the clergy. Johannes Gurlitt, the enlightened headmaster, fought and overcame the opposition of the school's guardians to accepting Jews. That he was a keen advocate of trying to convert Jewish boys does not lessen his example of tolerance. Here, for more than a century, many of Hamburg's Jewish leaders in politics, commerce and the professions were educated and formed ties with gentiles.

Hamburg's Jews were among the pioneers in promoting the education of the community's poor children. The *Israelitische Freischule*, the Free School for boys, was founded in 1815. The school taught German and, by example, 'elimination of all peculiarities in custom, speech and public behaviour'. A school for poor Jewish girls was also established. All this happened long before compulsory elementary education was a requirement in Hamburg.

II

When the community was looking for a teacher for the Free School, their choice fell on the well-educated young doctor of philosophy Immanuel Wohlwill.[9] He did not wish to limit education to an elementary level suitable for the positions Jews were able to fill. He wanted to prepare those boys capable of a higher education for the professions which he was sure they would be allowed to enter when they reached adulthood, but at the time were still closed to Jews. Wohlwill soon felt at home in Hamburg. Young and full of the joys of life, he set out on journeys through the countryside and described his wanderings in glowing terms. In the city, Jews and Christians could meet on equal terms at the Harmony club, which welcomed him as a member.[10] They gathered for good conversation, relaxation or a game of billiards, and ladies joined on social occasions. Wohlwill describes meeting there members of the Hamburg elite and a fellow Jew, Dr Hertz, who contributed much to institutions for the poor. Here, Wohlwill felt completely at ease: 'The atmosphere of the *Harmonie* I like very much. Officers, the nobility, scholars and Hamburg citizens all live together here on the most cordial footing.'

He preached for a time in the *Tempel*, but his reforming zeal went too far for the liberal-minded congregation. He was one of a group of intellectual reformers who wished Jews to abandon Talmudic thinking and distinctive external Jewish practices while preserving the universality of Jewish ethics. Harmony was his guiding passion. In the search for truth, Jews and Christians would come together sharing a common 'church' under one God for all. But his critics believed that such a vision would lead to the loss of Jewish identity altogether. Reform Judaism, which grew in strength during the century, rejected Wohlwill's vision.

Wohlwill could not escape the negative aspects of Hamburg life for a Jew.[11] Although there was no ghetto in Hamburg, Jews were required to live in specified streets. Popular riots were incited against Jews from time to time. In 1835 there was a renewed outbreak along the fashionable Jungfernstieg, where well-off young Jews relaxed in coffee houses and the Jewish banker and philanthropist Salomon Heine lived. The authorities restored order. As a trading city, Hamburg frowned on such disturbances. The senate, though privately sympathetic, admonished Jews in public 'not to cause conflict by their behaviour … in public places to behave with reticence and modesty … to avoid putting forward demands which cannot be accepted in their relationship to the state so that no mischief is caused thereby'. Jews, no longer just a frightened, pliant community, responded with a robust complaint. All was well in good times, but in times of stress Jews did not find much public support from those in power, save protection of person and property.

For Wohlwill, these were years of domestic fulfilment. His marriage to Frederike Warburg linked him to a well-to-do and philanthropic Hamburg family. From the happy union five children were born – Fanny Henriette, Wolf Emil, Daniel Theodor, Anna and Adolf – all suitably adorned with German first names. Wohlwill left Hamburg in 1838 on his appointment as director of the *Jacobson Schule* in Seesen which he had attended as a boy. The school now educated not only Jewish boys; the excellence of its education attracted boarders from all over Germany. Wohlwill died prematurely in 1847, just one year away from seeing his dream of Jewish emancipation seemingly fulfilled.

III

The 1840s marked a new beginning for Germany's Jews.[12] The dead hand of conservatism in reaction to the Napoleonic upheavals began to ease. In Hamburg, the elite merchants for the first time admitted Jews to their association of *Ehrbaren Kaufmann*, 'honourable merchants'. The lesser traders were now also able to join the organisation established for them, the *Krameramt*. But the craft guilds remained resistant, fearing Jewish competition. They became less important as time went on. Nevertheless, the difficulty of placing Jewish apprentices and the denial of recognition of the status of mastercraftsmen was a problem. Creative solutions were found for such skilled workers as tailors and shoemakers, for whom equivalent approbations were devised. Street trading and hawking declined. What was happening in Hamburg happened too in Berlin, Frankfurt, Leipzig – indeed, all over Germany. Jews were now highly regarded in the 'free' professions. They had long been practising medicine; journalism, music and entertainment also opened opportunities.

In politics, Jews were prominent among the Hamburg liberals. Immanuel Wohlwill, Isaac Wolffsohn, Dr Anton Rée and the most celebrated of all, Gabriel Riesser, all became powerful spokesmen of reform nationally. And it was the *Johanneum* that had provided them with connections and a sound and thorough German education.

The mid-century years were not, however, the dawn of democracy. Hamburg, Hanseatic and free, an independent state for centuries, small in size but with its merchant and seafaring tradition open to the world, was a republic surrounded by kings and princes. With pride in its history, the merchant and financial elite were the rulers of the city-state. They were a close-knit group of families determined to preserve their privileges. They looked upon themselves as custodians and guardians for the good of Hamburg, entitled by their wisdom, as evidenced by commercial success and standing, to govern for the people. Complicated constitutional arrangements ensured power lay in the hands of the twelve (later sixteen) senators, who were appointed for life; only death or decrepitude would require their replacement. The senators were generally men of real ability, who devoted their energies and time for the good of the people as they saw it. Unlike in princely realms, descent by family was not enough; these guardians had to prove themselves by showing the ability to take on the activities of their fathers.

The elites defended their privileges against the agitation of the excluded majority. Why, then, upset the common crowd unnecessarily by openly defending and promoting the unpopular demands for equality put forward by Jews? The pace of reform should not outpace what was acceptable to the prejudiced majority.

By the mid-century Jews of Hamburg were no longer overwhelmingly poor but began to form a part of the higher social classes. The Jewish population had grown from 6,000 to 10,000, living among 140,000 gentiles – a minority at every social level, but as a community active and well organised. A network of charitable foundations looked after the needs of the disadvantaged. Though more than half of the Jews would by any standards still be regarded as poor, most earned enough to contribute something to the exchequer. Only four of every hundred Jews fell below the poverty line. The Jews thus were making proportionally a greater contribution to Hamburg's finances than the rest of the population. The better off among them could no longer be distinguished in manner or dress from their fellow Germans – this the achievement of just one generation.

The social progress of the Jewish community would not have been possible without the goodwill of their Christian fellow Germans. Archaic restrictions appeared increasingly absurd in modern times. In 1842 the great Hamburg fire led to new demands for reform. Why reject Jewish help to rebuild Hamburg? The Jewish banking house of Salomon Heine provided large credits at normal interest rates to help the city, which otherwise would have taken much longer to recover. It was hoped that the wealthier Jews would acquire the land of burnt-down dwellings and build new houses, so their restriction to certain streets and prohibition from owning property was removed. They also gained the right to participate in all trades.

Wealthy Jews responded to the support given by enlightened Christians by charitable giving to causes benefiting all the people The most magnificent bequest was the money Salomon Heine provided for the building of a new hospital in St Pauli, the harbour district in the old part of the city. For a hundred years the Jewish doctors and nurses of the *Israelitisches Krankenhaus* tended to both Jews and gentiles, the poor, sailors and prostitutes, and Jewish midwives delivered their babies. That toleration had its limits in Hamburg soon became evident. When it was proposed that the philanthropist Salomon Heine be made an honorary citizen, this was turned down by the senate as not compatible with the Lutheran republic. Jews could not be citizens.

Progress step by slow step: suddenly the Jews were granted all they had hoped for. The all-German parliament meeting in the Paulskirche in Frankfurt in 1848 promulgated the fundamental rights of every German, manhood suffrage and the end of discrimination on grounds of religion. All over Germany constitutions had to be revised. Jews were now eligible to become citizens, to vote, to be elected to the parliamentary assembly and to participate in government. But the high-minded aspirations of the parliamentarians were not much understood by the common people. Too much freedom too soon? For the Jews, 1848 was also a time of violent anti-Jewish outbreaks, and reaction came a year later.

The best years of their lives

Following the heady year of revolution, Hamburg's Jews could become citizens and be appointed to positions in the service of the state.[13] A few, like Gabriel Riesser, became judges. But prejudice persisted. Independent careers in law, journalism, the arts and, above all, business were more attractive than hoping to secure a position requiring appointment by the state.

I

Immanuel Wohlwill's five children took advantage of the new times. Adolf became a distinguished historian of his native city and was the first academic in

Hamburg to be granted the title of professor. He too had been educated at the *Johanneum*. Daniel Theodor was a wealthy merchant and philanthropist. Fanny Henriette became the founder and director of a Froebel school in Belgium, Anna was a much beloved schoolteacher, and Emil made a significant contribution to Hamburg's industrial development.

Jewish middle-class life is exemplified by the changes Emil experienced. He was born in 1835.[14] Brought up in a liberal Jewish home, he worshipped with his father in the *Tempel*. They were a close family, with Rachel, a Warburg who had married Immanuel in 1831, presiding over the household. All the children were brought up to be proud and observant Jews and also to be Germans with love for their fatherland and its culture.

Emil's early years were happy and secure. His time in the Jacobson School in Seesen was free from corroding conflict and religious prejudice, and he mixed easily with the boys from Christian families. Emil's horizons were constantly being widened and not confined to traditional Jewish studies. The death of his father, when Emil was only twelve, was a devastating blow. Without his father's influence he began to drift away from Judaism.

After leaving the Jacobson School he had a less happy experience in a state grammar school. Here, the only Jewish boy, he was singled out for crude harass-ment. Emil stood his ground and battled it out. His talents and drive then earned him a place in the *Johanneum*. But wide interests were frowned upon in the *Johanneum*, where a strict curriculum was taught: Latin, Greek, history and liter-ature. Knowledge was inculcated as through a funnel into restless adolescent heads, imagination regarded as youthful aberration. Emil complained of the school as an 'academic filtration machine', but it prepared him well for later life.

Over several years he wrote lively letters which recapture the feelings of an educated German Jew in changing times. At the *Johanneum* he was accepted by his classmates and teachers. There was no overt anti-Jewish atmosphere. Just now and then there were reminders: 'Some of the people of Christ remembered in time that I was a Jew',[15] he wrote, when the boys did not vote for him to act as president of the philosophy society. He probably was oversensitive.

An unpleasant experience brought home to Emil, at the age of eighteen, that what really mattered was not the identity a person chooses, but how they are identified by others.[16] A friend had drowned in the Elbe. Emil could not accom-pany him to the graveside:

> Because I was a Jew, I could not be a friend to my friend, and that is some-thing that makes me regard it a sin ever to allow myself to be baptised … I have the right to speak at the grave of my friend … and regard it as my duty to fight for it … I cannot give in to escape the unpleasant inconveniences which are unjustifiably imposed on me.

What did he believe? Emil put it succinctly: 'I know nothing of Judaism any longer, I know only the Rights of Man.'

Emil's attitude to religion corresponded to that of many of the better educated Jews, as well as of many Christians who regarded religion and literal interpretations of the Bible as superstition. Ethical conduct should no longer be linked to any one religion. Freethinkers, like Emil, believed there had to be a better way, not bound by past bigotry.

Conversion was out of the question for most German Jews. Although Emil no longer observed any Jewish ritual, he did not wish to deny his Jewish descent. This did not make him feel less German. When his sister Fanny decided to marry her Belgian fiancé, Emil was aghast at her abandoning her homeland.[17] Should not love of country come before romantic love? Emil's letter to her reveals his inner feelings:

> I do not wish to be anything but pure German. I belong to Judaism but, as the Jews are no longer a people, although I have the greatest respect for my ancestors, I regard it as inevitable to leave my origins to the past and to belong to my country.

That, though, was problematical. There was no quick solution to adoption as a citizen of Hamburg and the wider fatherland.

His struggle for emancipation met with obstacles.[18] The Hamburg constitution of 1860 had separated state and church, and Emil was sufficiently well established to qualify for the right of citizenship. He filled in the application. The rubric 'religion' he left blank. That would not do as far as officialdom was concerned, and he was asked to complete the form. A Jew, he was told, could only become a citizen if he was a conventional Jew, a member of the Jewish community; should he not be a Jew, would he please produce his certificate of baptism. There followed a heated exchange. Emil declared he was neither Jew nor Christian. In the upper reaches of Hamburg society Jews had been accepted as citizens now for ten years, but those Christians and Jews calling themselves freethinkers were not. They rated below the Jews as having no belief at all. The freethinkers organised themselves. There was a debate in parliament (*Bürgerschaft*). Emil's application became a *cause célèbre*. The senate, the government of Hamburg, decided to reject it on the grounds that he was a Jew and should so declare himself to be. For Emil the consequences of rejection were serious. Without citizenship he could not be registered as a qualified research chemist, the career of his choice. But in 1865 the senate finally gave way, and Emil was the first of the Wohlwills to become a citizen of Hamburg.

Despite his religious detachment, Emil Wohlwill married Louise Nathan, the daughter of a Jewish doctor. Very few Jews formally left the community. Emil Wohlwill was one of the few who, as soon as the new law allowed, declared his intent to cease to be a member. But he remained a Jew proud of his descent and baptised none of his five children. Emil's chosen course reflected the attitudes of an increasing number of educated Jews. Whether religious or not, orthodox or liberal, they all felt German.

Emil was appointed as a research chemist in the old established smelting concern of precious metals founded by Marcus Salomon Beit in 1770.[19] The Beit factory amalgamated with the Elbkupferwerk, which was in business to produce purified copper. After amalgamating with another Jewish firm, the industrial concern dropped the family name and exchanged it for Norddeutsche Affinerie. Emil Wohlwill's discoveries of how to apply an electrical current to separate precious metals enabled the business to grow into an industry of global importance.

Emil Wohlwill worked for the firm for the next twenty-two years. His outstanding scientific contribution was acknowledged when the Norddeutsche Affinerie won the gold medal for its electrolytic purification method of gold, silver, copper, platinum and palladium at the World Electrical Exhibition in Paris in 1881. In 1900, at the age of sixty-five, his contract was ended – the reasons for this are not clear – and his son Heinrich was appointed to take his place. Heinrich Wohlwill carried on his father's work and succeeded in patenting many improved processes.

II

Another industrial concern in Hamburg, which owed its worldwide success to two Jews and a Christian working in trusting partnership was Beiersdorf.[20] Oscar Troplowitz was born in Prussian Breslau, now Wrocław. He began his career in a pharmacy and later studied in Breslau and Heidelberg, gaining his doctorate in 1888. The following year he joined his uncle's pharmacy in Prussian Posen. Meantime, Carl Paul Beiersdorf had opened a pharmacy in Altona and established a small laboratory in Hamburg. The profits from this business were modest even when Paul Gerson Unna, a young Jewish doctor working in the *Israelitisches Krankenhaus*, formed an association with Beiersdorf to patent medical discoveries to treat skin complaints. Their partnership was sufficiently successful to enable Carl Beiersdorf to give up the pharmacy and devote all his efforts to the laboratory. After the suicide of his son, Carl Beiersdorf decided to sell the factory-laboratory to Oscar Troplowitz, who became the sole owner in 1890 but retained the Beiersdorf name.

Troplowitz was not only a good researcher but had a brilliant grasp of business. His first success was to invent a paste that could be inserted into a tube to clean teeth. Soon the Beiersdorf *Pebeco* toothpaste brand sold worldwide. Another development was a plaster that adhered to the skin without causing irritation. It took years of research before Troplowitz finally succeeded. *Hansaplast* is better known outside Germany as Elastoplast. Well known among doctors was Unna's development of a skin ointment, *Unna Paste*, which became the standard treatment for skin ulcers. He also perfected a nourishing skin cream, known as Nivea. Unna and Troplowitz launched Beiersdorf. Later Jewish and Christian board members worked together until the Nazis came to power, creating today's world-renowned pharmaceutical giant.

Troplowitz, in what was perhaps characteristic more of Jewish than of Christian owners of businesses at the time, showed concern for the social welfare of his workers – a model employer. Hours of work were first reduced to fifty-two and then in 1912 to forty-eight, without loss of earnings. Women did not lose their employment when they became pregnant, as was then usual; a room was set aside so they could breast-feed their babies. Paid vacations and free warm midday meals were other innovations. A social fund, contributed in part by the workers, provided additional help in case of sickness, marriage, burial and other costly events. What was unusual was that the workers were given control of decisions, though under Troplowitz's watchful eye.

In a full life he still found time to play an important political role in Hamburg. As a member of the *Baudeputation*, he played a leading role in urging the creation of the beautiful *Stadtpark* for the people of Hamburg to enjoy their leisure. Generous with his wealth, he did not confine his philanthropy to Jewish charities. He supported both the Catholic hospital, the *Marienkrankenhaus*, and the *Israelitisches Krankenhaus*. In his will in 1918 he left his twenty-six most valuable paintings, including a Renoir, a Sisley and a Picasso, to Hamburg's *Kunsthalle* museum. The Nazis auctioned the Picasso in Switzerland as 'degenerate art'.

III

Another Jew who served his city was Leo Lippmann, a young lawyer. Leo Lippmann was one of only two Jews admitted before 1914 to the higher civil service in Germany.[21] Lippmann held his head high as a Jew. He had long ceased to go to a synagogue but remained all his life a proud Jew. There were many German Jews who now no longer practised their religion but identified as and felt Jewish. Lippmann's schooldays in the *Johanneum* were happy. He mixed freely with all his classmates and got on equally well with his teachers.

After completing his studies at the university, Lippmann returned to Hamburg. Johann Georg Mönckeberg, a tolerant and farsighted patrician, was the mayor. Word of the young talented lawyer had reached him. In 1906 Lippmann received a personal invitation: Mönckeberg urged Lippman to make his career in Hamburg as a higher civil servant. Lippmann hesitated. As a Jew, could he expect promotion above the lower career positions? Would it not be better to make the same choice as other Jews and build up an independent private law practice? Mönckeberg reassured him. He would be appointed as councillor (*Rat*), not to an unimportant part of the administration, but to finance, the most important; as for his concerns about being an unbaptised Jew, 'I surely had never heard that in Hamburg anyone had been treated differently because he was a Jew.' Lippmann accepted and had no reason to regret his decision. He rose rapidly in the service to his city-state and reached its very pinnacle. In his memoirs he recounted that he had never met with a single instance of antisemitism during his long years in office.

IV

For secular Jews like Lippmann, it was nevertheless possible to remain a member of the community because of a unique compromise. The right to leave the community was of great concern to religious Jews at the time. To meet this threat, a reorganisation was undertaken in 1867. The Hamburg 'system' was the result.[22] It separated religious activities – the appointment of rabbis, the supervision of synagogues, circumcision, marriage, ritual slaughter and kosher food preparation – from the remaining activities of the community – education, social and cultural activities, the hospital, orphanages, charities, almshouses, finance and recreation. This enabled Jews without any synagogue ties to remain members of the community.

It was a far-seeing and wise solution. Well thought out, too, was the decision to place burial outside religious jurisdiction and so to allow those Jews who were not affiliated to a synagogue the right to a burial in a Jewish cemetery with their families. Non-religious Jews did not have to support the synagogues, but every community member was free to assign 10 per cent of his tax to the synagogue of his choice. The community ensured its dynamic survival in other important ways. Although Jews became eligible for state poor relief and welfare, there were separate Jewish welfare institutions, schools, orphanages and provisions for poor relief. Jews thus benefited from both Jewish charities and the state.

Ties to Judaism were weakened not so much by conversion as through marriage. The generally tolerant atmosphere of Hamburg is reflected in the high rate of inter-faith marriages, which rose to one in five by the new century and as high as one in three in the 1920s. The great majority of the children of mixed religious marriages were baptised at birth to spare them future discrimination. But these new Christians found that they were not completely accepted, as the vicissitudes of the Elkan family illustrate.

V

The Elkans lived in Pöseldorf.[23] Before the turn of the century Pöseldorf was a suburb of Hamburg separated by pastures on which cows grazed. Here lived the wealthier and well-educated Jews whose one ardent wish was to blend completely with their neighbours. Carl Elkan recalls that this probably explained why it was only when he was fifteen years old that

> I learnt that I was of Jewish blood. In the home of my parents, and presumably also in the homes of our friends, we never spoke about such things. Such issues were forgotten, needed to be forgotten and finished with. I cannot say whether among the majority of Hamburg's population the consciousness that we were outsiders, of different blood, temperament, history and tradition, had disappeared. Below the surface such feelings must have existed. When my brother, Otto, entered the University of Heidelberg just

at the time of the [anti-Semitic] agitation of [the court preacher] Stoecker, he found himself suddenly separated from his schoolfriends, who as Christians were able to join the feudal student corps closed to him, and he had to experience an army major who said to him that he was excellently suited to be made an officer, but not being a Christian he couldn't be promoted.

The younger brother Carl, too, was to experience the wounding impact of discrimination. To save his children from the same fate, to 'free them from the chains of oriental superstition so that they could stand shoulder to shoulder with their countrymen', they were baptised.

Jewish parents who baptised their children, usually themselves, did not convert out of respect for the feelings of their parents.[24] This created a dilemma in their own family. Carl Elkan thought it best to 'admit' to his baptised children that their mother and father were Jews rather than have others reveal this to them. Elkan explains: 'What a ten year old can accept with equanimity cannot be told without danger five years later.' Carl's life in the family home, shared with seven brothers and one sister, first in Rabenstraße 14 and later in the patrician Harvestehudeweg, was warm and happy. Harvestehudeweg 39 had been acquired from James Hardy, nicknamed 'Hardy the Wise', who before baptism was called Nathan. Carl served his one-year compulsory military service with the horse artillery and enjoyed the rough and tumble experience; he recalled no hostile feelings among his comrades. Corporal Elkan was without a care, enjoying young manhood.

Following his appointment to a junior position in the well-known Hamburg firm of G. Amsinck & Co., his colleagues told him how, soon after his arrival, the senior *Herr* Gustav Amsinck had asked one of his assistants, '*Herr* Otte, you know all about Hamburg; the Elkans are not Jews are they?', only to receive the reply that they were. Amsinck hesitated a moment before dismissing this blemish as of no consequence. 'Ah well', he rejoined, 'Hamburg Jews are not real Jews.' The Amsincks themselves were descended from Jews, which helped to explain their excessive later Germanic fervour, confided another colleague. Actually this large and powerful patrician Hamburg family was of Dutch Protestant origin. Gustav Amsinck was now on one of his periodic visits to Hamburg. He lived in the United States, where he headed one of the most important banking houses on Wall Street. Except among fanatical antisemites, to be a Jew did not turn you into some sort of pariah in Germany or Hamburg. Sent to New York by his firm, Carl Elkan experienced more antisemitism there than in Hamburg.

An important preoccupation of Jewish families was to arrange suitable marriages for their offspring. Whether religiously inclined or not, the majority of Jews before the First World War believed that it was not done for a Jew to marry a gentile – a feeling less strongly felt by prospective Christian spouses if an advantageous marriage was in the offing. After his earlier amorous affairs, where physical attraction had counted far more than social or religious considerations,

Carl conformed to tradition and settled down with the Jewish daughter of a family of similar social standing. For the better-off Jews like the Elkans, the years of the new century before the First World War were a golden era.[25]

VI

Their high profile creates a false image, as if all Jews were rich. There were many poor Jews – small shopkeepers, greengrocers, tailors and white-collar workers, as well as artisans – making only a very modest living. It is just that the wealthy Jews were more in the public eye. Those prominent in commerce offered an easy target.

Among the pioneers to develop the first department stores were Jews. The earliest was opened by Oscar Tietz in Munich at the close of the century. In Hamburg, in the then fashionable Großer Burstah, Tietz opened another branch. The idea of offering a wide assortment of goods at small profit margins in large, well-appointed stores had been pioneered by Bon Marché in Paris thirty years earlier. Prices were clearly marked, and summer and winter sales advertised bargains. Small shopkeepers tried to hold on to their customers by providing a more personal service; they felt their livelihood was threatened by the lower prices of the larger stores. Antisemitic propaganda exploited these fears and agitated against the Jewish department stores.

Another enterprise was to supply smaller traders with keenly priced goods through the purchasing power of wholesale traders. One of the best known in textiles was the Jewish Hamburg firm of M. J. Emden und Söhne, founded in 1823. Some traders developed into specialised department stores, providing linen, bedding and fine tablecloths. If you wished to purchase overcoats, furs, hats and dresses in Hamburg, a favourite store was Hirsch & Cie; fashionable ladies went to the Gebrüder Robinsohn or to M. Hirschfeld. At the turn of the century the most elegant establishments were situated along the Jungfernstieg or in the Neuer Wall. Many were owned by Jews, their success assured by their overwhelmingly Christian clientele.

Private banking was another area of Jewish prominence.[26] The phenomenal growth of Hamburg's commerce was dependent on ready access to credit. Among the best-known private banks was M. M. Warburg & Co., at Ferdinandstraße 75, founded in 1798 by the brothers Moses Marcus and Gerson Warburg.

The Warburg family traced their origins to an ancestor in the Westphalian town of Warburg in the mid-sixteenth century. In the seventeenth century the family moved to Altona. The Altona branch of the Warburgs played a distinguished role in politics, philanthropy and business but was later overshadowed by the Hamburg Warburgs, whose bank made solid strides in the nineteenth century, forging the foreign connections which were to prove of the utmost value for the Warburgs, for Hamburg and for Germany in the twentieth. Already during the financial crisis of 1857, the Warburgs came to the rescue of the city by arranging an Austrian loan of silver bars to shore up credit until the panic was allayed. It was characteristic shrewd business, but it also earned them the gratitude of the city-state. With only ten employees in the financial house, which only then assumed the title 'bank', it was still a modest conservatively run enterprise. Siegmund and Moritz Warburg laid the solid foundations of the business. Siegmund and his elegant ambitious wife Theophilie produced seven children, none of whom played a major role in the later expansion of the Warburg bank. Moritz and Charlotte were also blessed with seven children. At first none of them seemed particularly cut out for a career in banking. Aby, the eldest, passed up the opportunity to become a banker, and instead blossomed as an art historian of great distinction. Having extracted a promise at the age of thirteen from his brother Max to purchase any books he wished to possess in return for giving up the rights of the first born to lead the family bank, he founded the famous Warburg Library in Hamburg. At the time Max had no idea how expensive the bargain would prove. Brother Paul, a partner in M. M. Warburg & Co., moved to New York after his marriage to the daughter of Solomon Loeb, of Kuhn Loeb and Company. He became founder of the International Acceptance Bank and vice-governor of the Federal Reserve Board. Felix courted Frieda, the daughter of Jacob Schiff, and became a partner of Kuhn Loeb. Felix's career, too, was star studied. Love thus forged a vital double link between Ferdinandstraße and Wall Street.

Max remained true to Hamburg. As a young man, dashing and sporty, banking did not appeal to him. He enjoyed riding, the outdoors, the companionship of men, the flirtation and love of pretty women. For his compulsory year of army service, with an eye to his future he chose a Bavarian cavalry regiment. In Bavaria there was no bar against a Jew becoming an officer. When he enthusiastically wrote to his father of his plans he received a laconic reply in Yiddish – *mischugge*, 'you are nuts'. His destiny was to follow his forbears in the family bank. He later acknowledged that the paternal advice had been sound. He possessed the quality of leadership and charm, the ability to get on with partners, colleagues, employees and clients. A creative drive and inveterate optimism were his strengths. With the death of his father in 1910, Max took charge.

An ardent patriot, Max became one of the *Kaiserjuden*, the group of successful and wealthy Jews who liked to associate with Wilhelm II, though he was capable, too, of vicious antisemitism.[27] Supportive of overseas expansion and colonial empire, the bank M. M. Warburg & Co. gained prestige far beyond Hamburg. Between 1900 and 1914 its balance sheet almost tripled. In 1912 the bank moved into a beautiful new building on the corner of Ferdinandstraße, a reflection of the importance of M. M. Warburg. Max was far-seeing, attempting in vain to dissuade the Kaiser from launching a 'preventive' war. He did not share the Kaiser's worries of 'encirclement'. Commerce, he believed, was the best guarantee of peace. In this he was at one with his close friend Albert Ballin, head of the Hamburg-America shipping line (Hamburg-Amerikanische Packetfahrt-Actien-Gesellschaft), Hapag for short.

After the close of the Stock Exchange, Max Warburg and Albert Ballin would walk around Alster Lake. Symbolically, the magnificent Hapag building stood on the opposite side of the street facing the bank. Max Warburg was a member of Hapag's board of directors, which helped to finance the great liners the ship-builders Blohm und Voss constructed on the banks of the Elbe. To help ensure the viability of the shipbuilders, Max was appointed to their board of directors as well. Interlocking responsibilities multiplied the bank's business.

Max was not orthodoxly religious but followed Jewish family tradition as a member of the community, providing generous charitable support. Albert Ballin too took pride in being a Jew but was married to a gentile. Anonymously, through Max Warburg, he contributed large sums to Jewish causes. Largely due to Ballin's commercial genius, the old established and staid Hamburg-America Steamship Company, founded in 1848, overcame the competition of other Hamburg shipping lines. Ballin joined in 1886 and took charge of the passenger traffic to New York, and rose in 1899 to become managing director. Passengers worldwide increased tenfold to nearly half a million on the eve of the Great War, when the tonnage of the fleet exceeded one and a quarter million. Ballin ordered ever bigger ships, winning the coveted blue riband for the fastest Atlantic cross-ing. The largest were the three giants of the Imperator class. All of Germany took immense pride in the achievement of rivalling British supremacy on the high seas. Ballin too was an ardent patriot and saw no contradiction in competing and good relations with Great Britain. Peace and commerce went hand in hand.

The *Kaiser* was a frequent visitor to Ballin's palatial villa in the Feldbrunnenstraße. The visits were enhanced by his appearance on the balcony, where he would be serenaded by the Jewish and Christian children who attended the Loewenberg school in the Johnsallee close by. On the occasion of the launch of the Imperator, Ballin gave a luncheon in his home in the Kaiser's honour. A row ensued when the wives of Hamburg's senators refused to join a social occasion in the house of a Jew. A solution was only found by seating them at the Kaiser's table. Social antisemitism was very much alive. When Ballin and Warburg attended the Stock Exchange, friends and colleagues would greet them and converse. After it closed it was customary to adjourn for a coffee and a friendly interchange of views in one of the fashionable cafés close by. Although Warburg and Ballin counted many members as their friends, they were not invited to share a table.

The social elite and bourgeoisie of Hamburg prided themselves on their good taste and manners. They considered many Jews as partners of equal standing in business. Yet, at the private social levels, there still were barriers. Prejudices sur-vived – the feeling that Jews were not 'Germans' in the same sense as they were. Jews remained in the eyes of the Christians a distinctive 'other group', though this attitude was equally true in liberal Britain and was not peculiar to Germany. But Jews thought it only a matter of time before such prejudices were overcome.

Did they not already enjoy equal rights under the constitution of the newly unified German empire? Paragraph 166 of the Criminal Code made it a criminal offence to incite religious hatred. No other country in the world had enacted such a law to protect Jews. Germany's Jews vigorously defended themselves against racial antisemites and took them to court, though they did not always secure convictions. It seemed inconceivable that in a civilised country extremists would ever gain the upper hand. Such things might happen in Russia and Romania, but not in Germany, despite all the nonsense written about race.

There were, of course, races. Black Africans, the Chinese, the Indians were all recognised as distinct races. The children of mixed race were generally regarded as inferior 'mongrels'. So far such inappropriate science was not applied to Jews and Christians except by out-and-out antisemites. But the growing preoccupation with race spelt danger for the Jews in Germany.

Light and shadows

Intellectual debates about race could now be tested in the living 'racial' laboratory of German East and West Africa. Here, in today's Namibia, a young scientist, Eugen Fischer, examined 310 children of white Boer and German fathers and 'native' mothers, concluding that, 'without exception, every European people who have assimilated the blood of inferior races paid for this absorption of the inferior elements by intellectual, spiritual and cultural decline ...'[28] He followed his findings with chilling advice. The bastard inferior racial offspring were only to be protected, 'to continue their existence: nothing more, and only as long as they are of use to us. Otherwise survival of the fittest, that is, to my mind, in this case, extinction.' The publication of his study advocating genocide was the start of a glittering academic career. Nor was this all mere theory. That African lives were not regarded as of equal worth was brutally demonstrated by the suppression of the Herero rising in 1904 which decimated the Bantu people, with the survivors being incarcerated in camps in terrible conditions. Mixed marriages were banned in the German African colonies. A ban on interracial sexual intercourse was also considered but thought to be unenforceable. What had this to do with German Jews? Is there any link with the later perversions of the Nazi racial state?

I

A healthy race, the supremacy of biology over morality, preventing undesirable offspring of Aryan and inferior races, eradicating the physically and mentally handicapped as 'lives not worth living' – these policy aims were fundamentals of Nazi ideology. They began, however, not with the Nazis, but a century earlier, as part of the pursuit of 'eugenics'. They originated in Britain, not Germany.

Sir Francis Galton has the best claim to recognition as the father of eugenics. He defined it as the science to improve the race. His research began investigating generations of the 'best' of British families, those that had produced statesmen, literary giants, philosophers, judges, bishops and, of course, other great scientists, to substantiate his belief that high achievement was inherited. The ability of the superior to reproduce should therefore be furthered. The unfortunates of the other extreme of degeneracy, on the other hand, should be prevented from propagating their own kind. Welfare therefore needed to be considered not from an individual's needs but from the viewpoint of the good of society. Such ideas, however, were strongly challenged at the time and never won overwhelming support in Britain.[29]

In Germany, eugenics received an enthusiastic reception from a group of scientists whose authority lent spurious legitimacy to the crimes of the Nazi era. The father of German eugenics was Alfred Ploetz. With his pupil Fritz Lenz, he founded in 1904 an influential academic journal, the *Archiv für Rassen- und Gesellschaftsbiologie* (Archive for Race and the Biology of Society).[30] Ploetz was right to point out that there were no 'pure races', but at the same time he believed the human population was divided into predominant racial groups of descending desirability. The Jews he assigned a high place, second only to Aryans, because he thought that Jews were 90 per cent composed of Aryans! (He had to abandon that conclusion in the 1930s.)

Ploetz taught that, to further the good racial elements, war and revolution, with their indiscriminate bloodshed, should be avoided. He advocated ending the lives of 'weak' twins and handicapped infants, while defectives ought to be sterilised. Eugenic societies soon spread, with branches throughout the West.

In 1912 the first International Congress of Eugenics was held in London. A large exhibitor's space was taken up by the Germans. Among the distinguished participants were Alfred Ploetz, Ernst Rudin and Eugen Fischer. An interesting exhibit, of later notorious application under the Nazis, was the *Ahnentafel*, a genealogical map of defects traced through generations. As you followed it down from great-grandparents to your own living self, the inherited defects accumulated, until 'the whole burden of an individual's forbears crushed the single final victim beneath its weight'.[31]

An Englishman – this time not a scientist – Houston Stewart Chamberlain, who later became a German citizen, supplemented the message of the eugenicists with his 'philosophy'. He published in 1899 a two-volume indigestible work entitled *The Foundations of the Nineteenth Century*. Chamberlain was no rigorous thinker. What gave his work such popularity in Germany was his glorification of the German nation. The Germans, he said, were the descendants of the Teutons, a superior Nordic people linked to the ancient Aryans. Their cosmological enemies, the corrupters of civilisation, were the Semites, the Jews. All history was the outcome of racial conflict. The Aryans were now engaged, he warned, in a struggle to prevent the global victory for supremacy of the Jews. That was the historic challenge confronting them. Hitler became one of Chamberlain's most ardent followers.[32]

After the First World War, the loss of young manhood, 'the best of German blood', the crippling of hundreds of thousands, asylums filled with returning soldiers whose nerves had been shattered – all created fears in the 1920s for the decline of the nation's racial health. The inhuman aspects of eugenics would not have gained so much influence but for the devastating consequences of the war. The eugenicists now won a greater hearing. But, during the years of the Weimar

Republic, human rights barriers were strong enough to block their adoption into policies. That would change once the Nazis came to power.[33]

Crude Nazi doctrines had been propagandised during the Weimar years. The eugenicists, in part true scientists, found some of these theories impossible to accept but welcomed their general intent. What is striking, however, is how quickly so many were able to suppress their scientific reservations and lend their prestige to the Nazis' inhumanity.

Among Ploetz's pupils was his brother-in-law, Ernst Rudin. Rudin wrote the official commentary on the Law for the Prevention of Genetically Diseased Offspring. He also invented a statistical method of *Erbprognose* (foretelling the likelihood of mental or physical incapacity of descendants). His advice on the need for sterilisation of the handicapped perfectly matched Nazi ideology. Another eminent member of the group, Eugen Fischer, also adjusted. Appointed director of the prestigious Kaiser Wilhelm Institute for Anthropology, Human Heredity and Eugenics in 1927, he remained in charge until 1942. His institute was involved in evaluating gruesome medical experiments in Auschwitz.[34]

The science of eugenics by then had split into the beneficial medical and environmental researches, which have been pursued to the present day, and the human engineering which the Nazis practised in its most murderous form.

Before the First World War, German racists were not slow to draw parallels between sexual relations among white and coloured persons and Jewish–Christian marriages, which they condemned as degenerating the German race.[35] There was no bar to such marriages in imperial Germany; on the contrary, they increased at a fast rate. The influence of the radical racists had its limits, but anti-semitism was again on the march: the Jews were blamed for the social dislocation caused by imperial Germany's rapid industrialisation.

In Germany, the now widespread use of the word 'antisemite' also revealed a crucial change from 'anti-Jew'. A semite 'could no more change than a sly fox turn into a noble deer'. A Jew could never be a part of the German *Volk*. The message was drummed home in leaflets, in books, in speeches and by word of mouth. Wilhelm Marr, a querulous old man living in Hamburg, published a jumble of his half-baked ideas in a book he called *Der Judenspiegel* (The Mirror of the Jew). Then in 1879 appeared *Der Sieg des Judenthums über das Germanenthum* (The Victory of Judaism over the German *Volk*), which portrayed the corrupt parasitic Jew conquering the virtuous German and destroying all that was good and noble. It ran to eleven editions, which may sound impressive, but each was small and read only by the converted.[36] Marr's diatribe coincided with the onset of a global depression in 1873. Antisemites blamed Jewish financiers. The link between vicious antisemitism and economic hardship was deepened. In the early 1900s, with the return of more normal times, antisemitism weakened but, like a virus, remained alive in politics and society, ready to break out whenever disasters and hard times reduced resistance.

There was no coherent antisemitic ideology. The antisemites made much of it up as they went along. There were differences and bitter disputes, infighting within groups and between them. Some condemned all religion, and in particular Christianity, as Jewish. Others differentiated between the Jews before and after Christ. It was an embarrassment that Jesus had sprung from the Jewish people. One 'thinker' worked out an ingenious explanation to remove this misconception. Jesus, he wrote, was of German stock, descended actually from blond, blue-eyed forbears from the Rhineland who, as Roman soldiers, had settled on the shores of Lake Galilee.[37] A pity about his mother. Jesus's life, this author explained, exemplified the struggle between the Jew and the Aryan and the triumph of the latter.

Nor was there agreement between these antisemites how the Jewish 'problem' was to be solved.[38] A small fanatical wing spoke of extermination if necessary. The German people as a whole would have been horrified at murder and violence. One of Germany's more influential antisemites was Theodor Fritsch. What he grasped was the necessity of organisation and the need to reduce propaganda to simple propositions. He founded the *Reichshammerbund*, one of several burgeoning 'orders', leagues and associations. Fritsch and others were successful in spreading the falsehood of Jewish racial difference and the danger of their growing influence to the well-being of the *Volk*. Emancipation of the Jews had gone too far. It was time to reverse it before the Jews gained control of German life. Fritsch's populism did reach a wider public: his *Handbook of the Jewish Question* sold 100,000 copies.

Even more dangerous were the respectable Germans of social standing, such as the history professor Heinrich von Treitschke. No extreme racial antisemite, he coined the phrase, later repeated thousands of times, 'the Jews are our misfortune'. Treitschke inflamed antisemitism in universities whose graduates would be Germany's future administrators and professionals. He was reproved by the equally famous historian Theodor Mommsen, but colourful and pernicious accusations carry more weight than reasoned argument.

Among the vehement antisemites of social standing was the Kaiser's choice of his court chaplain, Adolf Stoecker.[39] Stoecker's original target was not the Jews, but materialistic atheistic socialism, to which the majority of the working class adhered. The Protestant Church was closely tied to the bourgeoisie and the ruling elite and had neglected social needs. Stoecker was influential in engaging the concern of the Church – a positive legacy. His discovery that antisemitism attracted the masses encouraged him down that dangerous path, and he denounced Jews as 'a foreign drop of blood in our racial body; a corrupting influence'. He was not advocating murdering Jews or expelling them from Germany, but limiting their influence. His increasingly violent antisemitic outbursts led to his dismissal, but the harm was done. His influence was long lasting especially on theological students, the Lutheran bishops and clergymen a generation later.

Antisemitism in Kaiser Wilhelm's Germany was a cancer in more hidden ways.[40] Political parties based solely on antisemitism had no chance of securing a mass following. But antisemitism could gain more votes for parties of the right. The Conservatives in their Tivoli party programme included 'combating this ubiquitous obtrusive Jewish influence which is rotting the life of our people'. More pervasive still was the antisemitism of groups who had lost social status in a modernising Germany, such as the white-collar workers. Their association, *Deutscher Handlungsgehilfen-Verband*, was openly anti-Semitic.[41] At the other end of the social scale of antisemites were the landowners, members of the Agrarian League, who condemned 'Jewish' free trade. Artisans and craftsmen fearing Jewish competition founded their own associations excluding Jews, possibly the most influential being the Pan-German League.[42] In an atmosphere of overheated patriotism it won a considerable following. Its chairman, Heinrich Class, was a rabid anti-Semite who proposed a reversal of emancipation. Jews who were not German citizens should be forced to leave and further immigration from the East should be stopped. Jews permitted to stay were to be placed under alien law. 'German' newspapers were not to employ Jewish journalists.

II

The phenomenal rapid growth of population, urbanisation and industrialisation lived through by two generations of Germans after unification created political and social tensions.[43] Hamburg's population burgeoned, becoming Germany's major port.

Prominent as some Jews were in trade, finance and politics, they dominated none of these. Jews were outnumbered by more than twice as many Catholics, who were also discriminated against and barred from becoming senators and so taking part in government. Hamburg was a 'Lutheran state'. But Hamburg's traditionally religious Jews were well represented in the parliament, the *Bürgerschaft*. The parties generally backed by Hamburg's Jews reflected their economic and social standing, with some notable exceptions. Dr Anton Rée, as had Gabriel Riesser, supported the more democratic liberal wing in the 1860s. Dr Albert Wolffsohn, from 1880 to 1910 a leading member, argued for a more representative franchise.[44] One of Hamburg's longest and most influential serving members in the *Bürgerschaft* – elected in 1871, its first vice-president (1880) and then its president until his death in 1902 – was the Jewish merchant banker Siegmund Hinrichsen. He also served as president of the chamber of commerce from 1889 to 1891 and as a religious Jew on the board of the Jewish community, devoting his efforts to helping persecuted Jews from Russia who had reached Hamburg.[45] Jews also supported the party of the workers, the Social Democratic Party, the staunchest opponents of antisemitism. But most upper-class Jews agreed with Max Warburg that 'politics' had no place in Hamburg, which should be governed in the interest of all by those best qualified. The openness of Hamburg's upper reaches of society to Jews in politics and trade strengthened their self-confidence despite the discords and hatred the antisemites were working so hard to arouse.

Prejudices against Jews climaxed, however, whenever a calamity struck the city. And so it occurred once again during the exceptionally hot summer of

1892, when a devastating cholera epidemic broke out.[46] The general public as well as the experts were quick to blame the immigrants from Russia living in the crowded halls of the American Pier for having carried the disease with them. More dedicated antisemites exploited the alarm. But when Dr Johann Julius Reincke, head of the Health Department, published the findings of his investigation, he correctly identified the inadequate polluted sewage system as the cause. More than 8,000 lives were lost, most of them in the crowded quarters of the city. Those who were better off, in the healthier districts, suffered fewer deaths. It is interesting that Dr Reincke made a point of repudiating the antisemitic claims, pointing out that the investigation had shown that Jews, on account of the better hygiene in their homes, had experienced fewer fatalities than their Christian neighbours. Jewish doctors were in the forefront of the fight against the scourge, which was finally mastered.

No other German city had been stricken. The oligarchic clans of the senate governing Hamburg, with their preoccupation with trade and commerce at the expense of welfare for the poor, stood condemned worldwide. Their belief was that wealth would trickle down. What was good for the merchants was good for all. The shock ushered in a period of reform before the First World War. The inadequacy of the sanitation system was effectively tackled, improvements in housing were started, and there was provision of new parks where leisure and fresh air could be enjoyed.

Jews were most at risk during times of rapid change, easy targets as scapegoats for those who lost out and were unable to adapt. But Jewish activists were not prepared to accept passively the assaults on their rights.[47] At the height of political antisemitism they founded in 1893 'the Central Association of German Citizens of Jewish faith' (*Centralverein deutscher Staatsbürger jüdischen Glaubens*), or CV for short. They used the courts to defend Jewry from libel and slander. More than 500 antisemites were tried for spreading their propaganda. Those convicted received prison sentences. Although cases were not always successful, public prosecutors were reluctant to proceed and witnesses were hard to secure, the fact that the law was applied regardless of social standing or religious faith made Jews feel that they were citizens of a law-abiding state. The name *Centralverein deutscher Staatsbürger jüdischen Glaubens* conveyed the message that Jews saw themselves as Germans, differing only in their religious faith. The Jews of Hamburg would prove their patriotism second to none when the nation was in danger.

Going to war together

August 1914, prayers held for victory in German, Latin and Hebrew; Catholic priests, Protestant ministers and rabbis, Jewish and Christian soldiers all in field, grey, with their buckles emblazoned with Prussia's crown motto, 'God with us'. The same God: now the only difference was that Christian soldiers attended field service with their heads bare, while Jewish soldiers covered theirs with a spiked helmet. All were Germans now.

For the Jews, the war had special meaning.[48] Germany was their fatherland too. Jews, from liberal to orthodox, from the CV to the Zionists, were at one in declaring, 'We will gladly as Germans give up our possessions, our blood and our life.' The Kaiser's rhetoric in the *Reichstag*, 'I see no parties any longer, I see only Germans', they applied to themselves – an end to discrimination, and not just to party conflicts. *Kriegserlebnis*, the shared experience of war, would sweep away barriers that remained. Just a few Jews had been appointed to high state positions in Wilhelmine Germany before 1914; now the needs of war would change that, and nowhere more drastically than in the Prussian army. The Prussian officer corps had kept itself rigorously *judenrein*, free of Jews; now Jews could become officers of the Reserve. There were also a few regular officers of Jewish descent. One of these was Captain Friedrich Wilhelm Solmitz, baptised at birth, the Christian names bestowed on him leaving no doubt about the patriotic sentiments of his parents.

Not just Jews, but Jewish forbears were still looked at askance in the army. It helped if you had some expertise to offer. Captain Solmitz was a trained engineer. Better still, Luise Stephan, his fiancée, was of impeccable Christian stock. Hamburg's soldiers were placed under the command of Prussia, and shortly before the outbreak of war Captain Solmitz was stationed in Berlin. In a letter home he recorded an important event, a Kaiser parade.[49] The All Highest was in a good mood, reviewing his soldiers and making jovial remarks in the worst possible taste. As he moved down the line and greeted the officer in charge of the locomotive transport company, Solmitz overheard him joking, 'Have you fired up your locomotives with the bones of Hottentots?' – a passing reference to the slaughter of the Hereros. Soon the time would pass for spectacles and 'pleasantries'.

A few days later came the order for mobilisation. Luise joined her fiancé in Berlin and vividly describes how the reservists passed along the famous broad avenue Unter den Linden, flanked by the lime trees planted in the days of Frederick the Great. She captured the mood: 'Everybody is very quiet; no one is joking, there is no laughter. The crowds came to life when the first reservists marched by. The men were greeted like princes with tears in our eyes.' Back in Hamburg, on hearing Britain's declaration of war, she wrote in her journal: 'In Hamburg-Altona everyone was very shocked and quiet. As long as it was a war against France and Russia there was confidence.' Now, with stubborn Britain in the war, 'it was another matter'.

People put on a brave face. They cheered the departing soldiers, but after they had gone the mood changed. 'How willingly and enthusiastically they all departed, but we, who are left behind', Luise reflected, 'are not laughing',[50] and, later, 'there was no mood of rejoicing in Hamburg over the victories', 'no hope of peace; everywhere German blood is flowing'. She swung from gloom to exaltation: 'These are great and glorious times after all the party haggling and conflicts over little things.'[51] 'A united *Volk*. And we all place complete trust in our Army!' United? Antisemitism was very much alive.

Almost from the day war broke out, Jews were accused of avoiding their duty.[52] Such slanders were circulating as early as September 1914.[53] When Ernst

Loewenberg joined his army unit, the company commander wanted to assign him to headquarters, pointing out that, 'with your education you will be far more useful there than in the trenches'; Loewenberg rejected the proposal, 'because, as a Jew, I did not wish to be in a position considered a "shirker's" posting'.[54] Jewish organisations were well aware that antisemites would spread such falsehoods and soon began preparing statistics to refute them. By the end of the war, 96,000 German Jews had fully played their part for the fatherland. But a bigot cannot be convinced even by facts.

On the home front they also played crucial roles. The single most important innovation, the production of nitric acid, without which Germany could not have carried on the war for lack of high explosives, was a process discovered by Fritz Haber, a physical chemist of Jewish descent. Working with Karl Bosch, Haber delivered to the munitions factories nitric acid in industrial quantities via the Haber–Bosch process, as it became known.

The critical shortage of many raw materials was a direct threat to the Germans being able to wage war for more than a few weeks. The head of one of Germany's major industries, the Allgemeine Elektrizitäts Gesellschaft (AEG), was Walther Rathenau. He set up within the Prussian War Ministry a central organisation for the distribution of raw materials according to the priorities of war needs. Albert Ballin, director of the Hamburg-America Line, headed the Central Purchasing Association, staffed with Hapag personnel. The economist Julius Hirsch was placed in charge of price control. Carl Melchior, a partner in the Warburg Bank, joined the Central Purchasing Association. The famous are cited often to the exclusion of the many too old to fight who served the war effort. Jewish doctors and surgeons, more than a thousand, helped to fill the huge needs close to the trenches and behind the front. In Hamburg the doctors and nurses of the *Israelitisches Krankenhaus* worked hours almost beyond endurance treating the flood of wounded. In their dire need, soldiers did not ask whether they were patched up by Jew or gentile.

In many government departments Jews met with the cool reserve of conservative civil servants who hitherto had not worked with Jewish colleagues. Walther Rathenau resigned in 1915, handing over the efficient organisation he had created. German Jews, he observed, should be careful not to expose themselves in prominent roles. It was advice he did not later heed. In 1916, Carl Melchior also withdrew. For the Jews, setbacks in the war once more threatened to turn them into scapegoats.

I

With the stalemate on the western front and no end of the war in sight, the mood in the country darkened.[55] The war had not gone as expected: were the Jews pulling their weight? The Prussian war minister announced in October 1916 an enquiry to ascertain how many Jews were serving at the front. For the Jewish soldiers it was a slap in the face. There was protest. The War Ministry back-tracked, but the damage of the notorious *Judenzählung*, the Jew statistic, was done. The information collected was never published.

The tradition of keeping the officer corps 'free of Jews' lived on, even though the demands of war made it impossible to remain so rigid. Jewish doctors and surgeons had to be granted reserve officer rank. But only 1,000 of the 96,000 Jewish soldiers were promoted. One of these was Lieutenant Hess.[56] He enters history only as the officer in charge of a corporal who changed the world. Adolf Hitler evidently respected Hess, his company commander. Bizarrely, he served under not one but two Jewish officers. It was unfortunate for Hitler that he owed his Iron Cross First Class to another Jewish lieutenant, Hugo Guttmann, who also wore this decoration.

Jews, Christians and non-believers all shared the hardships and dangers of the trenches and were killed in their tens of thousands at Verdun and in the fields of Flanders. Bullets did not discriminate. Daily life with no space to move awake or sleep and the constant fear of death bred comradeship and broke down barriers. 'Antisemitism among the people I never felt during the war, as long as I was with ordinary soldiers',[57] Ernst Loewenberg recalls, 'but once there was a prospect of promotion to the officer corps, that changed from one day to the next. On the day the non-commissioned became candidate officers they forgot we existed.'

From the start of the war the antisemites set out to destroy the acceptance of their Jewish fellow citizens.[58] One means was to revive fears of Jews from Russian Poland and Habsburg Galicia 'flooding Germany' and 'infecting German civilisation'. It evidently worked well. 'I wish that sharper frontier controls were put in place against the Jews from Galicia and Poland', Luise Solmitz wrote in her journal, 'otherwise we will not be able to save ourselves from these people.'[59]

Many established German Jews too were discomforted by the arrival of the *Ostjuden*.[60] The assimilated Jews were ready to provide funds for welfare but avoided social contact. The established Jewish community looked askance at these foreign Jews who threatened their acceptance as Germans. It was a typical reaction of established minorities towards newcomers, not peculiar to Jews. But there was another side. Eastern Jewry brought about a renaissance of Jewish culture and a revival of religious observance.

Prejudice did not stop the German and Austrian high command when entering Russian Poland from appealing to Polish Jews for help. Tsarist discriminatory laws against Jews were abolished. 35,000 Polish Jews were recruited to man factories in Germany. Another 35,000 arrived in Germany as Russian prisoners of war.

II

Polish Jews early in the war regarded the German and Austrian soldiers as liberators. Jewish soldiers who now made contact with their co-religionists for the first time were welcomed. The soldiers marched through towns and villages sunk in dire poverty. One Jewish soldier wrote home from Olkusz that conditions were a hundred years backward, but that the Jews performed an essential function for the occupiers; 'as the Jews could speak German, much of the trade was now in their hands'.[61] German was the language of the educated Jews. Jewish communities had established German *Gymnasien*, preferring to send their children to them rather than to Polish schools. The poorer Jews, with only a few books in their homes, were sure to have on their shelf Friedrich Schiller, whose *Wilhelm Tell* was a gospel of freedom.

German-Jewish soldiers were invited to share their bread and a simple meal on the Sabbath. Prejudices were dispelled. From Brusz, a soldier wrote home that there was great poverty everywhere. The Poles were living among unbelievable dirt and hated the Germans. The life of Jewish families was different. They faithfully follow the requirements of religion, 'they keep their houses clean and honour their wives'. But the German administration gained no such insights, and their bias against the Jews increased with the agitation of the antisemites in Germany. At headquarters officers stereotyped them as inferior, as carriers of disease and creators of strife.

In Germany they were blamed for fomenting unrest among working people, accused of being the wire-pullers behind demands for a negotiated peace. The war-weariness of the workers had nothing to do with 'Jewish' influence. Hamburg suffered particularly badly.[62] Overseas trade was cut by the blockade. The port workers lost their jobs, but shipbuilding was booming, making near impossible demands on an exhausted workforce. The workers did not even earn enough to feed their families. Strikes broke out, the first in 1915. The following year hunger protests drove women and youths into the streets, and shops were plundered. Women who had worked for twelve hours stood in long lines outside food shops. Men were working even longer hours. Mass strikes held up production for several days in 1917. That winter was one of the worst: food became so short that it was christened 'the turnip winter'.

Despite victory in the East, Germany was close to breaking point.[63] To win over the disaffected workers, long overdue franchise reform was promised. Victory would no longer mean rule by the old elites. These in turn now blamed the Jews for the strength of social democracy. Worse followed. The *Reichstag* in July 1917 passed a resolution calling for a compromise peace without annexations or oppression – an end to war without the fruits of victory. The war would last another year before the supreme command finally accepted that all resources, human and material, were exhausted. It was clear the fighting would not last much longer. Unwilling to sacrifice their lives uselessly in a suicidal battle with the British fleet, the sailors of Kiel sparked off a revolution when the warships were ordered to sea. Within days it was all over. In Berlin, on 9 November 1918, the Social Democrat Philipp Scheidemann proclaimed the 'German Republic'. That evening the Kaiser took flight for asylum in the Netherlands. Living in a mini-castle at Doorn, he wrote his memoirs and turned bitterly on the Jews, blaming them for his downfall. What would happen in Hamburg? Would their fellow citizens turn on them too?

2

THE SHADOW OF THE NAZIS

Revolution and after

For *Frau* Solmitz, the very foundations of her orderly world were crumbling. Mechanically she followed her routine. She went to teach her class of girls as usual on 6 November 1918. That evening, she sat down to write in her journal:

> Today it has started in Hamburg. The mood among colleagues this morning is below zero. Some believe that revolution is imminent, others hope it will all settle down … life is dreadful, everything unstable, no one knows what the next day will bring … disgust and abhorrence seize one's throat … sorrow and apprehension for the shattered fatherland, indignation at the 'Germans' who have betrayed us.[1]

Who were the traitors – Bolsheviks and Jews? The 'stab in the back' legend did not have to be invented by the supreme command, let alone by Hitler; it was widespread early on.

The day *Frau* Solmitz made that entry in her journal the sailors from Kiel reached Hamburg. They set up a 'Workers' and Soldiers' Council', but this was not a Soviet revolution – it only borrowed the Bolshevik name. All over Germany, 'Workers' and Soldiers' Council's sprang up and for a time filled a power vacuum. The pressing need was to ensure the supply of necessities for the population. In Hamburg the workers soon realised that they could not manage without the skills of the state bureaucracy. Faced with everyday problems, the continuing blockade, shortage of food, returning soldiers, the needs of the war widows and the disabled, theoretical socialism gave way to pragmatic measures to cope with the catastrophic situation. Hamburg followed its own path. But ultimately what would happen in Hamburg would become dependent on the outcome of the political struggles in Berlin.

I

A revolution practically without bloodshed: the socialists now in command. To give some semblance of legitimacy to the transition, the last imperial chancellor, Prince Max von Baden, handed power over to Philipp Scheidemann, leader of the Social Democratic Party, who on 9 November 1918, from the window of the *Reichstag*, proclaimed the 'German Republic', only to be challenged by the radical left when Karl Liebknecht declared the foundation of the 'Free Socialist Republic of Germany' from the balcony of the imperial palace. Thus the fracture that ultimately doomed the republic was manifest from the beginning.[2]

For a short time the two wings of the socialist party cooperated as they faced enormous practical problems. But very soon the fissures between them widened. For Liebknecht and his followers, the priority was to carry the revolution further, to establish a socialist society breaking the power of the owners of industry, the imperial reactionary military command and the old imperial administration. For the Social Democrats, with the support of the bulk of the working class, the priority was to establish a stable parliamentary democracy. The transformation to socialism would have to come later, and, as it turned out, was never accomplished.

On the eve of Christmas 1918 tensions heightened between a militia of sailors of the left and the military in Berlin. In January 1919 the conflict escalated to open fighting in the streets. What became known as the 'Spartacist Rising' had not initially been planned by the leadership of the left, who had formed the Communist Party of Germany (KDP), but once it had broken out the majority of its leaders backed the use of force with the intention of overthrowing the Reich government. Reichspresident Friedrich Ebert and his defence minister, Gustav Noske, called on the army to restore order. The soldiers were joined by undisciplined right-wing Free Corps militias, who murdered on 15 January 1919 the two communist leaders Rosa Luxemburg and Karl Liebknecht. What followed was lawless brutal repression in Berlin and much of the rest of Germany. The legacy was hatred and the irreparable split of the socialists.[3]

Hamburg escaped the worst of the violence during the years from 1919 to 1923.[4] In March 1919 the Workers' and Soldiers' Council handed their powers back to the elected Hamburg government and its traditional institutions. Henceforth, until 1933, Hamburg was governed by coalitions of the moderate socialists (the SPD) and parties of the centre. Here a tradition of compromise and moderation prevailed, despite all the challenges on the economic and political fronts the city shared with the rest of Germany. Neighbouring Prussia too enjoyed a stable government headed by moderate socialists.

Elections for the all-German National Assembly had been held in January 1919, four days after the murder of Rosa Luxemburg and Karl Liebknecht. The immediate task of President Ebert and the government was to meet the challenges of the radical left and right to its existence. In fact it was in greater danger from the right than the left. A rightist attempt to seize power in March 1920, known as the Kapp coup, found the government to be so weak that it had to flee from Berlin. This time the army refused to restore order. The army command could be relied on to fight the communists, who attempted a number of smaller further uprisings until 1923, but not against the extreme right. It was the solidarity of the majority of the working people and the trade unions, and, it also has to be added, the bulk of the judiciary and civil service, that put an end to the coup.

As if these internal conflicts were not enough, disputes over reparations payments and deep resentment at the unjust *Diktat* of Versailles brought the republic to the very verge of ruin. The conflict reached a climax with the French and Belgian occupation of the Ruhr in January 1923. The occupiers imposed a harsh military regime, and the German government answered with 'passive resistance'. Industrial production plummeted and the German currency, already in a parlous state, collapsed to a degree not previously experienced in modern times, becoming practically worthless. Now everyone was a millionaire and a pauper – actually not quite everyone: those with tangible assets, industrial plants or houses rescued something from the crash; those with debts saw them reduced; but the patriots who had subscribed to war loans, Jews and gentiles, and those with their savings in the bank, saw their wealth practically wiped out.

From these depths, recovery came more swiftly than could have been expected. The years of Weimar were full of surprises and contradictions. A monarchist politician of the centre-right, Gustav Stresemann, became the saviour of the republic and its most outstanding statesman until his death in 1929. He broke off the policy of civil disobedience in the Ruhr and undertook to follow a policy of 'fulfilment'. Reform of the currency created new economic stability, reparations were scaled down and loans at attractive rates, subscribed by foreigners, relaunched industry. Germany's international standing was also restored when she was accepted as a member of the League of Nations. In 1925, the Locarno Treaty guaranteed the western frontiers agreed in the Versailles Treaty between Germany, France and Belgium, promising stability with security. The following year, Gustav Stresemann accepted the hand of friendship extended by Foreign Minister Aristide Briand. The age-old enmity between France and Germany was buried. This set the scene for the phased Allied withdrawal from the occupied Rhineland. It was an astonishing transformation not conceived to be possible two years earlier.

The stability of the republic seemed assured by another surprising turn of events. The death of Ebert in February 1925 necessitated new elections. The electors now placed the future of the republic, and the considerable powers of the president that went with the office, into the hands of the arch-representative of the Kaiser's military, Field Marshal Paul von Hindenburg. Unexpectedly, the old man loyally performed his duty until it seemed that the republic could no longer function on the basis of its constitution. While weaknesses could not be hidden, it had overcome the first five traumatic years of multiple challenges, but it would not prove equal to survive a second shock five years later.

II

In this cauldron of instability, the extremists got a hearing. Hitler's National Socialist German Workers' Party in Bavaria attracted 55,000 members; his violent oratory mobilised thousands more. His attempt on 8/9 November 1923 to seize power in Munich and 'march on Berlin' failed, but it was not the end as it should have been. Hitler enjoyed the protection of the political right and of the army in Bavaria. In Hamburg, the earliest local National Socialist group would have fitted into a single street car.[5] They did not in the beginning gain the sympathies of the merchant elite and bureaucracy and could muster only a hundred members. In November 1922, the senate ordered a cessation of their political activities. But the Nazi movement was not doomed. The fanatical right gained a firm hold in German society, becoming a springboard for the later Nazi breakthrough. Many organisations fighting each other burgeoned like poison mushrooms; they prepared millions to accept the racial ideology.

From the very first, the assault on the republic and democracy was linked with the assault on the Jews. A symptom of the distress during these early years was an explosive growth of antisemitism. Far more important than the Nazis in Hamburg in the 1920s was the *Deutschvölkischer Schutz- und Trutz-Bund* (German-*völkisch* Defend and Defy League), with its headquarters in Hamburg.[6] The league, from its foundation in 1919, flooded the whole country with vicious antisemitic propaganda pamphlets, booklets, and stickers that could be attached to shop windows; swastikas soon appeared crudely scrawled on bare walls.

The Defend and Defy League was the offshoot of the Pan-German League. With not many more than 20,000 members, it adopted a well-tried path to win mass appeal. The Jews would be made 'the lightning conductor' for all Germany's ills. The league denounced the democratic republic as the Jew republic; its slogan, 'Germany belongs to the Germans'. Imperialist and nationalist as well as antisemitic in the Kaiser's Germany, it transformed and adopted new tactics. Radical antisemites became its organisers. The membership grew rapidly and in 1921 reached 150,000. In such pamphlets as 'The Jews in the Army' and 'The Jews in the War Economy', they spread their lies. One novel, entitled *Sünde wider das Blut* (Sinning against the Blood), sold 200,000 copies.

The active organisations of German Jews[7] vigorously opposed the lies of the league with their own publications and appeals to tolerance and reason. Dr Albert Holländer, of the Hamburg branch of the Central Association of German Citizens of Jewish Faith, wrote a counter-pamphlet, 'Germany for the Germans': 'We also demand Germany for the Germans and have the right to do so since we have lived for centuries on German soil … [we too] love Germany as our fatherland.' Against the barrage of antisemitic slander, the CV achieved little. Antisemitism struck a chord also among many decent Germans who would not personally have harmed a fellow Jew. It was effective because what the racial antisemites preached was not new, only an escalation of previous beliefs.

III

Luise Solmitz describes a scene in her journal at this time which is trivial yet revealing.[8] A small family group – father, mother and their son, a young man, carrying a heavy suitcase – were waiting at a tram stop. By their appearance they were clearly recently arrived Jews from Poland. First the parents entered the streetcar, then the youngster tried to follow; the conductor barred his way because of the suitcase. Angry words were exchanged. The parents stood up and got off again – their son was still standing in the street – and as the tram started to leave the conductor loudly shouted after them, 'pack of Jews', so all could hear. Luise Solmitz could not help feeling sorry for the family, '*even* if they are Jews'. The conductor should have let them into the half-empty carriage.

What does this little scene tell us? It shows something of the split state of mind typical of so many educated and morally upright Germans. Ready to agree with what was said in general about Jews, few did not believe *something* disreputable about them, but most knew a good Jew. No one in the tram protested at the conductor's behaviour. In his uniform he represented authority. Such small everyday incidents were repeated many times.

Much more serious were terror attacks on prominent Jews. These terrorists usually belonged to several *völkisch* and antisemitic organisations, some shadowy and secret. One of the most sinister, code-named Consul, incited its members not just to 'educate' and open the eyes of the people to its racial enemies, but to murder them.

Matthias Erzberger was the *Reichstag* party leader who had co-sponsored the Peace Resolution in 1917. A Catholic, he became a prime target. Five attempts to kill him failed, but the sixth succeeded. The following year, in June 1922, the first prime minister of the Weimar government, the Social Democrat Philipp Scheidemann – not a Jew – was also the target of a failed assassination. Jews who had been prominent before the collapse of the Wilhelmine Empire and now supported the republic were in double danger. Walther Rathenau in 1919 accepted ministerial office. As foreign minister, he followed a policy of seeking agreements with the Allied victors while stoutly defending Germany's interests. It was Rathenau who stunned the Allies by concluding the Rapallo Treaty with Russia, mutually relinquishing claims to reparations. By the right he was labelled a traitor; his enemies chanted, 'Strike dead Walther Rathenau, the god-damned Jewish sow'.

Max Warburg knew Rathenau well and in May 1922 paid him a visit.[9] Rathenau asked Warburg whether he would join the government. It was not the first time Warburg had been offered high ministerial office. He always refused for the same reason. Jews, he believed, could not afford to occupy prominent positions in the state; to accept would simply provide more ammunition for the antisemites, who would heap blame upon them, irrespective of whether they succeeded or failed. His recent experiences only confirmed that. With much reluctance, Max Warburg had given in to pressure to join the peace delegation at

Versailles as one of the financial experts. When the peace conditions, in the form of an ultimatum, were presented by the Allies to the German delegation, he and the other experts advised in vain that they should be rejected. The German delegation, however, bowed to the Allied threats and signed. This did not stop the antisemites subsequently from accusing Warburg of selling out to the enemy in the interests of world Jewry. So, not surprisingly, Warburg's response to Rathenau's question was that he thought that more than one Jewish minister was simply inviting trouble – little guessing how soon he would be proved tragically right. Rathenau half agreed but was fatalistic. He told Warburg that he had received many death threats, but had refused the police protection an anxious government tried to persuade him to accept. Four weeks later, on 24 June 1922, while he was returning from the Foreign Ministry in an open car, assassins riddled his body with bullets, and for good measure threw in a hand-grenade that tore him to pieces. His death was the one event that briefly aroused the political parties and trade unions to rally to the republic and to condemn violence.

Shortly after Rathenau's murder, Warburg tried to bring together influential people in Hamburg. 'I considered it proper', he recalled,

> to urge my Christian friends to take a public stand against the lawlessness, to make a plea for tolerance and mutual affection and to put their names to such a declaration … But it soon became clear that the number of people who were courageous and decent was small. After a great deal of effort the declaration was made public, signed by very few though distinguished people.

This was an illuminating episode during the early days of the Weimar Republic – how much more difficult it would become to persuade anyone to speak up for the rights of Jewish citizens after the Nazis had demonstrated their strength.

Max Warburg that autumn was himself in danger.[10] Hugo Campe, the police president of Hamburg, warned him that the police had received information that an assassin was planning to make an attempt on his life. He should take care to vary his routine, to use different streets to reach the bank or the Stock Exchange and restaurants. Max Warburg took refuge with his sister-in-law. For his protection, the Hamburg police assigned a police lieutenant to guard him. The young man was devoted. He slept in the same bedroom with Warburg or close by, his pistol always at the ready. At such close quarters Warburg got to know his young protector well, but evidently not well enough. Only later did he find out that the policeman sent to guard him was a National Socialist. Warburg speculated that this explained why he was so well informed about their clandestine plans. 'Of all the dangers to which I was exposed', Warburg wryly remarked, 'not the least of them was my protection.' Fortunately the lieutenant took the view that his duty as a policeman had to take precedence over his party association. He was a war veteran who had suffered head wounds. When he opened fire on his own police unit a short while after, it became clear he was not accountable for his eccentric behaviour, and he ended his days in a mental institution.

IV

Stabilising the currency in 1923 resulted in more hardship. Who was to blame? The Jews of course, the foreigners, the Bolsheviks – all linked to world international Jewry. In Berlin, there was a pogrom against the 'Eastern Jews' in the Scheunenviertel close by the Alexanderplatz. A Berlin newspaper reported 'howling mobs in all the streets. Looting is going on under the cover of darkness.' In Hamburg, there were rumours of plans for a Nazi uprising. Max Warburg left again, remaining in the United States for a few weeks. He was back by Christmas. The police now became alarmed that they might find themselves unable to protect Jewish property in time if it was suddenly attacked by a determined group. The Warburg bank was an obvious target, and a group of bank employees were allowed firearms in readiness to repel an assault. Darting in and out of Hamburg, Max Warburg remained robust. Like other German Jews, he had no intention of giving up.

Political developments in Hamburg became more reassuring.[11] Hamburg was governed by parties, from centre-left to centre-right, which were solidly democratic. The city's Jews in the main supported the German Democratic Party, whose leading local politician was Carl Petersen.[12] Petersen made no secret of the fact that one of his forbears was Jewish and condemned the antisemites. In 1925 he assumed a leading role in the city-state as mayor. That democratic politicians secured a majority of the votes at elections might lead to the comforting conclusion that this reflected the firm support of the people for liberal democracy and a constitutional republic. It was not so. The popular spread of antisemitism in the 1920s and the lack of public protest shows how little democratic values were really understood.

The so-called golden years of the mid-1920s were not so bright when looked at more closely. The Achilles heel was the economy. In his annual reports Max Warburg was full of misgivings.[13] He could not shake off the feeling that the recovery was not soundly based. The country was living on borrowed money and time, on short-term loans at high rates of interest to tempt foreign credit. How would the loans be repaid? Unemployment remained high. The prospects for the younger generation leaving school or university were far from rosy. Professions like the law and medicine were already overcrowded.

Nor did the political omens look better. The Social Democratic President Friedrich Ebert died in 1925. He had helped Weimar to weather the crisis of the early years. In his place, incongruously, the most celebrated of the Kaiser's soldiers, Paul von Hindenburg, was elected and sworn in as the republic's president.

In Berlin, one Reich coalition government followed another. In the federal *Länder* there was more stability, and in Prussia, the most important, the Social Democratic government was in control. In Hamburg, something of an old tradition that government was less about ideology than about good administration prevailed. Coalitions between the Social Democratic Party, the German Democratic Party and, later, the more right-wing German People's Party here provided stability.

The constitution of Weimar granted Jews equal rights. That was not new. What changed was that they could now enjoy these rights in practice. Life for the Jewish population of Hamburg – predominantly middle and lower middle-class professionals, shopkeepers and employees – during the Weimar years was just as difficult as for the rest of the population. Only a few Jews belonged to the wealthy upper classes. All social classes suffered in Germany, and recovery to pre-war standards of living was not reached until 1928, and then only for a short time before the devastating Depression began. For the Jews, the Weimar years had two faces. While antisemitism spread alarmingly, on the other hand, Jews gained full legal emancipation and equal rights; they could now be, and were, appointed to high offices of state previously closed to them. In Hamburg, Leo Lippmann as head of the Finance Office became the leading civil servant.

V

Although he held one of the top positions in the state civil service, Lippmann's career exemplifies the ambiguities Jews felt.[14] Beside his responsibility for Hamburg's finances, he also had the financial oversight of opera performed in the *Stadttheater*. Largely due to his efforts, the opera survived the difficult years. Jewish artists played a prominent role in Hamburg's cultural life. From 1917 until 1931 Egon Pollak was musical director, and from 1922 until 1933 Leopold Sachse, renowned for his Wagner *Ring* productions, was the director of the opera. His replacement, chosen early in January 1933, was Heinrich K Strohm, days before Hitler became chancellor. Lippmann was still a participant on the selection committee which agreed that no Jew should be chosen; he thought this prudent, given the times they lived in. Nor had judges in Hamburg been promoted simply on merit. Religion entered into the consideration, 'so that', as Lippmann recalled, 'the percentage of Jewish judges should not be too high'. 'I cannot remember', Lippmann added, 'ever having proposed a Jew in Hamburg for promotion' – an extraordinary admission of how Jews disadvantaged themselves.

How little rhyme or reason there was in the general public's attitude to Jews in Germany is shown by their popularity in the theatre and concert hall and on the silver screen. To mention just some popular Jewish artists, favourite actors and actresses were Rudolf Schildkraut, Elisabeth Bergner and Fritz Kortner. In Hamburg, Mirjam Horwitz made Wedekind's Lulu her own role; with her husband, she founded the *Hamburger Kammerspiele*. Julius Gutmann sang the role of Alberich in Wagner's *Rheingold*.

A strange state of schizophrenia also afflicted the university,[15] founded in 1919. In all faculties a number of professors who were Jewish or with Jewish forbears achieved world fame: in psychology William Stern, in physics Otto Stern, and in international relations Albrecht Mendelssohn Bartholdy, grandson of the composer. The Warburg Institute became world renowned; Aby Warburg, Max's elder brother, had established the library and centre of study of art history and philosophy; professor Erwin Panofsky was closely associated with the institute and occupied the chair of art history at the university.

Jewish professors faced antisemitic abuse early on. William Stern met the threat head on. In 1919, before starting to lecture he told students:

> At the meeting of the student association the day before yesterday a large number of pamphlets by the German-*völkisch* Defend and Defy League and the *Reichshammerbund* were circulated … I am personally concerned by one passage: 'as a German student avoid as far as possible the lectures of Jewish professors but if you have to attend be critical'; the intention is nothing less than a call to boycott some university teachers and an attempt to drive a wedge between students and teachers … Ladies and gentlemen, as I am one of the few Jewish professors at the university and at present the only one in the faculty of philosophy, I consider this injunction is directed against me; when I read this sentence I felt shame that such a thing is possible in a higher educational institution. I have been a university teacher for decades and always enjoyed the warmest relations with my students … as a teacher and scholar I have contributed to my German fatherland at least as much as those who wish to deny us the right to belong to Germany and wish to bring the students in conflict with us.

He then invited those students who did not know that he was a Jew and now wished to leave to do so and receive back their lecture fee, appealing to the rest 'to uphold the atmosphere of goodwill and cooperation that had always existed between teachers and students and to combat the poison designed to destroy it'.[16]

The *völkisch* antisemitic students were not just a few. Together with conservative groups, who were antisemitic though not *völkisch*, they made up almost the majority and were later able to associate with the Nazis. They were the generation that had passed through the conservative nationalistic *Gymnasien* of the Wilhelmine years. More remarkable is the fact that just over half the student body still rejected a motion to exclude Jewish students from the student's union. A Jewish scholar was carefully taking note. The distinguished philosopher Ernst Cassirer had made his acceptance of a professorship in Hamburg dependent on the outcome. In 1929 he became *Rektor*, chancellor, of the university for the year.

Among Cassirer's professional colleagues in Hamburg, only one, the geographer Siegfried Passarge, agitated openly against Jews,[17] Marxists and pacifists. Cassirer ignored Passarge's outbursts and agreed charitably with his colleagues that he was a crackpot. That appeared to be confirmed by Passarge's attempt to exonerate his colleague from blemish. Passarge assured Cassirer that he was not included in his racial condemnation, explaining that a small sub-racial group of

Jews to which he was certain Cassirer belonged were actually Bedouins, adding for good measure that these Jews neither looked like other Jews nor shared their bad characteristics. Cassirer thanked him for the compliment but asked him to spare him racial theories. Assuring Jewish acquaintances that they were an exception to the general rule was actually quite typical of many relationships. The university authorities told Passarge to stop his diatribes, which he did for a time, but he was an incorrigible antisemite. In 1927 he delivered a popular lecture series, 'The Racial Science of the German Volk and the Jews'. His was the only department that did not dismiss Jewish academics in 1933, as he had appointed none. Held in high esteem during the Nazi years, he retired in 1935. After the war, in 1957, on his ninetieth birthday, the university bestowed on him an honorary doctorate.

Voting for the representatives of the students' union from the first produced conservative majorities.[18] These students found National Socialism increasingly attractive. They believed with the help of the National Socialists they would regain their proper role in society as leaders and face down the socialist masses. Jewish students formed their own associations and voted for a social democrat pacifist coalition which enjoyed stronger support in Hamburg than in other German universities. There were not many Jewish students at the University of Hamburg, only just over a hundred out of a student body of over 3,000. They threatened no one. Student attitudes were an indicator of the future, but for the present Hamburg's government remained resolutely opposed to vulgar prejudice and discrimination.

Unequal struggle

August 11th was Constitution Day.[19] In 1928 the Hamburg senate marked the occasion as usual with a festive ceremony in the town hall. But all was not well with this democracy long before Hitler came to power. *True* democrats were fewer than the voters who until 1931 gave the senate a democratic majority. The conservative elites accepted the republic but without heart or warmth. They were known as *Vernunftrepublikaner* – republicans not of conviction but seeing the republic as the best option. How shallow was the understanding of democracy was shown by the vicious campaign of extremist groups against Jewish citizens. Too many good people quietly tolerated these attacks, even if they did not openly support them. There was little popular understanding that democracy was based on human rights, on the acceptance of those with whom you differ for political, social, economic, religious or cultural reasons. Hamburg's senators were well aware of the shortcomings of the people's civic education. So it was no mere chance that the senate chose a Jew to deliver the keynote speech on this particular Constitution Day.

The invitation to Professor Ernst Cassirer was unanimous.[20] *Frau* Cassirer urged her husband to decline: 'I was against his involvement in politics even at the university; I did not want him to further the prevailing allegations that Jews were playing too large a role, intruding into the fate of the nation.' Ernst disagreed. The senate, he said, had placed on him a responsibility he could not shirk.

Cassirer, with his shock of white hair and blue eyes, attired in the traditional university black robe and contrasting brilliant white ruffled collar, Dutch burgher style, stood out as an unmistakably commanding figure. The largely conservative audience he addressed, Hamburg's elite in politics, government and business, did not particularly want to hear what he had to say. Cassirer extolled the virtues of democracy. His theme was that democracy was not un-German, not a foreign import from the French Revolution, but was imbedded in German thinking and philosophy and represented what was best in Germany. The message missed its mark. His audience heard only what it wanted to hear, *Frau* Cassirer observed shrewdly.

In 1928, however, the Hamburg senate was still sufficiently confident of public esteem to throw its weight against the rising tide of intolerance and antisemitism. In the city-state the patrician tradition prevailed that the overriding duty was to provide for good government and not to allow political passions to dominate. It was this attitude that enabled senators of different parties – socialists and conservatives – to work together in fulfilling practical tasks long after in Berlin at the Reich level such cooperation had become impossible. Typical was the police force, crucial for the preservation of law, order and civic rights.[21] The responsible senator was Adolph Schönfelder, a Social Democrat; the police president, Hugo Campe, was a member of the conservative People's Party, and the commander of the special militarised security police, the *Ordnungspolizei*, Colonel Lothar Danner, was a Social Democrat.

The governing coalition still felt able to lead with the increasing electoral support they had won. After the recent elections they enjoyed a comfortable majority. Although only two out of every hundred had voted for the Nazis, it was ominous that fourteen people in every hundred supported the antisemitic German National People's Party. And that was before the Depression had affected Hamburg severely. Two and a half years later the writing was on the wall. The elections for the *Reichstag* on 14 September 1930 left no one in any doubt that a political upheaval was under way. Nationally the Nazis won 18.3 per cent, the communists 13.1 per cent. In Hamburg the Nazis polled 19.2 per cent and the communists increased their vote to 18 per cent. These results left the governing coalition parties in Hamburg just hanging on to power.

I

This huge increase in Nazi support alarmed democratic politicians and Jews. The Nazi movement was spreading like a cancer, infiltrating the police and the civil service, disrupting democracy from within. The majority of the higher civil servants, the judiciary and army officers had been hostile to the republic from the beginning, though they avoided open identification with anti-republican parties for fear of blighting their careers. Among the officers of the police, the Nazis gained many sympathisers, especially in the militarised force. The ordinary civil police force supported the Social Democrats. But here too the Nazis were increasingly able to attract the younger policemen.

In November 1930 the governing senate summoned enough strength to try to meet the threat from the anti-republican left and right. Following the lead of the government in Prussia, the senate issued a decree threatening disciplinary proceedings against any state employee joining either the Nazi or the Communist Party. Democratic control nevertheless crumbled. A few months later this prohibition triggered a violent occurrence which sent shock waves through the Jewish community. Otto Pohl, a policeman, was being interrogated by his senior, Oswald Lassally, about his secret membership of the Nazi Party. Pohl drew out his revolver and at point blank range shot Lassally, severely wounding him. What had so enraged the policeman? Pohl declared that he was not going to allow a Jew to question him. The Nazis claimed that it was provocative for a Jew to have been chosen to undertake the investigation. Conservatives, liberals and socialists alike condemned the brutal attack. Dr Erwin Garvens, head of the state's Audit Office, called the crime, in his diary, a 'filthy outrage'.[22] In the hospital, Lassally was said to be very depressed: 'no wonder when shot after baptism and confirmation only because of his Jewish descent'. A few days later, *Frau* Solmitz recorded another Nazi outrage:

> Yesterday was a dreadful and bloody Sunday. Ernst Henning, a communist member of Hamburg's parliament, was shot travelling on the night bus from Bergedorf. This is a uniquely bloody deed in Germany undertaken by three National Socialists. The bus was full. A schoolteacher sitting next to Henning was wounded in her legs. One can only imagine the panic of the other passengers.[23]

Hamburg's Jews felt isolated and threatened.[24] Shortly after the shooting, Alfred Levy, the chairman of the council of the Jewish community, received a letter from a prominent member. Jacques Meyer lived in one of Hamburg's best avenues, the Mittelweg, which, unlike the streets in the poorer Grindel quarter close by, was not exposed to daily provocation by the Nazis. Meyer, a man of wealth and substance, was not given to alarmist views or exaggeration, but now he wrote:

> The situation is deteriorating for our fellow co-religionists so seriously that only one more short step is needed for a pogrom. The life-threatening wounding of *Regierungsrat* Lassally, who was fulfilling the duty of his profession, should serve as a *Menetekel*; it is high time that the leaders of our community present a common front to combat the brutish degeneration of public morality, which dishonours everything our fathers have fought for so hard and attained. The impact of the incitement which we are

experiencing is tearing down all barriers; parliament, open meetings, even schools have been infiltrated and everywhere can be heard the cry, 'Judah perish!' …

Neither the Reich government nor the government of our state have taken any steps up to now to check the degeneration. The leaders of our community have a duty to remind the government of the Reich and the state of the necessity to ensure that our rights are maintained, that what we possess is not taken, and that our lives are not sacrificed.

In my judgement of the situation, a delegation from the executive committee should call on the two mayors [of Hamburg], Ross and Petersen, without delay, pointing out the dangerous agitation taking place within our city walls and the threat this poses not only to our co-religionists but to the people as a whole. We have to demand that all means at the disposal of the state are employed to put an end to this dreadful situation.

The Jewish community issued a dignified public declaration a few days later demanding that the senate halt the defamation of its Jewish fellow citizens. The democratic party leaders responded by accepting an invitation to a public protest meeting in the Heinrich-Hertz *Gymnasium* organised by the Association of German Citizens of Jewish Faith. The hall was filled with Jews and committed Christians. Obviously larger and more impressive meeting places like the auditorium of the university were thought unsuitable. The risk of disturbance and disruption was there too great despite the distinguished platform. The mayor of Hamburg, Carl Petersen, first addressed the expectant meeting: 'I regard it as my duty as a German to protest against what is happening in Germany today'; 'we all need to stand up for a just, humane Germany and condemn the passions, hatred and base spirit convulsing our beloved fatherland.' The leader of the Social Democratic Party in Hamburg, Hans Podeyn, next assured Hamburg's fellow Jewish citizens that his party would fight for their right to equality. The uniformed Social Democratic Ex-Servicemen's Association declared its solidarity, as did the Centre Party, a crucial partner in the Reich government though of little political weight in Hamburg. Significant was the condemnation of the Nazis by Dr Richard Behn, the representative of the conservative German People's Party, who attacked the similar-sounding antisemitic German National People's Party. Many ties, he said, had previously bound them, but not any longer now that they were working hand in glove with the Nazis. Outside the hall the words of tolerance and reason fell on deaf ears, drowned by Nazi rallies of thousands and fired up by speeches promising a new age and an end to Marxists, Weimar democracy and Jewish dominance.

II

Up and down the country Nazis were calling on people to boycott Jewish businesses. Threats against their lives and property were no longer uncommon. With increasing desperation, Jewish leaders attempted to put some backbone into politicians and their fellow citizens. The Zionists, the Jewish Ex-Serviceman's League and the Association of German Citizens of Jewish Faith put aside their differences to fight the menace. While Hitler opportunistically toned down his verbal onslaughts against the Jews, his party and its Nazi propaganda machine went all out to stir up the masses.

The best hope for stemming the tide of abuse seemed to be an appeal to the highest Reich authorities.[25] In the spring of 1931 the leaders of the CV and the Zionists decided to approach Chancellor Brüning directly. They were politely received by his state secretary and told him Germany was perceived in the world as a cauldron of antisemitism thanks to the activities of the Nazis. The Jews had previously counted on the liberal parties to defend them, but those parties had lost the support of the nation, and they now placed their hope in Brüning's Centre Party. Germany's Jews needed reassurance that the Reich government would uphold their rights. They asked the chancellor to include a passage in a forthcoming speech to defend them. He should declare that any citizens of whatever religion enjoyed equal rights and that differences enriched German culture. He should emphasise that 'our Jewish fellow citizens need have no doubt that the majority of the German people will not tolerate injustice against religious and national minorities in their midst'. This stirring passage remained between dusty covers in the files of the Chancellery. The weakness at the heart of the Reich government laid bare the increasing moral bankruptcy of the politicians. Fewer and fewer voices spoke out on behalf of the beleaguered minority. The democratic parties doubted whether the defence of Jewish human dignity was the best way to safeguard the republic, fearing that voters would be alienated if they stood up for Jewish rights. The moral high ground was abandoned step by step for political expediency. It did not save the republic.

III

In the Reich, after the spring of 1930 no government enjoyed a parliamentary majority and minority coalitions could enact laws only with President Hindenburg's authorisation, reserved to him in emergency situations. So far, in Hamburg, the democratic senate still had a workable parliamentary majority.[26] But would the Nazis achieve success when Hamburg elected its new parliament in September 1931? They did. The results were disastrous for democracy.[27] The coalition no longer commanded a majority, since the Communist Party and the Nazis could muster more votes and cynically cooperated to destroy democratic government, each expecting to inherit power. The government survived only because no other could be formed, but it was virtually powerless to alleviate the Depression by following independent policies as it had to rely on subsidies from Berlin to save the city from bankruptcy. The Reich government's dictated reductions in expenditure deepened the Depression – the cure worse than the disease.

Hamburg's democratic politicians were in a blind alley from which there was no escape.

The Depression hit Hamburg later than other German states but then all the more harshly.[28] Jews and Christians both suffered. It peaked in the summer of 1933: 17 per cent of the employers had lost their businesses and almost half of the workers and nearly a third of the shop assistants were thrown out onto the street. Statistics do not convey the misery and despair, as everything got worse, seemingly without end or hope. To begin with, the unemployed received for the first six months between 40 and 60 per cent of their previous income from insurance, but by the end of 1932 it was only for six weeks and just 20 to 30 per cent. After the insurance ran out they received so-called crisis payments, after a means test had deprived them of all but a few belongings. Finally, there was only the humiliating welfare to fall back on. Families went hungry in their thousands. Crisis support just kept body and soul together. 'Benefits', surely a misnomer, were enough to buy 500 grams of margarine, 500 grams of meat, sausage or fish, 250 grams of sugar, one litre of milk, and coffee substitute for each adult once a week; bread and potatoes had to fill empty bellies. The health of children suffered. There was no money left for clothing, shoes or medicines. Men out of work gave way to despair, wives starved themselves to provide for their children; for the pensioners, the old and the sick, there was no comfort. You were lucky if three times a week you got a warm meal for a few *Pfennige* at one of the welfare kitchens set up in the city. By the close of 1932 times became even more desperate. Now unemployment compensation was restricted to about a quarter of their previous income and lasted for only six weeks.

Those in work suffered as well, as wages were cut; they lived in fear – how long would their workplace last? The state had always relied on its own employees, the civil servants, the policemen, and a host of others. They too could no longer be sure that their income was secure. Their resentment was great; for the second time in their lives since the hyper-inflation of the early 1920s their salaries were cut and the retirement age was lowered. A class-conscious middle class descended to the income level of workers and deeply resented their loss of status.

The democratic culture in Germany had not taken sufficient root to withstand the shock. People asked why such a catastrophe should overtake them through no fault of their own. Their daily lives turned on immediate needs. The government was failing to put food in the mouths of their children. Contemporaries were in no doubt about the close link between the Depression and the end of Weimar. The Nazi Party drew voters from all social groups but secured especially the support of the middle classes threatened with poverty and of those who had not voted before. The parties which were deserted by the bulk of their supporters were the liberals and conservatives.

The days of democracy in Germany were numbered. In the spring of 1932 presidential elections were held. Hitler stood against Hindenburg and lost, but 13 million had voted for him. The fate of the republic was in the hands of an old man. Violence became pervasive: 400,000 storm troopers filled the streets and battled against the communists. Everywhere Nazi sympathisers had infiltrated the pillars of the state – the police, the army, the judiciary and the state bureaucracy. Although the Nazis were in the minority, millions were afraid to commit themselves openly to oppose them. The Nazis waged a blackmail campaign, threatening retribution once they came to power. Best not to show too much friendship to Jews, perhaps advisable to loosen any former ties, to do your shopping elsewhere if you could be identified as giving your custom to the Jewish greengrocer or dairy. Opportunists saw the light and joined the winning side. The Nazi core was augmented by tens of thousands of cautious fellow travellers who did not show their hand openly so long as the republic was still in being.

IV

On 17 July 1932, the Nazi Party staged a monster demonstration, a march through the streets of neighbouring Altona, the stronghold of the Marxists. The clashes that then occurred on Altona's 'bloody Sunday' mark a climax of violence on a single day.[29] It was something of a miracle that not more than eighteen were killed – communists, storm troopers and bystanders – but sixty-one people were injured as firing began from the rooftops. Order was restored the following day. The bloodshed in Altona changed the political landscape in Hamburg. Jews looked on helplessly as two weeks later, in the election for Reich parliament, the Nazi Party gained substantially, becoming the strongest party and overtaking for the first time the Social Democratic Party. The government was weakened to the point where bringing the Nazi Party into a new coalition was considered by the Conservatives to be the only way out. It would have meant dropping the Social Democrats and so a breach with Hamburg's post-1918 tradition. But the feelers came to nothing and the old coalition struggled on.

Normal life in Hamburg was degenerating. Marches and counter-marches, beggars on the street – the contrast became more and more stark between the well-dressed and unemployed workers in ragged clothes. Police tried to keep law and order while paramilitary formations of storm troopers, of the uniformed Social Democratic *Reichsbanner*, of the *Stahlhelm* and communist reds, frequently carrying arms, marched with flags and symbols, clashed and fought, breaking up each other's meetings. Violence became a means to an end to beat opponents and win the backing of the uncommitted. Although the Nazi thugs in Hamburg were the smallest group, they made up for this by fanatical devotion. Whenever a march or a demonstration was planned, there was a good response from party members and supporters. Their hyperactivity conveyed the impression of an unstoppable movement.

Storm troopers, the SA, were recruited largely from the unemployed.[30] More than half of them were without work and on welfare. The socially disadvantaged, unemployed office workers and blue-collar employees were attracted to the party.

Unemployed workers tended to remain loyal to the Social Democrats or swelled the ranks of the communists, though some also joined the Nazis.

V

Hitler took advantage of every grievance, however contradictory. In 1926 he paid his first visit to Hamburg.[31] He courted the 600 members of the conservative *Nationalklub von 1919*, most of them dedicated to ending Weimar and its social-ist support, and appeared before them in full morning cutaway at the renowned Atlantic Hotel. There was not a storm trooper in sight. Hitler behaved with due modesty. But once he began to speak he mesmerised his listeners. With sure instinct, he spoke about what was dearest to their heart: the need for national revival, rejection of Weimar democracy and the republic, and death to Marxism. There was nothing to choose between the Social Democrats and the communists, he claimed. They were Marxist revolutionary bedfellows. But he was careful not to attack the conservative parties to which his audience overwhelmingly gave their support. He also soft-pedalled his racist beliefs. His contempt for the masses – 'they are feminine and stupid' and require a strong leader to detach them from Marxism if Germany is to recover – won him the stormiest applause of the eve-ning. Not with one word did he single out the Jews. His usual primitive invective would not have gone down well with drawing-room antisemites.

By the time of his second visit to the *Nationalklub*, in December 1930, Hitler was the leader of a powerful movement and his standing had been transformed. He delivered a long diatribe on the ills of the economy and its causes: the hae-morrhage of reparations and the lack of discipline and organisation that had brought Germany to the brink of collapse. He promised salvation, to end the 'international thinking' of the people, democracy and pacifism. The masses had to learn to understand that Germany must rely on its own strength. Class identifi-cation, bourgeois and proletarian, was outworn. Germany as it existed would decay; the National Socialist mission, Hitler declared, was to unite the nation. He spoke for two and a half hours – a speech strong on emotion, weak on the specifics of policies. Once more he failed to mention Jews as the incarnation of evil. The majority of the good and great of Hamburg punctuated his oration with loud applause.

Erwin Garvens was present again and recorded on the following day his impressions.[32] The hall, he wrote, was filled to capacity: 500 had dined in the Atlantic Hotel before the speech. Hitler had not joined them, pleading indiges-tion. Outside the hotel his followers, dressed in their best, had waited for hours for their *Führer* – office employees, small traders, a few schoolboys and some workers. Hitler did not bother with them, avoiding contact with the 'proletariat' while busy impressing the capitalists. 'Surely', they thought, 'if Hitler only knew that we were here he would come out and greet us.' When someone in the crowd excitedly exclaimed he had just glimpsed the *Führer* in the lobby, they all raised their arms and shouted '*Heil!*' Still, even Garvens thought that Hitler's speech had been so sensible that everyone could subscribe to 90 per cent of what he said.

More Nazi speakers were invited: Joseph Goebbels in March 1931 and in February of the following year the popular Great War air ace, Captain Hermann Göring. What many prominent merchants and bankers feared was that the Nazi Party showed dangerous 'socialist' tendencies and that Hitler's proletarian followers were violent and ignorant. Hitler allayed their fears by focusing on the dangers of Marxism. Hamburg's mercantile elite nevertheless remained doubtful about embracing the unpredictable populism of Hitler's appeal. It was a case of hedging your bets. Garvens and only a few others considered giving up their membership. Garvens was scathing about Göring's rhetoric. The most perturbing aspect was the reaction of the distinguished audience: 'Whenever he [Göring] drew breath in pauses between his bellows, older members, like [the banker] Max von Schinkel, and the most prominent businessmen applauded as if possessed … Their completely uncritical attitude', he observed, is 'shameful.'

Antisemitism was secondary in the appeal of the Nazis among these well-to-do adherents of the *Nationalklub*, who rejected rabble-rousing racism and the violence of the street, where bands of storm troopers shouted: 'Judah perish!', 'Jewish blood will spurt from our knives!' They did not wish to harm Jews physically, but the verbal assaults on their fellow citizens did not turn them away from the Nazis, whose success with the masses they wanted to employ to weaken the socialists and the trade unions. With the Nazis as junior partners, when necessary, you hold your nose; they expected to regain their rightful influence in politics. It was a misjudgement of colossal proportions. The Jews, gypsies, 'asocials' and other undesirables, such as the mentally weak, were the victims. Where could they look for support? Would not at least the churches speak out against the assault on common ethical values?

VI

Individual churchmen did so, but the leadership of the twenty-eight Protestant state churches, *Landeskirchen*, bound only loosely together, remained silent. Antisemitism was deeply rooted in Protestant and Catholic theology, the German variety worse than most. The Protestant Church was also strongly national, its prayers for victory in 1918 unanswered. The old certainties of the Wilhelmine state were gone; the new republican constitution cut the link between obedience to the 'prince' and protection from him that had existed since the Reformation.

The transformation of post-1918 Germany after defeat and revolution plunged the Church into crisis. How to recover authority, to win back the support of the people? Leaders of the Church had no love for the republic, which they held responsible for defeat and for their own condition. Bishops discovered the virtues of the *Volk*. It needed but one more step to 'recognise' the importance of race. Language not so different from that of the Nazis began to be heard, not just from fanatical clergymen but from respected theologians.[33] The Berlin professor

Reinhold Seeberg called on everyone who wanted to preserve the *Volk*, the German way of life, morality and the Christian religion 'to fight the international power of Jewry'. A vicious series of articles also appeared from the pen of Hans Meiser, who a few years later became Bavaria's bishop. '*Zersetzen*' was a favourite cliché the antisemites used to describe Jews as an element that brought about the 'decomposition' of decent German values. 'God did not give each *Volk* characteristics to be bastardised through mixture with inferior races.' Only a few churchmen would oppose the antisemitism of the Nazis. They saw in the *Führer* a leader who would re-establish their influence. When conflict did break out later, it was not over the persecution of the Jews. The prevailing voice of the German Evangelical Church placed few moral obstacles in Hitler's path. The Catholic Church held out a little longer until it too capitulated.

An incident in Hamburg only confirmed how little support the Jewish community could expect. During the night of 18 August 1931, a synagogue in the Marcusstraße was desecrated.[34] The silver vessels were demolished but nothing was stolen. The perpetrators were never found. The silence of the Protestant Church authorities was for Jews another of the discouraging signs of the time. The Church's hypocrisy is revealed in a remarkable correspondence with Rabbi Arthur Posner, whose synagogue in neighbouring Kiel had been attacked with dynamite, when compared with their own internal exchanges of how best to deal with his appeal for the Churches to say an open word against the flood of public abuse by Nazi gangs. In August 1932, Rabbi Posner wrote to the *Deutsches Evangelisches Kirchenbundesamt* (DEKB-Amt) and the Lutheran authorities of Schleswig-Holstein. Why was the voice of the Church not heard? It was their duty from the pulpit and in schools to counter the hatred, to support religious adherents of another faith, when 'Jews, men and women, children and old people, are threatened with violence and abused in the streets, in the parks and on the beaches'. Rabbi Posner received replies assuring him of the Churches' condemnation of such attacks and of the steps being taken. The truth was very different. In the internal exchanges between the two church authorities of Schleswig-Holstein and of Germany with the press office of the German Lutheran-Evangelical Church, the latter, noting receipt of copies of the correspondence, replied, 'We conclude from the correspondence that the church authorities have weighty reasons not to take a public position on these issues, which we completely agree with.'[35]

Graves in the Jewish cemetery on the Rentzelstraße were defiled in October 1931, gravestones upturned and broken. A week later the wall surrounding the graveyard was covered in swastikas. The police apprehended a number of suspects but did not prosecute for supposed lack of evidence. In November, and then again two months later, the sacrilege was repeated. Finally, the miscreants were caught, one of them a member of the National Socialist Party, the other a sympathiser. They received sentences of six and nine months, which on appeal were reduced to four – no more than a slap on the wrist.

Early in 1932, the Jewish community tried to organise a joint declaration of rabbis, Lutheran pastors and Catholic priests to condemn such sacrileges. Max

Warburg approached Pastor Heinz Beckmann with the plea that he should organise the response of the Lutheran Church. His reply was apologetic. He said he
had no authority to initiate anything but would pass the appeal to the head of the
Church council. Personally, of course, he condemned desecration of graves but
did not think that public pronouncements would do much good. Nothing more
was heard of the proposal. Without support from Hamburg's Protestants it was
useless to try to carry it further. Too many parishioners sympathised with the
Nazis and would be alienated from the Church if it took an open moral stand for
the Jews – all this a year before Hitler came to power.

VII

For opponents of the Nazis it was difficult to understand the mass appeal of
Hitler. Was it just a temporary aberration? Erwin Garvens met an enthusiastic
colleague who could not exactly explain what was so bad about the Weimar
'system' and why he supported the Nazis;[36] he was, Garvens comments, typical
of 'hundreds of thousands of fellow travellers who had no more idea either. …
National Socialism', he concluded, 'is sustained by the complete lack of any critical judgement of the mass of the people and their unfulfillable expectations that
under Nazi rule everything will change, and therefore will be better.'

In Hamburg, the Social Democratic Party, the *Staatspartei*, and leaders of the
German People's Party did their best during the last three years of the republic to
enlighten people that a Nazi or a communist victory would lead to the destruction
of justice and of democracy. Once in power Hitler would never give it up; the
independence of other parties and the trade unions would be extinguished in a
totalitarian state, whether Nazi or communist. Three arrows began to appear on
posters and on walls. They symbolised the 'Iron Front' – an alliance of the Social
Democratic Party, its uniformed formation the *Reichbanner Schwarz-Rot-Gold*
and the free trade unions – which stood for the defence of the republic against its
opponents, the Nazis and the communists. In the November 1932 elections,
nationally only about a third of the electorate voted against the totalitarian parties
and in support of the republic. In Hamburg the percentage was a little higher
(37 per cent). Still, it does mean that nationally 14 million people opposed the
Nazis, their allies, and the communists. Nazi myth would later depict the German
people overwhelmingly hailing Hitler as their saviour; enough did, but millions
opposed him.

Jewish organisations provided support for Social Democratic Party attacks on
the Nazis. In Berlin the CV worked surreptitiously, supplying information and
propaganda material through an office known as the *Büro Wilhelmstraße*, housed
in the government quarter. Any more open help the parties feared would lose
them voters.

The Nazis engaged the idealism of youth. The young unemployed men and
women ending their school years during the Depression years, students without
prospects of gaining a foothold in their chosen career – young people from every

class were attracted by Hitler's promise of change and the birth of a new Germany. They had nothing to lose. The rootless joined the party and swelled the ranks of the storm troopers,[37] whose strongholds provided comradeship, restored a sense of purpose and pride, and offered material help. Their meeting places in cellars and beer halls, the largest of them in an empty factory in the Barmbecker Straße, became like second homes, where torn clothing was mended and wounds suffered in street battles were dressed tenderly by the admiring Organisation of Nazi Women. Outside support was provided by party subventions and the gifts of well-wishers. Potatoes and vegetables for their soup kitchens were delivered by farmers from the surrounding countryside, who themselves were suffering badly from the effects of the Depression. Owners of lorries provided the transport free. In this way a basic network of assistance was built up.

Paradoxically, at the same time as the Nazi Party surged in popularity, the obituaries of illustrious Jews in the Hamburg press were full of praise. German Jews enjoyed the esteem of their colleagues. Despite all the tumult on the streets, many Jews continued to maintain close relations with their fellow citizens – friendships and cooperation that had lasted for decades. That only a few socialised with Christians in each other's homes was nothing new, and just as true in Britain and other countries. But these were not normal times. Once normal times returned, surely the heat and fevered agitation would cease and support for Hitler would weaken.

VIII

Leo Lippman, among well-placed Jews, who was not particularly alarmed.[38] Isolated in high office, responsible for Hamburg's deteriorating finances, he was unfamiliar with the lives of *Ostjuden*, the poor Jewish traders in the streets of the Grindel. A contemporary photograph shows him as tall, conservatively and elegantly dressed, with stiff white collar, tie and pearl tie pin, and reveals a stern face enhanced by rimless spectacles – a man used to command. Justice, correctness and hard work for the common good were his guiding principles. He treated civil servants of lesser rank as underlings as he grappled with the problems to make ends meet, earning respect for his expertise and his devotion to Hamburg. That he was now needed more than ever was a view widely shared. On his fiftieth birthday in May 1931, Lippmann received many good wishes. Typical were those printed in the *Hamburger Anzeiger*.[39] Lippmann, the paper attested, was an exemplary civil servant who had worked with unrivalled mastery with a succession of city mayors and senators for the good of Hamburg for almost twenty-five years: 'How fortunate that he is only fifty, so that we can safely leave Hamburg's finances in his sure hands.' No inkling here of what was to come less than two years later. In the autumn of 1931, two leading Nazi members of Hamburg's parliament, Wilhelm von Allwörden and Georg Ahrens, were elected to join the committee overseeing finance. Lippmann spoke with both of them frankly, asking them whether they felt able to work with him in good faith or whether because he was a Jew they would treat him with a lack of respect. Allwörden and Ahrens reassured him 'that they and their party, now and later, once they came to power, were willing to work with me and they hoped I would be willing to do the same'. Allwörden, who was the leader of the Nazi Party in Hamburg's parliament, on another occasion told him that he did not think the issue of the Jews would be important for the party later on. It was just used to arouse people; once the Nazis were in power, Jews would no longer be permitted to teach small German children and no more Eastern Jews would be allowed to enter Germany, but 'Jews settled in Germany for a long time who, like myself, had given all their strength to our Germany would not be molested or slighted in any way'. Lippmann was convinced that Allwörden and Ahrens were sincere, and they probably were.

Superficially some things remained reassuringly unchanged. Every year representatives of the state and the armed services gathered in the Ohlsdorf cemetery to honour the Jewish war dead. The commemoration was organised by the Hamburg branch of the Association of Jewish War Veterans, RjF, which in the Reich had 35,000 members and took every opportunity to emphasise its German patriotism. The previous November the roll of honour of the Jewish dead, perpetuated in a memorial volume containing almost 12,000 names, had been presented to Hindenburg. Hindenburg added a dedication: 'I receive this book in reverent remembrance of the comrades from your ranks who have fallen for the fatherland and incorporate it in my war library.'

In the higher social classes, Jews continued to enjoy the esteem of their colleagues. Professional associations of lawyers and doctors still elected them to their ruling councils; Jewish professors brought distinction to the university, and Ernst Cassirer was chosen as rector for the academic year 1929–30. In banking and commerce, Jews were prominent and, like Max Warburg, played important roles at the Stock Exchange and served on the council of the chamber of commerce; in the theatre, opera and concert hall they were patrons and performers. But Jewish shopkeepers, the small greengrocer or tailor, were painfully aware that their custom was shrinking. The Nazis stridently called for a boycott. In some districts lists were circulated identifying 'Jewish' shops and businesses. Perhaps it was better not to be seen shopping there in case a Nazi made a note of the Jew friend? Some Jewish concerns even began to 'Aryanise', voluntarily appointing no more Jewish employees. What this shows is that the Nazis succeeded well before 1933 in spreading apprehension. Too many otherwise decent people lacked civil courage and gave in to moral blackmail.

The Jews were exposed to two misfortunes: the rising tide of antisemitism coinciding with the economic recession. It is difficult to see how they could have done more to defend themselves. They were only a small minority. In Hamburg there was some discussion as to whether they should set up their own defence militia on the model of the *Stahlhelm* or the republican *Reichsbanner*. The idea was fanciful. What could formations of maybe a hundred or so achieve when faced with thousands except to invite a beating.

Self-discrimination became common. It was no longer thought 'healthy' for the individual to follow his or her chosen career. In the university, Jewish colleagues agreed it was best not to appoint a Jewish front-runner to a professorship that had fallen vacant as there were already too many Jewish professors. And Leo Lippmann, too, when involved in appointing a new director for the Hamburg opera, thought it wise to reject the best candidate because he was a Jew. There was widespread acceptance that the Jews had an 'unnatural social structure' that needed to be rectified so that it corresponded more closely to that of a 'normal' population. Were there not already too many scientists, artists and musicians, lawyers and doctors? Jews needed to behave modestly, they were told by other Jews.

On the high holidays in the autumn of 1932, when dressed in their best clothes, the community's leaders urged Jews not to draw attention to themselves, not to congregate outside the synagogue in conversation, but to go home quietly. They must avoid all cause of 'offence'. It was better for the ladies not to wear fur coats or jewellery. All forms of 'ostentation' became taboo. That was the state of affairs months before Hitler became chancellor.

Jews were forced to accept that the number of colleagues and friends who would stand by them, the political leaders who would defend them, had shrunk to a few. The mass of the people looked elsewhere, had more pressing concerns. Carl Melchior, Max Warburg's banking partner, noted in August 1932: 'We can only hope that the people, who after all are decent and sensible, will overcome the present symptoms of high fever.' A few months later, just days before Hitler's appointment as chancellor, Max Warburg spoke at the graveside of the Jewish banker James Simon. The scathing words expressed his bitter feelings:

> Those who know no better and have been misled we should forgive. But not those who know the truth but lack the courage to declare themselves openly against the scandal of antisemitism, who with their feeble and carefully formulated declarations of support avoid stating with clarity the reality of the situation, for them we can have nothing but contempt, and as Germans we can only feel shame for their lack of honour and courage.[40]

The Jews in Hamburg and the rest of Germany had effectively lost the struggle for equality and acceptance well before 30 January 1933.

A vote for Hitler?[41]

Luise Solmitz belonged to the *Bürgertum*, the educated social class spanning from moderate to sometimes considerable wealth. Her husband was now a veteran career officer receiving a pension for his war disabilities. One would hardly have expected such a family to be attracted to the Nazis. Luise had strong moral convictions, and by any standards would be regarded as a decent church-going German. That is what makes her feelings as she recorded them in her journal so fascinating. Even before she had fallen for Hitler she was waiting for him.

'Only a miracle can save us, one man, a deed, a striking event', she wrote in her journal in 1928. The working classes, *Frau* Solmitz thought, were being pampered at the expense of the better educated members of society for the sake of gaining their votes. She admired the right-wing veteran association the *Stahlhelm* and was attracted to disciplined marching men in uniforms with all classes united, workers following their 'natural' leaders, their officers and the Hohenzollern princes, Eitel Fritz and August Wilhelm, sons of the Kaiser. To each class its allotted place, otherwise the stable *Bürgers* would find themselves swamped by the envy of the masses. In an entry in December 1928, Luise Solmitz expresses views about Jews similar to Nazi propaganda, except that she would not have read the Nazi gutter press.

The Nazis were still insignificant. It did not need Nazis to establish anti-Jewish feelings in Germany. The notion of the Jews 'decomposing' German society was peddled far and wide. That someone of Luise Solmitz's education and social commitment as a schoolteacher could believe in such warped ideology shows that the Nazis would not be rejected by otherwise good and sound people. What is more surprising is that Luise Solmitz was in close contact with Jews who in no way substantiated the theory. She taught Jewish children with the same kindness as all the other children in her class. Like so many Germans, she was able to have good relations with Jews she knew and to harbour prejudices about them in general.

> 30.12.1928. In Berlin recently, in a secondary school, modern youth assembled to discuss their right to love between the same sexes and other forms of sex. It is a news report as if from a lunatic asylum. The famous and notorious Dr Magnus Hirschfeld appeared and explained to the boys and girls this was an issue of free choice, that virtue was not situated below but above the navel.
> The spokesmen of decomposition and of shamelessness are the Jews. They dominate wherever lack of morality, the assertion of rights without responsibility, weakness, decomposition and mental vacancy exist. That is where they have their mastery. Our sickness makes them our masters.[42]

Another constant theme in her journal was the injustice of Versailles and the burdens of reparations. Fear of 'Bolshevism' tormented her. Would it spread westward? It was the work of Jews, though she had to admit that 'Stalin was not a Jew'. By the summer of 1930, with the Depression deepening, Luise Solmitz began to be attracted to the Nazis 'because they hold the promise that they will be strong and that is what really matters'.

> 6.9.1930. Whether in practice the National Socialists can achieve anything, one cannot yet tell. But can it get worse? Hitler spoke in Hamburg. The crowds recently with Frick and Göring are said not to have compared with the rush to hear Hitler. All tickets had been sold already days ago.

In one entry (12 September 1930) ideology and reality conflicted jarringly. On a visit to a small town Luise came across a Jewish burial ground: 'Next to the old cemetery there is a Jewish graveyard, absolutely on its own. In the first rows of graves three men fallen in the war lie buried.'

Millions of Germans like Luise Solmitz no longer believed salvation would come from a parliamentary democracy that could not provide even the basics of life.

> 11.9.1930. ... Will National Socialist ideas cleanse? Will salvation come from the unity of the people [*Volksgemeinschaft*] in harmony with the *Bürgertum*? Will we today place fatherland above private interests? One thing is for sure, the strong attraction of National Socialism.
>
> 14.9.1930 (Election day) We have twenty-eight parties ... I decided to vote for the two Nazis; it is a dangerous experiment. What can be said in favour of the Nazis is that they are hated by the left.

But misgivings surfaced from time to time:

> 22.10.1930. In Ulm, Hitler acted very unadvisedly in the court case against the army officers. Called a witness, he said that, if force is used against him or his supporters, then heads would roll into the sand. That is no way to behave in politics.

Luise Solmitz blamed the Jews for the misfortunes that had befallen her beloved fatherland. When the ex-crown prince tried to dismiss the myth of the 'stab in the back', she was indignant:

> 16.1.1931. He now pretends that Jews and Marxists were not the November criminals of 1918 ... the German Empire is a hollow vessel ... it is no longer German, but Jewish-Marxist.
>
> 25.2.1931. A communist hunger march. There are almost 5 million without work. The situation is becoming more and more critical. No one can see a way out ... Fredy's pension of 440RM has been reduced to 392RM – that means economies. On the other hand, everything has become cheaper; even so one cannot go out buying. As long as I can make use of it I buy from the poor people who come to the door and who, without hope, walk with tired feet from door to door ... misery everywhere.

Hope? Perhaps Hitler is the answer:

> 20.10.1931. What has this man achieved from nothing ...? He is able to catch hold of the poorest and most miserable for the national ideal, who have never followed this course – except in war. May Hitler's way be blessed. At least he brings us hopes of a new dawn.

4.2.1932. The lack of an ideal for which one is ready to sacrifice oneself and by means of which one can rise again. And so one comes again to Hitler. He is the only one who can have meaning for 15 million people and can offer them something – of no importance what that is.

During the elections for *Reichpresident*, Hitler, standing against Hindenburg, had flown from city to city, mesmerising huge audiences with his oratory. Luise Solmitz, caught up in the mass psychosis of the crowds who came to hear him, lost all her critical faculties. She estimated there were 120,000 crowded into a stadium in Lokstedt, a suburb of Hamburg. The orchestrated staging brought everyone to fever pitch.

24.3.1932. No one calls him Hitler, only 'the Leader' [*der Führer*], ... it's almost three o'clock. 'The Leader is coming', the crowd startles, around the speaker's platform hands are raised in Hitler salute ... a forest of swastika flags rises up. And there is Hitler in a simple black suit looking expectantly over the crowd ... jubilation greets him. Then Hitler spoke. His main aim to make one people in place of the many political parties. He condemned the 'system' [and exclaimed] 'I would like to know what is left in this state to ruin'.

With the November elections of 1932, the Nazis suffered a significant setback. The disappointed Solmitzes, too, turned away, and the journal reflects the voices of others. Hitler's siding with the communists in the Berlin transport strike cost him many conservative votes. The Solmitzes cast their vote without much enthusiasm for the German National People's Party.

Luise Solmitz's rejection of Hitler was short-lived. On 30 January 1933 she exulted:

Hitler chancellor! And what a government!! A government we hardly dared dream of last July. Hitler, Hugenberg, Seldte, Papen!! On every one of them rest my hopes for Germany. National Socialist vitality, German national prudence, the party independent, *Stalhelm* and the never to be forgotten Papen ...

Her husband was more reflective. True, he felt completely German and had given ample proof of his loyalty to the fatherland, but, with all the vilification of Jews in the street, he could not obliterate the thought that he too was descended from a Jewish family. The future for anyone with Jewish connections was veiled in uncertainty. Some said it was better with Hitler in power forced to act responsibly; others feared the worst.

Although there was no ghetto in Hamburg, the early Jewish arrivals had to settle in parts of the *Altstadt* and the *Neustadt* with limited trading and property rights. The centre of bustling Jewish life until the 1870s was the Elbstraße, ironically referred to in a Jewish poem of 1842 as 'the Jewish stock exchange'.

In the early seventeenth century, Jews worshipped in their private houses. From 1671 to 1811 they formed a triple community of Altona, Wandsbek and Hamburg. This ended with a French occupation from 1811 to 1814. The earliest Hamburg synagogue was in the Elbstraße, built between 1788 and 1789 and demolished in 1906.

About 1850, the German-Jewish Ashkenazi community, by then some 8,000 members strong, was the largest in Germany. The small but influential and more liberal *Tempelverein* was founded in 1817. The members built their synagogue in the Brunnenstraße. After bitter disputes with Chacham Isaak Bernays over ritual and a new synagogue, the senate permitted its construction in the Poolstraße (1842–4). The Jewish bourgeoisie was no different from their Christian neighbours in dress or manners. The large, more orthodox, German Israelite community built their new synagogue (1857–9) in Kohlhöfen, facing the street openly.

Between 1870 and 1920, Jews moved to the better quarters of the Grindel, Rothenbaum, Eppendorf and Hoheluft. The great Bornplatz synagogue was consecrated in 1906. A new *Tempel* was consecrated in the Oberstraße in 1931. In ritual observance, the New Dammtor Synagogue, founded in 1894 and moderately conservative, stood between the orthodox *Deutsch-Israelitischer Synagogen-Verband* (German Israelite Synagogue Community) and the liberal *Israelitischer Tempelverband* (Israelite Temple Community).

Gabriel Riesser (1806–63), the leading advocate of Jewish emancipation, who in 1848 was elected to the Frankfurt pre-parliament. He fought for the idea that there was no freedom or liberty without the complete equality of all Germans. In 1859, after the establishment of a higher court in Hamburg, he became the first Jewish state judge in Germany. Until his death in 1862 he was also vice-president of the Hamburg *Bürgerschaft*.

In gratitude for Jewish emancipation in Hamburg, the merchant Lazarus Gumpel (1770–1843) founded the Schillingsverein, which provided free apartments, six for Jews and six for Christians, in the Eichholzstraße, opposite the Landungsbrücken. They were handed over in 1851. Hamburg's Jewish benefactors founded many more such apartments, most of them without any religious restrictions.

The banker and merchant Salomon Heine (1767–1844) took financial risks to set up Hamburg as a financial centre once more after the great fire in 1842.

The *Israelitisches Krankenhaus*, the munificent gift of Salomon Heine, was opened in 1839 close to the poor harbour district and looked after sailors, prostitutes and poor women who were in need of midwives. For close on a century the hospital provided some of the very best medical facilities, irrespective of the religion of the patients, and some well-to-do Christians did not hesitate to make use of it even during the Third Reich.

Betty Heine (1777–1837), the aunt of Heinrich Heine, was among the most generous benefactors of welfare for Jews and Germans alike.

Ferdinand Beit (1817–1870), whose grandfather Marcus Salomon established the gold and silver foundry in the Elbstraße, by the middle of the nineteenth century one of the foremost foundries in Europe of pure silver. Ferdinand played a leading role in the foundation of the Norddeutsche Affinerie in 1866 and became chairman of the board. It is one of many examples of institutions in which Jewish and Christian financiers and scientists collaborated.

The renamed Norddeutsche Affinerie (today Aurubis) owed its rise to Dr Emil Wohlwill (1835–1912), inventor of the electro-analysis of pure copper. His son, Dr Heinrich Wohlwill (1874–1943), technical director of the Norddeutsche Affinerie (1913–33), was deported in 1942 and murdered in Auschwitz in 1943.

The Norddeutsche Affinerie before the First World War. It rose to become a leading global copper refinery.

Professor Paul Gerson Unna, a world-renowned dermatologist, who invented many skin products used globally – among them Nivea and Unna's Paste, the latter for the cure of skin ulcers. He first collaborated with a small factory pharmacy owned by Paul Beiersdorf and later with Oscar Troplowitz.

Dr Oscar Troplowitz (1863–1918), scientist, mercantile genius, social reformer and one of Hamburg's biggest benefactors. He was a co-founder of the Beiersdorf empire, which went on to international success.

Troplowitz pioneered both toothpaste in tubes and Elastoplast.

Kaiser Wilhelm's visit to Ballin's palatial home, 1913. Ballin counselled the Kaiser against war.

Albert Ballin's Hamburg–America Line enjoyed friendly rivalry with Cunard, from whom he wrested the blue riband for the fastest Atlantic crossing. At the turn of the century he inaugurated the first Mediterranean luxury cruises.

Jews have always prized education. The senate early on permitted classes for poor children indoors. Teaching was limited to religion and arithmetic. Among the oldest schools was the *Talmud-Tora-Armenschule* of 1805, which moved first to Kohlhöfen with a synagogue and then in 1912 to the Grindelhof. The curriculum encompassed orthodox education, German culture, natural sciences and sport. Christian teachers were appointed also. Fees were adjusted to family income.

The *Israelitische Töchterschule* of 1798 and the *Mädchenschule* of the *Deutsch-Israelitische Gemeinde* of 1818 were founded by bequests. A large benefaction moved the schools jointly to modern premises in the Karolinenstraße in 1883. Another pioneering foundation was the *Israelitische Freischule* of 1815, which taught Jewish children German subjects as well as religion. Anton Rée overcame resistance by the community to admit the first Christian children in 1859. Over the following years the Christian children became the majority. The elite *Johanneum* had already admitted Jewish children since 1802. In the twentieth century the majority of Jewish children entered state schools.

Pupils of the *Talmud-Tora-Schule* with Arthur Spier, Rabbi Joseph Carlebach's successor, in 1926. Spier ensured the survival of the school under the Nazis. The school was forced to combine with the girls' school in the Karolinenstraße, to be known as the *Judenschule* in Nazi language from 1940. Spier was sent by the Gestapo to New York in 1940 to extract money from the Warburgs, ostensibly for Jewish schools in Poland. Alberto Jonas, the devoted headmaster, was deported and murdered with his last remaining pupils when all Jewish schools were closed in June 1942.

3

HOW WILL IT END?

Thirty-four days

'A thousand years of Jewish history have come to an end', exclaimed rabbi Leo Baeck, the foremost representative of German Jewry.[1] But was the die really already cast on 30 January 1933?

The month of February was a strange twilight period. What was going to happen? Who controlled the country? The Hitler coalition cabinet reassuringly enacted no anti-Jewish laws. Vice-Chancellor Papen promised that there would be no discrimination. In Berlin, violence was directed against known opponents of the Nazis – socialists, communists, anyone who had worked against them. If there were Jews among them, the worse for them. Old scores were settled. Jews in general were left alone. Hitler even expressed regret to his cabinet colleagues at outbreaks of violence by 'irresponsible elements'. Jews could only wait and hope.

In Hamburg, it was even more difficult to discern the future. The old democratic senate was still in place and did all it could to stand up to the Nazis and their threats.[2] Mayor Carl Petersen continued to speak out against *Kulturschande*, the 'cultural disgrace' of antisemitism. The second mayor, Rudolf Ross, was a Social Democrat. The democratic socialists, predominantly a party of workers, and the parties supported by the middle classes, cooperating together, had been Hamburg tradition since the Great War. But Hamburg was just a small state. Power lay with its neighbour, Prussia, and with the Reich cabinet in Berlin. Hamburg had no hope of maintaining its independence and of defying Hitler for long. The struggle put up by the democratic senators was nevertheless a remarkable tribute to their moral convictions.

On 6 February, a week after Hitler became chancellor, the Association of Jewish War Veterans held a service of remembrance. Representatives of the Reich and of the Hamburg state attended. The armed services were all represented, as was the Reich War Ministry and other Reich ministries. Members of Hamburg's parliament and senate were there too. They had assembled to honour the Jewish war dead. A memorial book was handed to Senator Platen by Dr Siegfried Urias, the chairman of the association, inscribed with the names of Hamburg's 460 Jewish soldiers who had given their lives for the fatherland. As Dr Urias began to speak, everyone rose from their seats. Senator Platen was handed the memorial book and responded:

> The senate would take good care of this book with its tragic but proud contents, a precious document in the history of Hamburg. He was especially gratified that all Hamburg's war associations had sent representatives. He hoped that this would also be the case in the future. The senate rejected with indignation the persecution of thousands and thousands of good Germans. Racial and religious hatred was contemptuous. The Jews were members of the German *Volk* and a valuable element of German culture …[3]

The voice of Hamburg's tradition, it would not be heard much longer.

Open antisemitism had never been the style of Hamburg's patrician world. But only a handful of the city's upper classes showed solidarity with their Jewish friends and colleagues. Max Warburg recalled how acquaintances and associates began to avoid him, crossing the road and passing on the other side in embarrassment. Once at the centre of social life, those Christian friends who still invited the Warburgs to their homes now chose the other guests with care. Reactions among those working-class people who were not Nazis were less hostile. That was particularly true of women in domestic service, whose relations with 'their Jewish families' had frequently lasted over a generation.

Inside the Warburg Bank there was little change. The employees revered their chief, and when the Nazis insisted that they had to elect an employee's council they chose those suggested by the partners. Nazi blackmail to stop social contacts with Jews, though not forbidden or punishable in any way, took many forms, such as written and verbal warnings – even the publication of photographs where important people were involved. Max Warburg had always been a favourite target. When a Nazi photographer trailed him and took a snapshot of him and Victor Hübbe, director of the Dresdner Bank, exchanging pleasantries outside the Stock Exchange, Hübbe took fright and was careful not to be seen with Warburg in public again. The behaviour of many people was less than courageous, predictably so in some cases, surprising in others. It was difficult for Jews to know how people would react. To avoid hurt and unpleasantness they turned to their Jewish friends and relatives.

I

How differently it all looked to millions of Germans not blighted by the Nazi vilification of Jews is reflected in Luise Solmitz's journal.[4]

2.2.1933. Hitler … intends to govern constitutionally. New *Reichstag* elections. The *Hamburger Nachrichten* [newspaper] fears that the new government will run itself to death in consequence of the Weimar constitution, just as all the previous ones. They want to break with the constitution which was given to us by the representatives of the people, authorised by no people whatsoever …

6.2.1933. Torch processions of Stahlhelm and National Socialists [in Hamburg]! A wonderful uplifting experience for all of us …

Gisela saw the reds on Sunday wading through the mud of a constant rain. They lengthened the procession by adding women and children. The Democratic Socialists and the Red Front are forced to cooperate.

Then new doubts:

19.2.1933. The scale of the political equilibrium does not come to rest. I can see next to Hitler party bureaucrat fighting party bureaucrat, exchanging the membership book of one political party for another, hear him speak in a socialist way … Käthe Kollwitz, Heinrich Mann have withdrawn from the Prussian Academy … 'because they did not wish to fall back into barbarism' …

There were shootouts between Nazis and communists, with several dead and wounded. But the police, still under command of the Social Democrats, did not lose control. The attempts by the Nazis to take charge of the police were rebuffed by the senate. It was quite different in Prussia. Göring, as assistant commissar and acting Prussian minister of the interior paid no attention to his superior in office, Papen, the acting Prussian prime minister. On 4 February, after Hindenburg had signed the 'Decree for the Protection of the German People', Göring unleashed a reign of terror against political opponents and 'cleansed' the civil service and police of Social Democrats. He gave orders to the police not to attempt to restrain storm troopers and to show no mercy to Marxists, communists and Social Democrats. Those who shoot down opponents, Göring promised, would be protected by him; those who 'failed in their duty' would be punished. A few days later he 'strengthened' the regular police by drafting in as 'auxiliary policemen' 25,000 storm troopers and 15,000 SS. The freedom of the press was abolished, meetings of opponents were disrupted; capriciously, those who had fallen foul of the Nazis were dragged into cellars, manhandled, and a few beaten to death.

The Great War hero Captain Göring had been a special favourite with the Solmitzes. 'Fredy' too had served in the air corps and, being a major, was actually his superior in rank. Göring's meteoric rise to field marshal came later, as rapid as the increase in his girth. Cloaking corruption with gallows humour, Göring was brutal. Luise Solmitz became aware of this dark side when Göring let the mask slip.

21.2.1933. Göring is not only permitting the police the right to shoot at rebelling communists and will protect them from repercussions, but also will regard 'failure to do the necessary' as a dereliction of duty …

25.2.1933. We listened to Göring's inspiring speech [over the radio] but I found it was wrong of him to say that German children should not grow up like negro vagabonds. Every race within its own sphere has to be granted its rights and respect. The negro in his own culture is worthy of respect when he is without a civilisation alien to his nature, which has been forced on him. What the black soldiers for four long years did to Germany, Germany and especially Hitler, must never forget. The bad negroised European outcome is not the fault of the negroes!

All thought and feeling among most Germans is dominated by Hitler. His fame rises to the stars; he is the saviour of an evil and tragic German world … The question we put to people of different education and different social standing is, 'How will you vote?' Well, everyone is voting for List One, only Hitler. But some like us are undecided between 1 [National Socialists] and 5 [Nationalist allies].

A respectable young man passed us, saw nothing, heard nothing, and loudly sang a Nazi song all to himself. 'It is turning into veneration, it is becoming a religion', was Fredy's comment. Fortunate for us that, at the head of this mighty people's movement, there stands a good man, a man without stain or blemish![5]

Nazi propaganda reached new heights after the *Reichstag* fire.

1.3.1933. The *Reichstag* fire was to be just the beginning. Their [the communists] intention was to take hostages of women and children, … send murderous bands to the villages to start fires, use every weapon in the cities from the most refined to the primitive, boiling water to poison. It all sounded almost unbelievable were it not for Russia, Asiatic torture methods, orgies such as a German brain could not imagine. Göring assured us he had not lost his nerve.[6]

Luise Solmitz hoped the people would not lose theirs and would vote on election day. When Hitler stopped in Hamburg on 3 March, two days before the elections, Luise Solmitz's devotion to Hitler knew no bounds. What was hidden from the Solmitzes and the people was the struggle going on behind the scenes to subvert democracy in Hamburg, just as it had been already in Prussia, before election day.

3.3.1933. … No *Kaiser* is received like Hitler – an ocean of enthusiasm, love, belief, faith and loyalty to the death … [afterwards] I was so restless, my blood was boiling with inspiration as I ambled through the streets …

5.3.1933. The great day. Our Kippingstraße [the house, no. 12 Kippingstraße, was owned by Friedrich Solmitz] black–white–red [the old imperial flag] and swastikas wherever one looks. A festive mood as never before. Should no majority be reached with Lists 1 and 5, we hope that Hitler will not give way by the breadth even of a little finger ... It was noticeable that in the Heimhuderstraße there were only half a dozen black–white–red flags, otherwise throughout its length nothing one way or the other. What kind of people live there now? [The Heimhuderstraße was situated in the expensive Alsterquarter of Rotherbaum; quite a few Jews lived there.]

　　The result of the elections ... a wonderful, unexpected and intoxicating victory. A victory, which we all, those who love their fatherland, have struggled to achieve for Hitler. We of little faith, we now admire Hitler's will for agreeing to elections. Once again this man was more of a believer, more intelligent than we.[7]

The rude awakening and realisation of what they had voted for, the inhumanity of the regime, was not long in coming. But the Solmitzes were blind when it mattered, on election day. Hitler promised many things; everyone could select what they wished and shrug their shoulders at the rest. Millions found that they had *something* good to say for Hitler even while they would not agree with everything. There is a handy German proverb to get over any little difficulty: 'Wood cannot be planed smooth without making many shavings'. It would often be repeated in later years.

There was no doubt that political opponents would be early victims – no bad thing if they were communists and were prevented from causing harm. It was not enough reason anyway to oppose the Nazis. Centuries of antisemitism and vicious anti-Jewish defamation after the Great War had immunised middle-class Germans against protesting the infringement of their fellow citizens' rights. That Nazi Germany would discriminate against Jews was obvious. How far would discrimination go? Would not those Jews who had proved their loyalty to the fatherland and long been settled in German lands be spared humiliation and worse? Jews were divided in their reactions – a question too of generations. Those who were older still held on to the hope of a better future after a Nazi interlude. In Hamburg, unlike Berlin, it was still easier to harbour such illusions for a short time. All here remained comparatively calm.

II

The democratic senate was resisting the clamour of Nazis who wanted to take over control.[8] The Nazis bombarded Berlin with demands to install a Reich commissioner, falsely claiming that the police force was no longer able to maintain law and order. The senate hoped to reach a sensible compromise. Discussions began. The Nazis proposed they should nominate five of the ten senators. They appeared to be moderate, requiring only four of them to be Nazi Party members, the fifth being Carl Vincent Krogmann, head of a well-known merchant family, who had inherited the business two years after the death of his well-respected father. Krogmann, the Nazis proposed, would preside over the senate.

Krogmann was physically courageous and patriotic, sporting decorations from the Great War. In the elite chamber of commerce he represented a minority view, urging Hindenburg to appoint Hitler as chancellor. Krogmann hoped to win some influence over Nazi economic policy. He was in favour of state direction, but Nazi aims of self-sufficiency were anathema in Hamburg, as the local economy was dependent on overseas trade. The discussions failed. The democratic senators balked at handing over the police to the Nazis, who had nominated a storm trooper, Alfred Richter.

That left the Social Democratic Party senators in place, causing fury in Berlin. All the threats from Wilhelm Frick, the new Nazi Reich minister of the interior, were repulsed by Mayor Carl Petersen. The first breach in the democratic front, nevertheless, occurred after the *Reichstag* fire. On that day in Hamburg a policeman was shot by a communist. The senate acquiesced now to demands from Berlin to ban communist propaganda and meetings, hoping to prevent a total Nazi takeover. Seventy-five communist functionaries were arrested. For Berlin this was not enough. The Social Democrats had to be denounced as fellow Marxists. A new pretext presented itself when the *Hamburger Echo*, a paper supporting the Social Democrats, published a critical article on the *Reichstag* fire headed, 'What lies behind it?'. Frick ordered the paper's suspension for fourteen days – a crucial period just before the elections. When attempts failed to have the order withdrawn, the Social Democratic senators withdrew from the senate. In the remaining rump senate, Senator Paul de Chapeaurouge of the German People's Party, a determined opponent of the Nazis, took over control of the police. Under pressure from Gauleiter Kaufmann he sent the Social Democratic commander of the militarised state security police, Colonel Lothar Danner, on leave of absence, but the Hamburg senate still would not replace him with Alfred Richter, as Berlin was demanding. On the eve of the elections, despite the Hamburg Nazis' hysterical messages to Berlin, law and order was maintained. It was now up to the people.

III

What happened on 5 March, election day, just thirty-four days after Hitler was appointed chancellor, was going to be decisive for Germany and the Jews.[9] In his whirlwind campaign from city to city, Hitler had not dwelt on Jews or racial ideology, but no German could be in ignorance of what the Nazis stood for. The rank and file inundated every town and village with their propaganda, with leaflets, and with posters large and small. Nothing could exceed Julius Streicher's *Der Stürmer*, which spread the most rabid antisemitism.

Hitler's coalition allies in the election, the 'Fighting Front Black–White–Red', consisting of the *Stahlhelm* and the German National People's Party, did not hold back either. They counted on fanning hatred of Jews to increase their vote.[10] Their crude election pamphlets sported swastikas, their message:

Germany is the land of freedom … Jewish capitalism has destroyed the achievements of Bismarck and the Hohenzollerns by decomposition from within and encirclement from abroad. The German people did not in the past realise the Jews were their slavemasters … the ignominy of 9 November 1918 and the shameless politics since the collapse is the work of the Jews, rule by parliamentary democracy the Jewish form of government over the peoples of the earth …

Hitler's calculated reticence not to raise the Jewish question in his speeches did not silence the streets or raucous party propaganda, as he well knew. A day before the election, 4 March 1933, Goebbels's infamous Berlin paper, *Der Angriff*, with a portrait of Adolf Hitler and his facsimile signature, spelt out the message:

The Jew today is the biggest agitator to bring about the complete destruction of Germany. Wherever in the world we read about attacks on Germany, the Jews are the originators, just as in peace and in war the Jewish Stock Exchange and the Marxist press enflamed hatred of Germany until one country after another gave up its neutrality and, in disregard of the true interests of its people, entered into the service of the world coalition [against Germany].

A quite different language was used when government spokesmen addressed foreign correspondents. Vice-Chancellor Papen, the respectable face of the coalition, told the press corps: 'Jewish citizens in Germany can be assured that they will be treated in the same way as all good citizens. Every German-Jewish citizen can count on equality of treatment by the authorities of the state.'

Did Hitler personally have to be reticent? The voters were not put off by the vilification of Jews. Their fate was not going to move the overwhelming majority one way or the other. But for Hitler to have dwelt on the issue would have been a wasted opportunity. He had to address himself to the more immediate fears, concerns and hopes of the people. He hammered away at a few issues; he stressed over and over again the failures of the party politics of Weimar, *das System*, which had brought Germany to its knees; he dwelt on the need for unity, galvanising the energies of the *Volk* to overcome the destitution of millions of unemployed; he warned of the danger of ruthless Marxists, communists and Social Democrats, 'whose bloody sword of destruction hangs over Germany'. He promised the German people would once more hold their heads high, so that Germany would cease to prostrate itself before the victors of 1914 and instead demand equality and respect. Millions voted for bread and national revival.

The disunity of the party was swept under the table. Was it a 'socialist' party, as its name National Socialist Workers' Party implied? Was it really a workers' party, or indeed a party at all? Or was it a party that upheld a capitalist structure? The Nazi mission of racial purity in people's minds was equated with excluding

Jews from the *Volk*. Jewish influence would be 'pushed back', something to be welcomed. What people did not vote for was a party, let alone a non-existent party programme. They voted for one man, in whose hands they placed their faith.

IV

Nazi voters came from all groups and social classes. Despite deep conflicts and divisions, the great majority were agreed on one thing: the Weimar constitutional democracy, the *System*, had failed; it was necessary to end it. What could fill the vacuum? The liberals were fatally weakened. The Catholic Centre Party could not hope to gain a majority, and the workers' allegiance was split between the Social Democrats and the communists, as hostile to the democratic republic as the Nazis.

It took courage to vote for the communists. Who could be sure that the Nazis would not scrutinise the returns to discover their 'enemies'? But Hitler followed a different tactic; there were to be no martyrs among rank-and-file followers. In Germany there were too many communist voters anyway, almost 5 million. They could not all be sent to concentration camps. Hitler counted on converting the 'deluded' workers. Their enlightenment would go hand in hand with the ruthless treatment of any activists and functionaries.

Of benefit to the Nazis was the higher voter turnout nationally and in Hamburg. The local Nazi Party had strained every means to take voters to the polls. Volunteers supplied cars to convey the old and the sick. People were carried to the booths even on stretchers. Party members on foot knocked on doors. Electoral lists in every district were scrutinised to detect the missing voters. The devotion and effort of the rank-and-file Nazi Party members helped to gather in every possible vote. But the great increase in their support was the result not of higher participation at the elections but people switching from the other parties.

When the votes were counted on 5 March the Nazis had done enough, with over 17 million votes - four out of ten people - supporting them nationally.[11] Together with their allies, they had gained a majority. In Hamburg, the Nazis did less well, and here with their allies they fell just short of a majority. Nevertheless, far more had voted for the Nazis than for any other party.

When all the votes cast against the so-called Weimar system are added together, those of the communists as well as of the Nazis and conservatives – and by no means all those who voted for the Social democrats, unlike their leaders, were greatly concerned about democracy – somewhere between two-thirds and three-quarters of the German people were unwilling to support parliamentary democracy any longer. They either did not realise that a dictatorship would undermine the traditional *Rechtsstaat*, the independence and impartiality of the law, or they did not care.

This is what placed the Jewish minority under threat, for law and democracy were the bastions of their human rights. And, if the Jewish citizens could be discriminated against with impunity, it opened the door to discrimination against any other minority group the Nazis chose to identify and attack. The election of 5 March was not about what should be done with the Jews as far as the great majority of Germans were concerned, though they thought it all to the good if their 'prominence' were pushed back. Even those voters who opposed the Nazis, with few exceptions, did not do so because of Nazi intentions to discriminate against their Jewish fellow citizens. Even fewer were now prepared to stand up for them.

Why were the Jews defenceless? It was not for any lack of effort by Jewish organisations or of liberal and socialist leaders warning the people of the dangers. The warnings fell on deaf ears. Many Germans felt some antipathy towards Jews. The prominence of the few wealthy and successful Jews aroused envy. Jews were resented not so much individually, more as a group supposedly all sharing unpleasant characteristics. Most hostility was shown to the recent *Ostjuden*, some of whom continued to live, as they had done in Poland and Galicia, strangers to German customs. They, too, would in time have assimilated. Intolerance extended to other minorities, especially the Roma and Sinti. In hard times the argument also proved persuasive that the severely mentally and physically handicapped were a useless burden on society when so much of the 'best blood' of Germany's manhood had been killed and crippled on the battlefield. Surely, was it not common sense to eliminate from the *Volk* all those who were defective?

The traumas successively suffered by Germans – defeat, hyperinflation and the devastating Depression – created a moral vacuum which Hitler was able to fill. There was a readiness to discard the old and accept the 'new', whatever that turned out to be. That this meant setting out on the road to barbarism few realised as they started on the journey. And the new masters of Hamburg began the descent in the city without even a day's delay.

New masters

It quickly became clear that there was no turning back. How would Jewish lives in Hamburg be affected? The Nazi takeover was swift and brutal.[12] The polling stations had barely closed when lorry loads of storm troopers drew up before Hamburg's town hall. They were there to make it clear to the senators inside who the new masters were even before the votes had been counted. Inside, the senate was debating how to preserve order and fulfil its constitutional obligations. The police were still under its authority, even though some police stations had demonstrated their subordination by hoisting swastika flags. So far the Nazis had been kept out of power in Hamburg. Frustrated and angry, they planned revenge; they were not going to wait any longer. Control of the police was the prerequisite to enable them to unleash a reign of terror on their opponents. Why delay? Their nominee, storm trooper *Standartenführer* Alfred Richter, should be made acting chief of police immediately. One hour after the polls had closed, the minister of the interior, Wilhelm Frick, sent orders from Berlin that Richter was to be appointed forthwith. The senate held out. Could the minister issue such an order without the full approval of the Reich cabinet? Dramatic final hours: the curtain was about to fall. Crowds had now assembled in front of the town hall on the Rathausmarkt, soon to be renamed Adolf-Hitler-Platz. *Gauleiter* Kaufmann and his deputy Harry Hennigsen arrived, young men full of arrogance. For Kaufmann, the senators of the '*System*' were history. Hennigsen demanded they act: 'It's time to end all your chatter. You are just delaying the outcome. Now it's our turn. We are not going to negotiate with you any longer.' The senate caved in and Alfred Richter was placed in charge of the police. To mark the Nazis' victory, the swastika flag was hoisted over the town hall. Cheers and cries of '*Heil*' rose from the crowd.

Getting rid of Hamburg's representative constitution took only a month. The parliamentary chamber met on 8 March. The communist members were missing, hunted down or already under arrest, Ernst Thälmann, their leader, in a concentration camp. The 'parliamentarians', many in brown SA uniforms, elected a new ruling senate with no Social Democrats for the first time since 1919. Headed by Carl Vincent Krogmann, it now consisted of six Nazis, four Nationalist allies and two from the parties of the right who had sat in the previous senate. By the Second Law of the Coordination of the Länder of 7 April, the basis of the constitution was hollowed out. The elected parliament lost control over Hamburg's government and the *Führer* principle was introduced. The parliament actually met three more times and then simply disappeared. An amazingly outwardly quiet revolution had taken place. How many people in Hamburg really cared about the death of democracy? Nazis did not play a parliamentary game for long in the Reich either. With the passage of the Enabling Act on 23 March, Hitler secured dictatorial control.

By terror and arrests the active opposition had been practically eliminated by the autumn of 1933. The political parties other than the Nazis had succumbed. The trade unions were forced to dissolve, and in their place the Nazis organised and controlled the Workers' Front. Most of the underground communist cells were mopped up. Some rank-and-file Social Democrats carried on distributing anti-Nazi literature, but this too soon came to an end. The state police could rely on informants. The communists were particularly vulnerable, as their membership cards had fallen into the hands of the Gestapo. Information was also extracted under threat or torture from recent recruits.

In the elections on 12 November 1933 the people gave Hitler a ringing endorsement. No doubt there was skulduggery: the referendum issue had been cleverly chosen. These were pseudo-elections, as people had no choice; all parties except for the NSDAP had been forbidden. The opponents of the Nazis, among them many Jews, rejected them and might have stayed at home had Hitler not combined them with a referendum on Germany leaving the League of Nations. The decision to leave the League was quite popular even among anti-Nazis and Jews, as it was identified with the Versailles Treaty. Thus, if they wished to support this foreign policy decision, they could not boycott the elections.[13] Secret party records in Hamburg show how much importance was attached to the outcome.

Hitler was so confident that circulars from Berlin warned local zealots against any sort of pressure: 'By adopting forcible means, the Nationalist Socialist movement does not gain loyal followers with conviction but bitter opponents. We only want National Socialists who come to us freely. We don't want short-term successes but results that will last for centuries.'[14] Two days earlier, on 10 November, at 1 p.m. throughout Germany the sirens had sounded: block leaders were told to make sure that every householder had access to a radio and that every beer hall and restaurant installed loudspeakers to hear their *Führer* speak. In the words of the party, this was Germany's hour of destiny. The referendum would demonstrate to the whole world 'that the regime internally is supported by all the people and that its life is guaranteed for all time'.

I

Not everyone was dragooned. The incessant propaganda was turning people off, as the Solmitzes discovered:

> We went to the Nazi beer house the Senator and heard there Hitler's wonderful speech … what I cannot forget is how the men playing cards at two tables continued to thump them on the tables … The cards thudded, the coins clanged and the players gossiped while Germany's future was in the balance.

One customer was so outraged that he complained to the landlord:

> how, as the owner of a Nazi beer house, can you tolerate that people play cards when the *Führer* is speaking? When he was outside, he said to us, 'They were Jews.' No, we replied, they were not Jews …. Since the behaviour of these philistines was deplorable they were immediately supposed to be Jews. We told him to think about the fact that the innkeeper did not just make his living from our glass of beer, thanks to Hitler's speech, but was dependent on the card players.[15]

That Sunday the people of Hamburg delivered their votes. Participation was high: 755,126 voted 'yes', but a still pretty astonishing 112,666 voted 'no', and almost 30,000 spoilt their papers. Nationally Hitler had triumphed, with over 90 per cent acclamation. Only by comparison were the results in Hamburg 'a disgrace', one in six voters having said 'no' to Hitler. The Nazis in Hamburg immediately sought to pinpoint the traitorous voters, 'the Marxists', and began analysing the returns district by district. Their suspicions were confirmed; the reds still had their strongholds in working-class districts, but the zealous Nazis had to stop the witch hunt. The Ministry of the Interior sent out instructions not to investigate further.

> A suggestion has been made by various authorities to identify the people who deliberately absented themselves from voting on 12 November 1933.

In view of the fact that the overwhelming majority of the German people have supported the *Führer* Adolf Hitler, it seems small minded and unnecessary subsequently to establish who did not vote. Under no circumstances should this be done.

This was obviously viewing the vote for the one-party *Reichstag* correctly from a wider perspective. The contrast between the voting on 5 March 1933 and eight months later is striking. Even in the former communist strongholds of the city almost three-quarters had voted 'yes', which, though it probably exaggerated the support, did not do so by all that much. What the referendum confirmed was that the majority of the people had fallen under the Nazi spell. What is more, the campaign against Jews and 'non-Aryans' and the destruction of democracy – Germany's transformation into an authoritarian state – had not turned the overwhelming majority against the regime. Admiration for Hitler was one thing, but would this necessarily transfer to local *Führer*s?

II

The *Führer* of Hamburg was Karl Kaufmann.[16] He owed his rise to Hitler. He was the head of the party and after 16 May, as *Reichsstatthalter*, head of the state government. Below him were an array of executives and senators, vestiges of old Hamburg, now responsible to him, a mayor, civil servants, party functionaries, and a host of special administrators he appointed to advise him on a bewildering array of problems. Beyond were the Reich ministries in Berlin and, as Himmler's star rose, the centralised machinery of the SS, the terror regime with a satellite organisation in Hamburg over which Kaufmann had no effective control. Efficient administrative leadership from the top was impossible even had Kaufmann possessed the superhuman abilities to oversee and coordinate the myriad activities. Corruption reigned, with Kaufmann a principal beneficiary. It was extraordinary how quickly the Hamburg tradition of good government could be undermined once gangsters and crooks gained key positions. But government continued to function under the Nazis.

Most of the state employees remained.[17] Many competent civil servants, judges and administrators neither resigned nor were dismissed, even though some accommodated themselves only minimally to the Nazis. Only at the top were Nazis on whom the regime could rely to follow blindly. Hamburg also needed all its policemen, and few of the lower ranks lost their jobs even though they were previously socialists; only the senior policemen were removed. The administrative machinery could function with some degree of independence, but on the whole tried to fulfil the Nazi directives faithfully. Many opportunistically jumped on the bandwagon and offered their skills to the regime, not caring where it led. Still others were newcomers, corrupt Nazis. It was difficult for anyone, including the Jews, to have any certainty about what the future held. You could obtain some support and advice if you knew the right person. That was especially true for all the *Volksgenossen*. Anyone with access to an important Nazi was fortunate, and in Hamburg at the top of party and state stood Karl Kaufmann.

Born in 1900, Kaufmann was baptised a Catholic. At the age of seventeen he volunteered for the Flying Observation Corps, though too late in 1917 to be sent to the front on active duty. After the war he joined the Free Corps and pinned to his uniform an active Great War service medal to which he was not entitled. His political associations early on showed his leanings towards radical extremism. He joined the *Deutschvölkischer Schutz- und Trutzbund* (German-*völkisch* Defend and Defy League) in 1923 during the French occupation of the Ruhr and became a member of the terrorist underground organisation Heinz. Early on he found his way to Hitler, who appointed him, at the age of twenty-four, *Gauleiter* of Northern Rhine and in 1926 *Gauleiter* of an amalgamated Rhineland-Westphalia *Gau*. But soon ructions started – accusations and counter-accusations of thefts of party funds. Kaufmann could not avoid examination by a Nazi court of honour, which found that he had entered a false date of birth to make it appear he had been old enough to have fought in the First World War, thus 'lied to the *Führer*', and that he had also worn a war decoration to which he was not entitled. Hitler intervened. He dismissed the wearing of the medal as youthful folly, sent one antagonist, Erich Koch, as *Gauleiter* to East Prussia, and in May 1929 Kaufmann to the unrewarding *Gau* of 'red' Hamburg. In 1931 Kaufmann was further embarrassed when the investigation of his medal became public knowledge in the press.

Hitler was not much concerned about the character deficiencies of his party organisers. What mattered was that they were young, active, hungry for power, without scruple, when necessary ruthless and violent, and above all unquestionably loyal to him. Kaufmann qualified. That these men often had a need to compensate for their weakness and previous lack of success in life through self-assertiveness to a pathological degree, that they lacked stability, were given to violence and lack of self-control, and found it difficult to form stable relationships within the party and outside it, made them all the more dependent on Hitler as their ultimate authority and father figure.

Kaufmann was a chameleon, and not without talent. He could be accommodating, acting not at all like the usual Nazi thug and gangster, but he could equally be brutal, encouraging the savage beatings of opponents. The cultivation of an image of moderation stood him in good stead after the war, reinforcing the legend of how different the National Socialist years were in Hamburg thanks to him. In his attitude to the churches he did show his more tolerant side. He sent his two daughters to a Catholic school and retained through his mother contact with the Church. Protestants too had nothing to complain of. This did not endanger his position, as he was not acting contrary to Nazi policies. When it came to the Jews, he showed no softness. On the contrary, Kaufmann, a hardened anti-Semite, was at the forefront of *Gauleiters* wishing to deport them. The anti-Jewish measures were carried out as thoroughly in Hamburg as elsewhere in the Reich.

Kaufmann earned a reputation for looking after the 'little man', the worker. Many had lost their jobs in the purge of 1933 because they belonged or had belonged to one of the two socialist parties. Soon the Hamburg practice was to reinstate them if no party member was available for the job, provided they received a positive political reference. Kaufmann was ready to defy Berlin's direct orders forbidding their re-employment. He could fall back on the claim that 'the *Führer* constantly stresses that, especially the junior employees and workers who previously were on the other side, should be won over to the movement, as the great majority had been misled by their leaders.' A significant number of state employees in Hamburg consequently were not party members. Especially in the technical branches of government, it did not hinder their promotion or careers. Given the chaos in his own administrative office, there needed to be efficiency elsewhere to get things done. Kaufmann courted popularity. He used a slush fund collected from businesses and individuals to set up his own foundation; from it he made charitable grants to party members who had fallen on hard times. By promoting a number of populist social measures he skilfully created an image of concern for the disadvantaged. Individual men and women could appeal to him to rectify injustice, harping back to an old tradition of the paternalist head of state. Kaufmann also cultivated relations with the mercantile elite, defending Hamburg's economic interests in Berlin. By such means he earned a good reputation with all classes of people. This overlooks the thousands of victims of political and racial persecution. The treatment of the Jews was not the uppermost concern of the people, which was actually a problem for the Nazi leadership they were determined to address.

Kaufmann's right-hand man was Georg Ahrens.[18] He was one of the more unusual leaders of the Hamburg Nazi mafia. Thirty-six years old when Hitler was appointed chancellor, the son of a Baptist preacher, he remained in the congregation of the Hamburg-Altona Baptist Church until 1940. His education had ended with elementary schooling. A volunteer in the Great War, he was wounded three times. After the war, trained as a bookkeeper, he worked for a number of companies. His attempt to found an independent business failed in the mid-1920s. He finally acted as the representative in Hamburg of a Cologne construction company until that too went bankrupt. Certainly this was not a normal background or preparation for high office but typical for many Nazis. Actually Ahrens's record was rather better than most. He had reached by his own efforts middle management positions and had tried to better himself and earn a decent living.

The success of the Nazis in the *Reichstag* elections of July 1930 persuaded Ahrens to throw in his lot with them. He soon made his way among the even less qualified Nazi 'elite', entered Hamburg's parliament (*Bürgerschaft*) in 1931 and became deputy leader of the Hamburg group. He was not an antisemite by conviction. Even after 1933 he could be helpful to Jews dismissed from state positions or actors who performed in the Thalia theatre and were married to 'Jewish' wives. When Ahrens was asked to provide a reference for Professor Wohlwill, who had emigrated to Portugal and was being considered for a position in the Cancer Institute in Lisbon, he wrote: 'His work was free of all criticism, his academic achievements were outstanding as one of the leading doctors in the

St Georg Hospital. He was highly valued by the medical professions. He left the Hamburg state service on 30 September 1933 on account of paragraph 3 (non-Aryan or Jewish) of the law for the Restoration of the Civil Service.' Wohlwill secured the appointment.

Ahrens's advancement was rapid: *Senatsrat* on 8 March 1933, state secretary in May and Mayor Krogmann's permanent deputy the following year, though in reality doing Kaufmann's bidding. Ahrens was placed in charge of the administration. Krogmann, Hamburg's mayor, became the fifth wheel of the coach. With an unfailing sense of timing, Ahrens joined the SS when Himmler visited Hamburg in the autumn of 1933. Thereafter on formal occasions he appeared in black uniform. Ahrens was fully aware of the tortures and beatings in the Stadthaus and Fuhlsbüttel and was present on some occasions. Power hungry and vain with a brutal streak, he tried to overcome chronic dyspepsia with copious amounts of alcohol and coffee. He prospered materially. His income doubled during the Nazi years. From an ugly apartment in the Hansastraße in 1940 he moved to a beautiful villa, BarmbeckerStraße 136, which he acquired from its Jewish owner for a ludicrously small sum. During the war his became the best-known voice on Hamburg radio. It earned him a new sobriquet, 'Uncle Baldrian', for his broadcasts to 'my dear Hamburgers' now living under the hail of British bombs (Baldrian is German for the nerve-soothing herb Valerian).

The new masters of Hamburg held together throughout the Nazi years. They were criminals steeped in corruption. They saw themselves as the leaders of a new world, a thousand-year Reich. They took the credit for bringing about this glorious transformation. Success inflated their sense of importance. Against the background of such stupendous achievement, the fact that they personally enriched themselves seemed insignificant. They deserved, surely, all life had to offer after their early years of hardship. Behind their backs, Hamburg society laughed at their social gaucheness but also courted them for their power and influence. For twelve unbroken years they were indeed Hamburg's undisputed masters and destroyed the old Hamburg the Jews had loved.

III

Kaufmann and Nazi police unleashed brutal attacks on political opponents immediately after the election. Communists and Social Democratic leaders, anyone who had fallen foul of Kaufmann, was arrested. Jews were among those taken into custody if they had played a role in politics or as lawyers prosecuting Nazis, but they were not general targets. Arrests followed a spate of denunciations when a remark in a shop or a casual conversation was overheard. There were so many people now anxious to prove their loyalty to the new state, including some wanting to wipe clean their past membership of a socialist party.

Knowledge about the brutal incarcerations was widespread, but the general atmosphere in Hamburg was not one of dread and terror. The great majority of people, including communists, had nothing to fear as long as they ceased political activity and kept their mouths shut. For those who did fall into the claws of the Gestapo it was a different story. They would be lucky to escape with their lives and not to suffer lasting injury. Within hours after the elections of 5 March, Kaufmann had set up two special police units.[19] Peter Kraus led one of these *Sonderkommandos*, and lieutenant of police Franz Kosa was in charge of the notorious 'Command for Special Purposes', KzbV for short, a second group some forty men strong.

The victims were singled out for 'special treatment' with a brutality in Hamburg second to none. The hit squads were determined that blood would flow. They would avenge their comrades killed by communists in street battles. Altona's Bloody Sunday was not forgotten. Carefully selected by Kaufmann, these sadists could be relied on; they were mostly old adherents of the Nazi Party, members of the security police or recruited from the SS or the SA with a background of violence in the Free Corps and in extremist right-wing organisations. Their education was limited to the level of the elementary *Volksschule*. Before the Nazis came to power they generally had led a precarious existence.

Typical was Heinz Emil Eggers, born in 1903, unemployed, the son of a schoolteacher. He had joined the extremist Nazi paramilitary Roland group in the early 1920s, then entered the Hamburg police in 1923, but because of his political background he was not considered for promotion to officer rank. In 1934 he joined the state police.[20]

Helmuth Deutschmann was another notorious torturer. Born in 1908, he was just twenty-five years old when he was selected by Kaufmann. The son of a butcher, he attended elementary school and then was apprenticed. In 1928 he shot his bride and then attempted suicide. On psychiatric grounds he was set free as not accountable for what he had done. He entered the Kraus command as an old fighter, SA 1926, and Nazi Party member, SS 1928, and rose in the ranks of the state police, but had to be moved to a 'safer' position in 1937 after a wild shooting spree in a beer house.

Ernst Jansen had been one of the three conspirators who had shot dead a communist parliamentary deputy in a bus in 1931. Released from prison in 1933, he was promoted until he received another prison sentence for severely injuring a policeman in a drunken brawl on New Year's Day, 1935. Born in 1909 the son of a farm worker, he was known to be unstable and excitable. He entered the security police in April 1928 but was dismissed in December 1930 for illegal support of the Nazi Party membership, which at that time had been declared inadmissable by the senate. During the Depression he too experienced hard times and found his only 'home' with Nazi comrades.

The unstable lives of these men recruited to smash the Marxists were typical of the whole group. Their skills and education were limited, and they could only prosper in the Nazi regime. Those placed in charge were better educated. Their commander Franz Kosa had enjoyed a higher education and a respectable war record as an officer in the Kaiser's navy during the Great War. A member of the Nazi Party only in November 1932, with a background in the security police, he was chosen to command this special unit. But his education did not make him less sadistic than the men under him.

The 'Command for Special Purposes' was housed in the Große Bleichen, now Stadthausbrücke 12.[21] Here, and in the empty women's prison in Fuhlsbüttel designated in the autumn of 1933 as a concentration camp, the interrogations and incarcerations took place. The brutal behaviour of the interrogators, no 'ordinary' policemen, defies imagination. Men were stripped of all dignity, shouted at, lain naked across tables, beaten with oxhide whips and canes, trodden when unconscious, revived with cold water and beaten again. This could go on day after day. The torture would end only when the victim had provided the information the Stapo were seeking, or was so badly injured that he died, committed suicide in his cell or was transferred close to death to the prison hospital. Several hundred men and even some women passed through this hell. They could secure their release only by satisfying their captors and informing on colleagues. Kaufmann was present at such beatings and, according to one witness, participated in them. After the war, descriptions of the tortures suffered by communist functionaries, as well as by Social Democratic Party leaders, became public in a series of trials. There were also Jews among the prisoners, who were beaten senseless and spared nothing.

What was happening was no secret either at the time. It was probably through an underground socialist group that an anonymous detailed description of beatings, with names of the victims and torturers, was sent in the summer of 1934 to the public prosecutor, clergymen and lawyers, appealing to them to protest. It was not the only communication of this sort. The creation of a storm trooper's concentration camp, KZ Wittmoor, which functioned for a few months until the prisoners were transferred to Fuhlsbüttel in September 1933, was reported in the Hamburg newspapers.[22] When victims were released they were warned not to talk about conditions, under threat of being brought back. No one could avoid seeing how they looked after a spell in 'Kola-Fu', the popular gallows humour description of the Fuhlsbüttel concentration camp. Among the victims were the leaders of Hamburg's Social Democratic Party.

They had called a meeting in June 1933, for which they had secured the permission of the Nazi authorities. Thirty assembled at their headquarters in the Fehlandstraße; here they became sitting ducks for the SS and storm troopers, who broke into their meeting and took them to the notorious Stapo headquarters in the Große Bleichen. Karl Meitmann, the first chairman of the party, was held down naked across a table and severely beaten. Kaufmann, he later said, was in the Stapo headquarters at the time. Meitmann and his party colleagues were interrogated all night and then taken to Fuhlsbüttel, where beatings interspersed with interrogations continued. They were released five weeks later with the warning not to engage further in any political activity. Small groups continued to organise the distribution of pamphlets, but relentless Gestapo searches and arrests soon brought their activities to an end. The success of the Gestapo was possible because the underground activities of communists and Social Democrats were carried on only by a few, and they were surrounded by people ready to denounce them.

The majority of lawyers, public prosecutors, judges and civil servants, who had behaved quite properly during the Weimar years, remained in office. As far as they were concerned, the Reich government was lawful and their duty was to carry out its policies. They had served the Weimar governments; now they served the new Hitler government, and those that were allowed would again serve the Allied military government after 1945. The only difference in the files – kept without a break – was that the questionnaires asked different questions about their past associations. Theirs was not to reason why but to apply themselves conscientiously to the task in hand.

IV

At first, not everyone adjusted fully. When the maltreatment of prisoners in Fuhlsbüttel came to the attention of the public prosecutor, he wished to charge Kosa and the pKzbV and to take up the case of a doctor who had been beaten up. He was quickly disabused. Curt Rothenberger, responsible for the judiciary, explained, 'It is obvious that this is best avoided. Information about the activities of Kosa would reach the general public if there were court proceedings.' There were now two laws in Hamburg: the ordinary everyday administration of law and the secret state law, which was no law.

Who was Senator Curt Rothenberger? Another appointee without previous background and experience who owed his office to early Nazi allegiance? In fact Rothenberger had been highly regarded as a lawyer in the administration of justice before the Nazis came to power. There is nothing in his background to suggest that he would serve a criminal regime with diligence and without scruple. If the Nazis had not come to power and Weimar democracy had prevailed, he would no doubt have completed an unblemished career.

Rothenberger's career took off after 1933. He was educated in the Wilhelm *Gymnasium* much favoured by Jewish boys, who made up a significant proportion of the pupils. Rothenberger struck up a close friendship with a Jewish classmate, Kurt Enoch. Their friendship continued after the school years were over. As the Great War drew to a close, both were lieutenants in the Reserve and participated in the 1918 spring offensive. They remained in touch after the war until Rothenberger's sympathies for the Nazis made this impolitic. Enoch emigrated and made his career in publishing and was spectacularly successful in Britain and the United States. Rothenberger ended up in 1947 in Nuremberg and was sentenced to seven years' imprisonment.

Rothenberger owed much to professors of Jewish descent, the distinguished Kurt Perels and Moritz Liepmann, who took a particular interest in the students who had returned from the war. They supervised Rothenberger's doctorate and helped to launch his career. Like many conservative colleagues in the judiciary, Rothenberger was no enthusiastic supporter of the Weimar Republic, but there was no doubt about his abilities. When in 1931 the democratic Hamburg senate failed to gain him a place on the Supreme Court, ambition overcame any scruples. With the spectacular rise of the Nazi Party, he linked his career to their success. Kaufmann thought he would be more useful to them if he did not join the party, and instead he provided legal advice. He was rewarded, appointed justice senator on 8 March 1933 and then joined the party. Now he made sure that no one could accuse him of friendship with Jews. He removed two Jewish public prosecutors from office even before the enactment of the Reich law of 7 April, and thereafter thirty-one public prosecutors and judges who fell under the non-Aryan clauses. His old teacher Professor Perels was forced to retire from his university chair and in despair committed suicide.

The judges in Hamburg and Germany showed little backbone. What worried them was the threat to their independence. So they passed a resolution expressing their confidence that the Nazis would respect it. But the Nazis had already broken their constitutional rights by removing 'Marxists' and Jews. It was a breach that after the events they agreed to tolerate as 'special cases'. So much for the guardians of justice. Rothenberger would not find their resistance a problem. Only a few months later, he dispelled any remaining illusions.[23] 'We stand at the beginning of a new era', Rothenberger told the assembled judges and lawyers:

> Such a complete and radical change would not leave the administration of justice untouched. Only those who have not grasped the inner kernel of the National Socialist ideology, in contrast to the democratic liberal one that existed before, will be surprised that a change of personnel in the administration of justice in Hamburg [and the Hanseatic cities] has occurred to an extent never before experienced ... Out of 280 Hamburg judges and public prosecutors, fifty-five have left.

With their removal, he continued, the changes had ended, unless conditions altered with the stricter application of racial laws. Independence from the new state was no longer an option. Rothenberger reminded those who needed reminding that they 'were an insoluble part of the *Volk*'. The implied threat from this recent super-Nazi was crystal clear. They were required to act in conformity with National Socialist ideology or they would be removed.

Old traditions nevertheless died hard. Confusing parallel systems in the administration of justice emerged. The death of prisoners or their maltreatment remained in theory at least a matter for the courts to deal with, even though anyone could be arrested by the state police without benefit of committal by a court. Deaths in custody should have been investigated. This difficulty was overcome by reporting murders committed in Hamburg's concentration camp or in Stapo cells as suicides or simply as deaths from natural causes. To prevent the medical examination of corpses beaten to death, Kaufmann ordered they be cremated immediately. The murderers and torturers of the Gestapo had nothing to fear from the courts.

The Nazi state needed men of competence and experience. Few left of their own free will. Jews too, and so-called non-Aryans not subject to dismissal by the provisions of the Hindenburg exemption, clung to their positions. In such harsh times a secure income was everything. How else would a family survive?

Typical was Erwin Garvens, head of Hamburg's Audit Office, a scathing critic before 1933 of his conservative fellow members of the *Nationalklub* who had flocked to hear Hitler. Would they be allowed to remain in office? 'No civil servant knows whether tomorrow he will still be sitting on his chair', Garvens noted in his journal, adding, 'for the time being I can remain calm.'[24] In early August he was still in his post. He describes a happy gathering organised by the Nazis in the elegant *Winterhuder Fährhaus* restaurant: 'Senator Burchard-Motz delivered a nice speech ... there was dancing ... the only senior civil servants who expressed their close links with the *Volk* were Dr Hennigsen and myself. The others sat silent at their tables and left as soon as possible.' The blow fell unexpectedly. Five days later, Garvens was arrested on a trumped-up charge and interrogated with threats of violence, but he was released when nothing could be proved against him. He was retired but received a good pension and was not molested further. It was remarkable too how leading Social Democrats as well as Jewish employees were treated. Nazi thugs might beat you close to death, but the civil service pension laws remained sacrosanct.

V

During the early weeks the news media abroad created an impression that Germany was engulfed in terror and that the lives of the Jews were under immediate threat. The brutalities unleashed by Göring in Prussia and Kaufmann in Hamburg were real. The boycott of 1 April and the book-burning a month later displayed the Nazis as racist cultural hooligans. The image of intolerable persecution was reinforced in the public mind by the exodus of illustrious musicians, academics and actors. Albert Einstein, the most famous scientist of the day, was interviewed on reaching the United States in exile; filmed scenes were shown in cinemas all over the world. Those on Nazi blacklists, such as the Nobel laureate Thomas Mann and his brother Klaus, turned their backs on Germany. Marlene Dietrich, a pure Aryan in Nazi terminology, left in disgust. Had Germany been turned into a cultural desert by the Nazis?

For the most part, those who left did so because they were Jews, descended from Jews or politically hated by the Nazis. For them there was no longer any professional future in the Third Reich. In quantum mechanics, dubbed a 'Jewish science', the Nobel laureate Werner Heisenberg, impeccably Aryan, remained and later headed Germany's efforts to create a nuclear bomb. The cream of the professions – leading actors such as Gustav Gründgens, the conductor Wilhelm Furtwängler, the composer Richard Strauss, the Nobel laureate Gerhard Haptmann – accommodated themselves with Joseph Goebbels's Ministry of Culture, despite their earlier connections and friendship with Jewish colleagues.

Goebbels showered them with honours and rewarded them richly financially. The Nazis wanted to be seen as patrons of German culture. The cultural elite, with few exceptions, lacked moral compass and backbone.

There were Jews too on the blacklists, especially socialists and communists. Those who did not flee in time were tortured, some despatched to rudimentary concentration camps. Thousands left the country in panic in 1933. But here too the contemporary picture was misleading. At the close of the first year of Nazi rule it was thought that 63,000 Jews had left. Later more accurate figures showed that some had returned and the actual number was 37,000: 92 per cent of the half-million-strong Jewish community remained in Germany. No doubt some would have seized the opportunity to leave if they could have done so, but for the overwhelming majority they stayed because they believed life in Germany was still preferable to the uncertainties abroad.

1933 was nevertheless a dire time for professional Jews. It is estimated that, as well as hundreds of actors, musicians and journalists, some 12,000 in the civil service and other professions lost their jobs. Though dismissal for many did not mean penury, as they qualified for pensions, the sudden ending of a career, with lawyers, judges, doctors and employees of the state forced to sit idly at home or change their lives altogether, was a sudden and tremendous shock. Pensions were regularly paid even during the early years of the Second World War, though by then into blocked accounts. The reason, nevertheless, for strong Jewish survival before 1937 was that the great majority – as many as eight out of ten – were engaged in the economy and protected to some degree by the Nazi priority of bringing about a revival. It was worst for small enterprises in smaller towns, but in the larger cities like Hamburg, Munich, Berlin and Frankfurt, where most of the Jewish community lived, surviving Jewish firms shared in the general upturn. The community could still call on enough resources to supplement the state welfare aid (paid until 1939) of the members who were suffering hardship. The picture of the Jewish community during these years is not a broken one. It was holding fast with considerable success. Life was still normal in the cities and larger towns, but it soon became intolerable for Jews in villages and smaller places.

Visitors from abroad found it difficult to grasp the reality of Nazi Germany once the early excesses in public view had been reined in by the authorities. They took good impressions home. There was more confidence and hope for the future; there was less crime in the streets; unemployment was going down – though only slowly in Hamburg; groups of young Hitler Youth were well behaved and orderly, perhaps gathering for an outing to the countryside. Violence was visible only on isolated occasions in public. Beggars were no longer seen in the streets. Germany presented a picture of orderliness and purpose. Jews were still in business, and the more privileged remained as civil servants, lawyers, judges and doctors. The country appeared to have settled down. Hitler was seen as a moderate. On 15 July 1933, he declared that the revolution was over. The following year, during the Night of the Long Knives, Ernst Roehm, head of the SA, who had dared to challenge Hitler, was murdered along with companions. It was an opportunity also to get rid of others thought undesirable. Former Vice-Chancellor Papen was lucky to escape. There were few Germans who did not approve Hitler taking the law into his own hands and punishing 'perverts'. The revolution was not over. Hitler had simply decided on a tactical pause as he was passing through the 'danger years' of rearmament. The people had adapted quickly, which was hardly surprising; Hitler was only doing what most of them wanted. True, almost everyone disapproved of one thing or another, but the 'good' far outweighed the 'bad'. Now for the lucky ones there were marriage handouts, child support, prospects of work, vacancies created by Jews. The disadvantaged were a minority and millions did not miss democracy. The people could express their approval in plebiscites instead.

VI

For the Nazi leadership in Berlin, an immediate problem was how to gain control over the local and regional Nazi fiefs like Kaufmann's Hamburg. From the Berlin ministries came streams of instructions and requests for statistical information. Much of this had little effect in Hamburg, where Kaufmann went his own way. But there was one area, critical to all Jews, where Hitler delegated power to a trusted lieutenant and took control out of Kaufmann's hands.

Hitler turned to Heinrich Himmler to coordinate the police and the terror machinery. In Hamburg, Himmler thus gained control over the state police, but he did this without offending Kaufmann. Kaufmann had become uneasy when he found out that the security police were spying on him. Himmler, an old friend, promised to help. Bruno Streckenbach, a native of the city, was then chosen with Kaufmann's approval as the local chief.[25]

The son of a customs official, Streckenbach was thirty-one years old. He had received a good education in the *Johanneum Realgymnasium*. Too young to fight at the front, he joined the Bahrenfeld Free Corps in Hamburg in 1919 to protect the city against the reds. He too was attracted to the antisemitic radical right. Unable to gain entry into the 100,000-strong army as an officer cadet, he showed ability as a representative for a number of commercial concerns. In 1930 he joined the Nazi Party and in 1931 the SS, where he led one of the formations. Streckenbach's private life was dysfunctional, with already two failed marriages behind him. Where he was consistent was in his radical aims. He was typical of the young Nazis who moved from a marginalised status in society to the centre of power after 1933. Under Streckenbach the Hamburg Gestapo were no less brutal than before: beatings and deaths from torture were commonplace, and Streckenbach personally inflicted horrendous injuries on victims to secure confessions. 'Guidelines' laid down by the Ministry of the Interior on the conduct of interrogations – only a limited number of strokes with a cane in the presence of a doctor in special cases – were simply ignored. Streckenbach's conduct won him the approval of both Himmler and Kaufmann. But in Fuhlsbüttel the sadism under its first commandant became so embarrassing to the judicial authorities that he was removed in June 1934. Fuhlsbüttel reverted to a more normal police prison regime. The nearest concentration camp, on the outskirts of Berlin, was now Sachsenhausen. Those arrested by the Hamburg Gestapo were sent there until a 'satellite' camp was later established south-east of Hamburg, in Neuengamme.

These then were the new leaders of Hamburg. They bore no resemblance to the responsible city fathers and politicians of earlier times. Not everyone was a Nazi by conviction. The policeman at the corner of the street was still the same policeman. In the town hall people were likely to be dealt with by the same officials as before. So too in the tax office, banks, post offices – no great change anywhere at the counters. Only a few people would even notice most of the Jewish employees were gone. There had never been many of them anyway. The few still dealing directly with the public anxiously enquired how they should respond to a *Volksgenosse* who greeted them with a '*Heil Hitler*'. A façade of the familiar and ordinary were it not for many more brown uniforms and swastika flags. The familiarity was misleading.

It misled observers. There was normality in many aspects of life in Nazi Germany. Most Jews lived in the larger towns and in the cities. It was not so bad here in the beginning. Jewish and Aryan children went to school together and played with each other in the street. Their parents in their daily life were not abused or treated with disrespect. Below the leading positions the infrastructure of Nazi Germany remained largely in the same hands as before. The ordinary policeman was helpful to everyone. Violence was the exception and most Jews did not actually witness any. Jews still felt safe. All the propaganda flooding the media was not yet matched by the experience of daily life.

In the top positions there had been a clearing out of the old and a bringing in of the new. Here were men exercising authority, corrupt, without moral restraint, capable of anything – including murder, as it turned out, when it was required – to reach the Nazi utopia. Kaufmann, Himmler, Streckenbach, Ahrens and their trusted henchmen would not hesitate for a moment or feel the slightest pangs of conscience. They were part of the new generation without respect for what had gone on before. Had not the traditional older elites led Germany to defeat and disaster? Their leadership was discarded, their principles treated with contempt. Those who served Hitler now were younger men. Himmler, thirty-three years old in January 1933, was the youngest. Goebbels was thirty-five, Hess, deputy *Führer*, was thirty-eight, Goering forty. Frick, at fifty-six, was one of the few more mature of Hitler's inner circle. A revolution was unfolding whose ultimate end was still veiled from public view. That Germany was heading in a new direction, however, became speedily clear on boycott day, 1 April 1933. The 'Jewish question' ceased to be a matter of propaganda and debate and was transformed into hard action of publicly isolating and harming Jews. The people needed to be 'educated' to recognise that the Jewish issue was the most important of all.

Boycott

Boycotts were nothing new, of course, nor stickers identifying Jewish businesses.[26] That of 1 April 1933, however, was different. Official boycott committees were set up throughout the country under the overall direction of Julius Streicher, the Jew-hating *Gauleiter* of Franconia. Hitler had approved the boycott, ostensibly in retaliation for boycotts of German goods organised abroad. Jewish organisations were now pressured to telegraph overseas that stories of atrocities were false and that they deprecated foreign intervention on their behalf. Local committees published lists in the newspapers of which businesses to boycott.

The boycott was not to be extended to firms 'in which there is only financial participation by Jews' until further orders; if the owner is an Aryan but the spouse a Jew, then the concern is to be regarded as Jewish. In the definition of 'Jew', race, not religion, counted. A general boycott of department stores was not to be attempted, as many Nazi followers desired – only of those in Jewish hands. Local activity committees were cautioned that Woolworth's was not Jewish. Storm troopers and black uniformed SS were to station themselves in front of Jewish shops on Saturday, 1 April 1933, punctually at 10 a.m., their duty, 'to inform the public that the enterprises before which they stood are Jewish'. The public should be warned not to buy anything, but no damage was to be done to the shops and owners were not to be molested. In Hamburg, Kaufmann on 29 March raised the temperature with an inflammatory radio broadcast against the lying, traitorous Jewish atrocity propaganda. Shop owners, fearful of being mistaken as Jews, put notices in their windows that they were 'old Christian' or a 'German enterprise'. Enthusiastic mishaps nevertheless proved unavoidable.

The show of brown uniforms was designed to intimidate. The police stood by awkwardly, not quite sure where their duty lay. Secular Jews reacted with uncertainty too. Should they open their shops or close them? They were not permitted to dismiss their Aryan assistants. Jewish doctors found that some of their patients now went elsewhere, while others took the opportunity not to pay their bills. But the choice of Saturday for the boycott day was not accidental. Religious Jews would close their shops on the Sabbath, reducing the possibility of unwelcome incidents that might be seen by foreigners.

I

John Kehl, the American consul general, strolled around Hamburg's inner city with its many elegant shops to see for himself what was going on.[27] There was, he wrote, a profusion of brown uniforms, with two or three men picketing Jewish shops, holding placards: 'Germans, don't buy from Jews!' 'Don't visit Jewish doctors or lawyers!' 'Remember the atrocity propaganda of Jewry abroad!' Others were standing on the pavement carrying similar placards. Stars of David were daubed on shop windows. But for the curious bystanders who gathered, 'one would hardly have realised a serious boycott was in progress'. People who entered Jewish shops were 'jeered at by the onlookers, and in some instances photographed'. In Hamburg few Nazis carried weapons. In neighbouring Altona the boycott was more aggressive, with Nazis sporting revolvers and even bayonets. Kehl's overall impression was that, 'during my almost two-hour trip about

Hamburg and Altona along the leading thoroughfares, there was no evidence of disturbance'. The local Nazi machine was in control. But then Kehl was sympathetic to the Nazis; people in custody, he wrote, were detained 'in the interest of general order and personal welfare .... The Nazi Nationalist government have rendered invaluable service to the world in crushing communism in Germany.'

Another view comes from a Jewish source, Max Plaut, the energetic young administrator of Hamburg's Jewish community, who recalled that

> the Jewish shop owners all reacted differently. Tietz was shut. But Max Haak on the Neuer Steinweg offered a reduction of 10 per cent and gave every customer a balloon; he doubled his sales; the communists came and bought so that boycott day here looked almost like a festival; the owner, wearing his Iron Cross first class, stood in front of the shop; discomfited SA men with their placards stood around.[28]

For many, like Martin Kohn, the boycott meant the end of running a successful business.[29] Well known throughout Hamburg were the *Hammonia* butter shops. While Kohn was in charge he increased the outlets from twenty-four to 140. On the eve of the boycott he had to give up control. A little card in every shop window informed the public of his departure and that it was no longer a Jewish business. The butter tasted no different. Opening an import–export firm next, Kohn was assured that 'gentlemen who bring in foreign currency need expect no difficulties'. Opportunism over ideology, but only for a time. Kohn owed his survival not to business acumen but to his Aryan wife. The chain of Wolff's cigar shops in Hamburg also avoided the boycott. The Jewish owner managed to arrange a suitable reorganisation in time.

II

The Grindel quarter of Hamburg, close to the great Bornplatz synagogue, was home to many mainly poorer Jews from Russia.[30] At Grindelallee 10 was the well-known Café Timpe, where culture, politics and affairs of the day were discussed by Jews and non-Jews. The most celebrated and frequent visitor savouring the atmosphere was Carl von Ossietzky, a citizen of Hamburg, editor of the pacifist *Weltbühne* and not a Jew. An obvious target of Nazi hatred, he was arrested just before the elections of 5 March, sent to a concentration camp and died in 1938 from tuberculosis he had contracted there. Two years previously, to Hitler's fury, he had received the Nobel Peace Prize. Hitler thereafter forbade Germans from accepting Nobel prizes.

Further along the road, the owner of no. 79 could make no claim to fame.[31] He was the proprietor of a small shop selling eggs. It so happened that, two weeks before the boycott was officially announced, Friedrich Solmitz was passing by. Storm troopers already stood in front of the shop carrying placards. Later that day Solmitz met Police Commissioner Zille. Zille was troubled by the behaviour of the

Nazis, who were interfering with everyday life. He told Solmitz that he was a patriot who had fought on the *Lützow* during the battle of Jutland, 'but, *Herr* Major, I cannot go along with this. *Herr* Major, you won't talk about it, but what should I do?' Solmitz: 'Your duty, without excessive show; keep your opinions to yourself and stay silent. This is only an occurrence of overheated feelings.' Overheated? Did Solmitz expect that in time these excesses would cool off and not worsen? He was not alone. There were many who echoed the sentiments of Luise Solmitz.[32]

> Saturday 1 April 1933. A bitter April joke today which will continue to trouble us for years. At 10 o'clock posts were taken up. Ugly red signs identified the Jewish shops. 'Don't buy from a Jew', etc. Some shop windows were smeared over with red paint, 'Beware Jews'. Many shops described themselves as 'old Christians' – 'No Jewish capital, no Jewish employees'. Brown shirts in front of the Jewish shops. For one of them, Fräulein Levi's, it was no longer worth carrying on; it has existed for forty years and now it is bankrupt; the German shop assistant has been there for twenty-three years. One feels ashamed in front of shops with daubs of paint and before every Jew. So that has been happily achieved. The mood of the people appeared depressed, unhappy; most cannot really support this …
>
> In front of Reese and Wichmann stood a Brown shirt; the owner is called Aronsohn (or something like it) …
>
> I saw no one buying the pamphlet 'Fight the Jew' …
>
> My inner contentment, which I have only so seldom lost, is gone. I look into a future black and blacker.
>
> 5 April 1933. Letters from Ethel and the Sloans [English friends]. They are friendly and sympathetic in tone, but all that does not help. They cannot comprehend the anti-Jewish events.
>
> We and the German *Volk* are also blamed. It is as if we, the 17 million, had chosen Hitler as the leader in the fight against the Jews and that we wanted nothing more ardently than this struggle should begin, that Versailles should take second place and the unemployment problem, the two crucial issues on which our survival depends.
>
> 15 April 1933. … And the effect in Germany is that one feels shame towards the Jews and feels a need to make restitution, and so one furthers their interests. On the Monday after the boycott we immediately went to *Herr* Lippmann, who had always served us well and honestly, and we bought a little something from his blond pure Aryan shop assistant, who must be happy to be earning her bread. Then again, others feel compassion for all those thrown out of their careers, like the lawyers, etc.

Most knew their own good Jew, whether shopkeeper or the doctor of their children. No harm should come to them. But they expressed their disapproval only in private, often adding by way of explanation, 'if only the *Führer* had knowledge of this … .'

III

Moral protest might have been expected from the churches.[33] Rabbi Leo Baeck, the head of the hastily constructed body representing German Jewry, on the eve of the boycott sent a telegram to the *Evangelischer Oberkirchenrat* [Evangelical Church Council]: 'German Jews hope for an early word from the Protestant Church in the name of religion against the threats directed against Jews to prevent irreparable harm to the religious faith we have in common.' A similar telegram was sent to Cardinal Bertram, primate of the German Catholic Church. Bertram did not reply. From the Evangelical Church Council at least came a response, 'that it was following developments with great attention and hoped that the boycott movement would be ended after one day'. In public there was deafening silence.

Behind the scenes there were individuals who urged a different course. The provost of the Catholic Cathedral in Berlin, the later martyr Monsignor Bernhard Lichtenberg, urged intervention, with protests to be sent to Hindenburg and Hitler. Archbishop Gröber of Freiburg was also in favour of doing something. Not so Bertram, who dismissed their views, since 'what was in question was an economic struggle concerning an interest group which from the Church's point of view it was not close to'. There were also Protestant voices demanding the Church should speak out, prominent among them the former lay head of the council, the Munich banker Baron von Pechmann. He urged the Evangelical Church Council jointly with the Catholic Church to condemn Jewish persecution – again to no avail. When his repeated attempts had failed, he withdrew his membership of the Church, a remarkable and radical protest.

The silence of the Church was not due to lack of courage. The Confessing Church fought the Nazis on other issues, most prominently against the introduction of the 'Aryan Paragraph' in the Church, but it too rejected Jews as alien to the *Volk*. On this they were in agreement with the Nazis, and the few who opposed found themselves crying in the wilderness.

IV

The state-sponsored boycott was the first indication that the Nazis meant to do more than just rant about the evil influence of the Jews. The impact of the boycott varied widely.[34] Small shopkeepers suffered the most, dependent as they were on all their clients. If only a few nervous customers went elsewhere, chose another baker, greengrocer or tailor, slim margins of profit vanished. The well-established larger concerns, such as the fashionable stores Hirschfeld and Robinsohn, Neuer Wall, survived, even increasing their turnover as living standards slowly began to improve. They offered value; they sold what their customers wanted. In some businesses in Hamburg, such as textiles and clothing, Jews were particularly well represented. In women's clothing almost half of all the 115 shops were owned by Jews, 'racially' defined. The import of furs and leather was a speciality of Jewish traders in Leipzig; many shoe shops in Hamburg were owned by Jews. Bâta was the largest manufacturer of shoes in Europe, with several branches in Hamburg and Germany. As Czech Jews the owners were exempt from boycott. The rival Salamander chain pointed out that they sold Aryan shoes but failed to dent Bâta's sales. Jews were well represented as tobacconists and also in corset manufacture. Portly Nazi matrons squeezed themselves into 'Jewish' corsets sold by the euphemistically labelled Gazelle chain of fourteen establishments situated all over the city. Where there was a need, the price was right and the product good, antisemitism met its limits. All party circulars could do was to appeal to the SA and SS not to enter Jewish shops in uniform.

Competing businesses were not slow to point out that a rival firm was Jewish. One of the more bizarre instances was the campaign launched against the pharmaceutical business of Beiersdorf,[35] which owed some of its most successful products to Jewish researchers and businessmen, above all to Paul Gerson Unna and Oscar Troplowitz. For the Hamburg manufacturer Queisser & Co. of *Lovana* skin cream, standing in the shadow of Beiersdorf's *Nivea*, the knock of opportunity was loud and clear. Queisser launched the slogan 'Do not use Jewish skin creams any longer! Lovana cream is at least as good, cheaper and pure German!' Ten thousand stickers were distributed: 'Whoever buys a Nivea product supports a Jewish firm'. Beiersdorf's products, however, did not succumb to *Lovana*'s charms. *Nivea* remained the skin lotion of preference for Nazis and Jews alike.

The campaign launched by local Nazis – the pressure from below both before the boycott and after it had been supposedly called off – so frightened enterprises large and small that they fell over themselves in their haste to remove Jewish blemishes. Beiersdorf reorganised its management team only a few days after the boycott. The Jewish chairman of the board 'resigned', together with another Jewish board member. For good measure, Dr Eugen Unna, the son of Paul Gerson Unna, also departed, although in Nazi terminology he was 'only' a 'half-Jew'. Beiersdorf was one of M. M. Warburg's soundest early investments in Hamburg. They now gave up their controlling financial interest and withdrew the partners from the corporate board. The new head of Beiersdorf was Carl Claussen. The Jewish connection was not, however, severed, as Claussen had married Troplowitz's niece. Beiersdorf announced it was now a 'German business'. *Nivea* and *Elastoplast* could safely be used.

The largest department store chain was Karstadt, with ninety-one branches and over 23,000 employees. Panicked by the announcement of the boycott, the majority of the board decided to dismiss their Jewish employees without notice so they would be gone before boycott Saturday. This enabled Karstadt to stay open on 1 April without fear of reprisals. The Tietz department store on the Jungfernstieg, one of a chain of eighteen and second in size to Karstadt, with some 16,000 'Aryan' employees, closed its doors.[36] There were occasions when discrimination of Jews also harmed 'Aryans'. A particular crass example was the appeal by 'Aryan' shopkeepers who after the April boycott were deserted by their Jewish customers.[37] Nine owners of shops in the *Grindel* requested a reduction of their Hamburg taxes because, they argued, since the coming to power of the national government and the measures passed by it, citizens of the Jewish faith have continued to withdraw their custom from Christian shops in localities where many Jews live, resulting in the loss of so much business 'that their very existence has been seriously threatened'. The appeal was turned down, and when Hamburg's press office wanted to publicise the problem it was told that 'mention of this matter was not opportune'.

In 1933, Nazis were divided and uncertain how to handle the Jews. Rabid Jew haters like Goebbels and Streicher exulted that the boycott would educate the Germans about the Jewish menace. Hitler had agreed to the boycott, possibly even initiated the action. But soon wiser counsels predominated in Berlin. The boycott had not been all that successful anyway. Priorities were reasserted. The Jews were not to be hindered in the economy – a temporary reprieve. The two ministers Hitler appointed to oversee recovery, Hjalmar Schacht and Kurt Schmitt, were allowed a free hand to defend this policy against party attempts at local and national levels to take more drastic action.

Kurt Schmitt, managing director of the Allianz insurance company,[38] who succeeded Hugenberg in June 1933 at the Reich Ministry of the Economy, and the banker Hjalmar Schacht, reappointed *Reichsbank* president, were not driven by ideology, nor were they members of the Nazi Party, just opportunistic supporters. In July, Kurt Schmitt called together representatives from the regional states, including Hamburg, in an attempt to coordinate and lay down guidelines. *Gauleiter* Kaufmann did not attend mere ministry meetings and sent Krogmann, who kept a record. Schmitt lambasted the Nazi hotheads who threatened to cause chaos and plunge the economy into constant unrest. The feebleness of those in charge of businesses and of the professional middle classes, who gave in to the slightest pressure from 'any unauthorised source', was even more contemptible. That had to stop now. Surely he did not have to point out that the Reich government would stand or fall by its success in finding work for the unemployed 5 million. The secretary of state of the Ministry for the Economy was none other than Gottfried Feder, an early member of the Workers' Party, the forerunner of Hitler's National Socialists. Once he had been a radical ideologist. Now he asked where the 200,000 employed by department stores would find jobs if they were closed. Deputy *Führer* Hess and SS leader Himmler reinforced the instructions of the ministry, circulating an order to all party and SS units that they were forbidden to show any hostility to department stores on pain of severe punishment. In Hamburg, Kaufmann took no notice, urging all civil servants and employees to purchase goods not from large enterprises but from smaller shops.[39]

Few businesses resisted Nazi pressure. They dismissed directors on their boards and Jewish assistants in their shops. 'Better safe than sorry' was the motto, leaving little room for decency and principle. Some behaved better than others. They paid pensions or found less exposed positions for valued Jewish colleagues. Dr Heinrich Wohlwill was removed from the board of the Norddeutsche Affinerie but allowed access to the research laboratories while drawing his pension. The

Jewish chairman of the Beiersdorf board was transferred to run Beiersdorf in Amsterdam. Other leading employees were also found positions abroad.

But some Jewish employees still remained in contact with the public. Ardent Nazi customers complained if they were served by a Jewish-looking shop assistant, regardless of whether they were attended to well or not. Sniffing out Jews was not a rare occurrence. Young ladies with dark hair and a give-away look of apprehension in their eyes dreaded every moment. You were luckier if you were blond. Life could become petty and base, with serious consequences quite out of the blue; you could no longer be sure how long your employers would keep you.

V

Well-known Jewish institutions were not immune. The experience of the Warburg bank illustrates how differently clients who had profited from its help in the past now behaved. During the Depression years, Max Warburg, overriding the advice of his banker brothers in New York, had risked his bank to stand by his old clients. He had made a disastrous commercial decision in providing almost a fifth of the capital of a banking consortium brought together in 1931 to fund the ill-advised expansion of the Karstadt department store.[40] Only a huge loan from the New York brothers rescued the bank. Yet despite all Karstadt owed to a Jewish bank shortly before the boycott day 1 April 1933, its Jewish board members, including Fritz Warburg, 'resigned', having been put in the impossible position of knowing that the Jewish employees were to be dismissed. Commercial relations, however, continued. The Warburg loan had to be serviced. Fritz Warburg was replaced by Rudolf Brinkmann, the bank's most senior 'Aryan' employee. That solution was adopted several times. It helps to explain why the number of positions on boards lost was not greater. The cosy arrangement benefited Brinkmann's career. After 1936, all but a handful of firms cut their connections; Max Warburg was thrown out of many honorary positions as well. The 'withdrawal', he recalled,

> was accompanied sometimes by expressions of regret, sometimes cynically, sometimes without any communication at all. Friends tried to sugar the pill. Only in one case was solidarity shown, the Kieler Institute for Sea Transport and World Economy, whose chairman, Dr Heinrich Diedrichsen, and whose director, Professor Dr Harms, declared they would resign with me, which they did.

Max Warburg belonged to the elite 'Association of Honourable Merchants' who elected the members of the Hamburg chamber of commerce. Only merchant bankers and industrialists who were on the boards of their businesses were eligible to become 'honourable merchants'. For his contribution to the association, Max Warburg had received its gold medal. With its long tradition of close collegial relationships between Jews and Christians, one might have expected it to have had a more determined resistance to the Nazis.

Max Warburg and Heinrich Wohlwill, who was also a prominent member, had no intention of withdrawing after the Nazis had gained control, and at first they found some support. When the newly installed mayor, Carl Vincent Krogmann, pressed for swift 'coordination', there was a show of resistance.[41] But then the honourable merchants decided it was better to compromise than provoke an open conflict and risk dissolution. There were glimmers of good form and still hopes that valued Jewish colleagues could remain. When in April two Jews resigned, Carl Ludwig Nottebohm, who presided over the association, appealed to Jewish members 'not to anticipate developments'. Max Warburg needed no such advice and stayed put. But Krogmann had to prove his Nazi credentials. Both father and son in past years had cultivated good relations with the Warburgs. Now the younger Krogmann demanded his removal and that of all the Jews. Resistance swiftly crumbled.

Within weeks the merchant elite capitulated. Nazi commissioners were sent in to take over, declaring that the honourable merchants should now regard themselves as 'soldiers of their *Führer*'. Max Warburg was still present, but not for much longer. Seven weeks later, Nottebohm passed on Kaufmann's 'request' that the whole council should resign and then hold new elections for a smaller body. It was a transparent device to exclude undesirables, including, of course, the Jewish members. After the war the chamber claimed that Max Warburg was not 'thrown out' but had resigned. In the better circles of society, hypocrisy covered reality.

VI

The stuff of legend, were it not reality, was the manner of Max Warburg's departure in 1933 from the board of Hapag, the Hamburg-America line.[42] His business association was of even longer standing than that with Blohm and Voss and also based on friendship with Albert Ballin, the author of Hapag's prosperity. The Nazis had followed their usual technique of adding Nazi sympathisers to the board, who then proceeded to drive out the Jewish members. That is what also happened at Hapag. To sweeten the pill, the elderly chairman and another elderly member of the board were pushed out at the same time. The chairman began a valedictory address after a festive dinner but was so overcome that he had to leave the room. There was a painful silence. Max Warburg then got up and finished the speech in the sense, he said, the chairman intended, drawing lessons from the past as a future guide for the benefit of the younger members. At the same time Warburg bade his own farewell. Now there was even greater embarrassment. Two members of the board began to whisper behind his chair but could not agree who should reply. It was not easy to find the right words to thank a Jewish colleague, whatever his merits. So Warburg got up again, saying he would adjudicate the dispute as to who would have the honour to thank him, adding it was probably best if he did so himself. Then he called for three cheers. He went on to enumerate all his important contributions after the First World War: the bank had enabled the shipping line to recover, having financed its new Ballin class ocean liners and then, when Hapag was in financial difficulties, again had helped when other banks had failed to do so. By the time he sat down there was laughter and applause. The 'amusing' incident, however, scantily covered reality. It was a typical audacious gesture; Max Warburg refused to be humiliated or to leave in silence without remonstrance. He cloaked his bitterness with humour.

The reduction of the bank's share of business was gradual during the first two or three years of the Nazi regime.[43] Its financial power and foreign links were still valued. Max Warburg sought to compensate losses in Germany with more financial involvement abroad. Unilever, Rotterdam, the Dutch oil giant, was one client. There were close business links with the United States reinforced by family ties, and with Hungary, Turkey, Russia and Romania. Within Germany, the Warburg bank participated in Prussian state loans and received ever smaller entitlements. 'My office was quiet now', Max Warburg recalled.

> On my daily walk to my office I did not meet a single acquaintance any more, whereas before in Hamburg I had to hold my hat in my hand in greeting. My Aryan former associates avoided me so that they would not have to greet me, because this would be noticed and noted. Jews left their homes as little as possible.

If the prestigious and once powerful Warburgs could be treated so shabbily, it is an indication how Jews of lesser importance fared. Max Warburg had expected those long-time clients and friends to show more moral fibre; they all fell over eventually, he sadly reflected. Actually, not all of them: Paul Reusch, who headed the large German steel concern Gutehoffnungshütte, and who had joined the Nazi Party, remained a lifelong friend. Not every German capitulated to the racial phobia of the Nazis.

Blighted lives

Large resources were devoted by the Nazis to the study of the Aryan race and all its ramifications. 'Fortunately', much 'scientific' work had already been done. A leading race expert was Achim Gercke, doctor of philosophy, appointed in 1926 to check on the racial purity of party members.[44] Seven years later he was an obvious choice to advise the Reich Ministry of the Interior. Gercke was a man obsessed. He had amassed the results of his researches on 50,000 cards of the main index and 20,000 additional cards. Dismissed by the SS in 1934, a victim of the homosexual laws, he fought in the *Wehrmacht* during the war and disappeared from view. His young assistant Wilfried Euler carried on his master's work for the SS with just as much enthusiasm. As time went on Euler extended his investigation and began to cover the rest of Western Europe too. In Germany, church registers of baptisms back to the seventeenth century were scoured for 'Jews', 'Gypsies', 'Turks', 'Moors' and 'Negroes'. Soon Euler's devotion to the cause began to embarrass. He claimed to have found a million and a half Germans who were either full Jews or harboured a fraction of Jewish blood.[45] That was too many for the SS. Even worse, he could not be stopped from delving into the genes of prominent Nazis. The SS got rid of him, but he soon found another Nazi institution to house him – the *Reichsinstitut für die Geschichte des Neuen Deutschlands* – under the aegis of Dr Goebbels, which had a branch in Munich directed by Walter Frank devoted to research on the Jewish question. The work continued. Euler's 'valuable' researches survived the Holocaust and the war. Eventually, an old man and still at it, he received a high decoration from a grateful Federal Republic.

The 'grandparent test' did not satisfy everyone. Himmler required proof of pure Aryan ancestry back to 1800 for the SS. It was also necessary for farmers and even for students. Spurious family trees sprouted, embellished with imaginative crests for those who could afford to commission such fantasies; they could still be seen proudly hanging in hallways after the war. Besides Jews, who rejected being labelled as a race, there were also millions of good Germans who became anxious. They did not know what an 'Aryan' was. One enterprising person resorted to looking it up in the Brockhaus encyclopaedia. It was not of much help. The entry referred to an ancient people who were 'Indogermans' and lived in Asia Minor, Persia and Iran. He appealed to the Central Protestant Church Archive in Berlin to trace his wife's grandparents, explaining, 'I have searched for "Aryan" in my encyclopaedia. They live in Asia. We don't have any relatives there, we come from Prenzlau [a small town in Brandenburg].' A selection of these enquiries shows how bewildered people really were: 'because of the enforcing of the civil service law I need my great-grandmother'; 'because I have no knowledge of Hannover, I am coming to you with my birth'; 'please send me my Arabian grandmother with birth and death'; 'I am contacting you concerning a matter which is of no business of yours yet. I need my grandmother, but I have not received an official request'; 'would you please certify that I am of Agrarian descent' – no laughing matter for the desperate enquirers whose livelihood might depend on furnishing Aryan proof.[46]

I

The sudden need to prove they were an 'Aryan' struck ordinary people like a bolt from the blue. Not so the Nazi 'experts', who had studied the implications of race long before the Nazis came to power. The plans they drew up were not hidden in secret dossiers but open to anyone caring to read issues of the monthly *Nationalsozialistische Monatshefte*, edited by the leading Nazi 'thinker', Alfred Rosenberg.[47] To 'cleanse' the *Volk* raised difficult questions. There could be no quick fix: 'the racial sins and crimes of past centuries cannot be remedied in a few years. The racial mixing that occurred far back will have to be left to the natural process of absorption.' But how far back? – that was the first crucial problem; no one knew how many 'infected genes' would be involved as you delved into generation after generation. How far should they go? It was not ideal, but a practical policy would be to search no further back than grandparents. Earlier forbears would just have to be 'absorbed'.

The elimination of carriers of racial blood harmful to the *Volk*, the writer in 1930 concluded, 'can only be achieved step by step. Whether it can be achieved in a few years or over a longer transitional time, the future will clarify.' The first step to be taken was 'to stop Jewry further breaking into our *Volk* … this will create a dam for our *Volk*'. All those with too much Jewish blood, essentially 'Jewish personalities', would have to be separated from the Aryans, who alone could be true Germans belonging to the *Volk* community. Non-Aryans would be allowed no influence on policies at home or abroad and had to be removed from the economy, cultural life, the press and the teaching profession. Jews and non-Aryans would not have the right to vote or to serve in the armed services; 'further limitations' would be imposed as necessary. Once the Nazis reached power, the plans would be ready to adopt when the time was ripe. That the 'fractional' Jews were going to be one of the most tricky problems before a 'final solution' was satisfactorily reached had already become clear.

By April 1933 it looked as if doubts had been resolved, at least for the time being. The racial test to be applied would normally be restricted to the religion of the four grandparents, just as the 1930 plan had reluctantly suggested, which turned even Christians, so-called quarter Jews, into non-Aryans. Marriage to a non-Aryan, furthermore, condemned the whole family.

Aryan proof was demanded of lawyers and doctors and required for membership of sports clubs, teacher–parent associations, employers – hardly any sphere was left out. No one had any clear idea how many Germans were blighted. There were more than half a million Jews to start with, but earlier censuses had not included baptised Jews. The descendants of mixed marriages would now have to be added as well. Estimates varied widely; contemporary calculations were much higher than their actual numbers. Recent calculations suggest about 400,000 non-Jewish Germans or others of Jewish or partial Jewish descent, plus their spouses. Together with the so-called full Jews, the total was around 900,000. But Nazi leaders also took into account that the relatives of the Christian spouses would have been concerned at the persecution of the mixed Jewish side of the family. Counting in-laws, uncles, aunts and cousins, all impeccable Aryans, adds at least another 500,000 potential critics of Nazi race discrimination. Nor were Jews entirely isolated from friends and colleagues – altogether no small problem, as too many have subsequently thought. The problem of Aryan purification would only be solvable by limiting it and dealing with one group at a time. But this was not fully recognised by the Nazis in 1933.

II

What had previously been the theories of charlatans, the 'Law for the Restoration of the Professional Civil Service' of 7 April 1933 was accorded the imprimatur of the state. One Jewish grandparent and you were automatically a non-Aryan. Gypsies and blacks were also racially alien and inferior. The status of other 'races' was later opportunistically defined, depending on needs at the time. The Slav Wenden, for instance, who lived in the north of Berlin along the rivers of the Spreewald, preserving their own culture and language, were officially declared to be Aryans. The law discriminated not only against those thought 'racially' undesirable but also against 'Marxists'. Actually Jews and non-Aryans were treated better than the political outcasts. Jews received three-quarters of their pensions provided they had served ten years. They also retained such titles as 'Judge' or 'State Secretary', with the addition of two letters: a. D. standing for 'not in office' and later i. R., 'retired'. Furthermore, President Hindenburg insisted on exemptions for Great War veterans and state employees who had lost a father or son in the war or been appointed before 1914. That covered the majority and would have driven a coach and horses through the legislation. Ways to circumvent the exemptions were found by dismissing non-Aryans under other provisions of the legislation. The political dismissals were treated in an even worse manner. They lost their titles and had no automatic right to a pension, though in Hamburg most received one.

In Hamburg, to begin with, Jewish and non-Aryan civil servants and state employees continued to serve.[48] Georg Ahrens, in charge of implementing the legislation, issued instructions in 1934 that their Jewish and non-Aryan colleagues who had not been dismissed were to be treated with respect as forcible retirements had come to an end. There was a general belief that 'good' patriotic German Jews would be left alone.

III

For ardent Nazis this was not an acceptable outcome. A way around had to be found. Other clauses in the law of 7 April could be invoked. One of the earliest victims of such manipulation was Leo Lippmann, head of the financial section of the administration [*Finanzdeputation*].[49] The new Nazi senate at first confirmed him in office. He had served Hamburg with loyalty and distinction, so he expected no other outcome. Had not the leading Nazi deputies assured him that they wished to work with him? He would serve the new regime to the best of his abilities. A Jew, civil servant at the head of Hamburg's financial management! When Mayor Krogmann was shown the list he demanded Lippmann should immediately apply for leave of absence. Krogmann did not care that Lippmann fell under the Hindenburg exemptions. In his case, the clause 'political unreliability' was used. Lippmann saw this as a slur on his life's work, as he had served all political parties. He sent a dignified protest to Krogmann and tried in vain for more than a year to get the reason for his dismissal changed.

Worse even than the loss of his career was the tragedy of his nephew's suicide. As a medical student, Rudolph Lippmann now saw the prospects of qualifying blighted. His uncle delivered the funeral oration.

He could not bear the fate and defamation that befell the German Jews ... he was a German and a Jew, for centuries his ancestors had been settled in Germany. They were bound to Germany with all their hearts. They did their duty as Germans in good times and bad, in peace and in war ... You suffered deeply from rejection to be told your help was no longer wanted ... You wrote to a friend that what sustained you was the belief that no one could take away from you your feeling of belonging to Germany ... in your own words, 'I know I am German as long as I wish to be'.[50]

These were Leo Lippmann's feelings too.

IV

Following the death of his son Rudolph, Professor Arthur Lippmann, the leading paediatrician at the St Georg Hospital, lost his position after twenty-six years of distinguished and devoted service to Hamburg's children.

In Hamburg and elsewhere, Jewish and non-Aryan doctors were removed wholesale from the register of insurance doctors.[51] They then had to prove to local boards that they fell under the Hindenburg exemption and add a photograph to their application. What purpose could that serve if a 'Jewish appearance' was detected but to prejudice the application? The excluded doctors had the right of appeal to the Ministry of the Interior in Berlin, whose civil servants reversed many of the decisions. The outcome was that three-quarters of the non-Aryan doctors in Hamburg kept their insurance patients.

Arthur Lippmann had gained his professorial title for his pioneer treatment with ultra-violet light of children who suffered from tuberculosis.[52] Held in high regard by Hamburg's doctors, he was chosen as one of the five supervisory members of the *Ärztekammer* (doctors' council). In June 1933 he received his notification of dismissal. Two months later, although a war veteran, he was struck off the register of insurance doctors. Lippmann had to provide written evidence of his military service as a doctor in an isolation hospital in Russia before he was readmitted.

For Jews, 'the oldest profession' was medicine.[53] They had practised in Germany since the Middle Ages. In Hamburg the people had been looked after by a long line of Jewish doctors – the Gersons, the Unnas and many more – where medicine was a family tradition. The *Israelitisches Krankenhaus* had taken care of Christians and Jews without distinction already for a hundred years. It no longer counted. In March 1933, the National Socialist doctors and their Reich leader, Dr Gerhard Wagner, demanded the removal of all Jewish doctors. There were too many doctors for everyone to make a decent living.[54] Thus the removal of the Jews and non-Aryans would be popular. But Hitler in 1933 decided against removing them despite the plea of the Reich leader. Where the Nazi practice was radical was to deny future entry to the profession to Jews and non-Aryans. Thus it would be only a matter of time before there would be no more Jewish doctors.

One of the Nazis' spurious claims was that the medical profession was *verju-det*, overrun with Jews.[55] Even if it had been, all that matters is whether they were good doctors or not. In Hamburg and the whole of Germany, obsessive counts were made every year of Jewish and non-Aryan doctors and later on even of doctors whose spouses were non-Aryan. As all the professions would be cleansed of Jews sooner or later, there was really no reason to suppose this would not also apply to universities.

V

Professor Ernst Cassirer was in Münster on the day Hindenburg appointed Hitler chancellor.[56] He wrote to his wife that people like them had nothing more to hope for. That did not mean that Cassirer thought all the Jews would be driven out of Germany. Some would choose to leave; others would stay and have to make the best of it. As a renowned philosopher he had a choice. He no longer wanted to live in a country that had welcomed the Nazis. *Frau* Cassirer recalled:

> He told me that he would finish his lectures at the university and then immediately leave with us for Italy. I, who in the past had been sceptical and apprehensive, tried to persuade him to hold back. It seemed to me nothing essential had yet changed. I thought that one should fight back before all was lost. The elections were only due at the beginning of March. The ship could still be turned to follow another direction. The first pronouncements did not give cause for concern. There was no mention of Jewish persecution or anti-Jewish laws. But when he read, 'Whatever serves the *Führer* is law', Ernst said to me, 'If all the learned German lawyers to a man do not protest against this paragraph, Germany is lost.' Not a single voice was raised. I could only persuade Ernst to remain in Germany until the elections had taken place.

A week after the elections the Cassirers left for Switzerland; he wanted to decide his future away from Germany.

> As we left Hamburg from the Dammtorbahnhof we did not then have the feeling that it was a final parting. But it became only too clear that the country in which we had lived, and in which Ernst had achieved his work, had in just a few days changed radically. The bad elements were swimming on top. What until now they had only dared to say in whispers they now declared loudly, and it was the decent people who either began to whisper or to stay silent altogether.

On Saturday 1 April, the day of the official boycott, the Cassirers were in Lucerne. From there Ernst wrote to Professor Raape, the rector of the university, that in the prevailing situation he was no longer willing to continue and requested leave of absence. Raape promptly replied. He urged Cassirer to withdraw his request and not to reach a hasty decision. As yet what was to happen in the university was not at all clear. The civil servant responsible for the supervision of the university, who was not a Nazi, was of the same opinion. The letter concluded with the warmest expressions of esteem and feelings of solidarity and the hope that in the interests of the university Cassirer would stay. Cassirer also received other messages from threatened friends and colleagues urging him to return. Fritz Saxl, after Aby Warburg's death in charge of the Warburg Library, appealed to Cassirer to use his prestige in the faculty to defend his Jewish and non-Aryan colleagues. After all he had accomplished for philosophy and the university, Saxl thought, 'he was bound to be listened to with respect'. Such were still the illusions two months after Hitler came to power.

The Cassirers did return to Hamburg – not to put up a useless fight, but to organise their emigration. To a gathering in his house Ernst discussed the situation with his Jewish and Aryan colleagues, and they debated what to do. Already it was clear that those who could, the Aryans, were beginning to wobble to save their teaching posts. Fritz Saxl, like Cassirer, by then had a clear view where their future lay, and that was not in Germany. Saxl was determined to save the unique and cultural heritage Aby Warburg had bequeathed and move the library abroad. The transfer to London's Courtauld Institute was finally agreed under the cloak of a loan and in strict secrecy to avoid public protest. The exodus of prominent scientists, such as Albert Einstein, literary giants, Thomas Mann among them, film producers and actresses Elizabeth Bergner and Marlene Dietrich – by no means all Jews – which was widely reported and featured in newsreels abroad, was creating a bad impression. A fuss about the Warburg Library would have added more ammunition. Better let it go quietly. But the impact of removing the non-Aryans from the universities just could not be hidden. Germany's loss proved an incalculable gain to the universities offering them refuge.

Hamburg University suffered a haemorrhage of internationally renowned professors and younger talent.[57] Whole disciplines collapsed. With the departure of the 'non-Aryan' William Stern and the dismissal of his assistants, the Institute of Psychology ceased to function. One Christian assistant at the institute committed suicide. The loss of her work and the university's behaviour towards her Jewish colleagues was more than she could bear. Professor Otto Stern, who, after emigrating to the United States was awarded the Nobel Prize, was head of the Institute of Physical Chemistry. He and his two assistants were forced out. The caretaker wasted no time and replaced a portrait of Einstein in his office with one of Hitler. Once famous for the study of art, culture and philosophy, the university became an intellectual desert following the emigration of professors Erwin Panofsky, Fritz Saxl, Ernst Cassirer and Edgar Wind. Professor Albrecht Mendelssohn Bartholdy, during the Weimar years, had been a co-author of the multi-volume document publication *Die Große Politik der Europäischen Kabinette*, an immense scholarly effort to show that the outbreak of the 1914 war was not Germany's doing alone. He was also head of the university's Institute for Foreign Affairs, now condemned to a lingering death after his departure. The mathematics professor Emil Artin, though an impeccable Aryan, was removed and pensioned later because he was married to a non-Aryan, and Professor Hermann Krogmann, director of the Institute of Juridical Medicine, had to go because of his spouse's one Jewish grandparent.

No exceptions were made if Jewish ancestry was involved, however distinguished the academic. One could be more forgiving of non-Aryan blood that was not Jewish. Assistant Professor of Chemistry Hans Heinrich Schlubach had been a member of the Nazi Party before 1933; his Aryan ancestry was not immaculate, however. His great-grandmother Arii Taimaii was a dusky beauty from Tahiti.[58] She was said to be of aristocratic lineage; this helped a little. Nevertheless, the Tahitian blemish hindered Schlubach's promotion to a full professorship for years. The Nazi student leader thought he was making a reasonable request when he wrote to the local party branch that the students did not want to remove the professor, but that the university surely could not appoint someone as director of an institute 'who was descended from a Polynesian royal family'. Such craziness routinely occurred and provided Nazi bureaucracy with headaches. They spent their time behind desks making rulings without giving thought to how their decisions affected lives. The banished teachers felt bitter at the behaviour of their colleagues, few of whom had previously shown any personal animosity. In many cases they had worked for years together, and now they found themselves cut off, barred from even entering the university they had served with distinction, and all this in just a few weeks. Colleagues had adjusted unbelievably quickly.

For Jewish and non-Aryan students to continue studying became a trial of strength in the hostile atmosphere.[59] For the new summer session of 1933 there were still 110 Jews registered and thirty-six non-Aryans. That undesirable situation was speedily remedied. By the following winter session there were only twenty-six left, even though at least three times that number could have remained according to the law. Conditions had become intolerable. Students could not rely on any protection from their teachers, though a few might retain the support of a close student friend. On 10 May (in Hamburg on 15 May) the Nazis made a public display of their coarseness, burning the works of Jewish authors, Marxists and pacifists.

Civil servants, lawyers, judges, doctors and professors were only the most prominent victims of the racial laws. There were tens of thousands less in the limelight. Musicians in orchestras, office workers, shop assistants, nursery teachers – in every sphere of work Jews were shown the door. Employers did not even wait for any law requiring their dismissal.

VI

The lives not only of Jews but also of tens of thousands of unsuspecting Christian 'non-Aryan' families were blighted. Among these was the Solmitz family. In common with other Germans, Luise had many prejudices about Jews. Would her eyes have been opened but for the effect the Nazi racial legislation had on those

she loved, her husband and daughter? Or would it have remained for her something remote, justified to correct the 'excessive influence' of Jews? There was so
much else to enthuse her about Hitler.

The Solmitzes' daughter Gisela was just thirteen years old when Hitler came
to power and, like her mother, was caught up in all the enthusiasm for the new
Germany.[60] Unlike 30 January, 20 May is not an important day in German history. For Gisela's family, however, it was the day that changed their lives. In her
journal, Luise Solmitz called it simply their 'day of destiny'. What had happened? A catastrophic illness? A death? Nothing so dramatic. Gisela had come
home as usual from the *Emilie-Wüster-feldn Schule* that afternoon. She was
happy at school, a popular girl with her classmates. She also got on well with her
teacher, Fräulein Evers. In short, she was a well-adjusted teenager. As important
as school were the many out-of-school activities. These proliferated in Hamburg
as elsewhere in Germany. Hiking in the countryside was a favourite, many sports
clubs flourished, and then of course there was sailing on the beautiful Alster, a
large lake in the centre of Hamburg; there were also church associations and various patriotic groups. Like nearly all the girls in her class Gisela had joined the
League of German Girls, BDM for short, with their neat blue skirts, white blouses
and the embroidered swastika. They marched like the boys, the Hitler Youth,
sang songs, and gathered around camp fires. With youthful idealism, they too
were participating in the 'national awakening', the new Germany the *Führer*
promised the German people.

Then out of the blue a dark shadow appeared in Gisela's life. It began seemingly innocently. At school she was given a questionnaire for her parents to
complete, handed to every child in the classroom by the teacher. It contained only
two short paragraphs: the first, 'My daughter Gisela Solmitz is of Aryan descent';
the second explained that, if only one grandparent or parent was not Aryan – that
is, Jewish – then this would mean that Gisela Solmitz was not an Aryan. The parent was asked to cross out the paragraph that did not apply and to sign the form.
Gisela's father, with a heavy heart, crossed out the first paragraph. Gisela thought
he had made a mistake: 'You have crossed out the wrong paragraph.' But he had
not. Gisela turned deathly pale. Luise waited outside her husband's room, 'too
numb to feel anything. Gisela a 'half-Jew'? It was a catastrophe. The Solmitz
family was no longer to be regarded as belonging to the German people, but was
now identified with a 'race' with whom they had had no contact and with which
they shared no beliefs. Both Gisela's parents had been baptised, as was Gisela,
and they regularly attended church. What would the future now hold for Gisela
on the threshold of adult life? They told their daughter to keep her Jewish descent
secret even from her best friends. Gisela now returned to school with foreboding.
But, unlike some of the other teachers, her class teacher, Fräulein Evers, was tactful; she asked for the replies to be returned in sealed envelopes.

For Gisela every day at school now became a kind of torture. Would her secret
leak out? Would she be ostracised by the other girls? Would she be expelled from
the BDM? The deceit was a terrible burden which daily preyed on her mind. She

was afraid to associate with boys. Outwardly she tried to act normally. She was even elected class leader. Of course she could not accept without Aryan proof, so an excuse was found for her refusal. The other girls must not know. Fräulein Evers was discreet. Gisela remained in the BDM for another three years nursing her dark secret. Her father appealed for an exception to be made so that Gisela could stay because his war record proved he was a 'good German'. He even wrote to Hitler. All this and Gisela's tears are recorded in Luise Solmitz's journal. But Gisela in the end was forced out and, once gregarious, now withdrawn, fell into a deep depression. She was one of the few girls in her class not wearing the BDM uniform. Fräulein Evers remained true to her – an exceptional teacher in Nazi Germany. Gisela's thoughts turned to suicide. Luise recorded that, before going to bed, Gisela had said, 'I am quite clear in my own mind and have to accept in such times as these I will only have a short life; perhaps I will be dead before the end of the year and not as a consequence of a natural death.' That is what a sixteen-year-old teenager confided to her mother, and Luise Solmitz reflected, 'We three know with cruel clarity that we are just victims, powerless against whatever is going to come.'

With increasing bitterness and despair, Luise Solmitz chronicled all the humiliation, her fears for Gisela's blighted youth, the uncertainties of what the future would bring. Some of their best friends broke off contact. Fearful of each succeeding day, they held to the one certainty in their lives: the three of them would, if it came to the worst, end their lives together. It was just one family's experience, but there were tens of thousands of families like them suddenly turned into 'non-Aryans' – Germans and aliens, rejected by the bond now holding together the German 'race', the *Volksgemeinschaft*, the people's community. That made them all the more determined that their children should not be driven into isolation. It may seem surprising, but secular Jews too shared this feeling.

4

COURAGE IN ADVERSITY

To school

Despite the Nazi curriculum, Jewish parents continued to send their children to the state schools, not wanting Hans or Grete educated in a self-imposed Jewish ghetto. The state school would prepare them better for future life in Germany. Liberal and secular parents were also alienated by the religious orthodoxy of the Jewish schools. In 1933, twice as many attended the state schools, though in Berlin there were also excellent non-orthodox schools.

Ernst Loewenberg was one of the few Jews who taught in one of Hamburg's state grammar schools, the *Lichtwarkschule*, a progressive co-educational school.[1] The son of a famous father honoured in Hamburg, Ernst Loewenberg too was held in high esteem. Even so, he would not stand as a candidate for the headship, fearing that a Jewish headmaster could harm the reputation of the school – and this two years before the Nazis came to power. He got on well with pupils and parents. During the school holidays he took the children on outings. Unpleasantness was rare. But the excursions had to be planned with care. There were a few Jewish boys and girls in the group, and Jews were not welcome at a number of beauty spots. Jewish organisations provided annual lists of places to be avoided. 'That was nothing new', observed Loewenberg. 'Jews always had to expect this.' In Timmendorf on the Baltic, a favourite with holiday seekers of sea and sunshine, Jews could only find accommodation on the less popular beaches.

Ernst Loewenberg had become used to coping with anti-Semitism, and 30 January 1933 did not alarm him unduly. 'We still were active in our professions. No one gave a thought to emigration. It took a long time before our German roots were torn out and we were ready to consider leaving.' Actually the atmosphere at the *Lichtwarkschule* soon darkened. Left-wing teachers were dispersed to other schools. There was tension in the air; no one any longer felt free. Some of the young men had joined the Hitler Youth to avoid disadvantages. As one of them put it, 'My father is an elementary schoolteacher. I want to study music and to obtain a grant have to be a party member.'

The politically unsuitable headmaster was replaced. Erwin Zindler was appointed in his stead. Zindler, an eccentric nationalist, found his way to the Nazis without delay. He demonstrated his new enthusiasm for all things brown by the way he held the swastika flag parades every Monday morning, paying particular attention to the Jewish pupils and the three Jewish teachers to make sure they too raised their arms in Hitler salute. All had to join in singing the *Horst Wessel* Nazi anthem. Early in 1934 the Jewish teachers, including Loewenberg, were told they would be retired, notwithstanding their status as war veterans. Colleagues who had earlier promised to protest now avoided talking to them. Zindler would not meet them face to face either. Surprisingly, Loewenberg did receive a letter of appreciation from the school administration and was paid a pension. He then secured a post at the orthodox Jewish *Talmud Tora Schule*. Two years later, in August 1938, he left Germany and emigrated to the United States.

A number of teachers were denounced by Zindler for their negative attitude. The most outspoken was Fräulein Ida Eberhardt, who taught mathematics and physics.[2] She had joined the school under its previous head, Heinrich Landahl, not a Jew but a prominent adherent of the German Democratic Party (DDP) and a member of Hamburg's parliament and the *Reichstag*. She shunned the National Socialist Teachers' Association. Zindler found her contrary attitude insupportable. In a report to the authorities headed 'Concerning Jews', he complained that Fräulein Eberhardt had criticised him for his attacks on the way the *Lichtwarkschule* had been run during the Weimar years; then she had complained to his deputy because he had 'briefly' referred to the part the Jewish race had played promoting Russian Bolshevism – the Jewish pupils, she said, would be deeply hurt by such remarks; then she handed him a copy of *Der Stürmer* and asked him to take steps to prevent its public display as, she said, it undermined the moral feelings of the young, especially as Jewish pupils attended the school; and the final straw, after the request of the school administration that all teachers should join the National Socialist Teachers' Association, she had replied that she could not do so, 'as it would bring her into a relationship with the Nazi Party with whose attitude to questions of the economy and race she was unable to agree'.

One particularly serious offence was held against her. She had invited to her home the former head, Landahl, and other old teachers, including a Jewish teacher. Zindler could only have discovered this through denunciations typical of the times. He now sent a questionnaire to all the teachers to provide him with details. That nothing unlawful had occurred, that his questions were an outrageous intrusion of privacy, no longer mattered. In February 1935 Fräulein Eberhardt was retired on the grounds of 'greater efficiency' – clause 6 of the civil service law – and pensioned off. She survived the war a righteous German.

I

Particular attention was paid to nurturing the young, inculcating the supreme importance of race, the need for blood purity, and the danger of the Jew. But how could this be accomplished if they mingled and formed friendships with Jewish boys or girls who were their classmates? Even worse, their class teacher, whom they had to respect, might be a Jew. Some things could be done straight away, such as removing head teachers or introducing new curricula; other 'reforms' would take longer.

In April 1933 undesirable teachers were moved from one school to another.[3] Individuals in the administration were also purged, replaced by members of the Nazi Party or the fellow travelling German National People's Party. But nothing is quite black and white. One *Schulrat* who had supported the 'Marxist' Social Democratic Party was suspended but then reappointed. Another, *Oberschulrat* Dr Wilhelm Oberdörffer, a conservative and not a Nazi before 1933, also kept his job. Race instruction now took a central place in the curriculum, together with physical training and adulation of the *Führer*. History, geography and German were distorted through the Nazi prism.

Some Jewish parents removed their children from schools where they were made to feel 'inferior' before they were forced to do so. Dr Wilhelm Unna made his reasons clear in September 1935.

> Dear *Herr* Zindler,
>
> According to a decree of the minister of education made known in the daily papers, the racial separation in elementary school will be announced and in higher school is being contemplated. As I and my family wish to emphasise our Jewishness in every respect and on every occasion, and as such a step only arouses in us a feeling of solidarity in respect of all Jewish children in all school years, and as we are not about to wait until it is decided to throw us out, I will withdraw my son Fritz in the Michaelmas term of this year from the *Lichtwarkschule*.[4]

Zindler was so angry. How dare a Jew write this? He passed a copy to the school authority, expecting it would be forwarded to the Gestapo. Nothing happened. The majority of Jewish boys and girls continued to be taught in German elementary schools, where there was no bar to their admission. What the letter shows is that many Jews were not yet intimidated and still relied on normal protection in Germany. There were also private secondary schools which continued to treat their Jewish pupils well.

II

The *Paulsenstift*, a school for girls in Hamburg, was such a private foundation. Here young women had received a sound education for more than half a century. The first headteacher was Anna Wohlwill, the daughter of Emil Wohlwill. The school flourished under Anna Wohlwill's direction, becoming a well-known *Lyceum* with 900 pupils.[5] In 1911, after forty-two years, at the age of seventy, Anna Wohlwill retired. Her successor was Hanna Glinzer, who had already been head of the school for twenty-two years when Hitler came to power. She held the memory of Anna Wohlwill in honour.

The school, attended largely by Christian girls seeking a good education, received generous donations from the Warburg bank, and Max Warburg's partner, Carl Melchior, was a member of the board of governors. In April 1933, to make it easier for the school in Nazi times, he resigned. Hanna Glinzer replied robustly. She asked him to withdraw his resignation, adding,

> Should we from outside be forced to accept it, and we hope this will not happen, then we will have to act as vassals in accordance with the dictate. Please be assured we would only act thus unwillingly. We regard it as an honour for our school to count you as a member of our board of governors.

He remained on the board until his untimely death later that year.

Nazi intrusion into the daily life of the *Paulsenstift*, however, could not be kept out. Schools were forced to detail the names and addresses of all the Jewish girls attending and whether their father had fought at the front in 1914–18. Details of mixed Jewish–Christian parentage had to be listed as well. In 1935, there were just nine Jewish girls and twelve *Mischlinge* left in the *Paulsenstift*. Almost all the thirty teachers had joined the National Socialist Teachers' Association by then and two the Nazi Party. But only about half the girls belonged to the BDM, a poor showing. One day, a particularly ardent parent complained to *Reichsstatthalter* Kaufmann about the school and withdrew his daughter. What outrageous incident had occurred? The gym teacher, Fräulein Mayer, had asked her class to give three cheers to a Jewish girl who was withdrawing from the school as her family was leaving Germany. Later the class received a letter from her which was read out aloud, and the whole class, all except the complainant's daughter, signed a warm letter in reply. The school authority called Hanna Glinzer to account. She was not intimidated:

> The Jewish girl was a good pupil and very good comrade in the class. The rest of the class expressed sympathy for the girl who was leaving the school with a heavy heart. This reflected their own human fellow feelings which is surely still acceptable to the leadership of the [Nazi] movement.

No compromise there. But, by Easter 1937, Nazi pressure and lack of parent support became too much to resist. There would be no start of a new school year at the *Paulsenstift*, and Hanna Glinzer gave up teaching altogether rather than swear an oath of loyalty to the *Führer*.[6]

Dr Puttfarken was a less admirable headmaster at the most renowned school in Hamburg, the elite *Johanneum*. It could be proud of its tradition, its tolerance and the famous alumni, Christians and Jews, who had passed through its portals. It was a conservative nationalist school, devoted to traditional learning. Here no enthusiasm was felt for the Weimar Republic. There was no affinity with the Nazis either or for the violence of the lower strata of society recruited into the ranks of the storm troopers. In 1933 all that changed. Fearing the school would be taken over by the Nazis, the association of former pupils and parents hastened to anticipate such a calamity. 'Our Vow', published in a special issue of the school magazine in June 1933, fervently welcomed the new Germany and its *Führer* with assurances that the school would fully and 'joyfully' cooperate in the great work that lay before the German people. The Hamburg elite, who sent their children to the *Johanneum*, turned their backs on the school's ethical tradition with alacrity and ease.

A number of teachers joined the party; life became difficult not only for the Jewish boys but also for the Christian so-called half- and quarter-Jews. 'Regrettably', the law which limited the new entry of Jewish children to secondary schools to 1.5 per cent of Aryans did not apply to non-Aryans with one or two Jewish grandparents, an oversight. Few teachers were as ardent Nazis as the headmaster. Puttfarken's theatrical gestures of loyalty at the obligatory 'raising of the swastika flag' on Monday mornings were so over the top that at other times he would not have been taken seriously. Ralph Giordano, a 'half-Jew', recalls:

> The six hundred pupils were drawn up on parole shortly before eight o'clock, together with all the teachers, secretaries and caretakers. Precisely as the clock struck eight, Puttfarken appeared, looked over the assembly briefly, raised his right arm and bellowed 'Heil Hitler'. From the chorus of pupils arose a mighty echo of 'Heil Hitler'. With hands behind his back, eyes right and left, he marched forward, looking to heaven; striking a pose half Napoleon, half Caesar, he pauses with pregnant concentration before shouting out the military command 'Flag raised'. *Deutschland über Alles* and the Nazi national anthem, *Die Fahne hoch*, was sung in unison. Puttfarken made sure that all the Jewish boys raised their right arm as well.[7]

The ceremony was not finished until Puttfarken addressed the whole school, lauding the *Führer* as time went on with ever-increasing enthusiasm.

Dr Puttfarken was no newcomer to the *Johanneum*. He had been a respected teacher and was installed as headmaster by the Nazis to bring the school into line. Whatever reservations he may have harboured about the many Jewish boys he had taught, there was no indication of his attitude before the Hitler years. But the Nazis must have known of his sympathies. Puttfarken never passed Ralph Giordano without making some wounding remark. The worst antisemite was Giordano's mathematics teacher, a leader out of school of a storm trooper unit whose vindictiveness became so extreme that the fifteen-year-old contemplated suicide. It was a matter of chance into whose hands a boy might fall. There were also teachers who behaved 'correctly' and a few who were friendly to their Jewish and 'non-Aryan' charges. Many of the Jewish children were already the second generation, some the third, born in Hamburg, their fathers and grand-fathers having been in the *Johanneum* before them.

The *Wilhelm-Gymnasium*, the *Heinrich Hertz-schule*, the *Lichtwarkschule* and the *Johanneum* were the schools of higher education which always attracted many Jewish children. In 1936 some fifty 'non-Aryans' still formed a consider-able contingent at the *Johanneum*. The parents of eligible Jewish children were still applying for admission a year later. Puttfarken wanted to exclude them, explaining to the school authority, 'Because of the large number of Jewish and half-Jewish pupils, I have great difficulties in the political education of the pupils. None of my teachers and pupils understand how Jewish children can now still be admitted.' The school authority sympathised with Puttfarken's predicament. Even if a comprehensive bar of Jewish children could not be announced, perhaps he could get rid of them some other way.

Starting in the school year 1937–8, Jewish boys in the *Johanneum* were assigned separate desks. They were no longer allowed on school excursions or gatherings which promoted 'comradely feelings'. Puttfarken personally made sure that every class understood the 'Jewish question'. He noted with evident satisfaction that in one class the 'German' pupils so isolated the only Jewish boy among them that his father withdrew him. Puttfarken studied the racial class lists with care. In October 1938 there were still eleven Jews and nineteen *Mischlinge* in the school. Puttfarken thought those figures 'still much too high, especially the number of half-Jews, whose Jewish looks arouse repulsion in public'. He managed to get rid of Oswald, a Jewish boy, who was expelled in October 1938 because he had attended a school festivity. He need not have bothered. Only two weeks later, a new law expelled all the Jewish children still attending German schools.

Puttfarken displayed a cruel streak towards young and vulnerable children in his charge. He was not pressured by Hamburg's school authority. His attitude provides just one example of the Jews being the victims not only of Hitler and his henchmen but of their fellow countrymen. The decrees often fell short of what Puttfarken and other individual Nazis hoped for, so he 'supplemented' them. The first Jewish boy had been admitted to the *Johanneum* in 1789; the last four left 149 years later.[8]

What was it like to be a Jewish boy or girl in a German school in the 1930s? It is not possible to generalise. Schools and teachers varied in their attitudes, as did the behaviour of classmates. The character, looks, physique and attitude of the child also made a difference. A blond, extrovert, self-confident Jewish boy expe-rienced far fewer problems than a sensitive dark-haired child of 'Mediterranean countenance' or 'Jewish looks', who was more likely to be victimised. It was rare for a Jewish child to be completely isolated; friendship with classmates coexisted with discrimination. Age was important. 'Racial consciousness' scarcely existed among children under ten years old. Older children in secondary schools, members of the *Hitler Jugend* and the SS, made life unpleasant. The Hitler cult made less headway in elementary schools, unlike in the higher schools, where headmasters were carefully selected to give a lead and where elaborate Nazi ceremonies were played out and Jewish children were debarred from extra-curricular activities. Little Jewish Hans or Grete in the elementary school was not generally excluded from anything and sang Nazi anthems in a chirpy voice with raised right hand without thinking anything of it. Nor was every headmaster a real Nazi, even though a member of the party.

The *Wilhelm-Gymnasium* was much favoured by Jewish parents. When Rudolf Heymann was accepted in 1936, his father was unsure whether his son would not suffer, so he went to see the headmaster, Dr Bernhard Lundius. Lundius told him, 'As long as I am headmaster I can reassure you', and, until he left the school in 1938, Rudolf was happy there.[9] Most of the teachers were conservatives like Lundius, not Nazis. He was as decent as the times allowed without imperilling his position as the school's head. That too was not an uncommon attitude.

As for the boys, the obligatory chores of the *Hitler Jugend* were not always welcome. The brainwashed ardent minority were a headache for everyone. Schools complained that the demands made on the youngsters by the *Hitler Jugend* interfered with their schoolwork. Tension between party and schools was common.

The Jewish boys in some schools like the *Wilhelm-Gymnasium* were not treated differently. Of course there were exceptions if the teacher was a rabid Nazi. Fellow classmates did not usually turn on their Jewish classmates either. What they could not escape was the world outside. Some became withdrawn and suffered; others, the more confident, overcame negative surroundings, feeling good about not having to follow the sheepish crowd. Most Jewish youngsters avoided these extremes. Despite the difficulties, many Jewish parents continued to send their children to German schools. Only 16,000 Jewish boys and girls had attended the Jewish private schools in the whole of Germany when Hitler came to power and more than double that number were in German state schools.[10] Only over time did the proportion change, as parents reluctantly concluded that only in a Jewish school would their children grow up confident and unashamed of their heritage.

III

The oldest Jewish boys' school in Germany was Hamburg's *Talmud Tora Schule*, founded in 1805. When the Nazis came to power, Dr Arthur Spier was the headmaster. His appointment in the mid-1920s, at a time of growing anti-Semitism, had been an inspired one. Spier was an orthodox Jew and had been a courageous fighter pilot in the Great War. No one could point a finger at him saying that he lacked patriotism. At its foundation the school had provided teachers for poor

Jewish boys. Later the intake reflected the social structure from the wealthy to poor parents looking for an orthodox Jewish education. But right from the beginning the ethos of the school was to equip the boys for life outside the community. At the celebratory opening in 1911, when the school moved to its fine new building, the headmaster called on the boys to become 'exemplary Jews, exemplary Germans and exemplary citizens of Hamburg. *Das walte Gott* – May God grant this.' Orthodoxy did not make Jews less German. Not only was Hebrew and Jewish religious practice central to the curriculum, the boys were also taught to live at ease in their Jewish and German home. The instruction was extended to middle-school and finally to upper-school levels, the *Abitur*, which entitled entry to the university. Reforming headmasters introduced lessons in German literature and culture. Christian teachers taught side by side with their Jewish colleagues even during the Nazi years.

The *Talmud Tora Schule*, a private independent foundation, was closely linked but not run by the Jewish community.[11] Fees were paid by those who could afford them; about half the boys attended free. No one was denied a place on grounds of inability to pay. The Warburg family, one of the principal benefactors, was represented on the board of governors. In the 1920s fees and private benefactions no longer covered all the costs and adequate salaries and pensions could no longer be paid to teachers. In 1921, for the first time, the school had to appeal to Hamburg's school authority for a grant to meet the shortfall. The senate agreed to provide funds. This successful outcome was largely due to the support of *Schulrat* Dr Wilhelm Oberdörffer, the civil servant responsible for the supervision of the school. The state of Hamburg now agreed to pay 80 per cent of the teachers' salaries and also took over responsibility for paying their pensions. Oberdörffer's goodwill continued during the Nazi years. Annual financial grants from the state became essential to keep the school open. Nazis paying large sums to an orthodox Jewish school? How this came about is an extraordinary story.

Reichsstatthalter Kaufmann ordered, as expected, that the subvention should end. Dr Spier then arranged to see him. Spier was the kind of Jew Kaufmann and the Nazi authorities respected, a war veteran, a survivor of aerial combat. His excellent negotiating skills helped to smooth the path of agreement. He persuaded Kaufmann that it was advantageous to the state for the school to absorb Jewish children. It saved the state money and separated Jews from Aryans. Kaufmann saw the point and the subvention was restored. It continued to be paid annually until the spring of 1939, despite frequent challenges from local Nazis.

In April 1933, Spier also had his first contact with the state police. A teacher one Saturday was arrested. Spier went to the offices of the school authority in the Dammtorstraße, where he asked to see Oberdörffer. Would he intercede with the state police? Oberdörffer was reluctant: 'Who can be expected willingly to enter the lion's den?' But he did write a letter of introduction. Spier next proceeded to the state police office in the Düsternstraße. After he had been kept waiting for an hour, a man in civilian dress appeared and without introducing himself asked

Spier what he wanted. Spier explained. An SS man was then called in and told to find out where the teacher was and why he had been arrested. It turned out that he had committed a traffic offence some years earlier and was in a storm trooper concentration camp. That was how Spier first met State Police Commissioner Claus Göttsche, who had been placed in charge of the Jewish affairs in Hamburg. Göttsche ordered the teacher's release. The encounter led to an extraordinary sequel. Göttsche said he was surprised that a Jewish school was still receiving financial help from the state. Spier recounted his discussion with Kaufmann. Göttsche was still curious; he wanted to learn more about Jews and asked Spier whether he could visit the *Talmud Tora Schule incognito*. Spier was happy to agree. Soon afterwards, Göttsche was shown round the school. The following week, Göttsche asked Spier to return to his office. He told him he had been very satisfied with what he had seen. Now he wanted Spier to explain citations allegedly from the *Talmud* which Streicher's *Der Stürmer* had printed. Spier replied that he could find a German translation of the *Talmud* in the state library and that he should look up the citations himself. Göttsche was evidently not happy about the idea of being seen in public studying the *Talmud*. Would Spier personally instruct him? On successive Fridays, Spier was collected from the *Talmud Tora Schule* by an SS limousine and introduced Göttsche to the finer points of Jewish religious philosophy. A relationship developed. It enabled Spier from time to time to intercede with Göttsche to release a number of Jews from concentration camps.[12]

It was a bizarre episode in Jewish–Nazi relations, but not unique. Individual Jews in prominent positions were sometimes able to establish tolerable one-to-one contact, winning the respect of a Nazi bureaucrat. But goodwill could not be relied on and did not protect a Jew from arbitrary abuse or physical violence at the hands of the Gestapo. Göttsche was capable of lenient gestures to individual supplicants when he felt inclined.

Who was Göttsche?[13] Göttsche was no ordinary civil policeman. In 1921 he had joined the order police, a militarised force housed in barracks set up to protect the fragile Weimar Republic from revolutionary upheavals. He gained promotion to middle rank and so by 1930 was on the threshold of a career in the higher service ranks. His social family background was modest, his formal education even more so. His father was a master shoemaker and his mother the daughter of a small farmer. As a child, Göttsche attended the local village school from the age six to nine and then worked in the fields as a farm labourer. In 1917, aged eighteen, he was conscripted to fight in the Kaiser's army, subsequently wounded, and in 1919 was demobilised as a private. It was the Weimar Republic that gave men and women of ability regardless of social origins real chances of advancement.

In 1932 Göttsche's career began to take off with his transfer to the political police, which under the Nazis in 1936 became the precursor of the *Geheime Staatspolizei*, the Gestapo. Hamburg's state police, *Staatspolizei*, already in 1933 had spearheaded the violent suppression of all opposition, assisting special units like the brutal Kraus Command. Early on, Göttsche also had some supervision over Jewish affairs, as the Jews were seen as the deadly biological enemies of the Reich. His responsibilities were extended and formalised when in 1935 he was placed in charge of the state police division for monitoring 'Jewish Affairs, Freemasonary and Sects'. Gaining a reputation as a Jew specialist, he headed the division of Jewish affairs, which was separated from the rest in 1938, and until 1943 dealt with Max Plaut throughout this period spanning Crystal Night to the Holocaust.

Göttsche was a ruthless opportunist. He joined the party in May 1933 and was ready to carry out all orders without scruple to further his career. But he also developed a style of his own in dealing with the Jewish leadership in Hamburg, personally avoiding outright cruelty and reassuring Jews about to be deported about their future so that the whole process would run as smoothly as possible. At the same time he made no effort to restrain his subordinates from maltreating Jews. Among the worst were Walter Wohlers and Hermann Kühn, known in the Jewish community as the 'bloodhound' for his violent assaults. A personal relationship did develop over the years between Göttsche and the Hamburg Jewish leadership, especially with Max Plaut. Göttsche and Plaut each tried to manipulate the other, though obviously not as equals. Plaut's lack of fear and black humour helped, though he knew if he overstepped the mark he could be dispatched to a concentration camp at a stroke of Göttsche's pen.

IV

Girls attended the other Jewish school in Hamburg which had survived the Depression, the *Israelitische Töchterschule*.[14] Unlike the *Talmud Tora Schule* in the largely middle-class part of the town, Karolinenstraße was in a working-class district, but this did not shelter the girls from taunts. The school developed in parallel with the *Talmud Tora Schule*, harmonising an upbringing in the Jewish religious tradition with German culture and love of the fatherland. Its classes expanded from elementary to higher education and finally to recognition as a *Realgymnasium*, leading to the leaving certificate at the age of sixteen. The few girls who wanted to take the *Abitur* at eighteen then transferred to the *Talmud Tora Schule*.

Dr Alberto Jonas, the dynamic headmaster of the *Israelitische Töchterschule*, deplored that more children did not attend Jewish schools. 'Frequently the reproach is heard', he wrote in the *Gemeindeblatt*,

> that the Jewish school leads the young back into a new ghetto. Those who say this believe that Jewish children are better prepared for later life in the state schools where they mix with all social groups, even though, regrettably, at some schools more and at others less, they have to experience hurt because they are Jews. It is claimed this prepares them for the struggles of later life. But children should not have to become hardened.

'In the Jewish school', Jonas continued, 'children did not have to worry and could develop normally in happiness ready to face life with confidence.'[15]

One remarkable aspect of Jewish education in Hamburg was the excellent relationship with the state school authority, which continued during the Nazi years on account of Dr Wilhelm Oberdörffer.[16] Oberdörffer supervised examinations and visited the schools. Accounts of his visits recount his warmth and friendliness when talking to teachers and when congratulating children, whose names he had memorised beforehand, on their success. His reports on the achievements of the *Talmud Tora Schule* and the *Israelitische Töchterschule* were always positive. Teachers knew that in Oberdörffer they had a reliable friend to whom they could go in case of difficulty. Yet Oberdörffer had joined the Nazi Party in 1933.

A Nazi helping and protecting Jewish institutions? Unlike Kaufmann, Oberdörffer was not motivated by cold calculation. He was in his mid-forties when the Nazis came to power. Only for a short time a teacher in the *Heinrich-Hertz-Realgymnasium* before the First World War, he chose a career as a civil servant in Hamburg's school authority (*Schulbehörde*). Politically, he supported the conservatives during the Weimar years but not the antisemitic *völkisch* right wing. He had made many Jewish friends with whom he shared cultural interests. His efforts on behalf of the Jewish schools during the difficult economic years of the 1920s had enabled them to survive. Of equal importance was the backing he gave to their progression in higher education, which required state approval. Oberdörffer had personally travelled to Frankfurt to persuade Arthur Spier to accept the headship of the *Talmud Tora Schule*. He was also the guardian of two orphans who, according to Nazi terminology, were 'half-Jews'. He even sent one of his daughters for a time to a private Jewish school. And during the Nazi 1930s he continued discreetly to help Jewish acquaintances.

Oberdörffer had acceded to pressure to join the party, fearful that he would otherwise be forcibly retired. The decisions he reached on school matters show he followed the letter rather than the spirit of the law. There were men in authority who were happy to go beyond what was required, justifying their 'initiatives' by claiming they were acting in conformity with the 'healthy instincts of the people'. Oberdörffer was not one of them, but then in 1940 he suddenly resigned. There is one clue why he had behaved so well. Among his hobbies was genealogy. His great-grandmother was Jewish. He is likely to have discovered this and not considered it a drawback in the least. But in 1940 he explained to *Reichsstatthalter* Kaufmann that even this small amount of Jewish blood made it impossible for him to supervise German teachers. Was it the real reason? He did not have to resign. One Jewish great-grandparent could be overlooked, especially when no one knew about it. Oberdörffer only had to keep it to himself. So why did he go when Kaufmann tried hard to persuade him to stay and even recommended that he be permitted to remain in the party? The persecution of the Jews had turned to murder in Poland. Their treatment – being forced into a ghetto, humiliated and worse – quite possibly made Oberdörffer feel that he could not remain even in a minor position serving such a regime. It was clear, too, that the conditions for German Jews were worsening month by month. His feelings of guilt by association became intolerable. He left the civil service and secured a position in the Reemstma business empire. Although reinstated in 1945 to restore Hamburg's school system, he was removed again by the British Control Commission after only a few weeks because he had joined the Nazi Party so early on – typical of the rough post-war justice. Today a street in Hamburg is named in his honour.

Despite all the efforts and pressure, the Nazis never entirely succeeded in isolating Jews. Every Jewish family knew someone who sympathised and a few even who would help them. There was 'another Germany', whose existence tragically persuaded many Jews to stay until it became too late to leave. There were also still a few associations and societies which did not expel their Jewish members. One of these in Hamburg was the Civic Association (*Bürgerrein*) of Harvestehude-Rotherbaum.

Self-help in difficult times

The more prosperous middle-class Jews lived in Rotherbaum-Harvestehude, with its many fine houses. Here a few gentiles, impeccable Aryans, gave ostentatious support to Jews, even though, paradoxically, the Nazis had been particularly successful in securing votes in the elections of March 1933 in this prosperous quarter of Hamburg. The courageous behaviour of the voluntary Civic Association, the *Bürgerverein*, of Harvestehude-Rotherbaum was certainly an uncommon occurrence. Local Civic Associations existed throughout the towns of Germany and concerned themselves with cultural and patriotic interests. The members also exchanged information and met once a year in one of their member towns.

The meetings of the local Harvestehude-Rotherbaum branch were held in the premises of the restaurant Klinker.[17] They were convivial affairs. The record of talks provides an insight into the issues that concerned the members. Senator Platen in March 1933 spoke about 'the political situation', Professor Dr Josephy about the law of sterilisation to prevent hereditary diseases, which in his opinion was a 'beneficial and necessary measure'. In 1934, Professor Dr Walther Fischer expounded on 'the New Spirit of Justice'; the unpolitical topic of 'three centuries of the Low German dialect in Hamburg's theatres' was the subject one evening; and in December that year Miss Elisabeth Pape gave an illustrated lecture on the preservation of 'Germanism in Siebenbürgen (Romania)'. The chairman of the association, Max Eichholz, thanked the speaker and stressed that, 'especially at the present time, talks which contribute to the preservation of Germanism inside our country and abroad are especially welcome'.

Max Eichholz took pride in being a Jew. A lawyer by profession, a brilliant speaker and a prominent politician of the Weimar era, representing the German Democratic Party in Hamburg's parliament, he was a thorn in the side of the Nazis. He was also a decorated veteran and possessed courage. Not many would have dared to take an SS man to court in November 1934 for calling them a 'dirty Jew'. He reminded the judge that, as a lawyer, he was 'a member of the administration of justice' and so could call on the special protection of the public prosecutor's office, which 'makes no distinction between Aryan and non-Aryan'. It tells us something about the ambiguities of Nazi control in the mid 1930s that he won his case. The SS man was required to pay a fine or serve a token two days in prison. After this, the Gestapo was out to get Eichholz.[18]

The Harvestehude-Rotherbaum Civic Association was associated with the *Bürgervereine* of Hamburg, to which all branches sent representatives to form a joint executive. No sooner had the Nazis won the March elections than a Nazi delegate with the appropriate name of Richard Wagner attacked the membership of the all-Hamburg executive for 'lacking the holy flame of renewal of the fatherland'.[19] What so angered *Herr* Wagner was the fact that not a single member of the executive was in the Nazi Party. He demanded new elections. The executive feebly resigned. But the local Harvestehude-Rotherbaum Association was made of sterner stuff. In the records of its meeting on 13 May 1933, Max Eichholz was thanked on behalf of the members for acting as chairman: the remark 'May he continue as leader of our association for many more years' met with warm applause. Then in April 1934 the association faced a crisis. The new central executive of Hamburg's *Bürgervereine* had introduced the Aryan paragraph. Jews could no longer belong. Max Eichholz proposed that the Harvestehude-Rotherbaum Association should reject the Aryan paragraph and dissociate itself from membership of the central executive.[20] This was unanimously supported. A year later, the Harvestehude-Rotherbaum Association was closed down on orders of the Gestapo, who cited the Emergency Law of 28 February 1933 for 'the protection of the people and the state'. Max Eichholz challenged the decision in court. The Law of February 1933, he argued, was directed against the threat of the communists. The association was national and patriotic. He also cited the Nazi newspaper, the *Hamburger Tageblatt*, which had explained the real reason the association had been forbidden was because it was led by a Jew and many Jews belonged to it. Jews could no longer be considered citizens of the state. But Jews, Eichholz asserted, were citizens, and, until laws were passed to the contrary, there was no difference between Jewish citizens and other citizens. The three judges were Nazis. They rejected Eichholz's arguments and denounced the Harvestehude-Rotherbaum Association as consisting mainly of Jews and Jew-friends who mocked the state. 'The national government and the *Führer* reject the cooperation of those of foreign race in the upholding of German values.' How times had changed in just twelve months.

Eichholz was among the better-placed Jews who could have left Germany in time. But his struggle for what he believed right, his defiance and his resistance kept him in Germany. The support he received from the Civic Association of Harvestehude-Rotherbaum had reinforced his belief that the 'other Germany' was worth fighting for. It did exist: unorganised, decent individuals who were neither blinded by propaganda nor by Nazi success, but they had no chance of unseating the Nazis, who held the reins of power. During the first four years of the Nazi regime, the Jews robustly asserted their rights; only with hindsight did this prove an illusion.

I

The Jewish community did not throw up its hands in despair. Most Jews were expected to stay in Germany. The community would have to take stock of the new situation, defend their position, and plan realistically for the future.[21] They could count on the help of men and women of ability and experience from within the community, and the greater part of their wealth still remained intact. The leaders were resilient and were determined to create order. The Jewish political organisations now settled their differences so they could unite their efforts and create a common front to face the Nazi authorities and to tackle the problems now facing them.[22]

It proved more difficult to persuade the community organisations of Berlin, Frankfurt, Breslau, Hamburg, Cologne and Leipzig, and numerous smaller ones, each independent with their own financial resources, to create one organisation to speak for all. Berlin, with its community of 175,000, was by far the largest and demanded the leadership role, but this was vehemently opposed by the smaller communities.

Rabbi Leo Baeck, the Jewish sage with a reputation throughout Germany, crafted a compromise. It took the Nazi threat to overcome all the internal barriers. The first step in March 1933 was to create a central executive for assistance and reconstruction – the *Zentralausschuss für Hilfe und Aufbau* – to deal with immediate problems facing Jews who had lost their jobs, providing advice, financial help and social assistance. Funds were collected at home and abroad, especially in the United States through the American Jewish Joint Distribution Committee. A centralised Jewish organisation was established, the Representative Council of German Jews (*Reichsvertretung der deutschen Juden*), which, however, did not begin to function until six months later, in September 1933, when final agreement was reached. The Berlin community had to make the largest sacrifice in accepting under representation. Actually its leaders never did fully acquiesce, and this became the cause of tension in the years that followed.

The *Reichsvertretung* made representations to the Nazi ministries and even directly to Hitler. It acted courageously but usually in vain. The *Reichsvertretung* was of importance nevertheless, studying the problems facing all the larger and smaller communities and making suggestions how to deal with them. It also acted as a funnel for the large funds being contributed by Jews abroad and was recognised by the Gestapo and government departments in Berlin as the body with whom they would deal. Over time its stature increased. The achievements of the Jewish organisations still lack the recognition they deserve in helping tens of thousands of Jews.

One of the oldest Jewish relief organisations was the *Hilfsverein der deutschen Juden*, founded in 1901 to assist foreign, mainly Russian, Jews to migrate overseas.[23] After 1933 it expanded greatly, now advising and helping German Jews to emigrate all over the world except to Palestine, which was organised by the

Palestine Office. The community's social services for the poor, sick and elderly also had a long history and were increasingly in demand during the Depression years. Thus experienced Jewish social workers were available to take on the new tasks faced by German Jewry. Professional salaried community staff were reinforced by volunteers. Their struggle to cope while holding their heads high, until they lost all control when deportations and mass murders began, is a tragic and honourable chapter in the final phase of German Jewry. In the properties of the Jewish community there were separate offices to deal with the specific needs of Jews who came for advice and help.

II

In Hamburg, an Advisory Service for Economic Assistance was set up in Beneckestraße 2. Its rooms were soon crowded with anxious enquirers. The financial section provided advice on welfare assistance, and there was a department concerned with career planning and a section approving loans. The emigration department was sub-divided into divisions dealing with emigration to Palestine and emigration to the rest of the world. A third office dealt with training for school leavers and training for those no longer able to follow their professions.

The advisers knew there was little demand in Palestine or in other countries for the professions which these middle-aged men and women who were coming to their office had followed before losing their jobs. They would need to retrain as skilled workers and craftsmen or turn their hands to agriculture or housework. In Germany the professions were now closed to young men and women, opportunities in commercial life were limited and, as most Jews were still expected to continue living in Germany, learning to do the work which was still permitted became the practical goal. Some Jewish scholars believed this was not altogether a bad thing. But the vision of Jews becoming more accepted in Germany through 'occupational restructuring', *Berufsumschichtung*, was yet another illusion.

The daunting task of retraining was tackled energetically, but there were not enough funds to meet the needs of the young. As for the middle-aged professional men, they found it even harder to adjust, lawyers becoming carpenters, locksmiths or agricultural workers. Most did not try. Their wives were more adaptable. They had already mastered the arts of housework and the skills of bringing up children. The wife of a judge would offer her services as nanny and cook to a household in Birmingham or New York. Many a family able to emigrate now depended on the resources and hard work of wives and daughters.

The Hamburg community enlarged existing training facilities such as the botanical training college in Wilhelminenhöhe outside the city and created new ones. In Weidenallee 8, thirty young men received one-year courses in carpentry and, in Heimhuderstraße 70, thirty young women were trained in tailoring; the *Talmud Tora Schule* instructed a group of fifteen-year-olds to become carpenters and locksmiths. Not only did money have to be raised for these purposes, but most of the trainees also needed the wherewithal to live, to buy food and other necessities. All in all, only 130 young men and women could be taken on in Hamburg every year and prepared for emigration – a drop in the ocean of need.

The agricultural settlements set up by the Zionist organisation nationally now found themselves overwhelmed with young applicants. They prepared the young for *aliya* – emigration to Palestine. They were called 'pioneers', *hechalutz*. The Zionists trained the whole person – not just in agricultural skills, but in preparation for a new way of communal life in the *kibbutz*. In the whole of Germany there were some 1,500 places, again not nearly enough. Near Hamburg only thirty-three places were available in settlements in Blankenese and Ahlem. The likelihood of acceptance further away was slim. The Zionists did not have a monopoly, for there were agricultural settlements for young Jews wishing to emigrate to other countries. Jewish organisations were also able to persuade some 'Aryan' farmers to take on Jewish trainees.

III

In Hamburg, a most unusual *Hachschara*, a training for Palestine, was organised, where young Jews were taught their skills by good German Aryans.[24] These young Jews formed a small group of cadets among a large number of German sailors. The *Hachschara* afloat was the brainchild of Lucy Borchardt, a formidable lady, stout in stature, tough in character. After the death of her husband she had taken charge of the management of the Fairplay tug boat company engaged in towing boats up the Elbe into Hamburg's harbour. Fairplay also owned two merchant ships. Together with the Bernstein Line, it was one of the only two Jewish shipping lines in Hamburg. Lucy Borchardt, 'Mother Borchardt', was held in affection by her Aryan crew and captains. She was able to persuade the authorities that to promote emigration she should be permitted to place up to ten young Jews on her boats to be trained as sailors. Her ulterior motive was to provide for the nucleus of a Jewish Palestinian merchant fleet. Later the Jewish-owned Bernstein Line also took on board six young Jews. By keeping the training period short, a number of sailors were brought to Palestine with at least a rudimentary knowledge of seafaring. Their training was then continued in Palestine on ships sold by Lucy Borchardt to her son, who had founded a shipping line based in Haifa. Some later served in the infant Israeli navy. The end for the Borchardt Line in Hamburg came in 1938, with Aryanisation on unusual conditions enabling Lucy Borchardt to take two tugs and one merchant ship abroad. Lucy Borchardt's story is typical of enterprise and initiative in face of all the difficulties. It is also an example of Jewish employers held in esteem and affection by their Christian employees. That was by no means an exception despite Nazi propaganda.

IV

Leaving the country of your birth was no easy decision. Where could you go? There were barriers everywhere at a time of high unemployment. You did not speak the language. If you were a lawyer, your knowledge of German law was useless abroad. If a doctor, you would need to pass examinations again before being allowed to practise. Musicians were not permitted to join orchestras. In other words, if you left without means, you had to rely on charity or your wife taking on domestic labour. The pensions of state employees continued to be paid but only into special German accounts. For a time, close relatives could make withdrawals from them.

Until the outbreak of war, Jews emigrating could transfer only ever diminishing capital abroad. To secure the best rate of exchange required negotiation between Jewish representatives and German officials. You were fortunate if you had a good Jewish negotiator, such as Max Warburg, to help you. Max Warburg through the years made frequent use of his contacts with the *Reichsbank* president, Hjalmar Schacht. But Schacht's opposition to the radical extremists did not extend to any generosity of treatment when it came to the transfer of Jewish money abroad. There was little room for manoeuvre. It was not a negotiation between equals. The Nazis wanted to drive out as many Jews as possible. That provided a chink of leverage, as the Jewish bankers and the *Reichsvertretung* pointed out that foreign countries demanded hard currency before allowing Jews to enter.

To cite exchange rates as a cold statistic, however, misses the point. A life in Germany that was still tolerable before 1938 had to be exchanged for poverty abroad. The state simply confiscated what people wishing to emigrate rightfully owned. First there was the flight tax, which had been thought up in 1931 before the Nazis to discourage money leaving Germany. Then what remained had to be exchanged. This was not calculated at normal exchange rates, and the state helped itself to another slice. What was left was half the original value in 1934, a fifth in 1936, and by 1939 just 4 *Reichsmark* in foreign currency for every 100 exchanged. Depending on the size of the family, a small amount was allowed to be transferred at a more favourable rate. If in the case of the very wealthy this still left too large a sum in foreign exchange, fines and impositions reduced even millionaires to penury. Those who had not got out in time landed on foreign shores as beggars and usually without the prospect of being able to earn a living. Jews who emigrated to Palestine were treated more favourably – on the face of it a curious anomaly. It was even stranger, perhaps, that the one country not joining the boycott movement was the British Mandate of Palestine. Here Jewish importers organised themselves to promote trade with Germany throughout the Middle East. The Nazis in return allowed German manufacturers to do business with them.

The Zionists needed capital and people to develop the *yishuv*, the Jewish community in Palestine. Jewish immigrants, limited by British-imposed quotas, were listed in different categories, the most important of which were 'workers' and 'capitalists'. The 'capitalists' needed to bring with them at least 1,000 Palestine pounds, which required Nazi collaboration. In August 1933, a trade agreement was concluded called after the Hebrew for transfer, *ha'avara*.[25] The transfer was of an unusual kind. German goods exported to Palestine were paid for in foreign currency, Palestine pounds, then placed in a special account in Palestine. These were in turn made available to the immigrant. In Germany, the manufacturers were paid for their exports in *Reichsmark* from a special account in Germany into which the Jewish emigrant paid *Reichsmark* he wished to transfer at an unfavourable exchange rate. The net effect was that the *Reichsbank* lost the foreign currency it could have received for those exports. The total allowed was not, however, without limit, as the annual amount was a fixed sum – 3 million *Reichsmark* in 1933.

There was deep division among the Nazi authorities about *ha'avara*. Some favoured it because it enabled more Jews to leave Germany; others pointed to the loss of foreign currency which was so urgently needed to import raw materials as rearmament accelerated. By 1937, few arguments were any longer advanced in favour. That the scheme was allowed to continue was thanks to Hitler. Hitler made known in January 1939 that *ha'avara* was to go on, and it continued until the outbreak of the war. Goodwill was not Hitler's motive. To create a better impression abroad in the early years, *ha'avara* could be cited as showing that the Nazis were helping Jews. It was also good propaganda to stress the breach in the worldwide boycott, especially as it occurred in Palestine. Nazi support of Zionism, the creation of a Jewish nation, justified Nazi claims that the Jews were a separate people. Not least important was the removal of Jews.

Ha'avara – a pact with the devil, certainly; significant assistance to the German economy, hardly; in the overall export trade, it accounted for only a tiny proportion. In preventing an increase in Germany's foreign currency reserves its impact was harmful to the Nazis. It saved 52,000 German Jews who were enabled to emigrate to Palestine. That the Zionists were right to negotiate and conclude an agreement with the Nazis was certainly the view of the thousands whose lives were saved. In all, 8 million Palestine pounds were paid to the immigrants. That more Jews did not reach the safe haven was due to the restrictions imposed by the British government.

There was a steady exodus of emigrants to Palestine and other countries, but the panic of early 1933 was not repeated until 1938. It would take nine or ten years to reduce the Jewish population to what was considered by the Jewish authorities the irreducible minimum of 200,000 – the very old, the sick and those too young to depart on their own. A sufficient number of Jewish men and women able to work and to support their dependants in Germany would also need to stay behind. The idea of no Jews in Germany in the near future was unimaginable. The three overriding aims of the Jewish leaders were to ensure orderly emigration, to keep Jews working and earning in the economy for their own livelihood and for those who could not work, and to maintain social, cultural and religious institutions offering quality of life for the Jews who did not emigrate.

Should they have foreseen that time was running out for every single Jew – the able bodied, the old and sick, and even babies with a whole life before them? Did not their very success in making the lives for German Jews more bearable, inspiring false hopes for the future, deaden German Jewry to the dangers facing them until five minutes to midnight? Yes, with hindsight, but the abyss simply could not have been envisaged, and even if it had been, half a million Jews could not have found refuge elsewhere in the world, as their entry in large numbers was resisted by every country.

The accounts of the early Nazi years do not generally convey what is hard to believe, that many Jewish Germans were still better off than most other Germans. The rich were still very rich. A large middle class had to make economies, but life in Germany was still tolerable for most. But the careers of employees of the state, which included civil servants, judges, public prosecutors and doctors in state hospitals, were abruptly ended. A pension does not compensate for their sudden unjustifiable dismissal. The young did not even have the prospect of a career. Jewish life in Germany had become an ambiguous existence depending on what a person had done before the Nazis came to power.

V

Better-off Jews took their holidays abroad to escape for a few weeks the Nazi surroundings. Hamburg's Jews did not have far to go. The Danish border was only a short distance away. Jews also continued to visit spas in Germany for their health and relaxation. Lists were annually published by the CV, where they were still welcome. Some, like Bad Homburg, even for a time issued official statements that Jews would find peace there and would not be molested, and that all paying guests were welcome.

During the first five years of Nazi rule there was no bar to Jews continuing to attend theatres and concerts, but not everyone felt comfortable enjoying concerts and plays after Jewish artists and musicians had been thrown out. The Jewish community was now supporting the unemployed musicians and actors and received permission from the Gestapo to arrange concerts and to provide academic lectures and literary readings. Although called 'Jewish', the Culture Association, the *Kulturbund*, was also open to Christians, provided they were descended from at least one Jewish grandparent.[26] In one respect Jews were more fortunate than the Nazi public. They could enjoy so-called Jewish music – Mendelssohn's violin concerto, proscribed in German concert halls, Max Bruch and non-Aryan composers.

The very first concert in Hamburg raised an important question never really resolved. Clearly, audiences and performers were overwhelmingly Jewish. But should their offerings be particularly Jewish? Hamburg's opening concert included Mendelssohn's violin concerto but pointedly began with Beethoven's *Egmont* overture and closed with Schubert's seventh symphony. Lessing, not a Jew, had written *Nathan der Weise*, praising Jews, which was frequently performed. The Jewish culture associations, *Kulturbünde*, were more German than Jewish; it was their links with German and universal culture, Shakespeare, Molière and Ibsen, which they emphasised while also featuring Jewish culture.

Cabarets, humorous evenings of entertainment and dances were interspersed with classical theatre. The Nazis wanted to show to the world that they were sponsoring a separate Jewish culture. Although the Gestapo instructions were to promote Zionist attitudes, the *Jüdische Kulturbünde* remained resolutely German. In Hamburg, the *Kulturbund* could look with pride on what was accomplished: 5,800 members had joined by the summer of 1936. Ernst Loewenberg, writing in the *Hamburger Gemeindeblatt* on the *Kulturbund*'s success, struck a realistic note: 'Jews have to accept they live in a new world. Some may still feel they can attend theatres and concerts untroubled, but we cannot rely on the past ... our future will be more confined yet still full of light and sunshine.'

That the *Kulturbünde* were able to flourish was due to the collaboration between Kurt Singer, the director of the *Kulturbund* in Berlin, and Hans Hinkel, Goebbels's culture commissioner. In his early thirties, Hinkel was typical of opportunistic Nazis. He forged close links with the Gestapo, and Himmler promoted him to the rank of SS *Oberführer*. The dual connection was his power base. Hinkel was two-faced: at heart a rabid antisemite, he also wanted to make a success of his own Jewish cultural sphere. He purged Jews from 'German' – that is, 'Aryan' – cultural life, but developed good personal relations with Kurt Singer, until recently assistant manager of the Berlin City Opera. In 1935, Hinkel brought all the various *Kulturbünde*, including Hamburg's, under his centralised control. He achieved this cleverly not by coercion but by being reasonable. All performances had to be approved by the Gestapo beforehand. In many cities the Gestapo acted far more restrictively than Hinkel in Berlin. In Hamburg, for instance, theatrical performances were not at first permitted, whereas they were in Berlin. Then in many ways the party pressured owners of premises, even if they were willing, not to hire their halls to Jews. By centralising, Hinkel explained, local interference would be reduced. Life in Nazi Germany had many facets: the Gestapo could be polite and reasonable if they needed cooperation and unpredictable and brutal on other occasions when not in the public eye. This helps to explain the records of the meeting of twenty-four of Germany's *Kulturbünde* on 27 and 28 April 1935.[27]

> *Dr Kurt Singer* (Berlin): Ladies and gentlemen ... I thank *Herr* State-commissioner Hinkel and the gentlemen of the Gestapo who are here so that we can examine our future, and how best we can accomplish our cultural aims within our Jewish society. The support of *Herr* State commissioner Hinkel, observing and looking after us, and the supervision of the Gestapo are very valuable to us ... *Herr* Statecommisioner Hinkel has in a most helpful way placed himself at our disposal to guide us.
>
> *Herr Hinkel*: ... I can assure you that the working relationship with the Berlin *Kulturbund* on the whole has been without any difficulties except on a few unimportant occasions, so that I was able to report to my superiors that everything was at all times in the best of order, making any intervention unnecessary. But we know that elsewhere in the Reich there were a

few instances when it looked different, but then you have to remember that the whole Jewish cultural question and how it should be handled is relatively new ... Please tell me from your own practical experience what your attitude is. Don't accept how we do things here as inflexible. It is in your hands whether you want to come together by forming a Reich organisation or not, but I would welcome it in the interests of both ...

    Dr Singer: I would like to thank *Herr* Statecommissioner for his address .... For my part I would wish to confirm ... that the cooperation with the authorities has proceeded without friction, but only thanks to the personality of *Herr* Statecommissioner Hinkel and thanks to the gentlemen of the Gestapo who supervise us ...

Despite all this bizarre show of goodwill, performances of 'Aryan' works were increasingly prohibited. Wagner and Richard Strauss were forbidden, and in 1936 Goethe and the German classics; Beethoven could not be performed either, and two years later Mozart was added to the list. Only Handel remained to the end, perhaps because he was considered more English than German. Perforce the *Kulturbund* had to turn to foreign dramatists and Jewish composers. The *Kulturbund* in Hamburg also provided light entertainment for young and old – escapism from the worries of daily life, at least a few hours of normality.

VI

What would the next day bring? Information about the cascade of laws and regulations could frequently be discovered only in Jewish newspapers. The oldest was the Zionist *Jüdische Rundschau*, founded in 1896, which appeared twice weekly.[28] In Hamburg, the *Israelitisches Familienblatt*, a weekly paper with a national circulation, was politically independent and privately owned. The largest circulation was reached by the weekly *C.V. Zeitung*. The Jewish Veterans' Association also published a weekly, *Der Schild*. Practically every Jewish family after 1933 subscribed to one or other of these or to the newsletter of their community, the least censored of the German press. Displayed in the early years on newspaper kiosks along Hamburg's Jungfernstieg and along Berlin's Kurfürstendamm, their headlines free from dreary Nazi uniformity attracted passers-by. Only in the Jewish press could people still read authors like Stefan Zweig or Franz Werfel and reviews of books by Thomas Mann and Romain Rolland. Nazi efforts to isolate Jews were still remarkably porous.

    The crucial question facing the readers of Jewish papers was whether to prepare to leave Germany or not. The advice given by Zionists and non-Zionists during the early years differed less than might have been expected. The Zionists were staunch Germans too and thought that most Jews would remain in Germany. Their appeal was to young Jews to come to Palestine, to give up thoughts of professional careers, to build up the Jewish home by joining an agricultural *kibbutz*. Most of the older generation would be a burden, and their emigration was not encouraged.

The Association of German Citizens of Jewish Faith, CV, advocated planned emigration and a 'reform' of the 'unhealthy' career structure of Jewish society, so it found much in common with the Zionists. But differences also remained. The *C.V. Zeitung* emphasised that German Jews were indissolubly bound to their native soil.[29] Though a great change had occurred, Jews should remain steadfast: 'We have the patience developed over a thousand years … with inner resistance we will overcome.'

The *C.V. Zeitung* attacked Nazi experts advocating expulsion, especially Dr Achim Gercke, who in the *Nationalsozialistische Monatshefte* had set out his 'final solution of the Jewish problem'. Germany's Jews were to be forced to leave for Palestine, where they perhaps could 'become a *Volk* and a nation'. In the same issue Goebbels's protégé, Johann von Leers, preferred Madagascar but rejected more radical solutions:

> only a barbarian, someone not recognising the divine order of world history, could propose a struggle leading to annihilation, the extermination of the Jewish *Volk* … superior peoples do not chose solutions of hate *where a decent solution of the problem is still considered possible* [author's italics].

What if a 'decent solution' was not possible? And this was written already in 1933. Clearly the measures so far taken in Germany did not comprise a 'solution', but just the beginning.

The CV asserted that forced emigration was neither possible nor likely: 'The majority of German Jews will and must remain in Germany.' The CV envisaged a different future. Once the National Socialist state was consolidated and strengthened, the CV leaders argued, it would cease to feel threatened by minorities like the Jews, who would find a place in an ordered structure. Jews would need to wait for laws still to come, but though 'torn from the mainstream of Germany's destiny', they should hold on in the expectation 'that they will be able to construct a small Jewish space at the edges of Germany's future'.

The Zionist *Jüdische Rundschau* did not share the CV's patriotic fervour but also tried to raise Jewish morale, which found its most memorable expression in the call of the editor, Robert Weltsch, for 'Jews to wear the Yellow badge with pride'.[30] It was prophetic in a way; Jews were not actually ordered to fix the Star of David to their clothes until eight years later. What Weltsch meant was that they should hold their heads high despite the denigration all around them. Later he regretted the sentiment of encouraging Jews to meet Nazi defiance and remain in Germany. But Weltsch too was deeply attached to the 'other' humane German tradition. 'We know that generations will remain true to what they have received from the German spirit', the *Jüdische Rundschau* wrote. 'We believe that German Jews also must find their place and be integrated into this state, and we hope it yet proves possible to find the form for this, one that is in harmony with the principles of this new state.' The paper warned that emigration to Palestine was no easy option:

> Zionism is not a welfare office … it would be a mistake to say whoever has
> lost his job in Germany should go to Palestine … As paradoxical as it sounds,
> we have to advise many Jews nowadays not to go to Palestine, because
> there will necessarily be disappointments arising from such decisions.

The Zionists, like the CV, at the outset did not believe that the Jews were in any
physical danger; they discounted the prophecies of the firebrand Nazis as rhetoric not representing official policies and aims, believing Hitler was more moderate than his followers.

Germans as a whole could not envisage mass murder either. Their reactions to
the discrimination of their non-Aryan – not just Jewish – fellow citizens differed
from one to another; most were neither consumed with hatred nor appalled by
what was happening, and there was every gradation between the two. But even
well-meaning Germans felt there was some justification for reducing 'Jewish
influences'; the helpful Jewish baker or the owner of the shoe shop or their next-
door neighbour was, of course, not meant by that.

The long shadow of Nuremberg

After the drama of 1933, the new year was one of consolidation. It began reassuringly when Hitler declared, on the anniversary portrayed as the heroic
Machtergreifung, the capture of power, that Nazi policy claimed not superiority
of one race over another but only the need for blood separation. The CV hailed
his 'statesmanlike' pronouncement as a confirmation of its views. Hitler was at
pains to emphasise how bloodless and disciplined the revolution had been. He
boasted of the mass support of 40 million Germans, while 'only a contemptible
two and a half million' opposed the revolution; it was criminal emigrants who
were spreading lies abroad, besmirching the Nazi Reich.

In Hamburg unemployment stayed stubbornly high.[31] By the end of 1934 one in
seven were still without work. Temporary work creation had made a dent, but new
secure jobs were few and far between. Hamburg had traditionally been a stronghold of the socialist and communist parties, and a core of brave men and women
recorded their opposition. On 19 August 1934, after the death of Hindenburg,
Hitler called for a vote of mass confidence. The plebiscite asked voters to approve
the fusion of the offices of head of state (*Reichspräsident*) and chancellor. The noes
rose in Hamburg (compared to March 1933) from one in six to one in five, a sham-
ing result for local Nazi leaders. In any free society, 80 per cent approval would
have been judged an overwhelming success. Many Jews thought better Hitler in
control than firebrands like Goebbels or the sinister Himmler.

I

In the mid-1930s the Jewish community did not meekly surrender. The leadership
was still confident that it could call on the authorities for protection; this did not

seem to be an unreasonable expectation. In June 1934, the Grindel graveyard was again desecrated, gravestones uprooted. Max Plaut took photographs and showed them to the Gestapo. The Gestapo inspected the cemetery, confirmed Plaut's report, and promised they would provide adequate security. They also told Plaut not to take any more photographs; none must get into foreign hands – a thinly veiled threat. An even more serious issue arose at the close of that year when the state of Hamburg demanded that the Jews vacate the Grindel graveyard and hand it back to the state so the land could be built on. The Jewish cemetery was the last still in existence in the area between the Dammtor and Grindel, which had once been the main burial ground for the people of Hamburg, Christians and Jews. This land was no longer situated on the outskirts, as earlier in the nineteenth century. A new large cemetery, further out in Ohlsdorf, for all, irrespective of confession, was created. The Christian graveyards close to the Dammtor had already been transferred to Ohlsdorf. Now it was the turn of the Jews.

Orthodox Jewry was placed in an impossible position. If the remains were left where they were they would be trampled on and built over, but to disturb and exhume the dead was equally repellent and against Jewish law. The Jewish community hoped that, as before, the Hamburg state would show understanding. It was a vain hope. Mayor Krogmann, to whom an appeal was sent, refused even to receive a delegation. Legal action was considered but rejected. There was no chance of success in Nazi Germany. The Hamburg state even insisted that the expense of the transfer of the remains had to be borne by the Jews. The community could not meet the cost. Descendants would have to do so if they wished their relatives to be individually reinterred. For the remainder, and those who could not be identified, there was a mass grave. The rabbis accepted they had to bow to the inevitable, only able to insist it should all be done decently. A descriptive list of all the identifiable gravestones was made; some 260 could not be identified. The transfer to Ohlsdorf was completed in 1937. Nothing more clearly exemplified the change of the times than this callous disregard for Jewish feelings and religious requirements.

The material decline of Hamburg's Jews is mirrored by the worsening financial state of the community. The *Gemeinde* was slipping into a crisis: expenditures threatened to outrun income again, as they had done during the Depression. Just at this point the one person who was possibly the most able and experienced expert in finance, *Staatsrat* (retired) Leo Lippmann, took charge of the community's complex financial problems.

Leo Lippmann had finally abandoned the hopeless dream of being reinstated to supervise once more the financial affairs of the Hamburg state. Vigorous and only fifty-four years old, he took on a new demanding responsibility. On arriving at the offices of the Jewish community in December 1935, as recorded in the minutes, he thanked the other members of the board for placing their confidence in him and then chose the occasion for a characteristic personal declaration: 'he was happy at the prospect of being able to serve the Jewish community with all his strength. He had always identified himself with it with pride but also wished to state with emphasis that he continued to feel as a German.'[32]

Leo Lippmann's skill and unrivalled experience were now invaluable to the beleaguered community.[33] He became responsible for negotiating financial issues with the state, which brought him in touch again with the civil servants who had once served under him. His manner did not change. He acted as if he was still their chief, addressing them by name without their titles, expecting deference in return. He got away with it, state secretary to the bitter end. At least marginally his masterful handling won for the community a few concessions.

The shrinking capabilities of funding hit hard all those institutions that depended on subsidies. In the early Nazi years some bizarre efforts had been made to gain access to state funds. The prize has to be accorded to the orthodox Jewish Altona community, which applied to the Adolf Hitler Fund in 1934 for a new ritual purification bath, a *mikveh*.[34] The request was politely declined on the grounds that a synagogue was not a business. The *Adolf-Hitler-Spende* was intended to be spent on work creation.

An unusual expenditure arose in the spring of 1935: the Hamburg state ordered that an air-raid shelter should be constructed for the Jewish children in the *Israelitische Töchterschule* in the Karolinenstraße;[35] this was on a parallel with the provision later on of gas masks for the Jewish population. The one bright spot was that the state subsidy to the orthodox Jewish schools continued. The Jewish community was making plans to expand educational provision against the day when all Jewish children would have to leave the state schools. In the event, their expulsion announced as imminent in 1935 was postponed for another three years.

An institution of particular renown not just among Jews but throughout Hamburg was the Jewish hospital, the *Israelitisches Krankenhaus*, a benefaction constructed in 1841 close to the harbour district. It was held in high esteem by the sailors, the poor and the prostitutes living in the streets of St Pauli who visited the *Poliklinik*, the outpatients department. Doctors administered to the sick, midwives to the mothers and babies. But patients also came from all over Hamburg to be cured by the well-known Jewish specialists. In 1933 six out of ten of the inpatients treated were Christians; in outpatients there were even more. In 1937 more than one in five Christians still chose the Jewish hospital. By a typical opportunistic doublethink, the Welfare Administration insisted that Jewish patients had to be referred to the state hospitals; Jewish patients in the Jewish hospital would no longer be funded unless they required ritual catering. All the doctors were Jewish, though a number had intermarried. With its own nursing school, the hospital provided the majority of nurses, but Christian nurses too had to be employed. They formed a Nazi union, and some caused trouble by making unwarranted accusations of uncleanliness which the Hamburg state rejected. But the days of the hospital were numbered.

II

For the Jews, discrimination was nothing new. One learnt to live with it. But, for the so called 'non-Aryan' Christians, the change in their situation was unexpected and hard to bear.

They reacted with disbelief and bewilderment the further they had moved away from their Jewish roots.[36] In 1933, one Jewish grandparent sufficed to brand them and to share all the discrimination against the Jewish community, with whom they felt nothing in common. Nor did they have anything in common with each other. Wives, husbands and children were all involved – the children, that was the worst of it. These non-Aryans were baptised Christians, patriotic Germans identified hitherto by the norms of society: class, education, profession, nationality, politics. Now more important than all of these was 'race', plucked as if out of the clear blue sky. Among them, to begin with, there had been plenty of supporters and admirers of Adolf Hitler. They had 'overcome Jewishness'. About 400,000 Germans were now 'non-Aryans' or married to 'non-Aryans' and cast out of the *Volk*. At the time it was thought there were many more, possibly even several million. No one was keen to advertise an awareness of a Jewish ancestor if there was a good chance of losing the unwelcome forbear in the mists of time. Thus many a worthy ancestor remained hidden, unrecorded. Today, they are unearthed with pride.

Most of the Christian non-Aryans in Hamburg were Protestants, though there were also a few Catholics.[37] Hamburg was important for non-Aryan Catholics in Germany, as the *St Raphaelsverein* established there its central administration, charged originally with the welfare of Catholic emigrants; it now took on the care of Catholic-'Jews'. Pater Max Groesser was the general secretary. Incarcerated for two months in 1938 and arrested in March 1940, he died of a heart attack on his way to the Gestapo in Berlin. The *St Raphaelsverein* was constantly harassed by the Gestapo and Bishop Berning of Osnabrück, though the president of the association gave it little protection. During Catholic services money was collected for its work, but not by name. The help was limited to Catholic non-Aryans. There was no care for the Jews, as Bishop Berning fully subscribed to the idolatry of the unity of blood and *Volk*. Still, the good deeds of the *St Raphaelsverein* were not negligible, as it helped over 10,000 racially persecuted Catholics to escape Germany.

The needs of the *Mischlinge* were much the same as those of the Jews,[38] as civil servants were dismissed from their posts, doctors were taken off insurance registers, the careers of young men and women were blighted, and entry to professional associations and sports was denied. But, unlike the German Jews, they had no organisation or community of their own to fall back on for moral support, no experienced social welfare workers to assist them in the crisis of their lives, while the community of which they were a part, the Christians, with one notable exception in Hamburg, failed them. Whether members of the Confessing Church or the German Christians, or the pastors who stood in between, there was a general consensus that the discriminatory racial decrees were a proper sphere for the state. The majority of Lutherans assured the regime of their positive support in all except the state's interference in the government of the Church. Admittedly there was also a theological problem; baptism in the eyes of the Church signified that Jews had found their way to Jesus. But the sprinkling of water over their heads had not changed their 'blood'. Baptised Jews in Germany were known as *Juden-Christen*, Jew-Christians, a concept much older than the Nazis.

III

In Hamburg, the Jerusalem *Gemeinde* was one independent church that rejected hatred of Jews.[39] It was not a German foundation. In the mid-nineteenth century the Presbyterians in Belfast had started a mission to convert Jews. The community in Hamburg, with its own church, took the name Jerusalem *Gemeinde* and adopted as its wider mission *Dienst an Israel*, service to Israel.

But for a few loyal friends, the converted Jewish Christians and the *Mischlinge* and their families were isolated in Nazi Germany. They had no contacts with the Jewish community and found cold comfort in Hamburg's Lutheran churches. Only the Jerusalem *Gemeinde* received them warmly, whether they were its members or not. As long as they were able to do so, the *Gemeinde* regularly advertised in Hamburg's newspapers invitations to afternoon teas and social evenings. Sausages and rolls were handed out. Funds were raised abroad from sister communities in Ireland, Switzerland and the United States. In June 1934 it is recorded that 200 'non-Aryans' joined in a 'family evening'. At Christmas a special festive spread was provided. The Jerusalem *Gemeinde* was not what was called a *Juden-Christen* community; some of its communicants were impeccable German Aryans, but in the 1930s embraced converted Jews and *Mischlinge* without distinction. The *Gemeinde* published a monthly magazine called *Zions Freund*, remarkable for its sympathetic reporting of Jewish life in Palestine and the diaspora. The *Mischlinge* and converted Jews sought to help themselves. These 'non-Aryan' Christians, unlike the Jews, had to start from scratch.[40] In July 1933 a 'Reich Association' with the unwieldy name of 'Christian-German citizens of non-Aryan and not pure Aryan descent' was formed. Included were Christians defined by the Nazis as Jews because of their descent from four Jewish grandparents as well as *Mischlinge*. All members had to attest to love of fatherland; their common bond was Christianity. By including 'racial Jews', the association did not follow Nazi doctrine until they were forced to do so; they then had to expel the baptised 'full Jews'.

The regime did not like the cumbersome title of the association – at once German, Christian and non-Aryan – so it was obliged to change its name to *Paulus-Bund*. During the six years it existed, it was a kind of miniature copy of the Jewish *Reichsvertretung*. There were departments providing legal advice and help to members who lost their positions. The patriotic fervour lessened after 1935. Now information on opportunities to emigrate and life abroad first appeared in the *Mitteilungsblatt* (Information News). Courses were offered in foreign languages and workshops established for those who had to change their occupation; advice was available on schooling and on holidays; there were youth and sport associations, talks, cabaret and dance evenings, and cultural affairs; and welfare assistance and help was provided in finding employment. The pages devoted to advertisements in the *Mitteilungsblatt* included offers of secretarial work; families advertised for nannies and home-helps. The columns of people seeking jobs tell their own story.

> Trained chemist, 21 years old, looking for a position as a commercial traveller.
>
> Owner of a landed estate, former cavalry officer, 39 years, Lutheran, single, who has sold his property, is looking for any kind of position, capital for later investment available, good horseman, huntsman, own typewriter and car.
>
> State-registered nurse wishes to find private nursing position, have worked for 15 years in a state hospital, best references.
>
> Police sergeant, retired 31 December 1935 after 17 years' service in Berlin's police force, 36 years old, in good health, likes work, writes well, is looking for office work, as messenger, or chauffeur, in a post requiring trustworthiness, driving licence.

Then there were the advertisements for marriage partners in conformity with the racial laws. Choice for young men and women was now limited. It was best if you did not look too Jewish.

> Businessman, mid-20s, ambitious, blond, is looking for a pretty, sympathetic girl, slim, if dowry is available that would be an advantage but not a condition, discretion assured.
>
> Young 21-year-old girl, no dowry, looking for life's companion not over 30 years.
>
> For my daughter early 30s, slim, sporty figure, wish to find a serious gentleman with a view to marriage, marriage will link him to an old established export firm in Hamburg.

It seems bizarre that in 1935 their exclusion also from the *Wehrmacht* was reconsidered.

IV

In March 1935 Hitler introduced conscription. As long as the armed forces were restricted to 100,000 under the Versailles Treaty it was not a problem, the army could cheerfully do without Jews and *Mischlinge*. The Aryan paragraph had been introduced in 1934. Now there were second thoughts. Conscription had drawn attention to them as a serious problem.[41] A meeting was called in May. It was agreed that Jews would continue to be excluded from the active fighting force – but what about the *Mischlinge*? How many *Mischlinge* were there in Germany? Expert calculations differed wildly. The most authoritative source was the

Reichsstelle für Sippenforschung (Office for Genealogical Research), which on 3 April 1935 came back with the response that there were 475,000 'full observant Jews', 300,000 full Jews who were not attached to the Jewish community, and three-quarters of a million *Mischlinge* with one or two Jewish grandparents. This was unwelcome news. It added up to a total of more than one and a half million. When the closest relatives of Aryan descent are added, the wife or husband, that figure could increase to at least 2 million, without adding uncles, aunts and grandparents – let alone cousins of the in-laws. Great care would have to be taken in handling this question without causing unrest. It was one thing dealing with half a million Jews; millions more disaffected Germans was quite another. The army command was more immediately concerned with the shortfall of recruits of military age and concluded that, if all were excluded on racial grounds, the loss of over 300,000, half of them *Mischlinge* and half of them Jews, had to be expected – far too many.

What should be done? It was unthinkable and irreconcilable with the party programme to accept Jews for active service. That would concede to them rights of full citizenship. They would be used only as an auxiliary labour force in war. The Military Law of 21 May 1935 and decree of 25 July 1935 assigned them to the Reserve II, a camouflage for whatever was decided to do with them. But as for the other non-Aryans, the *Wehrmacht* began to backtrack. Inconsistently, the Aryan paragraph was reconfirmed but exceptions were to be allowed. *Mischlinge* with one or two Jewish grandparents could volunteer for active service. They would have to appear before a commission, which had the unenviable task of taking a good look at the young men in order to reach conclusions of how 'Jewish' their appearance and demeanour was. Clearly, anyone with supposedly 'Jewish looks' need not bother to apply. Paradoxically, there were plenty of Jews with 'Aryan' features who would have passed muster had it not been for their excessive number of Jewish grandparents, and there were pure Aryans who seemed to look like Jews according to the Nazi stereotype. Alas, there was no safe way of making a judgement based on looks. Neither could Jews be caught parading as *Mischlinge* with certainty by inspecting them naked in front of the commissioners; circumcision for religious reasons had been abandoned by large numbers of Jews.[42] To reduce the numbers to be excluded, and so the problem, piecemeal attempts began to be made to distinguish *Mischlinge* and sub-divide them into those with just one or two Jewish grandparents. The Reich Ministry of the Interior paved the way in June when it became possible for newly qualified medical students who were one-quarter Jewish to be admitted as doctors.

The complexity of laws and the stream of directives that followed allowed room for different interpretations. There were times when the bureaucrats discussed at length the precise percentage of Jewish blood of an individual: on the outcome depended livelihoods and perhaps later even life. The bureaucrats behaved as if resolving purely technical problems. Jews and non-Aryans worried how and when, if ever, the party programme would be fulfilled.

V

That further legislation was intended had been rumoured and expected for months. Different proposals were put forward in articles, speeches and publications by ministerial spokesmen, knowledgeable professionals and party experts. It was widely expected that Jews would be deprived of citizenship and treated as aliens, that sexual relations and marriages between Jews and 'Germans' would be banned, that Jews still holding public office would be removed, that Jewish and German children in schools would be separated – beyond this there was uncertainty. Would the Jews be left in possession of their capital? Would they be allowed to continue in business? It was a pity they could not all simply be made to disappear. The talk was all about Jews, but in reality hundreds of thousands more people were involved, the so-called non-Aryans and anyone married to a Jew as well as their children. For these, knowing that their situation would only get worse, waiting for laws and decrees created stress when all they wanted was to be allowed to be German.

None of this clouded the days of Aryans. There were other grumbles. But Hitler was not blamed. He could not be everywhere at once. He was given credit for reducing crime and fighting in the streets. No one saw or wanted to know what happened behind the closed doors of the Gestapo cells or in the concentration camps. It affected only a few thousand anyway who, the rest thought, probably deserved to be there. Soon the world would be coming to the Olympic Games. Hitler was adulated from afar; Göring, approachable, with his black humour and expanding girth, was popular, and the little doctor, Joseph Goebbels, who spoke such beautiful melodious German that clothed his odious words, was not exactly loved but admired for his cleverness. Other leaders were less liked. Hess acted like a puppet on a string when he introduced his *Führer*; Robert Ley, head of the German Labour Front, was frequently drunk in public; Himmler kept himself in the background and was feared. The rest were less in the public eye. Party men who feathered their own nests and the army of bureaucrats were blamed for the ills of everyday life. Coffee and butter was in short supply, prices outstripped wages, but then, on the plus side, unemployment had fallen significantly. Hamburg's elite businessmen were nevertheless apprehensive as to where it was all heading. Mayor Krogmann thought they did not show the requisite enthusiasm for what had already been achieved.

With the fanaticism of a recent convert, Krogmann now had no time for weaklings not wholly committed to the Nazi cause. There were still too many doubters in Hamburg's mercantile circles without requisite conviction and enthusiasm. So, inflated with self-importance, unexpectedly made mayor despite his lack of experience or success in his own business, Krogmann seized the opportunity to lecture his more senior business colleagues. The occasion was the festive dinner of the East Asian Association in March 1935.

Krogmann got to his feet and began by praising the achievements of the Nazis. Admittedly they had rather passed Hamburg by, but that was a sacrifice that had to be made for the fatherland. His listeners were calculating and sober businessmen who were not easily impressed by so recently a junior colleague. He lectured them on 'the stupendous struggle of national socialist ideology ... a struggle without compromise ... of life and death'; then he went on to criticise their half-hearted attitudes. In one respect he was absolutely right; they could not simply pluck National Socialism into pieces, picking out the raisins, currants and almonds, 'they had to swallow the cake whole'. The German *Volk* would recover unity and greatness only when it grasped the crucial importance of race. Calling history to his aid, Krogmann pointed to Japan and England, 'which had closed its shores for a long time to foreign peoples'. The Jewish question was decisive, it had existed worldwide from the beginnings of time and not just in Germany: 'self-preservation demands that the *Volk* solve this question uncompromisingly.' The applause was no more than polite.

When Max Warburg read Krogmann's speech he sent a letter of protest to Emil Helfferich, the chairman of the association and head of the board of the Hamburg-America Line, one of the most influential businessmen in Hamburg, an opportunist of the first order.

> In the past two years, I have read so many sharp attacks on Jews that, sad to say, I am accustomed to much. What shocks me is not the manner of Mayor Krogmann's speech, but that such a speech could have been delivered by someone so prominent, especially in Hamburg. Whether such words will prove helpful for Hamburg's portal overseas, you and other exporters belonging to the East Asian Association can judge better than I ... Since when are the English one people stemming from a single race? Is not the population of England composed today of the descendants of Celts, Angles, Jutes and Saxons, and have they not mixed with Romans and Danes? And while we speak of England, can we ignore that Westminster Abbey houses a monument to one of England's most successful statesmen, Lord Beaconsfield, who before he was ennobled was called Disraeli? ... it is true at other times in world history 'solutions' of the Jewish problem have been less humane than now in Germany, as for instance in the pogroms of the Middle Ages ... but these were times when witches were burnt and the darkest superstitious beliefs prevailed ... True there are no bloody pogroms in Germany ... But what we have is a cold pogrom that has the cruellest consequences for the destiny of German Jews ... is it a solution of the Jewish question to destroy the way Jews and Christians have worked with each other? No solution can be found which simply ignores the proper claims of Jews that Germany is their home and fatherland.

The robust rebuttal was characteristic of Max Warburg. He continued to fight for the right of Jews to be Germans, for their place in the country of their birth. He felt sure that no personal harm could touch him. Nazi dominance would not last forever. Jews must hold on.

Max Warburg concluded from his experiences: 'What this shows, as I constantly stressed, is that friends at best behaved correctly, but never with courage.'[43] Among the longest associations going back to before the Great War was the bank's relationship with the shipbuilders Blohm & Voss, on whose board Max Warburg had sat for more than twenty years. He remained on the board until the age of seventy in 1937 and then was granted his wish to resign rather than fail to be re-elected. That same year Daimler-Benz also broke off their connections with the bank.

VI

The general public was not aware that the party and state were at loggerheads on the Jewish question, especially when it came to the role of Jews in business, as many still were in Hamburg. On 20 August 1935 a ministerial meeting took place in Berlin.[44] Hjalmar Schacht, minister for economy and *Reichsbank* president, was determined to gain the upper hand and began by complaining about the unauthorised excesses committed by the party which were damaging the German economy; antisemitic propaganda was to blame and was endangering the rearmament programme. Schacht agreed that the party programme had to be fulfilled, adding that this would have to be done on the basis of law and order, not by the arbitrary behaviour of individuals. Crucially important, raw materials – cotton, copper, nickel – could in many cases only be bought from Jews, as world trade was virtually in Jewish hands.

Wilhelm Frick said that there were measures his ministry was preparing but that they still had to be discussed with the deputy *Führer*. Adolph Wagner, Hitler's personal representative, rose next and conceded that excesses were doing harm; they showed up, he said, the differences that existed between the state and the party, but 80 per cent of the *Volk* were pressing for a solution to the Jewish question in accordance with the party programme. He continued that it was not necessary to do everything at once. It would suffice for the time being to take a few steps forward; it would be best to begin by concentrating on measures against 'full Jews', so that the drawing up of laws was not again held up over whether or not to include the *Mischlinge*.

Franz Gürtner, the justice minister, made an interesting observation: all Reich instructions would prove fruitless if the people believed that the regime really wanted to see official measures against Jews exceeded. Heydrich, waiting until the end of the discussion, weighed in with the demand that 'the influence of the Jews should be completely annihilated', mixed marriages forbidden, extra-marital intercourse between Aryans and non-Aryan, *Rassenschande* (racial defilement), punished, and restrictions placed on Jews who wished to move to larger cities.

On 9 September, the opening day of the Nuremberg Rally, Heydrich followed this up with a detailed memorandum sent to all the participants, headed 'Proposals for the Solution of the Jewish Question', which also now included placing restrictions on their role in the German economy. Hitler could not postpone action much longer.[45] Party frustration at the lack of progress had led to organised open attacks on Jews on Berlin's fashionable Kurfürstendamm. There were more attacks in Munich. In Hamburg people were just as keen to see 'progress' made. Drift could not continue, especially with the Winter Olympics due to open later that year in particularly Jew-phobic Bavaria.

It came as no surprise to anyone that the Jewish question in 1935 therefore took centre stage at Nuremberg.[46] Captured on film and newsreels, scenes from Nuremberg were shown all over Germany. Tens of thousands of Germans old and young, in many uniforms of brown, grey and black – Hitler Youth, workers, SS and party members – gathered to renew loyalty oaths and express their adoration for the *Führer*. On the stage-managed set Hitler delivered the opening oration, singling out Jewish Marxists at the head of Germany's internal and external enemies which would be vanquished. The party would take matters in hand if the state bureaucracy created too many obstacles. Hitler was playing to the gallery. Actually, he was far more circumspect, carefully weighing the alternatives. On the final day of the party rally, on 15 September, the ornamental *Reichstag* was summoned to meet in special session to be told to pass a flag law. There would be something more substantial as well now. Before the *Reichstag* met, Gerhard Wagner, Reich doctor leader, had already promised the party activists in a speech that a law would shortly be introduced to 'protect German blood'. The following day Hitler instructed the state secretaries of the Ministry of the Interior to summon their racial experts to Nuremberg to draft such a law. It was unlikely that Wagner spoke out of turn; Hitler was the initiator. The second law to be passed was the law on Reich citizenship, which Hitler in an earlier speech in Koenigsberg had declared was part of the party programme ripe to be fulfilled. Over the next six months, in heated debate, what was decided was not arcane detail but affected hundreds of thousands of Germans. Both the citizenship and blood laws raised similar problems: whether and how to distinguish between Jews and other non-Aryans. This had held up legislation before. Hitler wanted to end the long acrimonious debate.

The Reich Citizenship Law, 'unanimously' approved by the *Reichstag* on 15 September, was brief and simple. It distinguished between those who had the status of simply belonging to the Reich and full Reich citizens. Only those of German blood or compatible blood could be Reich citizens. That excluded Jews for sure, though they were not mentioned by name, and perhaps other non-Aryans as well. Future legislation would decide further ramifications.

The Law to Protect German Blood and German Honour, approved the same day, did specifically mention 'Jews' and forbade their marriage to those of German or German compatible blood, as well as 'intimate relationships' outside of marriage. That was vague. Did it mean only sexual intercourse? It was prohibited for Jews to employ in their households females below the child-bearing age of forty-five. Jews could no longer run up the German or swastika flag; they could, however, display 'Jewish colours'. Not many Jews were likely to draw attention to themselves by hoisting blue and white flags.

To hammer out the problem of the future position of the non-Aryans took a further two months of debate and draft after draft until a compromise was reached. The first supplementary decree of the Blood Law of 14 November was a complicated affair and needed to be read in conjunction with the supplementary decree of the Reich Citizenship Law of the same date. The decisions reached, though later refined, proved fundamental and decided whether tens of thousands would live or die during the war. The two Nuremberg Laws, for the Protection of German Blood and German Honour and the Reich Citizen Law, interlink and were progressively changed by thirteen subsequent decrees. Some non-Aryans benefited from the laws. Non-Aryans were now divided into two major categories, Jews and *Mischlinge* (those of mixed blood), who in turn were divided into two further categories, first and second degree. The *Mischlinge* did not suffer the same severity of discrimination as the Jews, as they remained, 'for the time being', full citizens of the Reich. Ominously, however, the *Mischlinge* of the first degree (two Jewish grandparents) were placed closer to the full Jews, in that they could only marry each other, and if they married a Jew would be treated as Jews, whereas the *Mischlinge* of the second degree could only marry Germans, and so would be even further removed from discrimination. The anomaly, because not dependent on the degree of Jewish blood, were the so-called *Geltungsjuden* – those descended from only two Jewish grandparents but who would be 'counted as Jews' because they had belonged to the Jewish community before the passage of the law (thus subsequent baptism would not help) or after – and *Mischlinge* who married a Jew or were descendants of an illegal union – *Rassenschande* – between a Jew and a German. The most significant decision in 1935 was to absorb the non-Aryans with only one Jewish grandparent into the German *Volk*. Hitler had drawn a red line here that was never changed. Though not freed from all discrimination, at least their children would no longer be classified as *Mischlinge*.

The Nuremberg Laws did hit one defenceless group of good Germans (Aryans) particularly hard. Domestic service was a major employment opportunity for women from poor families. Some had served their Jewish families for decades and bonds of affection and intimacy had developed. Hitler, to emphasise the principle of the Blood Law, had been keen on the provision that no women under the age of forty-five could be employed in a Jewish household. This was felt by the Jewish families to be a particular slur, implying the master of the house might seduce the domestic. But there were second thoughts between September and November. The supplementary directive lowered the age to thirty-five. The Reich employment office had calculated that between 100,000 and 150,000 employees in Jewish households would lose their jobs. Lowering the age limit reduced the number. Hitler was angry at the bureaucrats but allowed the change to stand.[47]

In Hamburg, there was a bizarre sequel. The Welfare Office tried to reduce its burdens by requiring unemployed Aryan women over the age of thirty-five to take up the domestic positions in Jewish households vacated by the younger women. One 'German' lady, however, refused to work for Jews. Should she be required to do so? In the end *Reichsstatthalter* Kaufmann had to decide, and he found in favour of the recalcitrant domestic.

For the overwhelming majority of millions of Germans, the Nuremberg Laws were just an affirmation of the Nazis' stand against the Jews. It did not affect them. True, many knew a decent Jew – a shopkeeper who had served them well, or perhaps the doctor who used to look after their children. It was a pity that the sins of some Jews should fall on all of them. The Christian partners of mixed marriages and their children who were directly affected by the laws scrutinised them fearfully, no one more so than Luise Solmitz.

VII

Luise anxiously read the newspapers and listened to the radio to discover where the next blow might fall.[48] Then on the eve of the Nuremberg rally she came across a newspaper article that made her fear for Gisela and even her marriage:

> Berlin, 10 September telegraphic communication. Reich Minister Rust has issued a decree that Jewish schools are to be set up Easter 1936. The criteria which determine who belongs in them is not the Jewish religion but the Jewish race. The Jewish schools will admit not only racial full Jews but also half-Jews. But pupils who have only one set of Jewish grandparents will not be forced to go …. It is clear from the decree that secondary schools for the time being are not affected. But a decree applying to secondary schools is in preparation ….
>
> As this news was broadcast over the radio … Gisela sat behind me and saw my face in the mirror on the dressing table. We acted unconcerned. That evening she said she would leave school …

On 15 November 1935 The family stayed glued to the radio. At 9 p.m. the *Führer* spoke: three new racial laws, the details would be announced later. Gisela had gone to bed. When later Luise went upstairs to Gisela's bedroom, her daughter was wide awake. 'Has he already said anything? I am so afraid. I am not only thinking about myself but also of the others who will be affected.' And then at around midnight the racial laws were announced over the radio. Luise's reaction was that they were 'the death sentence of our civic life'. Jews racially defined could no longer be Reich citizens. Future marriages between Germans and Jews were forbidden, as were sexual relations outside of marriage. Jews may not raise the Reich flag, hoist 'the Jewish' colours, nor employ domestic help under the age of forty-five. Lore, their domestic, had worked for them long and happily. Luise Solmitz gave vent to despair.

> 15.9.1935. For the second time our black–white–red flag is gone. Whoever marries my daughter goes to prison and she as well; our domestic help has to be dismissed; we are no longer permitted to hang out our flag – Jewish

flags we have no knowledge of, just tolerated – I may live in my fatherland as a foreigner … At least a feeling of happiness that we carry the
burden together … and in the end there is for us three a last escape possible. How comforting this last possibility is one only realises on days such
as these … up to now we still have our house and pension and are thankful
for that.

25.9.1935. Cousin Ernst telephoned from Berlin … He was in Berlin,
they have progressed further there. No one talks to a Jew or offers him their
hand, in Kempinski [a well-known restaurant] they sit by themselves in a
corner.

30.9.1935. Information over the radio. Marriages concluded before the
19.9.1935 are not included in the law forbidding marriages [of Jews and
Germans]. Apparently there was apprehension, doubts and even despair on
that score. That was something that never entered my head and I refuse to
consider even if it became law.

13.10.1935. Dr Frick [minister of the interior] announces that the
detailed regulations of the Nuremberg Laws will be published in the next
few days. We constantly live with a sword hanging over us. One has to for-
tify oneself for what is certain to come, that is all that is left …

Repeatedly she feared for her daughter. As husband and wife, Luise wrote,
they had had good lives, but Gisela's future was bleak. 'What did she have to
look forward to, fifteen years old on the threshold of womanhood?'

28.10.1935. That Gisela with a wan smile says to her own mother, 'I am
afraid. I am afraid every day.' To have to hear this and not to be able to
help. Normally parents are the protectors, helpers and comforters, but we
are just as helpless as she is … however hard you try to learn a profession,
you are not allowed to enter any … no friendly hand is permitted to help
you, no friend or relative can provide you with support. You may well be
afraid from day to day ….

6.11.1935. Fredy met Dr Rosenstein, our throat specialist; he told him
he is still entitled to see insurance patients, but he sits alone during surgery
hours. Too old to pass new state exams once more in a foreign country, he
is considering Russia, where this is not required … Dr R. was a doctor on
the front line. Gisela told me she did not want to go to school any more. It
was clear every day from the address of the headmaster that she would be
expelled. She looks terribly wretched and ill.

15.11.1935. The directives [covering the Nuremberg Laws] have been
made public …. I glanced quickly through them to find out whether there
was anything comforting in them. And there was something, the *Führer*
can allow exceptions. Gisela is not Jewish but a *Mischling*, and may with
special permission marry a German or a *Mischling* with only one Jewish
grandparent … I am writing all this down in a jumble without referring to

the newspapers as Fredy is at this moment writing his letter to the *Führer*. Maybe he will be successful, appointed a civil servant before the war, participated in thirty-three engagements, Iron Cross first class, etc. All Jewish civil servants are to be retired, but with full salary without enhancements until they reach retirement age and then will receive their pension! This lifts one of our great worries. What my position is is not mentioned – there is enough of bad news – Fredy has no right to vote, whether I have I do not know. No professional chances for Gisela. Still it does sound different than at Nuremberg [Party Congress] ... with the thirty-five age limit for domestics the situation is that anyone who already employs one above the age of thirty-five may keep her. While Fredy is writing his letter to the *Führer*, I am listening to Beethoven's sixth symphony in the darkness of the sitting room ... hundreds of thoughts and moods pass through my mind ... will bitterness or hope gain the upper hand ... whether one may breathe a little more freely, perhaps yes ...

Between hope and despair, the Solmitzes counted on the success of Major Solmitz's appeal to Hitler. They would then be able to rejoin their German roots and, above all, Gisela's future would be secured. He had already appealed in vain to Frick the interior minister on behalf of Gisela to remain in the League of German Girls. No reply was received from Hitler. One can only speculate how the Solmitzes would have reacted had the *Führer* shown understanding and leniency. Would they then have been able to turn away from the injustices inflicted on the Jews and the less fortunate in their eagerness to embrace the German fatherland? It was not to be. As time passed their situation deteriorated and the concessions made to the *Mischlinge* were one by one taken away again. Their situation seemed even worse than that of the Jews, whom Luise Solmitz almost envied:

18.12.1935. ... they find support in relations with each other and their belief. We have nothing, nothing, nothing in common with them, those to whom we do belong will allow us to be driven into isolation because that is what is desired ... all the relatives in Berlin are successful, and moving forward we may not retain a domestic ...

17.9.1936 'In the name of the *Führer* and chancellor I inform you herewith that your application to be freed from the provisions of the supplementary requirements of the Reich Citizenship Law and the Blood Law out of considerations of principle can not be acceded to. The decision is final.' It is exactly a year on 15.11.35 since Fredy's first application ... A policeman gave to Gisela the important communication and enclosures. She brought it upstairs to us. We knew immediately that this was the decision. I had little hope. But we were silent, then spoke matter of factly and were silent again as the news hit us deeply. As we were opening the letter we had a glimmer of hope. When Fredy left the room I would have liked to have burst into tears. But only a few tears came, not comforting ones, tears of hopelessness … tears that are held back frozen in bitterness. Who can feel with me the isolation from the *Volk*, the rootlessness of a 'wife married to a Jew'; she must find from her inner strength the determination 'I will remain with you', my *Volk*, my fatherland. Most, like myself, will reject the Jewish association …

Before going to bed Gisela said to me, 'I am quite clear and accept that I will have only a short life; that is how times are. Perhaps I will be dead in a year and not a natural death' – that is what a sixteen-year-old girl says to her mother … A bitter day. Let us not lose faith with what is within and over us …

Luise Solmitz began to experience the abrupt ending of old friendships out of fear that association with anyone branded as belonging to a Jewish household could lead to unpleasant consequences.

29.9.1937. A peculiar day which I will never forget. Something has occurred which I could not have thought possible, nothing good, the end of a friendship of forty-eight years …

I visited Lene [name changed] at the institute and said to her I wanted to find out why we had not heard from her and her relatives for such a long time. She replied, 'Let's talk about this frankly. It is best as I am not allowed to visit you. You will know why and that it is not owing to anything personal. I actually continued to come to you although as a civil servant I was not allowed to. I thought about it frequently whether I should go on doing so. I came to the conclusion that it was impossible. Everyone has enemies and one has to reckon with the possibility this could be used against one. I can understand that this touches you deeply, but other times can come again.' I got up and replied, 'Then we have nothing more to say to each other.' … That my oldest blood-related friend and schoolfriend is the first zealously to hide behind a decree so that no one can officially attack her for not acting correctly, and is so weak from a human point of view, that hurts. But perhaps my opinion of her is not just. I cannot expect her to risk her living … but I do not wish to adhere to a *Volk* that allows itself to be ordered not to keep faith with a friend … do you have to move morally on all fours? All our friends and acquaintances holding positions in the state as well as the private people will be forbidden contact with us and then every *Volksgenosse* ….

Celebrating peace, preparing for war

1936 was an unforgettable year in Hamburg and throughout Germany. The Olympic Games symbolised friendly contest between athletes of all races and nationalities.

The teams from overseas would catch their first glimpse of Nazi Germany when they arrived in Hamburg. In July, the *SS Manhattan* docked at the *Überseebrücke* with the United States sportsmen and women. As they came ashore, a large crowd which had expectantly assembled cheered. A band struck up. There were welcoming speeches from the dignitaries in English and German. Then a fleet of buses took them to the impressive neo-Gothic *Rathaus*. After more speeches and toasts and a champagne reception, the team was taken to the station to board the efficient fast express to Berlin. A sea of swastika flags everywhere. So this was Nazi Germany – not what they had expected. Only the six Jewish members of the US team were left uneasy by their reception. The Nazis seized the opportunity to present the new Germany and made their visitors welcome. Perhaps the Third Reich was not so bad after all. Not everyone was so easily deceived, but who would have imagined that at this very moment Hitler and his helpers were laying the foundations for waging war and the 'final solution'?

War was the last thing on everybody's mind. After years of humiliation and weakness, Germans were thrilled by the ease of Hitler's successes. Exhilarating times: in March 1935 the Saar was reincorporated, and the same month, with conscription, the military restrictions of Versailles were unilaterally denounced. A year later, the biggest coup so far, another Hitler spring surprise, complete sovereignty was restored over the Rhineland, and all without sacrifice. The icing on the cake was the Olympic Games. Germany was riding high.

Hitler had promised to transform Germany within four years, and he had fulfilled his promise even sooner. From 6 million unemployed in January 1933, in the year of the Olympics the number of those out of work had fallen to just over 2.5 million, and when rearmament was accelerated Germany enjoyed full employment. It was less welcome that prices had increased and so cancelled out wage increases.

I

In Hamburg, times were less rosy.[49] Dependent on overseas trade, the city suffered badly from the economic policies of self-sufficiency and the lack of foreign currency. Twice as many families remained on welfare support than in the rest of Germany: one in seven in 1934 and over 100,000 in 1936, still one in twelve. So, as late as 1936, Hamburg was designated a special relief area. But the economic situation had significantly improved here too and the shipbuilding yards were busy again. One deficit – industry was now dependent largely on orders from Berlin.

There were other downsides. For those in work the standard of living was still modest. Not until 1937 were real incomes as high as they were before the Depression. There were shortages too with luxuries like coffee and butter, and overseas produce was obtainable only in small quantities. The rise of the price of potatos on which the working class relied as a cheap staple food to feed the family aroused particular resentment.[50] The hours of weekly work increased. Göring's slogan 'guns before butter' aroused little enthusiasm. The mood of working people remained dour, and they resented particularly the corruption and overweening behaviour of upstart party officials.

Welfare officers followed the attitude of the workers, and their reports make interesting reading.[51] In St Georg and Hammerbrook, previously 'completely red', greetings of '*Heil Hitler*' were met with 'good morning'. In the poorer part of Winterhude, the Rehmstraße was reputed to be communist, with many men in concentration camps; also in the BarmbeckerStraße and Geibelstraße the people were reported as 'strongly Marxist-communist and difficult to satisfy'. The welfare officers' efforts of 'persuasion' were of little avail. They were rightly suspected of acting hand in glove with the Nazis as spies for the Gestapo.

Amid all the fanfare, the 'other Germans' were in the shadows. The handicapped lived under constant fear of sterilisation. A communist hard core of workers had to be careful: if caught in now illegal activities, they were savagely sentenced; the worst offenders were executed, and the best outcome was a concentration camp. Reports of the barbaric behaviour in Gestapo prisons and of beatings in concentration camps were widespread. But was it not your own fault if you landed yourself there? Asocials, homosexuals and the Marxist leadership belonged in them, most people thought. If they kept out of active opposition, even the former rank-and-file Communist Party worker was left unharmed. The *Führer* could not be blamed for everything that went wrong.

Propaganda tried to cover the defects. Every family would one day drive their own people's car, the *Volkswagen*; the 'Strength through Joy' organisation offered worker holidays on cruise ships – once a luxury confined to the rich; the German Workers' Front (DAF) provided cut-price affordable entertainment. The DAF organised the free time of its 23 million members – theatre performances, excursions, concerts, talks and educational courses – everything at minimal cost. It was bribery on a grand scale. Jewish property could be advantageously acquired, replacing a Jewish superior secured professional advancement – opportunities which provided benefits by happy chance. Tens of thousands profited from the racial state.

You could either choose to support the Nazis, take advantage of opportunities that came your way – provided you were not a Jew – or just go along with the tide, risking nothing by 'inner dissent'. Active opposition was the choice of a brave few. The great majority backed Hitler. Plebiscites and elections were rigged to show 90 per cent support, but, even had this not been the case, Hitler would have enjoyed majorities democratic parties could only dream about.

But more than a million Germans were left out of the consenting *Volk* community. The fate of the racially unfit and those deemed biologically unfit would be decided by definitions, labels and the calculations of the state. What was not conceivable was that millions would be murdered when the opportunity of war five years later made it possible.

II

Five interlinked circles symbolise the Olympic ideals. Nothing was spared to make the German games a success. If 'bread' was short, 'circuses' lifted morale. The spectacle of the superior Aryan race was marred for diehard Nazis by the spectacular success of the black athletes. The games might never have come to Garmisch and Berlin. The racial Nazi ideology at first threw the suitability of Germany into serious doubt. Black athletes from the United States threatened boycott. The Nuremberg Laws passed three months before the opening of the winter games were an added shock. The regime did its best to play down the blatant discrimination. The German News Agency issued a statement on 17 September 1935 that the Nuremberg Laws had now established 'absolutely clear relations between the German *Volk* and the Jewish people'.[52] Had not the international Zionist Congress itself declared that the Jews are a separate people?

> The new laws give the Jewish minority in Germany their own cultural life, their own national life. In future they will be able to shape their own schools, their own theatres, their own sports associations; in short, they can create their own future in all aspects of national life.

What they would no longer be permitted to do was to interfere 'in the national affairs of the German nation ... The German people is convinced that these laws have performed a healing and useful deed for Jewry in Germany, ... [leading to] more tolerable relations between the two nations.' The announcement glossed over Hitler's statement two days earlier that a solution had been found of '*perhaps* creating a basis on which the German people might possibly be able to find a tolerable relationship with the Jewish people'. The laws were, he said, 'an attempt at a legal regulation of a problem'; but he then threatened that, if this did not succeed, the solution would be handed over to the party.

The *Reichsvertretung* also issued a declaration: 'The laws approved by the *Reichstag* in Nuremberg have most deeply disturbed the Jews in Germany', and added, more in hope and faith,

> They should, however, create a basis which will make possible a tolerable relationship between the German and Jewish people ... Conditional for such a tolerable relationship is the expectation that Jews will be allowed the possibility of a moral and economic existence with the ending of defamation and boycott.[53]

Was it perhaps an indication of a new relationship that the invitation to the participating nations was signed by a 'half-Jew'?

Theodor Lewald was a non-Aryan. Before 1933 he had been the most prominent civil servant promoting sport. It was Lewald who had been placed in charge of preparations for the Olympic Games while Kaiser Wilhelm was still on the throne. He worked tirelessly for the games to be held in Berlin. In 1932, as the Weimar Republic was entering its death throes, he succeeded. Lewald was made president of the German preparatory committee, which assembled for the first time just six days before Hitler became chancellor. He then offered to resign, but for the International Committee his continued presence was a test that Nazi racial ideology would not be allowed to infect the games. A year earlier, Hitler had denounced the Olympics as 'an invention of Jews and freemasons'; now he grasped its propaganda value and granted Lewald a personal meeting, shaking the old man's hand. However distasteful this was to him, Hitler kept his feelings under wraps. When Lewald complained about attacks on him in the *Völkischer Beobachter*, the official party paper, Hitler ordered they cease. Promises of no racial discrimination of Jewish sportsmen and women were given and broken.

Having by one means or another excluded most Jews from the German team, just three non-Aryans were invited to return from exile: the fencer Helene Mayer, fortunately blond and a model of Aryan looks, winner of the gold medal in 1928 and an exile in California; the champion high jumper Gretel Bergmann, who had emigrated to England; and Rudi Ball, recalled from abroad to join the ice-hockey team – a distasteful concession to dispel international suspicions. Rudi Ball's story is the most extraordinary of all the three.[54] Dropped in 1933 as a half-Jew by his ice-hockey club, the renowned sportsman found it easy to leave and join a Swiss team. An obvious choice for the German Olympics, the organisers tried to disbar him until a teammate threatened to withdraw. There was no chance then of a medal without both players, so Rudi Ball was reluctantly invited. The aftermath sounds incredible if it were not true. Rudi Ball stayed in Germany after 1936, played for the Berliner SC until 1944, and helped his team to win the German championship. After the war he emigrated to South Africa.

On 6 February 1936, Hitler opened the winter Olympic Games in Garmisch-Partenkirchen. The participation of a half-Jew in Germany's national team was all the more galling after what had happened in Davos just two days earlier. Wilhelm Gustloff, a leading Nazi in Switzerland, was assassinated by a Jew. Telegrams were urgently sent to Hamburg and *Gauleiters* all over Germany to prevent any 'spontaneous' demonstrations and attacks on Jews. With the games safely under way, a week later, at Gustloff's funeral, Hitler raged in a speech broadcast in Hamburg and throughout Germany:[55]

> An endless line of murdered National Socialists, assassinated in dastardly fashion march before our eyes … Behind every murder is the same power which is responsible for this crime, the hate-inspired influence of our Jewish foes … We have done nothing to harm the enemy, yet he tries to place the German people beneath his yoke and make them his slaves … a guiding hand organised these crimes and will continue to do so …. We understand the declaration of war, and we will respond. My dear party comrade, your death was not in vain!

But nothing was allowed to disrupt the games in Berlin that summer.[56] Forty-nine nations sent athletes. In round after round of glittering receptions Nazi Germany wooed the *Ehrengäste*, the guests of honour. The public were caught up in the excitement. Anti-Jewish notices disappeared for the duration in places where a foreigner might stumble upon them. In the stadium, Helene Mayer performed splendidly, won silver and, as a proud German, raised her right arm in salute. She was actually a Jewess according to the Nuremberg Laws. Although her mother was Christian, her father had inscribed his daughter in the Offenbach synagogue as a child, so she was classified a 'full-Jew', *a Geltungsjude*, which in later life she found a handicap and longed to be accepted as a German. Another Jewess, Gretel Bergmann, expected to compete after the German Olympic Committee had asked her to return. She was a natural choice. No one in the world had exceeded the height she had already jumped. She actually began training in Germany. But was it all a cynical ploy to counter the strong protest movement among American athletes? As soon as the US athletes had set sail she was dropped for spurious reasons. The spectacle of the crowd enthusiastically singing 'Deutschland über alles', while another Jewess was crowned with gold, would have been too much for the Nazis to stomach. Better to forego a precious gold medal. Black athletes, male and female, dominated the games. Jesse Owens was the popular hero, winning four gold medals. Good natured, he was the darling of thousands of Germans, who cheered his spectacular victories. Sudden surges of goodwill could overcome years of denegrating propaganda, but were just as easily reversed.

III

The games were scarcely over when Hitler empowered Göring to call a meeting to prepare the country for war, 'to meet the Bolshevik-Jewish menace'.[57] The stage was set for action on two linked fronts: to accelerate production of everything needed for war and to rid Germany of the Jews within the Reich. The overall direction of the economy was handed to Göring, the second most powerful man in the Reich, in the guise of placing him in charge of the publicly proclaimed Second Four-Year Plan. The true aim was set out in a long secret memorandum written by Hitler, read out to the assembled functionaries.

Hitler began the harangue with his repetitive cosmic ideology depicting the clashes of civilisations over the millennia. World Jewry and Bolshevism were the threat no nation could escape. The strength of the Red Army was growing, the democracies were feeble and Germany remained the bulwark of civilisation. Time was running out: the German people faced extermination unless they struck in time. They had heard it all before. What followed, however, was not nebulous.

The time had come for a ruthless mobilisation. Schacht's more orthodox approach was jettisoned. Priorities were the production of substitute gasoline and synthetic rubber. If private industry did not accomplish the targets, the state would take over; *Ersatz*, substitution, was the order of the day. Germany had to become 100 per cent self-sufficient. Laws would make economic sabotage punishable by death. The German people would have to accept sacrifices. The task of the Four-Year Plan was to mobilise the economy and the army to ready Germany for war in four years. Jews were not omitted. Hitler's visceral hatred spilled out. The whole of criminal Jewry would be made responsible for any damage to the economy if any single Jew dared to sabotage rearmament.

No time was lost. The state secretaries of the Reich Ministry of the Interior and the Ministry for the Economy, together with the representatives of the Deputy *Führer*, next met to discuss detailed laws to deal with the 'Jewish question'. The party spokesman made the simple point: 'The Jewish question can only be regarded as solved when there are no more Jews in Germany. Anything now decided would only be a partial solution. It is therefore just a question of pace and the extent of individual measures to be taken.' When they had all finished talking, Wilhelm Stuckart, state secretary at the Ministry of the Interior, drew together the consensus.[58] There were no differences of opinion about the final objective. It would only be attained by the wholesale emigration of the Jews. But this could only be achieved in stages. The pace would be determined by what was of greatest benefit to the German people. It would be limited by what was possible. The policy should be based on encouraging their emigration to the greatest extent possible. The participation of Jews in the economy should be permitted to enable them to exist but not to improve their well-being, which would weaken their desire to leave. '*In the last resort, the departure of the Jews by force would have to be considered.*' Their exclusion from the economy for the moment was not possible. There were still branches where they dominated and where an Aryan business could not be substituted. They were also essential in the export trade for earning foreign currency. Pressure would be exercised forbidding such groups as civil servants from purchasing in Jewish shops, but Hitler had specifically forbidden that Jewish shops should be identified – a temporary reprieve.

A chilling phrase was now in the open: 'in the last resort', the Jews remaining would be removed 'by force' – in other words, deportation. To where? Somewhere outside Germany. What did Stuckart and the others have in mind? What if other countries refused to accept them all, which had become obvious in 1936. The island of Madagascar, talked about for many years, did not belong to the Germans. In the coming war, German *Lebensraum* would be won in the East with the destruction of the Bolshevik danger. There would be possibilities there. The millions of Bolshevik Jews would not be spared. The Jews would be gone one way or another. The ministers and their civil servants were happy not to think this through. That is how the fate of Hamburg's Jews and of the Jews throughout the Reich was being settled around the conference table by men in respectable suits.

IV

Prospects for the Jews rapidly grew darker behind the scenes while outwardly the year following the Nuremberg Laws was a 'quiet' one. For those in the know, what happened in 1938 came as no surprise. It had been planned, only the precise timing of the blows to be delivered depended on the international situation, the pace of rearmament and the unfolding of Hitler's war plans. From the grassroots there were plenty of suggestions, however.

Party pundits, lawyers, 'experts' and all and sundry put forward their own ideas of how to solve the 'Jewish question'. It was good to be seen to be working towards the *Führer*. They all reached much the same conclusion. Germany had to be free of Jews, who would be forced to leave by whatever means necessary. The special Jewish section of Himmler's Security Service also was just as unoriginal. The Jew, the Gestapo concluded in 1937, was the enemy of National Socialism, exercising his influence through the freemasons, liberals, Marxists and, not least, Christianity.

Hitler was content for the groundswell to grow. When he felt the time was ripe he communicated his decision often verbally; more rarely he initiated ideas. Usually he directed and guided the plans of others, choosing which of the options to follow and sometimes adding a crucial change to the proposals put before him. Among those engaged in working for the 'final solution' was the SD, the secret intelligence security service of the SS.[59] It was led by Reinhard Heydrich, assisted by Adolf Eichmann. The SD had been set up to provide surveillance of 'enemies', defined as Jews, freemasons, Jesuits and Bolsheviks. An ever expanding card index was built up based on reports from a network of unpaid informers. Among the enemies surveyed, increasing attention after 1936 was paid to the Jews by a sub-section of department Roman II, with a numerical identification 112. Serving on its staff was Adolf Eichmann, a young Nazi who had escaped from Austria. After the unsuccessful Nazi putch in 1934, he spent some time in the service of the SS in the Dachau concentration camp and was then transferred to the SD in Berlin. Initially assigned to the surveillance of freemasons, he was next moved to observe Zionism. Learning some elementary Hebrew gained him the reputation of an expert.

Underlying SD activities was unreality.[60] There were no nefarious plots to be unearthed either within Germany or by a worldwide Jewish-Bolshevik conspiracy. The periodic reports on the Jewish organisations and the freemasons compiled by the security service put together much information readily available in print, only adding their own observations. Eichmann's more ambitious effort in 1937 to coordinate intelligence with informants inside the British Palestine Mandate failed to produce any results.

The SD saw itself as an educated elite within Himmler's sprawling empire, a think tank on the Jewish question. The trouble was that their ideas before 1939, only repeating what others said, were too general to be of much use. The detailed legislation was drafted not by the Gestapo but by Frick's Ministry of the Interior and by the Ministry for the Economy and leading civil servants such as State Secretary Wilhelm Stuckart. It was civil servants and their ministerial heads who performed the bulk of the work before 1939. Despite his suspicions and occasional objections, Hitler left initiatives to them, adjudicating mainly on details and timing. So far, they were only dealing with plans for the future of German Jews and non-Aryans. They were all aware that there would be problems of quite a different order once war began; millions of Jews would then fall into their hands and would have to be dealt with. Research on the numbers was already under way. But, for now, the focus was on making the territory of the Reich *judenrein*, free of Jews. Everyone was agreed that emigration was the only practicable solution with Germany and the world at peace. Nor was there any originality in the proposition that the next phase was to exclude them from the German economy and make their life as unbearable as possible to hasten their departure.

Eichmann supported the idea of popular pogroms to intimidate the Jews.[61] The time for that was not yet ripe. But he did make one practical proposal. Emigration was delayed because the Jews had first to secure clearance from several different authorities: the Finance Office to verify they had paid all the taxes due; bizarrely, the police for a certificate of good conduct; the Passport Office – and so on. Eichmann suggested that the SD should set up a central office to coordinate all this efficiently. After the *Anschluss* (annexation) of Austria in March 1938, Eichmann was sent to Vienna to try this out. The office he set up began work in August 'processing' Austrian Jews and was judged a success. The SD had shown that it could get things done, knock heads together, forcing the civil servants to abandon old habits so as ruthlessly to subordinate everything to further the single aim to remove as many Jews as possible in the shortest time. Central organisations were later set up in Berlin and Prague. Heydrich and Eichmann had proved their organising abilities to Himmler and Hitler. Gestapo and SD increasingly coordinated their work.

The reports of the SD during the years 1934 to 1938 based on a network of confidential agents in Germany do contain some nuggets of interest about popular feelings.[62] From Erfurt, there was unreserved approval of the Nuremberg Laws but regret that the better off continued to buy from Jewish shops and, to avoid being seen, telephoned their requirements and arranged for their purchases to be delivered. In Bielefeld, placards were on display: 'Jews need not spy here'; 'Whoever knows a Jew, knows the devil'; 'Traveller rest here provided you are not a Jew'; and a Jewish grave was dug up by a group of young men who had heard a rumour that the deceased had taken with him 3,000 *Marks*. But in Brackwede, the attempt by two party followers to deter buyers from entering a Jewish department store misfired. A large number of people ostentatiously went in and left by another door without buying anything. In Paderborn a crowd demonstrated before the town hall because it was said that the wife of a city civil servant had purchased goods in a Jewish shop. Unfortunately, many *Volksgenossen*, the agent observed, were still friendly with Jews. The Jews everywhere were reported to be very quiet, as they now recognised after the Nuremberg Laws that they enjoyed only guest status. The trade of the smaller Jewish shops had shrunk by three-quarters, but the public still patronised the department stores. More interesting was a comment that Aryan employees in Jewish enterprises were anxious that boycotts of Jewish businesses would lead to the loss of their jobs and they hoped these businesses would soon pass into German hands. From Hannover, in November 1935, came an observation that the mood of the people, especially the working people, was unfavourable to the regime; meantime the Jews, the agent wrote, were anxiously waiting for the directives that would follow.

V

The Nuremberg Laws created a new crime, *Rassenschande*, racial defilement.[63] What exactly constituted the offence was not made entirely clear – whether intercourse, petting or just holding hands. The law cleverly absolved Aryan females from punishment for denouncing a Jewish male, but Jewish females were punished as well as their Aryan partners. The law was a serious danger to Jewish men entering new relationships and tragic for those in partnerships outside of marriage.

In competition with the Gestapo, judges were under pressure to prove their own Nazi credentials and competence to keep *Rassenschande* within their jurisdiction by interpreting widely what constituted sexual encounters. The sentences passed were arbitrary and could be severe or mild depending on the attitude of a particular judge. The courts worked in close collaboration with the Gestapo, which investigated and could initiate proceedings. Gustav Schmidt, an unsavory character of little education, headed the Gestapo unit dealing with *Rassenschande* in Hamburg and after 1940 became responsible for homosexual offences as well. Schmidt was the fifth son of eleven children, born in 1901 to parents of modest means. He had had a hard youth. At the tender age of eleven he contributed to the family income by working on farms. In 1921 he joined the Hamburg police force. As an interrogator of *Rassenschande* cases he took pleasure in threatening and abusing the female witnesses to extract confessions and forwarded the evidence to the public prosecutor.

Racial defilement was a favourite charge used by the Gestapo against Jews they wished to finish off. One Jew they never lost sight of in Hamburg was Max Eichholz. His courageous but foolish insistence on his rights as a lawyer had humiliated the Gestapo in 1935. Soon after this he was arrested but released. On 9 November 1938 he was sent with the other Hamburg Jews to the Sachsenhausen concentration camp, but once more was released. In March 1939 he was arrested again on the pretext of having had sexual intercourse with a German and sentenced by a judge to five years in prison. While other Jews were able to leave the concentration camps on being able to show that they had a visa enabling them to emigrate, when *Frau* Eichholz went to the Gestapo to appeal for his release from prison the official declined to intervene with the legal process and replied vindictively, 'We are delighted we have him at last. Make sure that you get away, or we will arrest you as well. Forget your husband. There are plenty of other men around.' *Frau* Eichholz emigrated from Germany and was able to save herself; Max Eichholz perished in Auschwitz.

There were a few old school officials in Hamburg and Germany to whom Jews could turn for advice, but many former Weimar civil servants embraced Nazi ideology with the enthusiasm of converts. In Hamburg, there were also new Nazi appointments of civil servants who had no previous Weimar positions. One of these was the senator, as Hamburg's ministers were called, responsible for the Welfare Office since October 1933, Friedrich Ofterdinger, a vicious Nazi, a medical doctor and an active member of the party since 1929. His responsibilites included the sterilisation of the undesirables pursued with particular vigour in Hamburg.[64] The 'supervision' of 'asocial' and 'gypsy' families as well as Jewish families was part of his remit.

Until 1938, the Nazi Reich authorities were careful how they depicted their treatment of the Jews to the rest of the world.[65] The vicious discrimination was presented as reasonable, as the justified defence of the 'German' people against the overwhelming 'Jewish alien' influence, and even as of benefit to the Jews themselves, by encouraging them to develop their own equal and separate cultural life as a people. Impoverished Jewish families still shared in the handouts of the street collections for the *Winterhilfe* (winter aid) until the winter of 1935. Thereafter they organised their own Jewish aid, though Jewish businesses had to continue contributing to the 'German' *Winterhilfe* as well. Jews in need were supposed to receive the same public assistance, but that was too lax for keen local Nazi administrators. How might the directives from the ministry be supplemented? Shared experiences would provide useful answers. In June 1937, representatives of municipal and state authorities met to compare their practices.[66] Dr Oskar Martini, head of Hamburg's Welfare Office since 1920, contributed his views that the Jews should be treated as if they were foreigners, that they should receive only the necessities of life and nothing more. He detailed good Hamburg practice: no training for young unemployed Jews, for the blind, the deaf and dumb or cripples to make it possible for them to secure employment. Since 1933, Hamburg's Welfare Office had cut the minimum support laid down by Reich laws and required the Jewish community to make good the shortfall. Two-thirds of the cost of sick children sent to the countryside for convalescence now had to be found by the Jewish community and poor Jewish children no longer received free school meals; assistance to pay the fees of Jewish children attending secondary schools was also no longer granted. Jewish adults required to work for benefits were placed in a separate work camp, foreshadowing wartime practice.

In Hamburg, the Welfare Office early on in 1933 cleared out from their positions Jews and non-Aryans, previously trusted and respected honorary guardians of young men and women in need of help and guidance and confidential Jewish doctors, to whom cases were referred. The 105 non-Aryan doctors advising the Hamburg Welfare Office were a problem, as twenty-one were veterans qualifying for exemptions. All had been removed already two months before the Nuremberg Laws; Hamburg was ahead of the times. The only medical practice left open to non-Aryans and Jews was private practice, including insurance work, if they managed to be accepted as having served at the front in the First World War.

Those in the civil service in Hamburg and Germany adjusted to new norms, conscientiously serving their new masters as they had done the old during the democratic Weimar years. For them it seems it was just a matter of new 'rules'. Typical of this type was the respected Dr Martini, whose relations with the Jewish staff had been close and friendly before Hitler came to power. His career continued onwards and upwards during the Nazi years. There was plenty of scope for making access to welfare more difficult for Jews than for *Volksgenossen*. Jews in need wherever possible were placed in institutions financed by the Jewish community. One welfare officer in 1937 thought it worthy of note that some Jewish mothers were still attending advisory clinics with their babies.[67]

> The behaviour of these Jewish mothers is modest and reticent, so that no particular difficulties are encountered in the waiting rooms. But mothers with babies or small children whose health requires more intensive care are told to come either before or after the official hours to avoid any incidents.

Why should there have been an incident? Was it feared that Aryan mothers would resent waiting if a doctor or nurse needed to take more time over a sick Jewish baby? Another welfare assistant found it an 'embarrassment if a Jewish mother comes unexpectedly'.[68] The conflict between her caring instincts and the hostile Nazi world can be sensed from the description of her feelings on visiting a Jewish family:

> From among Aryans of this district again and again astonishment is expressed that welfare officers are still concerned for Jewish children and provide family support. Frequently when I discuss some matter with a Jew in the street, I receive looks of disapproval and people watch to hear what is said. The most difficult group to deal with are the *Mischlinge*. They have no chance of securing work and no hope of better times. The Jewish community refuses to assist them and the Welfare Office denies them any special assistance so that they receive no help from anyone. These people are especially deprived and dealing with them is not always easy … if part of the family is Aryan particular difficulties arise, marriages break up, the raising of the children becomes difficult. The work among such families brings with it little satisfaction; they complain and one is powerless to do anything.

Can we discern perhaps some feeling of empathy in these comments?

But when others charged with the care of the most disadvantaged in the community turned against the needy, against mothers and babies because they were not of pure 'German' blood, what could be expected from the authorities of the Nazi state? These were men and women who had received their training during the earlier democratic years. They were Christians, and yet infrequently is a spark of humanity to be found in their reports. The profession was not well rewarded and attracted to it were young idealistic men and women. Yet many succumbed to the evils of the day. The Nazis were kept in power not only by psychopaths and gangsters but by consenting and decent Germans – the story not just of Hamburg but of Germany.

Steadfast in crisis

To remain in control, plan for the future, regulate the exodus and make life as tolerable as possible were the tasks the Jewish leadership in Hamburg and Berlin set themselves as problems mounted all around them. But had their advice against panic decisions to emigrate deterred many who otherwise would have left in time? Were their carefully devised emigration policies of 20,000 people a year too cautious, the emphasis of strictly adhering to legal requirements unimaginative and misplaced? In dealing with the Nazi authorities, had they not been turned unwittingly into collaborators? Why were the Jews not more militant?

Not everything done was right, but choices were limited. Armed resistance before the war, in effect terrorism, was out of the question. There was resistance, but with few exceptions of a more subtle kind. What would have been the fate of the women and children and the reaction of the rest of the world to violence in peacetime? Had 300,000 Jews been urged to leave during the first two or three years of Nazi rule, countries of possible refuge would have closed their doors sooner. Unless supported by earlier emigrants who had been able to establish themselves, it was virtually impossible for the elderly to emigrate. In most countries large funds were required to bring over adult Jews and children. Work permits were severely restricted. As for the charge of 'collaboration', again, the Jewish leadership had no choice if they wanted to accomplish anything practical. Given the times and the attitudes abroad, it was an extraordinary achievement to have saved as many as were saved.

The Jewish community had to rely on itself to make existence possible. The old, the sick and those made destitute had to be taken care of, and advice given to those who wished to leave. Life had to go on somehow – but, more than that, the spirit needed nourishment with the help of social contacts and cultural activities, while inspiring worship instilled hope. Leaving without means or prospects of a profession, without knowing the language to a country perhaps as alien as China, appeared a counsel of despair.

The indications as to what the future held in store for Jews were ambiguous. The Nazi regime before 1938 still appeared outwardly to accept that it had obligations to Jews even while discriminating against them. About their plans discussed behind closed doors there was only speculation. The Jews received their pensions, though these were reduced, Jewish doctors were still practising, lawyers continued to plead in the courts. The Jewish department stores were a prominent feature of the street scene, with names like Hirschfeld in Hamburg and Israel in Berlin; smaller businesses had also survived – none had been forcibly closed down, though many had sold their shops, sometimes even at a fair price.

Jews were still active in the economy and strong, well-established businesses shared in the recovery.

Jews in general had not been harmed physically. Attacks that occurred were isolated events. Thousands of Jewish children were taught in German state schools. In the larger towns, Jews went about their daily lives without fear and threat of abuse. It helped that most could not be identified by their fellow citizens as Jews anyway. They ignored the occasional restaurant sign '*Juden unerwünscht*' (Jews not welcome) if they wished to eat there. The tirades of Dr Goebbels, or Nazi black banner headlines, did not reflect the daily experience. The antisemitic atmosphere was more insidious. Jews went shopping wherever they wished and were treated as normal customers. They went to the bank to withdraw money from their accounts like everyone else, rented apartments or owned houses, and worshipped in synagogues without molestation. There was a large gap between Nazi diatribes and daily experience. Passers-by avoided looking at the *Stürmerkasten* on the street corner displaying Julius Streicher's antisemitic rag, with its pornographic drawings of a 'fat Jew' lusting after a blond girl in pigtails. Still, Jews did realise they were living in a potentially hostile world, of having to be careful, of not attracting attention, not behaving loudly in waiting rooms, the train, the underground, wherever they were in close contact with other Germans. Yet, with all the unjust discrimination, it still seemed possible to believe that the 'government' and Adolf Hitler were proceeding on a 'legal' path.

The Jewish leadership was concerned to meet the practical needs of the community. That could not change even when the true nature of Nazi violence first became openly evident on a mass scale. There was no avoiding the state bureaucracy, the police and the Gestapo. By skilful handling, and by knowing whom to approach, minor concessions could sometimes be won. When it came to emigration, interaction went further than that. In Hamburg, an important hub for those departing, there was close cooperation with the Gestapo. Here, Jews and Nazis shared a common purpose. Only someone not understanding the times would call that 'collaboration'.

I

Max Plaut, Leo Lippmann, Joseph Carlebach and Max Warburg, each in his own way, exemplified the courageous leadership of the Hamburg community during these years. They were supported by a large number of devoted men and women in community posts and by volunteers. There was no time for despair. Gathering all their resources, material and human, the Jewish leaders worked on the only assumption they could, that they would master the storm by careful planning. The record shows that over half of Hamburg's 20,000 Jews were saved from the Holocaust. Those that became the victims were helped until that was no longer possible.

The second syndicus or secretary of Hamburg's Jewish community in 1933 was Max Plaut. Administrator of the community since 1912 was the 54-year-old

Dr Max Nathan, trained as a rabbi, experienced in handling inner Jewish affairs, but with the coming of the Nazis not able to adjust to a new world.

Max Plaut was just thirty-one when he was appointed to assist him. He had been active in Jewish politics since the mid-1920s, conservative in politics and conservative in religious practice. A photograph taken in Hamburg in the 1930s shows a sturdy, thick-set man with a calm and confident expression, sure of the role he felt himself called upon to play. His background was patriotic German and Prussian. The family had settled in Upper Silesia on the borders of Poland, a province rich in Jewish culture. Grandfather Plaut was the first Jewish school-master appointed to a Prussian state school. His father went to fight in the First World War, a patriot who emerged severely wounded. Max was born in 1901, just too young to join the war. He made up for it, encouraged by his father, by joining the militia Free Corps in Upper Silesia, a region which the Poles were attempting to wrest from Germany. In 1921, he fought in the skirmishes around the Annaberg against the Polish militias and was decorated for bravery with the Silesian Eagle first class. After his training in the Warburg bank, he was recommended to the community by Max Warburg. Flexible and skilful at handling people, he was a good, inspired choice. Like Spiers at the *Talmud Tora Schule*, Plaut was the kind of German Jew likely to win the respect of the Nazis with whom he would have to deal.

One unusual features of the Jewish–Nazi relationship in Hamburg was the circumstance that, for the whole of Plaut's time, from 1933 to 1943, his opposite number at the Gestapo was the Weimar police inspector Claus Göttsche. It did not save Plaut from a number of arrests and physical assaults from Göttsche's underlings, but a certain respect and reliance on each other's word developed between them. This did not make Plaut a 'collaborator', though after the war he faced bitter and unjust accusations. Plaut was able to exploit his relations with Göttsche for the good of the community. He never doubted that the man he faced was the representative of a regime implacably hostile to Jewry. In this respect, there were no differences between Göttsche and his Gestapo superiors in Berlin. Though not a hardened antisemite, Göttsche was ready to do whatever was necessary to further his career.

The mid-1930s was still a time of illusion that a separate Jewish sphere would be able to coexist with the German *Volk* in a modest way. So preparations were made to provide schooling for Jewish boys and girls expected soon to be excluded from state schools. There were other pressing needs: adequate places in old-age homes for the rapidly ageing population, and the need to raise funds to meet the increased welfare burdens and to assist those who hoped to emigrate. The money was raised mainly by German Jews, supplemented by generous donations from abroad.

Among the more bizarre problems Plaut faced was the criminal offence created by the Nuremberg Laws of sexual relations between 'Germans' and 'Jews'. The Reeperbahn was renowned for the variety of sexual services on offer. What if a German prostitute denounced a Jewish client who might be identifiable when embarking on the pleasures on offer? The Gestapo showed understanding. Racial defilement had to be avoided. An exclusively Jewish *Bordell*, a house of prostitution, was licensed, staffed by a Jewish madam and an assembly of attractive Jewish ladies. It opened its doors at Winkelstraße 25 but did not prove a success; it closed again after only a few months for lack of clients.[69]

II

Five thousand Jews, about a third of the community, had departed from Hamburg before 1938, leaving most of their possessions behind to start a new life far from home. Nearly half of these had received financial assistance to enable them to emigrate. The majority were young people who entered the British Palestine Mandate. After the Arab unrest in 1936 and British restrictions in 1937 halved the exodus to Palestine, the United States, South America and European neighbours took in the majority of refugees. But as the pressure on German Jewry grew, so did restrictive barriers increase. Nevertheless, after the early exodus during the first year of Nazi rule, emigration was an orderly process until 1938. The Jewish leaders in Berlin took the view that illegal entry and the flouting of the laws of the receiving countries would lead to the closure of their borders. Plaut saw this differently and did not hesitate to make use of every opening, legal or not, to get Jews out of Germany with the connivance of the local Gestapo.

The outward calm after the Nuremberg Laws was spurious. The leadership of the Jewish community, faced with hostile state institutions, knew they would need to rely on themselves. The situation was no better in Hamburg than elsewhere. National policies were anticipated locally. Jewish orphans were removed from state children's homes; legal adoptions and fostering arrangements were reversed where Jewish parents had taken care of Aryan children, leading to heart-breaking family disruption. Jewish leaders after 1935 understood that there was no long-term future for German Jewry. They calculated that an orderly liquidation would take a generation.[70] The central representative body of German Jewry, the *Reichsvertretung* in Berlin, prepared plans to enable 20,000 Jews to leave each year. That meant that Jews would have to find refuge wherever possible. Ideology no longer ruled choice. Despite the troubles in Palestine and lower emigration there, the *Reichvetretung* exceeded its objectives.

Even so, there was now a mismatch between the Jewish planners and the Gestapo. For Himmler, Heydrich and Eichmann, the rate of 'progress' to make Germany *judenrein* was too slow and had even declined in 1937.[71] The Jews still had it too easy in Germany. New ways would need to be adopted to hasten their departure: organised pogroms, 'popular' violence, and the destruction of the community's economic base.

On the economic front, some progress was achieved by the Nazis. Local Nazi pressure induced Jews to sell their businesses at bargain prices. But other firms, especially the larger concerns, clung on, and those offering good value, both smaller enterprises and large department stores, continued to attract customers.

Nazi stickers tried to deter shoppers. Plastered on Walter Bucky's store was the message 'Whoever makes purchases from Jews is a traitor'; the owner stood before his shop and addressed the storm trooper holding the sign: 'Ah well, already this morning lots of traitors showed up.' Nor was the party in Hamburg successful in its demands for an official listing and identification of Jewish enterprises. This was resisted by Schacht's Ministry of Economics, as Hitler had forbidden it.

The process of change was gradual before 1938, but had taken its toll.[72] New employment for Jews dismissed from their workplace or for youngsters leaving school became difficult to secure. Most Jews were employed by the remaining Jewish businesses. Jews whose life was becoming intolerable in villages and smaller towns moved to the bigger cities, whose Jewish population did not therefore diminish as rapidly as local Nazis wished.

New Reich decrees in 1936 and 1937 drove out professionals performing 'semi-public' functions, accountants, foreign currency advisors, pharmacists, book dealers and publishers, among others. Practising doctors and lawyers were thrown out in the autumn of 1938, with the few exceptions of those now labelled medical and legal helpers for Jews only. All this happened in Hamburg just as in the rest of the Reich. To the burden of maintaining all the traditional work of the community, new responsibilities kept on increasing. Although the number of 'racial' Jews living in Hamburg had almost halved between 1933 and 1939, to just over 10,000, the number of those needing support had actually increased.

III

The most senior officer of the community after Plaut was Leo Lippmann.[73] Lippmann was responsible for finance, balancing the expenditure and income of the Jewish community. Before 1939, the funds gathered annually by tax were not enough. The community increasingly had to rely on voluntary contributions, Jewish *Winterhilfe* and large individual contributions from a small number of wealthy Jews in Hamburg. Lippmann was also responsible for administering the capital bound up in trusts and legacies set up by wealthy Jewish benefactors for relief of the poor.

When Lippmann took over the financial management the position was far from healthy and decisions on each item of expenditure were reached only after lengthy wrangling.[74] The reluctance to raise the tax rates had led to deficits just as needs increased, and emigration and general impoverishment reduced the ability of the community members to pay. Lippmann took the bull by the horns. In masterful and expert exposition born of long experience, he overawed the elected representatives. In the end, paradoxically, his good household management simply allowed more money to fall into the coffers of the Gestapo. Lippmann could not help himself. For him, sound financial management was an end in itself to which he had devoted his professional life. Dealing with Hamburg's state administrators, he could still command respect and secure minor concessions. The heavy expense of exhumation and transfer of remains from the Grindel burial ground to Ohlsdorf was initially to be entirely borne by the community, but Lippmann secured a repayment of almost half the cost. Thus, with Nazi help, splendid new gravestones for a hundred of the most illustrious Hamburg Jews were erected in Ohlsdorf.

It was a small success. The balance of expenditures and income deteriorated sharply, and Lippmann could not save the venerable *Israelitisches Krankenhaus*.[75] In 1938 there were fewer than a hundred patients occupying the hospital's 250 beds. The new hospital buildings constructed with the help of a state loan during the closing years of the Weimar Republic were efficient and modern. The hospital was plunged into financial crisis trying to meet loan and interest repayments. Despite large benefactions from the Warburgs and other well-wishers, the repayments completely exhausted reserves. The payment due in 1937 could only be made with the help of a loan from the Jewish community, and the payment due on 1 January 1938 was once more covered by a loan from the community. There was no prospect of further loans, although there was a need for a hospital for the Jewish population.

Lippmann, in negotiations with the state, managed to save something from the takeover of the hospital buildings.[76] A contract was concluded on 11 September 1939, ten days after the outbreak of the war, and the whole property was transferred to the state. It was worth of course much more than a still outstanding loan of over 1 million *Reichsmark*, which was cancelled. Leo Lippmann succeeded in securing what at the time seemed a big concession: the old buildings after the war, 'if there was such a need', would be rented as a hospital back to the Jewish community for a modest sum and the costs of modernisation would be borne two-thirds by the community and one-third by the state. In 1939, the civil servants did not imagine the grim reality of six years later. As a replacement, the small previously private clinic of the gynaecologist Dr Calmann on the corner of the Johnsallee and Schlüterstraße hardly provided enough beds in 1939. Even this building was later taken away. Soon few beds would be required anyway.

The liquidation applied to all the property owned by the Jewish community and to the legacies left in their care for charitable purposes. The Nazis were determined to seize any Jewish assets they could lay their hands on, but a façade of legality was maintained. The community property was not simply confiscated but 'valued' and 'purchased' by the state. Lippmann conducted these negotiations with Hamburg's civil servants. Sizeable wealth was involved in legacies made by wealthy Jews in the nineteenth century to support charitable housing for the poor. Most benefactions made no distinction of religion. They were an expression of gratitude for the acceptance of Jews as citizens of Hamburg. It was also a Jewish tradition to provide for the poor.[77] It was overwhelmingly Christians, good Aryans, who were the ones who now benefited. There were more than a thousand rooms and apartments provided in almshouses for little or no rent at all. Fewer than ninety of these were occupied by Jews. That came as a surprise to the Nazis. Still, it was no reason to deprive Aryans of Jewish gifts. Jews and Aryans could no longer share accommodation. A sorting out was necessary. There were too few Jews to need all of the homes. The community was allowed to retain three. Six large Jewish homes, together with their capital, were Aryanised and the Jewish trustees replaced by Aryans. The conditions of the bequests were simply torn up. The funds in all other legacies were taken over by the Jewish community, whose income and expenditure was controlled by the Gestapo. This proved perversely helpful in one sense, as the Gestapo did not wish to see this capital depleted more than could be avoided by payments to the Reich or to the Hamburg state. It would all be used for the purposes they determined and what was left over flow into their own coffers.

The community's capital was under heavy pressure for reasons beyond the control of the Gestapo. The number of Jews still in employment was declining all the time, more and more old and infirm men and women were left behind, and the wealthier members were losing their businesses and capital. Emigration reduced the number of wealthier Jews who had been the mainstay of the community. Then from 1 January 1939 a new law deprived Jews of state welfare benefits[78] and made them the responsibility of the community – an open-ended new burden, since Jews could no longer find employment in Aryan businesses and were unable to continue in the professions and trades. The remnant lived off their capital until it ran out. Those who still had sizeable bank accounts or were in receipt of state pensions had their accounts blocked and were permitted to draw out only a small sum every month to cover basic needs. In 1939, already more than a quarter of the community had become paupers or received paltry wages for menial forced labour.

In Hamburg there were transitional welfare payment arrangements until the summer of 1939. A special emigration tax, which had flowed from blocked accounts into those of the Jewish community since early in 1939, increased financial resources for a time, but that source ran out too a year later. For the Nazis the problem was that, inside Germany, they could not have people starving and dying in the streets. That would have upset the general population. What could be done in Poland was not possible in the streets of German towns. As long as they were still in view, the Jews were allowed to exist at subsistence level.

Among forced sales of community property to the Hamburg state was the site of the Bornplatz Synagogue. *Reichstatthalter* Kaufmann wanted to build a teacher-training college on the land. That meant demolishing the synagogue, whose burnt-out walls were a stark reminder for everyone passing by of the pogrom night of 9 November. The sooner a Nazi building could replace it the better. The 'negotiations' were between unequal partners, the forced sellers and the purchasers. Surprisingly, real negotiations did take place. Leo Lippmann behaved as if he had legal and financial rights to defend on behalf of the Jewish community, a small but extraordinary footnote showing old habits did not easily die. He conducted the discussions with the civil servants of the Finance Office with astounding assertiveness, addressing them as if they were still his subordinates. The community, he declared, was not prepared to demolish the synagogue and clear the site, nor was it willing to pay the whole costs of demolition; he offered to contribute one-fifth. The purchase price, he proposed, should be set against the welfare bill.[79] He then pointed out that, if the community received no state assistance, their funds would run out in two or three years' time, implying that the state would then have to provide for them alone. In the end Lippmann won some minimal concessions. Plaut, later on, adopted a different policy and sold community properties for such ridiculous low prices that, he calculated, the community would have no difficulty after the Nazis were gone in claiming them back.

IV

Hamburg's Jews were also fortunate in their Chief Rabbi, the charismatic respected Joseph Carlebach. The Nazi years for deeply religious Jews like Carlebach had their positive as well as negative aspects. If assimilated Jews had forgotten who they were, Nazi legislation forced them back to their roots. The majority of Hamburg's Jews retained some relationship with religious practice. More than half the male babies were ritually circumcised in Hamburg and three quarters of all Jewish marriages were conducted by a rabbi. The majority of Jews behaved like their Christian neighbours who were baptised, married in church and were buried in religiously hallowed ground, but otherwise only rarely, if at all, saw the inside of a church. What this reflected was the overall decline of religion in western society. It should have diminished the old antagonisms of Christians towards Jews. Instead spurious racial doctrines supplemented religious prejudices.

While relatively few in Hamburg left the community, intermarriage was the Achilles heel.[80] Jews who married Christian spouses did not generally convert, but their children were nearly always lost to the Jewish community. The low birth rate and interreligious marriages appeared to threaten the long-term survival of German Jews. The gloom was overdone. A core of observant German Jews would have ensured that Jews would continue to live in German lands.

Rabbis grasped the opportunity to provide leadership and restore self-confidence. They conveyed in their sermons the message that the Jews would prevail, that, after the days of shadow, sunlight would follow once more, that Jews trusting in God had overcome every enemy through the millennia and would do so again. They refused to be intimidated by the Gestapo spies they knew to be listening at the back of the congregation. Synagogue attendance for the first time in years increased. In Hamburg, Joseph Carlebach earned admiration for his steadfastness and knowledge.[81] He was kindly, with a great sense of humour, hard working and engaged in many community activities, especially for the young. As chief rabbi he presided over different forms of worship.[82]

Carlebach was orthodox but accepted the existence of the more liberal forms of worship in the *Tempel* and the Neue Dammtor Synagogue without making any concessions in leading his own congregation, the *Synagogenverband*. His blend of orthodoxy and tolerance was characteristic of this remarkable man, who saw no contradiction in being both a passionate moderniser and a traditionalist.

Carlebach's forbears had settled in the seventeenth century in southern Germany.[83] Joseph began his higher education not in rabbinical studies but followed a broad range of secular subjects: physics at the University of Berlin under the renowned Max Planck, and astronomy, philosophy and art history. He also found time to deepen his knowledge of the Talmud. Later he was drawn to mathematics and the natural sciences, completing the qualification required for a teacher in secondary schools at the age of twenty-two. Two and a half years teaching in Jerusalem left him with both positive and negative impressions. The isolation and intolerance of orthodoxy and rejection of his own wish to combine orthodoxy with secular involvement convinced him that orthodox Judaism as practised in Palestine was not the right path for him to follow. After returning to Berlin, he taught part-time in a Prussian school and continued his studies in both mathematics and Judaism. Then he immersed himself in studies for the rabbinate in the seminar which followed the new orthodoxy rather than entering a traditional *yeshiva*.

After the outbreak of the First World War, Carlebach volunteered as an army chaplain. The German military authorities recognised his abilities as an educator and posted him to occupied Lithuania to reorganise and Germanise the Jewish school system. He founded in Kowno the Carlebach *Gymnasium* and was now able to put all his learning and skills into practice.

With the death of his father in 1920, Carlebach returned to Lübeck as its rabbi. But when the headship of the *Talmud Tora Realgymnasium* became vacant in 1921, he was an outstanding choice. To the dismay of the more orthodox, he reformed the curriculum, giving more time to science and physical training. The gymnasium of the *Talmud Tora Schule* became one of the best in Hamburg. Carlebach enjoyed taking the children on excursions into the countryside and fostered a love of *Heimat*. There is a memorable photograph of the rabbi swimming, surrounded by eager pupils. Chosen by the Altona congregation as their chief rabbi, Carlebach left the school in 1926, but first had made sure that a thoroughly modern educationist and orthodox Jew, Dr Arthur Spier, would take over the reins. The next ten years were the happiest years of his life, fruitful as scholar, educationalist, rabbi and parent. Seven children were added in Altona to the two daughters born in Lübeck. In accordance with tradition, in 1928 Carlebach requested the Reich president to become godfather to his ninth child – Sara, his youngest daughter. Hindenburg graciously accepted. (It did not save Sara from being deported and murdered in Riga thirteen years later.) The official salary of a rabbi was not so abundant as to provide easily for such a large family, but half was set aside as a matter of course for good causes. In April 1936, Joseph Carlebach was chosen chief rabbi of Hamburg in succession to Dr Samuel Spitzer.

Now fifty-three years of age, Carlebach, recognised as a leading orthodox scholar throughout Germany, could look forward to many more years in high office, strengthening Judaism and holding the Hamburg communities together. In fact he was granted only five – the most onerous and difficult of his life. He got through an almost superhuman amount of work, meeting all the calls made on him by the increasingly desperate members of his congregation, conducting services, lecturing in his house to those who came to learn, and keeping in touch with Jews in prison or concentration camps. Sunday mornings were dedicated to Bible talks, where he expounded the uniqueness of the Jewish people, their mission, the grandeur of the past and the promise of the future. It took courage to declare in the synagogue in the presence of Gestapo stooges, who held him in grudging respect, that the people of God were eternal.

Carlebach's inauguration as chief rabbi on 22 April 1936 in the great Bornplatz Synagogue was the last splendid religious occasion celebrated in Hamburg.[84] As yet the future of Jewry in Germany did not appear doomed. The synagogue was festively lit. Rabbis from Hamburg's other synagogues and more than 200 honoured guests from further afield joined the members of the Hamburg community. Dressed formally, wearing top hats, they filled the synagogue to capacity. Those who could not find room listened to the transmission of the ceremony in the *Talmud Tora Schule*. It was an impressive and moving demonstration of Jewish solidarity and strength in the middle years of the Third Reich. The president of the *Synagogenverband* greeted the congregation as first speaker. His message was one of hope and confidence. Even though, he said, events had hurt everyone, there was no reason for despair: 'We look to a happy future for our people; the unnatural culture which had been allowed to develop for decades is broken and new life and strength will grow when it is transferred to our motherland, Palestine.' Rabbi Hoffmann from Frankfurt spoke of the need for will and action. The role of rabbis had become more difficult, but their influence had increased, as the community had become more ready to listen to the teaching and responsibilities of being a Jew.

Then Dr Joseph Carlebach delivered his address.

> When I look in your eyes and hearts, what are your expectations of the rabbi you have chosen? I don't believe my response will be mistaken in believing that the community is looking for a man in whom they can confide, who will be a mainstay to those seeking support, because we know God is with you. I have the courage to be the man you are seeking.

Carlebach spoke of his rabbinic ideal to care for all. The Hamburg community still suffered from the heritage of old rabbinical disputes. 'I ask you all in honour of Judaism to bury these conflicts and to work for unity, and I will do everything in my power to make fraternal conflicts impossible.' The most striking and challenging words came at the end: 'Just as Jeremiah commanded those carried off to Babylon to care for the well-being of the state to which God had banished them', so too the German Jews should not cease to pray for their country. It was a courageous challenge to the prevailing Nazi denigration. To ask Jews to care for the well-being of the Nazi state – was that not carrying love of country too far? Like Max Warburg, Carlebach still had faith that the German people would recover from the evil Nazi mirage that had seduced so many of them.

Carlebach wholly rejected the Nazi image of the Jews as alien among the German people, as parasites harming the society which sheltered them.[85] And yet, he did not dismiss out of hand the Nazi doctrine of race. It held a certain attraction for orthodox Jews. Two years earlier Carlebach had made known his views on this delicate issue in an article he contributed to Hamburg's Jewish community paper.

> Mankind's unity is created by its Godlike image, but differences between men is also the will of God. Everyone is equal; it is each individual's duty to further his race. The religion of the race is of indispensable significance for mankind as a whole. We too are decided opponents of mixed marriages, the senseless intermingling of races undertaken with indifference. In Israel one always valued most that part of the people who kept their families free of foreign blood … in the grandchildren and great-grandchildren grew the strength of the fathers to a higher level. Whenever one researches the great personalities of the past, it can be shown that such exemplary types of mankind were made possible by the higher development of certain genetic characteristics through generation after generation.

But then, in contradiction, he added,

> Blood is not the final and only decisive factor determining the worth or lack of worth of an individual. There is something stronger than race in man: his will, his inner strength and the strength of his soul. Our history shows examples of how, despite foreign blood, an individual has been raised to the highest level of the Jews: the foreign origin has been overcome.

He cited the mother of King David, first ruler of Israel, and also Ruth, whose mother was a Moab, and Rabbi Akiba ben Joseph. Anyone, he continued, who values mankind on the basis of blood and race alone denies the principle of freedom and that man is made in God's image. From the general he passed on to the particular, pointing out that German Jews living in these lands for 2,000 years were not of pure descent. This enabled him to end with the statement 'What we have in common with all German citizens is greater than what separates us.'

Orthodox Jews in one respect could not help expressing relief and even welcoming the Nuremberg Blood Laws. The real problem lay with accepting the premise of race. Although religious Jews oppose marriage outside their religion, notions of 'race' play no part in their rejection. There is no bar to a Christian convert to Judaism marrying a Jewish spouse (except for a Cohen in orthodox Judaism). In biblical times intermarriage was common. Carlebach was treading on dangerous ground, lending his authority by implication to any form of racial purity as an ideal. His observation led to some dissent and criticism.

V

It would be impossible to omit Max Warburg from the prominent personalities exemplifying Jewish leadership in Hamburg in the 1930s.[86] Max Warburg celebrated his seventieth birthday in 1937. It should have been a festive occasion. Under his leadership, M. M. Warburg & Co. had become the leading private bank in Hamburg of international renown through family links with the United States.

Max Warburg was not an orthodox cautious banker. Backing large loans to clients during the Depression years, particularly to the department store chain Karstadt, had brought the bank almost to its knees until it was rescued by the large Kara loan from his American banking brothers. His faith that Germany would recover, and that it was the bank's duty to support its clients loyally in bad times just as in good, was typical of the man. But now in the mid-1930s his robust strength and optimism were weakening. The happy synthesis he had forged in his life-time between being a German, a Jew, a banker and a philanthropist, proud of his native Hamburg roots, was disintegrating. He nevertheless got through a prodigious amount of work, directing the bank and involving himself deeply in Jewish organisations, while struggling to get on top of the problems facing his fellow Jews. Characteristically, he sought to exploit every opportunity and to create new ones, not allowing his deep disillusionment of former colleagues, once eager for his advice, to drive him to despair.

Not all German Jews wished to emigrate to Palestine under Zionist auspices, despite the more favourable currency arrangements negotiated under the *ha'avara* agreement.[87] In any case, by 1936 it had become clear that refuge would have to be found the world over if the majority of the Jewish community was to be enabled to leave Germany over time. Max Warburg had long been associated with the *Hilfsverein der deutchen Juden*, the Aid Society of German Jews, founded in 1901 to help the persecuted Jews of Russia and Central Europe to find new homes, mainly in the United States. After 1933 it became the principal channel to assist German Jews with information, loans, visas and practical help to emigrate to countries other than Palestine. The achievement of the *Hilfsverein* was considerable. In congratulating Max Warburg on his seventieth birthday, Hamburg's Jewish community paper praised the society for having helped almost 40,000 Jews to leave the country.

Max Warburg now had two passions: to serve and save the family bank and to do all in his power to help the Jewish community in Hamburg and Germany. The two aims dovetailed with each other. In the bank, Jewish clients replaced departing Christian ones. Commission was earned from representing Jewish interests. The arrangements and financing of emigration, the negotiations for transferring assets and the soliciting of funds from abroad provided the bank with a lifeline.

Shortly after the Nuremberg Laws, Max Warburg's most ambitious project was to create a transfer bank with large capital resources in order to rescue

168,000 Jews from Germany, one-fifth to leave for Palestine and four-fifths else-where.[88] A large loan would be raised, two-thirds from American and one-third from British Jews, secured on the property the Jews had to leave behind. The plan was based on the *ha'avara* arrangements. Warburg engaged in discussions with *Reichsbank* President Schacht in Berlin and bankers in London and New York, aiming to raise half a million pounds sterling. The scheme foundered when it received headlines in the *New York Times* in January 1936: 'World Jewry to be Asked to Finance Great Exodus of German Co-Religionists'. The conditions, the paper explained, were 'designed to restore economic and financial prosperity to the German Reich'. The final outcome was a pale shadow of Max Warburg's hopes, but he did not give up. Negotiations went on in Berlin, where his long-established contacts with Schacht gave him unique access to the top bureaucrats in the Economics Ministry and the *Reichsbank*. The discussions in Berlin, London and New York limped along, promising much but achieving little.

More successfully, the Warburgs used their own money and influence to help Jewish emigrants. Max Warburg and his son Eric contributed generously from their personal capital to assist individuals and Jewish causes in Hamburg. Eric Warburg was also active in raising funds in the United States. Generous grants from the Warburgs were channelled to the community's welfare causes. Poor Jewish children were provided with a breakfast of milk and bread at school; 200 children requiring fresh air were sent on holiday breaks; 300 children every day were taken on day excursions; nurseries and youth counselling were provided; the orphanage for girls, the *Paulinenstift*, received support, as did mentally hand-icapped young people in the institution in Beelitz; mothers could turn to Jewish advisory clinics; the difficult task of finding vacancies for apprenticeship was tackled; jobs were found in businesses; and Jewish teachers were employed in Jewish schools, though many first required some introductory lessons to acquaint them with Jewish culture. Increasing number of Jews who had become entirely dependent on welfare received supplementary help, as did the old and sick living out their last years in homes founded by Jewish philanthropy.

What made all this possible were the contributions from the declining numbers of the better off in the community to their less fortunate co-religionists. How German Jews helped each other during the Nazi years is one of the still hidden and finest chapters of German-Jewish life in dissolution.

In Hamburg, the Warburgs were very much in the forefront of this effort, despite all the problems facing them.[89] Max Warburg was chairman of the board of the Jewish orphanage, a member of the board of the *Talmud Tora Schule*, on the advisory board of the *Reichsvertretung*, and chairman of the *Hilfsverein*. In the unpublished manuscript of his memoirs he wrote that he never regretted not following the advice of the family to liquidate the bank during the early Nazi years, which would have saved at least a part of the family fortune. What held him in Germany was, first, the illusion that the Nazis would not last and, later, his sense of duty towards the community, while still hoping that he could preserve at least a shrunken family bank.

Remarkably, Max Warburg was able to rescue the bank from the losses it made during the early Nazi years and to retain most of its employees, half of whom were Jewish.[90] Besides new Jewish clients, some of Germany's elite firms continued to do business with the bank, among them the large steel concern Gutehoffnungshütte of Essen, the department store chain Karstadt, Hamburg's shipbuilders Blohm & Voss, the Krupps armaments giant, the well-known cigarette manufacturers Phillip Reemtsma, the coffee importer J. Darboven and the pharmaceutical business of Beiersdorf, just to name the best known. The bank even won new Aryan clients such as the Phoenix Insurance Company, but others progressively dissolved their commercial relations. As long as Schacht was still in control, M. M. Warburg also secured a declining share of the Reich loans.

Max Warburg, between bouts of frantic activity at home and abroad, describes his own black periods of despair in his memoirs. He had expected his former German associates in banking and commerce to show more fibre; 'they all fell over in the end', he sadly reflected.

Max Warburg had an extraordinary capacity to recover from troughs of despair as, with renewed energy, he served Jewish interests and maintained 'his fortress' M. M. Warburg at Ferdinandstraße 75. A particular stroke of creative genius was to protect the bank by renting the second floor to the United States consulate. Warburg laboured to stem the tide of declining account holders. Personally he felt secure from arrest until the autumn of 1938 and had no intention of following family advice to leave Germany. He was still a German determined to see the bank through every crisis. He also remained steadfast as a Jewish leader, concerned to make the life of Jews in Germany still worth living.

On 9 January 1938, Warburg opened the new Jewish community centre in the Beneckestraße. It housed a theatre, a lecture hall, a library and kitchens serving a restaurant, as Jews were no longer 'welcome' in 'German' establishments. The *Kulturbund* could perform in surroundings where young and old could meet without fear of unpleasant incidents, a centre for their cultural and social life. In the words of Max Warburg, Jews here could renew a feeling of self-worth and regain a sense of inner peace. It was a place where individuals could study or clubs could meet, an oasis, a shelter where the harassed would find diversion and relaxation.

Jungfernstieg, Hamburg's finest shopping promenade. On the middle left is the *Alsterhaus*, once part of Hermann Tietz's large chain of department stores, which had to be sold on 'Aryanisation' at a fraction of its value. However, the stores continued to be known into the twenty-first century as 'Hertie', so perpetuating Tietz's name.

The *Rathaus* on the renamed Adolf-Hitler-Platz was built between 1886 and 1889, its lead architect Martin Haller (1835–1925). The Hallers moved to Hamburg in the eighteenth century. By Martin's time the family members had been baptised through three generations, but had married Jewish wives, which made him a retrospect Jew. His father, Nicolaus Ferdinand Haller, was a leading senator and several times mayor of the city-state. The Hallerstraße was named in his honour.

Everyday life in Hamburg.

The Gängeviertel: this medieval slum quarter, whose politically active residents were divided between communists and Nazis, was demolished after 1933.

Nazi flags in front of the main station: they were hung in this manner only when a Nazi leader was visiting. Private apartments also had to show flags, and those whose flags were too small were likely to have their windows broken by enthusiasts.

Welcome to Hitler, 17 August 1934.

Another face of Hitler, attending the *Staatsoper* for a performance of Wagner's *Die Meistersinger*, 23 June 1935. On another occasion Luise Solmitz recounted that the family was looking forward to a performance of Lessing's *Minna von Barnhelm*. However, Hitler's introduction was so long that the audience fell asleep and there was no time left to perform the play.

Peaceable group of Hitler Youth – for many, their first camping trip in the beautiful countryside.

1936: an Olympic flag and two tatty swastikas. There was no fuss apart from the day when the American team arrived in Hamburg.

A well-known illustration of boycott day, 1 April 1933, with the placard saying: 'Germans do not buy from Jews'. Esek Getzler, aged twenty-eight, had only just opened this branch of his father's business. There was clearly no future for him, and so few weeks later he decided to emigrate to the United States.

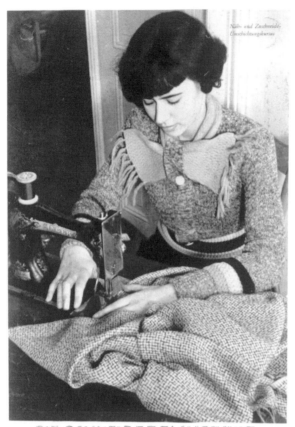

DIE SCHNEIDERFACHSCHULE

Jewish self-help: learning the tailoring business.

Training as locksmiths.

Working the land. However, the Jewish community couldn't finance anything like enough places.

5

SAVE YOURSELF IF YOU CAN

The beginning of the end

Sylvester, New Year, 1 January 1938, was celebrated by families with celebra-
tion wine. The children melt pieces of tin on large spoons over the gas fire, then
plunge them into cold water. Bizarre shapes are formed. What do they reveal?
Fortune telling was just a game. What did the future really hold? In every Jewish
family thoughts turned to the question of what the new year would bring.
Nothing good was expected, but nothing as bad as actually occurred.

168,000 Jews had already left the country of their birth, almost one in three.
Lawyers lost clients; few companies would any longer employ them, however
satisfied they had been with the service they had given. It was nothing personal,
they explained, just the times. Doctors lost their 'Aryan' patients and their
insurance-related work. Former civil servants sat at home, though a few tried to
learn a new skill as cooks, joiners, or bookkeepers – anything that might lead to
work abroad. Not all Jews were well to do; most were struggling to make ends
meet, and the elderly increasingly became dependent on welfare. The gap
between haves and have-nots was constantly widening. Middle-class lifestyles
became harder to keep up, and many Jews without other income were now living
off capital. They at least still controlled their own bank accounts and property.
A Jewish business sector survived but had shrunk during five Nazi years, from
some 110,00 enterprises to little more than 39,000, according to one estimate.

Unexpectedly emigration slackened. Many of the younger generation without
prospects of employment had already left. If you had transferable skills it made
sense to depart; doctors could overcome hurdles, take new examinations abroad
and, with luck, eventually find somewhere to practise. For the adaptable young
there were opportunities in agriculture. Business people had transferable skills
too, but would have to accept that they would receive only a much reduced price

for their German business when sold and would be able to transfer only a fraction of the proceeds abroad. For lawyers, prospects of remaining in their profession were practically non-existent. The majority of Germany's Jews hung on, reluctant to leave behind what they and their parents had built up over decades in order to become paupers in a foreign land whose language they did not know and whose labour laws restricted what they could do. The old and sick did not have any choice anyway. Foreign countries would not accept them unless their keep was guaranteed. Most stayed behind, as frequently did daughters to take care of their elderly parents. It was supposed that women and children would not be physically harmed. The Nazis were malevolent, but surely there were limits which even they would observe. Many still hoped that one day the Hitler years would pass. So far the democracies had allowed him easy victories, and when they ended the eyes of the German people would open.

Before the summer of 1938 arbitrary arrests of Jews were the exception, sporadic attacks outside the law, though they usually went unpunished, particularly if the Gestapo was involved. Hitler and the ministries frowned on *Einzelaktionen*, individually incited violence, even when started by Goebbels. They undermined central control and direction. Law-abiding Jews did not expect to be arrested. You had to denounce the Nazis openly, engage in clandestine activities, or break the law to place yourself in danger. More threatened were the so-called asocials, people who did not conform to expected lifestyles – a heterogeneous group of petty criminals, beggars, and the 'work shy'. Included in this category were Roma and Sinti if they were not settled. The concentration camps were known about and feared, but 'adjusted' Germans who kept their mouths shut and dutifully said '*Heil Hitler*' had nothing to fear. You had to be cautious: a careless remark overheard by the wrong person could have unpleasant consequences such as a summons to the Gestapo, but without sufficient proof you would be released. For a first minor offence a warning was usually regarded as sufficient. Apart from the exceptional and the unusual, Nazi Germany still appeared to be a *Rechtsstaat*, a state where law prevailed, if one overlooked the fact that new laws were perverting justice. But there was also constant pressure from below to fulfil the Nazis' ideological aims, the local civil servants initiating action ahead of decrees, especially when it came to discriminating and isolating Jews. A civil servant in Hamburg, for instance, thought it a strange anomaly in 1935 that synagogues were exempted from property taxes.[1] But legality still held sway. The Law Office explained that nothing could be done, as synagogues under existing rules were treated like the churches. It took time to catch up and issue all the necessary decrees to fleece the Jews.

In March 1938, the tax privileges of the community were removed, the start of an assault on Jewish organisations with serious consequences. This meant that the local communities no longer had a legal right to raise taxation as a proportion of state and Reich taxes. They of course had to continue to do so to meet the increased demands made on them. After more than 150 years of self-finance, bankruptcy now became a prospect. The economic base was shrinking and emigration of the wealthier members of the community was depleting income.

Jews before 1938 could still lead a dual existence in close touch with purely Jewish associations, attending the private Jewish *Kulturbund*, with its plays, readings, musical and social events, but also public 'German' symphony concerts and the theatre. Jewish parents continued to send their children to German schools. In everyday life, most Germans behaved reasonably; only a minority were openly nasty. Shopkeepers served their Jewish customers, and the general public did not hesitate to patronise Jewish shops if they supplied what they wanted at a better quality and lower price than the Aryan competition. The majority of Jews lived in the bigger cities, where life still followed a customary pattern. Here the Jewish organisations provided strong support. For the young there were Jewish sports clubs, since Jews were no longer allowed into German ones. But communities in the smaller localities found it difficult to survive, as more and more of their members moved to the larger towns where greater anonymity was possible. There were also places still where Jews could go on holiday in Germany. In Buttenhausen, a small township in Württemberg, Jews and Christians, the rabbi and the local priest, were on the best of terms even in 1938. This was unusual but not unique. Everyday life to all appearances remained surprisingly normal. That is why the majority of Jews were not ready to leave.

The months of January and February 1938 passed relatively quietly. There was, of course, the usual party pressure and abuse. In Berlin, storm troopers attacked the *Ostjuden* in the *Scheunenviertel*, but Hamburg was peaceful. The first massive breakdown in law and order did not occur in Germany, but in March in Austria.[2] Before even the Germans had taken control of Vienna, local Austrian Nazi thugs abused and humiliated Jews, attacked and plundered shops and forced Jewish men and women to scrub pavements, shouting, 'Down with the Jews! *Heil Hitler! Sieg Heil!* Perish the Jews'. In August, Eichmann put into practice the proposal of the previous year and organised a central office to speed up the emigration of Jews wanting to escape the intolerable conditions. It proved a success. Austria became a model for the *Altreich* (the pre-1937 Reich). But not everything worked so smoothly or could be centrally controlled.

I

Reich ministers were ignored by *Reichsstatthalters*, *Gauleiters* and local party leaders when it suited them. Some decrees were welcome; others did not go far enough and were creatively supplemented. Orders from the Reich Ministry of the Interior, for example, were issued, signed by Frick and Himmler, on the treatment of prisoners in Gestapo hands, detailing precisely when stricter methods of interrogation were allowed and how many strokes of the cane were permitted in the presence of a doctor. Locally not a blind bit of notice was paid. There was no shortage of torturers. Whether Berlin's decrees were followed or not depended largely on the whim of the local party, *Gauleiters* and bureaucrats. The men who wielded whips were beyond the restraint of orders from Berlin. In

the concentration camps the SS henchmen were given free rein, the comman-
dants even exceeding in sadistic brutality the rank and file.

Himmler gradually imposed his control over the police and the repressive
machinery of the state, pushing aside Frick, the minister to whom he was supposed to be responsible. In other areas, especially when it came to the economy,
there was little cohesion. Göring struggled to centralise economic policy to prepare Germany for war under the aegis of the Four-Year Plan. It had fallen far
behind its objectives. Even basic resources for conducting a war lasting longer
than a few months were lacking. There was a dire shortage of labour; another
key shortage was the foreign currency required to import raw materials. The
Four-Year Plan lurched from one crisis to the next. Casting around for a solution
as to how to plug the financial hole, it seemed that Jewish assets – shares, bank
deposits, property, jewellery, gold, silver and precious stones – were an obvious
target. The first need was to find out what the Jews still owned.

A decree dated 26 April 1938 required Jews to fill out a four-page questionnaire.[3] This asked for personal details, place of birth, citizenship, whether married
to a Jew or not, plus details of capital and ownership under four headings – land,
property, rents and pensions, money in the bank and shares – with a further listing
required of works of art, jewellery, stamp collections. Nothing of value was
omitted. Two pages of detailed instructions accompanied the form, which had to
be returned by 30 June 1938; any omissions or delay would lead to heavy fines
and prison. It would take time to scrutinise the returns. It required no imagination
to surmise that its purpose was confiscation. Meantime, Jewish wealth shrank during the course of the year and 'voluntary' Aryanisation made strides in Hamburg
and elsewhere. Göring also expected the Reich to share in the profit from taking
businesses away from the Jews.[4] By the summer of 1938 the majority of Jewish
business were already in Aryan hands, purchased at highly favourable prices –
profits all round for valuers, lawyers, banks, party officials and the new owners,
provided they knew how to run them. So far the Reich had derived little profit.[5]
Göring was determined to remedy that. According to local records there were still
1,200 mostly small Jewish businesses functioning in Hamburg in 1938, an estimated decline of only one-fifth, but that probably understated the loss.

What all this showed was that the pressure on Germany's Jews was gathering
pace. Pressure from the top, pressure from below. The party hate campaigns
were hotting up. Anyone showing friendliness to a Jewish neighbour began to
feel threatened from possible denunciation. Teachers generally still behaved
'correctly'. An incautious remark could lead to drastic consequences for the little
man. An electrician in Hamburg got into trouble for being overheard saying,
'The state does not pay decently, whereas Jewish firms like Robinsohn and
Alsberg pay properly and are really generous in such things as pension plans for
their employees', adding for good measure, 'If Hitler said from tomorrow everyone will wear a suit blue in front and red behind, then the German people would
act accordingly without hesitation … the *Volk* follows their *Führer*.' His punishment, despite his pleas, was to be excluded from work for the state.[6]

The party for years had demanded that more should be done to exclude Jews from any contact with the German *Volk* as employers. The state sector had cleared out the Jews; it was high time that the principle was extended to the rest of German life. Indirect influences had to be stamped out too, such as hiding the 'Jewishness' of a business using a German name, or employing Aryan partners and frontmen while influencing decisions from behind; the investment of Jewish capital in an otherwise Aryan enterprise should be stopped. Paranoia knew no limits. Signs in restaurants and hotels, 'Jews not wanted', sprouted everywhere. Jews were not yet externally marked with a yellow badge, so no one knew whether an individual was Jewish unless it seemed to be 'obvious' from their appearance – sometimes leading to unfortunate mistakes. None of this was authorised by the Reich government, but it was tolerated and encouraged in the regions. Some places, such as Nuremberg and Munich, were worse, others – Berlin and Hamburg – a little better; it was only a matter of degree.

II

Emigration began to increase modestly again during the early months of 1938. Since 1933 Jews with assets in business or capital had been liquidating them to transfer what they could, even if it was only a small proportion. When an invete-rate optimist like Max Warburg was 'voluntarily' contemplating giving up control of the family bank, which he had vowed to defend like his castle, the writing was on the wall. In an unpublished passage of his memoirs he reveals some of the agony and indecision he felt at this time: 'In my growing inner desperation, the one thing that kept me going was that I had to fulfil my duty to the family, the firm and my Jewish fellow citizens. I would not capitulate until I was forced to do so.'[7] He worked with undiminished vigour for Jewish charitable organisa-tions and for Jewish clients who tried to save a fraction of their wealth on leav-ing the country. Early in 1938 the time had come to hand over the bank, to 'Aryanise' it. On paper it looked like a more favourable outcome than might have been expected. Max Warburg wanted to preserve at least the bank's inde-pendence and not see it fall into the hands of a Nazi predator. By allowing friendly 'Aryans' a controlling partnership, he hoped he would be able to retain a minority family stake and an active role in running the bank. That too proved hopelessly out of touch – as if Nazis would have welcomed the retention of Warburgs. But Max and his Jewish partners were still able to choose new part-ners from loyal clients who now subscribed the capital to purchase the bank. At its head to run it was the existing Aryan general manager Rudolf Brinkmann, who owed his good fortune to having acted as 'frontman' for the Jewish partners on a number of boards. He was joined by Paul Wirtz, a Hamburg merchant brought in from outside. Neither were party members and so their acceptance by the *Reichsstatthalter* Kaufmann appears surprising. But Kaufmann was astute: he wanted to make sure that the Warburg bank remained a Hamburg business and that its Aryanisation should look benign in foreign eyes, as the role the bank played and could continue to play in Hamburg's overseas trade was important. Max Warburg explained in April 1938 to a banking client in Oslo that the new partners had subscribed 12 million *Reichsmark* and 'were all old clients, with some of whom the bank had worked for two generations'. The Warburgs were permitted to retain one-fifth of the capital, 3 million *Reichsmark*, and so would keep a 'sleeping' share in the business, as Kaufmann insisted that the Jewish partners had to go.

30 May 1938 was the day Max Warburg said goodbye to the assembled employees and associates.[8] There were tears as he moved among them, shaking hands with a genial smile, saying a few words to each one. He gave no hint of the bitterness he felt, praising the two men taking his place. By their side would remain Kurt Sieveking who had risked his career as a lawyer to join M. M. Warburg two years earlier.

Max Warburg did not simply wash his hands of the bank after ceasing to be a partner. He wrote to the loyal customers who had stayed with him, asking them to give their confidence to the new partners and owners. The responses he received were balm to his wounded feelings.[9] The well-known coffee importer Arthur Darboven sent a warm letter:

> My relations to your firm M. M. Warburg & Co. are for my part purely personal. During the many decades we have worked together, you have never let me down when I approached you with my wishes … I deeply regret the changes now taking place in your firm … I will visit you to keep in personal touch with you and your brother … I will continue my business with the present bank. In this way I transfer my personal loyalty and the gratitude I feel for you and your brother to the new firm.

On behalf of the Hamburg Charitable Society, Dr Gerda Feldner also conveyed deep regrets: 'Through our hands passed a large proportion of the charitable contributions made by your firm for the needy irrespective of religion or race … we felt ourselves as a part of your firm and identified ourselves with its existence and interests.' A final example of such testimonies, though not from a well-known industrialist, came from a single lady, Fräulein Eleonore du Bois-Reymond, who deliberately sent a postcard to the Ferdinandstraße so that everyone could read it; nothing could change her admiration and gratitude, she wrote, 'for everything you have done during the whole of your life for *our* Germany, achievements which today are falsely suppressed and denied'. These were the 'other Germans' in all walks of life who had enjoyed good business and personal relationships with Jews. They were outraged by the anti-Jewish measures but were powerless to do more than express their feelings.

Max Warburg was bitter at the terms of Aryanisation, explaining to his nephew James in New York, 'The negotiations changed course frequently, even though certain basic principles were maintained.' Even the money the Warburgs received for the bank was not theirs to dispose of. The Amsterdam bank fell into

German hands in 1940. So in the end nothing was left of the assets of one of Germany's wealthiest families – not an isolated case, but typical. 'In outward form Aryanisation did not mean confiscation', Max Warburg wrote, but 'the end result was just that.'[10] He was angry that the family name continued to be associated with the bank from which they had been expelled.

Almost to the end Max Warburg had not intended to leave his home and beloved Hamburg. He retained his faith in the German people. They were, he thought, fundamentally sound and would recover their traditional tolerance, and this would be especially true of Hamburg. The black mood he described in exile in his memoirs did not wholly reflect his feelings while still in Hamburg. During the summer of 1938, he wrote, 'My brother Fritz and I will remain in Hamburg. We will go on helping but not as much as in the past.' Whom did they propose to help? The Jewish community, obviously, but also the bank? In fact in the bank's archives an extraordinary epilogue is recorded, revealing Max Warburg's refusal to abandon ship, his courage, his audacity but, alas, also his misjudgement. In August 1938, Max and Fritz Warburg applied to Kaufmann to found a new firm in Hamburg to provide advice to Jewish businessmen having to deal with Aryanisation and other questions.[11] The actual financial transactions, he explained, would then be passed on to the Warburg bank; the proposal of acting as a consultant and agent was supported by the Aryanised Warburg bank, which was hoping to benefit from Jewish clients. Kaufmann's reply was curt and to the point: Jews were not permitted to start any new business – a definitive end.

A charitable Warburg foundation, the Sekretariat Warburg, survived until 1941, administering Warburg properties and the capital in blocked accounts. The Warburg house at Mittelweg 17 became a cultural oasis, with a reading room and library for Hamburg's beleaguered Jews caught in Germany by the war. The foundation also received support from the bank, an honourable gesture amid so much shameless exploitation.

Max Warburg left Hamburg for New York in August 1938 to raise money for Jewish emigration, intending to return.[12] His brother Fritz emigrated to Sweden. Eric followed his father to the United States. In early November, as chairman of its trustees, Fritz returned to Hamburg to assist the *Israelitisches Krankenhaus* in its financial crisis. During the pogrom of 9 and 10 November, Crystal Night, Fritz was arrested and incarcerated in Fuhlsbüttel. Not until May 1939 was he released from prison and able to return to Sweden. Max Warburg was warned in time by the bank not to go back. He would never again see the city to which he was tied by so many links. He died in his seventy-ninth year in New York.

The night of broken glass

During the summer of 1938 the atmosphere was becoming more oppressive. For those who did not close their eyes there were ominous signs that the Nazis were planning drastic new measures. The tempo of Jews giving up their factories and shops 'voluntarily' was increasing as they tried to get the best deal they could for what were in reality forced sales. 30 June was the date set for the *Vermögensabgabe*, the listing in minute detail of all a Jew still possessed. In July, the remaining Jewish doctors lost the right to practise after the end of the year, though a few war veterans were permitted to continue as *Krankenbehandler*, medical helpers for Jews. In Hamburg 195 Jewish doctors of the 300 remaining 'non-Aryans' lost their livelihood and profession; just fourteen were granted the status of *Krankenbehandler*. The same drastic expulsion removed Jewish lawyers; in Hamburg twelve were retained as legal assistants for Jews. Only racial Jews were affected by these measures in 1938; non-Aryans who were *Mischlinge*, half- or quarter-Jews, were excluded. Hitler was showing caution in dealing with the *Mischlinge*, overriding ideological diehards. He was focused on the coming war, the *Wehrmacht*'s insistence to conscript the *Mischlinge* and the reactions of hundreds of thousands of Aryan relatives. Old lists of non-Aryan doctors diligently drawn up in Hamburg were ordered to be removed from circulation.[13]

Public reminders of Jewish achievements had to be erased. And so, in August, Frick required the removal of Jewish and Marxist street names.[14] Hamburg was faced with a special difficulty. The city-state had been enlarged in 1937 with the additions of former Prussian Altona, Harburg-Wilhelmsburg and Wandsbek. There were some 1,600 street names that already needed to be changed to avoid duplication. The undesirable Marxists, Weimar politicians and Jews were an added problem. To manufacture so many street name signs in a short time proved impossible. In the end, it was decided that the changeover would have to be postponed with the exception of the most 'undesirables'. *Reichsstatthalter* Kaufmann asked for more time, but on orders from Berlin the 'undesirables' had to be tackled without delay.

In the centre of the city, Dr Nicolaus Ferdinand Haller had a fine thoroughfare named after him. The Hallers were a prosperous Jewish family who had moved to Hamburg in the eighteenth century. Nicolaus Ferdinand Haller, a prominent patrician and senator, six times mayor of Hamburg, was baptised but had married the Jewish daughter of a banker; his father too had been baptised and had married a Jewish wife. His son, Martin Haller, was also baptised; despite Protestant baptisms through three generations, he would nevertheless have been classified as a full Jew by the Nazis had he not died in 1926. Martin Haller had made a significant contribution to Hamburg's spectacular skyline. He was the leading architect of the *Rathaus*, the splendid neo-Gothic town hall which dominated the renamed Adolf-Hitler-Platz. It was one thing to dispatch Hamburg's worthies to oblivion, but the city would look ridiculous if it tried to abolish the internationally famous such as Heinrich Hertz, the physicist world famous for the discovery of the length and velocity of electro-magnetic waves named after him. His father was a Jew, so Heinrich was a post-dated 'half-Jew'. The *Reichsstatthalter* asked for an exception to be made. Frick would not allow it. Twenty-two streets proved racially impure. Street names were not the only problem. Stonemasons were called to remove six portrait medallions prominent inside the *Rathaus* of five 'full Jews': the philanthropist Salomon Heine, uncle of the poet; the lawyer and politician Isaac Wolffsohn; Moritz Heckscher, elected to represent Hamburg in the Frankfurt pre-parliament of 1848; Felix Mendelssohn; and Heinrich Hertz again. The obsession is revealed by the trivial. Jews were also shunned socially. A century earlier, at the elite *Harmonie* club in the Große Bleichen, Jews and Christians had mixed with ease; now Jews were no longer welcome.

During the summer of 1938 there were some open attacks on Jewish businesses in Berlin and elsewhere. Because they had been sentenced to a fine or a short term of imprisonment in the past, 600 Jews were sent to concentration camps without legal process. Heydrich was applying the lessons of Austria. The Jews had been added for the first time to so-called asocials – itinerants, vagrants, beggars, the homeless, pimps and petty criminals, as well as Roma and Sinti. There had been a previous *razzia* of asocials three months earlier, but the numbers caught in the net disappointed the Gestapo. On 15 June, in 'Operation Workshy', the criminal police were determined not to disappoint again. Heydrich's instructions were interpreted widely. Jews who had committed only traffic offences were arrested. In all some 10,000 men in Germany were taken to concentration camps, subjected to inhuman conditions, and forced to labour in SS enterprises. After only a few weeks came the first reports of deaths.

In Hamburg, Max Plaut secured the release of some of the Jews in Sachsenhausen. He negotiated with the Gestapo in Berlin, who agreed to let them go if they could prove they would leave Germany. Plaut succeeded in getting visas mainly to South American countries, and so they were saved – an important precedent as it turned out.

In September, the attention shifted away from the Jews as the world held its breath as to whether a war would be the outcome of the Sudeten crisis. It passed with the signature of the Munich Agreement on the last day of the month. Hitler was left in a black mood. The worst aspect had been the unmistakeable desire of the German people for a peaceful outcome. Even more galling was that an elderly gentleman with an old-fashioned stiff white collar and an umbrella that never seemed to leave his side had outshone in popularity the *Führer*. With peace assured, German audiences burst into demonstrative applause when Neville Chamberlain appeared on newsreels.[15] Jews took a different view of Munich. They saw the settlement as the last opportunity of checking Hitler. If the two great democracies were not prepared to defend Czechoslovakia, a small democracy they had created in 1919, what chance they would defend the German Jews? Hitler was robbed of easy military glory. The Jewish leadership feared the worst and did not have to wait long.

I

The Polish Jews living in Germany were the first to suffer mass expulsions. In October, thousands of Polish Jews were arrested all over Germany. Of the half million Jews in 1933, about 100,000 were not German nationals. It had always been difficult to secure citizenship, as the criterion was parentage, not place of birth. Just over half of the foreign Jews were in possession of Polish passports, though many had lived for decades in Germany.

When, early in October, Poles in Germany were required to have their passports validated at Polish consulates by the end of the month, the Gestapo realised that Germany would soon be landed with tens of thousands of Jews made stateless; no one actually knew how many.[16] When the Polish government refused to give an assurance that, even if made stateless, the Polish Jews would be allowed to return, Himmler, in coordination with the Foreign Ministry, ordered on 26 October their immediate deportation. Men only were to be arrested; their families could then be expected to follow. The result was chaotic. In the haste, in some cities like Hamburg, whole families were included to ensure maximum numbers; in others only the men were seized.

The Polish Jews who had settled in Hamburg and Altona for many years owned property, shops and a variety of businesses. They were caught unprepared. In the middle of the night of 28 October they were hauled out of their beds and forced to leave with no more than a suitcase. Children who had attended school just the day before, who spoke no word of Polish, afterwards sent pathetic postcards to their teachers of how much they missed their home, friends and classmates.

Among the Polish families were *Herr* and *Frau* Friedfertig.[17] They had lived in Altona for over thirty years. Just after 5 a.m. during the night of 28–9 October the doorbell rang. Two policemen appeared with a list of names. They said they had come to take the whole family with them. *Frau* Friedfertig explained that their eldest daughter was in Frankfurt and her other daughter in Berlin. In the end, they decided to arrest only *Herr* Friedfertig. 'Actually we are supposed to take you all with us': the policemen were solicitous and felt sorry for the family. '*Herr* Friedfertig, take your time and dress warmly and say your prayers, we will come back in ten minutes.' In the morning *Frau* Friedfertig took their youngest daughter to school and then went to the Jewish community offices in the Beneckestraße. It is easy to imagine her fears. The office was thronged with women. The community officers did their best to calm them. This had happened without any warning, the officers told them, but they were in touch with the Polish consulate in Hamburg and Berlin. In the streets of Hamburg there were scenes of men, women and children taken in custody. Policemen entered synagogues on the Sabbath to arrest men praying. The whole of Hamburg could hardly miss what was going on. Understandably but, as it turned out, foolishly, *Frau* Friedfertig went to look for her husband at police headquarters. There in the large gymnasium a scene of chaos met her eyes, with men, women, children and babies in prams milling about, not knowing what was going to happen to them next. The community social workers, alerted that morning, hurried to the police station with Max Plaut, bringing with them food and necessities hastily got together. *Frau* Friedfertig was able to find her husband and discuss with him what to do. Then she got up to leave. But the door was guarded and the police would not let her go, even though she explained she had not been arrested. In despair, worrying about her child left alone at home, she turned to one of the community social workers whose presence of mind saved the day. Fräulein Ellern, the social worker, went to the door with her, and when they reached the exit called out, 'You silly donkey, you forgot to bring my papers. They are in my desk.' The policemen, thinking she was one of the community assistants, let *Frau* Friedfertig pass. At home, she had just cooked dinner when there was another knock. A policeman again, this time to take her and her young daughter to police headquarters. The policeman allowed her time to pack and even helped to carry the luggage. In the evening they were all taken in lorries to the Altona railway station. On the platform, from which the public had been excluded, stood a normal passenger train, well lit and heated; community workers were there handing out food packets. The journey took all night. It was dawn when they arrived at Neu Bentschen, close to the border. Here they were met no longer by kindly Hamburg policemen, but urged on by the Gestapo. Those who fell behind on the march of 7 kilometres to the border were beaten; if the luggage was too heavy it was taken from them and just thrown away. Once they arrived at the frontier, men, women and children were driven into no-man's land. The Poles shot a few times in the air, but the whole group pushed on and eventually reached a wood on the Polish side. Here they remained all day and night in the rain. In the morning the Polish authorities finally managed to house them in the neighbouring town in stables, with just hay for bedding. Over the next few days and weeks, with help from Jewish organisations abroad, some semblance of living conditions was established. They had to rely on charity from abroad. This is the account of just one family, but 17,000 Polish Jews were expelled over the course of just three days – and it was happening not in war but in the midst of peace.

II

The third and by far the largest mass arrest this time of German Jews followed the pogrom of 9–10 November 1938, which has gone down in history as Crystal Night (*Kristallnacht*), a phrase coined in black humour to depict the millions of shards of glass from broken windows of Jewish shops and houses. The provoked violence was related to the Polish expulsions. Among those expelled had been the parents of Herschel Grynspan, an eighteen-year-old living in exile in Paris. On the morning of 7 November, crazed with anger and grief, he managed to get into the German Embassy and fired two shots at Ernst vom Rath, the first official he saw. Rath fell mortally wounded. He died on the afternoon of 9 November.

No one could have foretold this would occur.[18] In that sense the pogrom was not premeditated and planned to happen at that very moment. But what followed did fit the thinking of those Nazis who wanted to force the Jewish issue forward. The Gestapo and every ministry had their own ideas how best to achieve this, including the local Nazis in Hamburg.

What occurred is well known.[19] On 8 November, at nine o'clock in the evening, Hitler delivered a speech in the *Bürgerbräukeller* in Munich to assembled Nazi greats on the eve of the anniversary of the failed Putsch in 1923. He did not refer to the shots fired. The following day in the afternoon the news of Rath's death was known. At eight o'clock on 9 November the leaders and old party comrades gathered for dinner at the old town hall in Munich. Goebbels conversed with Hitler, who responded that demonstrations should not be hindered: 'The Jews should for once be made to feel the full fury of the people.' Then he left. Goebbels spoke and announced that Rath's death had led to popular anti-Jewish demonstrations; they should not be organised by the party, but if they break out spontaneously they should not be stopped. The hint was taken. The party leaders at midnight notified the local parties all over Germany to start the pogrom against the Jews. At one o'clock in the morning of 10 November, Himmler, after seeing Hitler, told Heydrich to issue instructions to the local SS to cooperate with the party. They should prevent the plunder of Jewish property and ensure both that the burning synagogues do not set neighbouring properties on fire and that as many Jewish men as could be accommodated, especially the better off, should be sent to concentration camps. Later that night further orders were passed on to public prosecutors and to justice officials that the perpetrators were not to be prosecuted – a green light for violence.

In Hamburg, there was widespread vandalism all over the city.[20] Jewish shop fronts were daubed with paint – 'Jew perish' – windows smashed and the contents thrown on the streets and plundered. The elegant fashion house of the Gebrüder Robinsohn on the Neuer Wall was trashed, its fifteen large shop windows broken to pieces, glass splinters everywhere. The Gebrüder Hirschfeld on the same street was ransacked. Close by, at Neuer Wall 30, the old established optical and photographic business owned by Julius Flaschner was vandalised. A contract for sale had already been agreed with the prospective new Aryan proprietor. The thugs were ignorant. Foreign-owned Jewish shops and some only rumoured to be Jewish were not spared. This was not the work of 'ordinary Germans' giving vent to their spontaneous anger, as Goebbels claimed, but of organised storm trooper gangs in civilian clothing who had assembled on the Adolf-Hitler-Platz in front of the townhall at 1 o'clock on the morning of 10 November. Armed with crowbars and bricks, they fanned out into the inner city in groups of six while the SS were asleep in their beds. Heydrich's instructions to the local Gestapo to prevent plunder reached them too late; they could not be contacted by phone at night by headquarters, as their home numbers were either out of date or missing: so much for efficient organisation. Soon 'ordinary Germans' followed the lead of the storm troopers, breaking into shops and joining the plunder; others just stood around, largely silent, interested spectators. Who now knows what they thought?

The destruction in Hamburg's inner city could not be hidden. There were still some thousand large and small businesses in Jewish hands in every district: clothing stores, shops selling valuable furs – such as Wolf Jägermann on the

Gänsemarkt – shoe shops, office suppliers, tobacconists, furniture stores, jewellers and drugstores. Few escaped the attention of the Nazi rowdies. The Hamburg press on 10 November tried to play down the damage. Foreign reactions still mattered when it came to exports and earning vital currency the armaments programme desperately needed. On 10 November, Goebbels published in the *Völkischer Beobachter* orders that all demonstrations and attacks on Jews were to cease. There followed similar instructions from the Berlin ministries and the Gestapo. But it proved easier to launch the thugs than to stop them.

From Berlin, foreign news correspondents sent back vivid reports. If they tried to take pictures they were arrested, taken to a police station and had their cameras confiscated. The ignorant mobs did not care much whether they were destroying the premises of foreign Jewish owners or German ones. The Dutch consul general, who tried to protect Dutch Jewish shops, was surrounded by an angry crowd and only just escaped lynching. He was rescued by the timely arrival of the police.

Smart milliners and dress shops such as Altaba and Rosner were reduced to a mass of torn materials, hats and other articles of clothing, trodden underfoot by the crowd with frenzied delight. In the Tauentzienstraße, one of the smartest shopping streets in Berlin, no fewer than twenty-four shops were demolished. Dobrin was a fashionable Jewish café. The mob smashed the counter and the tables and chairs and stamped cream cakes and confectionery into the floor. Another well-known restaurant, Weisz Czarda, owned by a Hungarian Jew, was invaded and wrecked by the mob.

The vandals also trashed the showroom of Citroën cars, a company once in Jewish ownership. In 1919, André Citroën, a brilliant entrepreneur, had set up the first European factory mass producing cars on the Left Bank in Paris. When he was forced into bankruptcy in 1935, one of his principal creditors, the Michelin Tyre Company, acquired the business. Compensation now had to be paid by the Nazis. The popular chain Etam was also wrecked. Booty was thrown from the first-floor windows to the street below, where women eagerly scrambled for it. All this took place in broad daylight. There were remarkably few policemen to be seen. Those who observed the pillage just shrugged their shoulders.

Mobs also broke into family apartments, threw furniture out of the window and terrified women and children whose fathers had been taken to a concentration camp. You heard the sound of broken glass come closer. Would they also break into your apartment? The long night passed; you were among the safe ones.

And what did the neighbours think? There was practically no public protest: that might have invited arrest. Vandalism does not fit the orderly German way. No doubt there was widespread 'inner' disapproval. Hiding a Jewish man you knew was also not so rare. But for the first time Germany's Jews felt utterly defenceless, their personal safety and their property at the mercy of the Nazis. The Berlin correspondent of the *Daily Telegraph* could hardly grasp what was happening, as he reported that 'Racial hatred and hysteria seems to have taken complete hold of otherwise decent people'.[21]

Synagogues in Berlin and elsewhere were burnt down. In Hamburg the synagogues had escaped during the night of the 9 November. Despite the order from Goebbels, arson was attempted, and a fire started the following day in Hamburg's main synagogue on the Bornplatz. It was extinguished, but the interior of the synagogue was demolished, as were other synagogues. The mortuary of the Jewish cemetery in Harburg was entirely burnt down. *Reichsstatthalter* Kaufmann could have stopped the arson and damage but allowed the pogrom to continue. Nazis in Hamburg wanted to make up for lost time; they did not wish to be stigmatised as soft on Jews. It was madness. The businesses were about to be Aryanised or closed down. The damage done was to the Reich. The Jews were only in temporary possession. It was irrational, as Göring and Himmler quickly realised, and they loathed Goebbels, who had stolen a march on them. Cold return to reason was overdue.

III

Luise Solmitz recorded these events in her journal.[22] On 7 November she referred briefly to the assassination attempt on the life of vom Rath, and two days later she voiced her fears, expecting reprisals:

9.11.1938. *Herr* vom Rath has died. This evening we heard the news from Paris. The infamous deed of a Polish Jew fills me with dread instead of abhorrence!

10.11.1938. A bad, bad day. Fredy first heard from the owner of the vegetable store that the Jewish shops were vandalised and closed. We went into the city to buy something … Much activity among the people, groups of them have gathered. Some roads are closed, all the large Jewish stores are shut, all the glass in the display windows of Robinsohn and Hirschfeld is shattered. The glaziers are working, and never before have I heard such constant jangle of broken glass. Some people are stupefied, others silent, and others voice their approval. There is an ugly atmosphere. One old lady said, 'if they shoot our people dead abroad, one has to respond this way'.

At 8 p.m. the radio announced that demonstrations and actions against Jews are to cease. Goebbels declared the *Führer* would give his answer to the murder of vom Rath by orderly decrees. What that means is that our fate moves unstoppably to its doom. Nearly all the windows of the synagogue [presumably the main synagogue on the Bornplatz] have been broken and the interior has been demolished. People looked through the doorways. The police stood in the front garden. People passed by in an unending stream ….

That evening Gisela and I brought a small dog to our police station. A Jew was being questioned; in the corner on a chair was slumped a man; his pallor was deathly white. The little dog sniffed the man. 'Pfui', said the policeman to the dog, 'that is a Jew.'

The three of us went with a companion to Baßler. Perhaps it was quite a good thing to do. The others there looked unconcerned, they know they have nothing to worry about ... all Jews are to report to the police by 6 p.m. and to bring their house and garage keys with them. It is said five hundred have been arrested.

From Berlin it is reported the synagogues were burnt down. The police and fire brigade did not intervene ... I always thought it could get no worse but, as it turns out, it was always just the prelude to what then followed. Now we approach the end.

11.11.1938. The day began with our cleaning lady making the following remark to comfort me: 'Now the mask has come off completely; now the Jews are finished.' I was fearful that she had heard something new early in the morning, but I was afraid to ask; but there was nothing new. Dark and bitter feeling. I went with Gisela into the city; instead of windows, wood covers the empty spaces. The damage is enormous. The people moved silently to and fro, no Jews among them ... Jews have to give up to the police all their weapons within four days. Fredy's beautiful hunting rifle and the weapons he carried in the war. One bitter blow is added to the other, not a spark of goodwill, of hope, of relief. Those whom this does not affect have no idea how happy, how secure their lives are. They do not have to fear for their possessions, the newspapers and the radio do not upset them ... Himmler threatens twenty years' concentration camp and imprisonment for anyone disobeying the order.

12.11.1938. I collected theatre tickets in the Alsterhaus. Before I entered I read, 'The Reich government will give its answer – legal but severe'. Our fate is sealed ...

Then I met Fredy ... and together we went to the Gestapo in the *Stadthaus*. Fredy had not read the order about the weapons or he would not have made the application to keep his dagger and pistol from the First World War. The two SS men who dealt with us in the hall at the bottom of the paternoster were somewhat perplexed – 'retired major?'. Then one said, 'That is all in the past now, and my advice to you is to give up every-thing ...

Just as we got home and wanted to go out again the doorbell rang. Two men in civilian clothing. Fredy said, 'Luise, the gentlemen are here from the Gestapo.' 'Come in', I said in a normal manner, as I entered the room with them. One of them said to Fredy, 'May we speak to you alone?' As I left the room I heard one of them say, 'Have you any medals from the war?' 'Yes, quite a lot.' 'Show us the documentation. Were you in the fly-ing corps?' 'Yes, one of the first flying officers in Germany and wounded with a 50 per cent disability ... what is the reason for your visit?' 'From the fact that we are leaving again you can conclude that everything is in order.' ... Fredy had to fight through a bad quarter of an hour ...

That evening the blow fell. Jews have to pay a thousand million Marks reparations for the murder in Paris. They are to be totally excluded from economic life. Now even Fredy admitted that we are destroyed.

In the next entry, Luise Solmitz refers to the 'final solution of the Jewish question', a phrase clearly in common usage long before the Wannsee Conference and not yet a euphemism for genocide.

> 14.11.1938. Discussions are being held on the final solution of the Jewish question … What will that lead to? Why do we have to tremble while 80 million can wait for it in peace?

There were adverse reactions to the vandalism even in the highest Nazi circles. Margarete Frick, the wife of Wilhelm Frick, minister of the interior, one of the most vicious instigators of Jewish persecution, wrote in her diary:

> Berlin, 5 December 1938. The stormy November is now past. Not the weather but the political horizon was stormy. This awful incitement against the Jews was terrible. One should send them out of the country in a decent manner, forbid them to earn their living here, but should not do things which are impossible for a people of culture! We are a cultured *Volk*, not Bolsheviks.

It is the only reference in her diary to the persecution of Jews.[23] In Munich, Cardinal Faulhaber noted only briefly the burning synagogues, but then at length described a threatened attack on his palace; the only damage, a broken window.[24] But there was one rare declaration of solidarity.[25] At their meeting in December 1938, a gathering of Protestants, the *Kirchentag der Konferenz der Landesbruderräte*, representing the Confessing Church, asked that a message should be read from the pulpits. Congregations were admonished to support fellow Christians of Jewish origin who were members of the congregation, as baptism superseded race. 'We are bound together as brothers with all those who believe in Christ. We do not wish to separate ourselves from them.' But there was no expression of support for Jews who were not baptised, no stand taken against the pogrom. Whether the message was ever read from the pulpits and by how many brave clergymen is not known.

The few individual clergymen, Protestant and Catholic, who spoke up paid for their moral conviction in concentration camps. In Hamburg there was silence. Bishop Franz Tügel boasted that he had been a lifelong antisemite. The one beacon of righteousness, the Jerusalem Church, was closed, its publication *Zions Freund* banned, and its two leading pastors driven out of the country. The pillars of a civilised state, the churches and the judiciary, utterly failed in Germany. And why? Because the majority agreed with so much the Nazis stood for.

IV

Something in public view more startling even than the destruction of the synagogues took place on 10 November. Lorry loads of men, all of them Jewish, were being driven through the streets. The arrest and brutal incarceration of 20,000 to 30,000 male Jews would rid Germany of 100,000 or more as their families followed. The better-off Jews were targeted because they were expected to find it easier to gain entry abroad. A further benefit was that their money would fall into the hands of the Reich, and some of it could be used to subsidise the exit of poorer Jews. Germany did not wish to be left with Jewish paupers.

In the early morning hours of 10 November, arrests began throughout Germany. The doorbell would ring. Two Gestapo men in black leather coats would ask the male Jew they found to accompany them. There was no time to take anything with them. No one had any idea why or where they were being taken, whether they would be away from home for a few hours or longer; most expected to be home before nightfall, knowing they had committed no offence. There were among them war veterans, businessmen, doctors, lawyers, retired civil servants in regular receipt of their pensions; so far in Nazi Germany they had lived a restricted but tolerable existence.

The wives with their children at home were left unprotected, not knowing what had happened to their husbands. Some hurried to the Gestapo and to police stations but could obtain no information. After a few days a message reached them from their husbands in the concentration camps. Middle-class German wives left big decisions to their husbands. Now all the responsibility fell on them. They had to enquire into the possibilities of emigration to secure the release of their husbands and make new arrangements for the children's schooling after their expulsion from the state schools. The difficulties were enormous, but they could not afford to give way to despair. On their shoulders now rested the lives of the whole family, and most rose to the challenge, securing the release of husbands, finding for them visas, transport and safe havens abroad. The children too had to be registered with the *Reichsvertretung* to be sent to safety on the *Kindertransporte*, the children's exodus. But thousands of wives later would not be able to save themselves and join their husbands, daughters and sons.

From Hamburg the Jews were taken first to a local police station or to Fuhlsbüttel, the principal police prison, more like a concentration camp. They were then transported to the railway station and from there to Sachsenhausen concentration camp in Oranienburg, just outside Berlin. Stripped of all respect and dignity, dressed in thin prison uniforms and with shaved heads, they spent hours standing to attention at roll calls, performed backbreaking labour, cold and hungry, driven by young SS guards. Some, in despair, ran into electric fences. Injuries were sustained, followed by infections of open wounds. There was no guarantee of survival after even a few weeks of this hell during a particularly cold winter.

People in the street witnessed the arrests as lorry loads of Jews were driven to the railway station or Gestapo quarters. No attempt was made to hide anything. Nor could news spreading abroad be prevented, though the newspapers in Hamburg avoided making mention of the wholesale incarceration of Jewish men.

The hunt for Jews had continued for a week after it was supposed to have ended. About one thousand arrests were made in Hamburg. The Gestapo showed real enthusiasm and were not too particular whom they caught. Max Plaut was among the first to be arrested to prevent him sending warnings to others to hide. He had a lucky escape.[26] The Gestapo put him in a prison cell, where he kept very quiet. No one came to see him, and he held out without food or water for a day and a half; not wishing to starve, he then called a guard. The policeman: 'What are you doing here?' Plaut: 'I was about to ask you the same question.' 'Are you a Jew? Don't you know that 1,200 Jews have been arrested and transported to a concentration camp?' Plaut replied that that was the first he had heard about it. 'What is going to happen now?', Plaut wanted to know. The policeman said he would ask the Gestapo. Soon a car came to collect him and brought him to Commissioner Göttsche. 'Where were you?', Göttsche wanted to know. 'We have been looking for you all this time.' Plaut: 'You should know. You collected me from the police cell.' Göttsche: 'I am not sure what to do with you, as there is no transport to the concentration camp.' Plaut helpfully suggested Göttsche should take his time to think it over but allow him meanwhile to go home; he would report twice a day to the police. The exchange was typical of Plaut's robust nature and black humour. It was fortunate for him that, after his many dealings with Göttsche, he had built up a rapport with him. Plaut returned to his community office. The chief rabbi, Joseph Carlebach, who had earned the respect of the Gestapo, was one of the few Jews not arrested.

The Gestapo could congratulate themselves on their general success. The 'rational' approach was working. There was now a mood of panic in the Jewish community. Any thought of staying in Germany was gone. Anyone who had the possibility of getting out tried to do so. No one was any longer choosy about the destination – be it Shanghai, Santo Domingo, Bolivia or Cuba – if more acceptable havens were unattainable. The countdown to a ruthless resolution of the Jewish question in Germany had begun.

Meantime the state continued to pay pensions due each month, the 'correct' and the 'extra-legal', side by side. There was no intention of killing the Jews in the concentration camps. Himmler and Heydrich took pains to instruct the local Gestapo to exclude men who were elderly, sick or too young and to arrest only the healthy, but the instructions were not followed in Hamburg. The Jews who were incarcerated were to be harshly treated in the camps but to be released as soon as they could prove that they would leave Germany. The treatment in the camps was so inhumane that hundreds died from beatings, tortures, lack of nourishment and the winter cold. The young SS guards were not restrained in Sachsenhausen, where Hamburg's Jews were taken. Other camps, such as Buchenwald, close to Germany's cultural capital of Weimar, were even worse.

There was a wave of sympathy abroad. In some neighbouring countries, notably Britain, the Netherlands and France, immigration restrictions were eased, especially for children and men in concentration camps. On release the Jewish men were allowed only a short time to make arrangements to leave Germany.

Unable to take their families with them, once they had reached the country of rescue they made frantic efforts to get their wives and close relatives out. For most, time was too short. The outbreak of war closed the frontiers. Only a fortunate few could escape along the few routes still open, mainly through Italy to Shanghai. Husbands lost their wives in the Holocaust, children their mothers.

V

Crystal Night was terrifying for children too. Father was gone and mother was now in charge of the family. Should they leave and seek safety or stay at home? Nazi rowdies were breaking into unprotected homes. There were rumours everywhere, no sure information. Some sought safety by taking a slow train to somewhere distant – not the express trains, which might be inspected. Others were sheltered by a German friend. Most stayed at home and hoped for the best. Some children did not go to school the following day, but others went as usual. Quite large numbers of Jewish children were still attending state schools, and a law announced that they must all leave. Even in 1938 there were Jewish parents who made great efforts to place their children in German schools.

Expulsion was a shattering experience for the children, who did not know what they had done that was so wrong.[27] How could they face their parents? One little boy of eleven stood in the school courtyard that day on 10 November, all alone during the morning break, crying inconsolably. He had been so proud the previous year to have passed the test allowing talented children to enter the grammar school a year early. He had friends at school who sat next to him when the teacher was out of the classroom and accompanied him on his way home. He was happy and extrovert and not much bothered by the Nazi paraphernalia. Now it had all ended in disgrace. A teacher came over. He took the boy aside. In a quiet corridor where no one could see them he put his arm round his shoulder: 'Go home. Your parents will understand.' It was a gesture of kindness the boy did not forget. Schools generally provided the departing Jewish child with a fair leaving report and good marks. In some schools, boys and girls were able to stay a few weeks longer to enable them to pass the *Abitur*, the all-important school leaving examinations. Many teachers of the senior classes had known the children growing into young adults for seven or more years and did what they could for them.

Elementary schooling remained compulsory for Jewish children by Nazi decree.[28] Every child had to be found a place. The Gestapo cooperated in releasing teachers from concentration camps, but there were difficulties nevertheless. Jewish parents who had not brought up their children religiously found the orthodoxy of the *Talmud Tora Schule* unacceptable. The elders of the community had to forge a compromise in what became a surprisingly bitter dispute. Worse was the position of Christian boys racially defined as Jews. A pastor was brought in to provide religious instruction. There appears to have been less trouble in the girl's school in the Karolinenstraße. These were extraordinary times, but quick adjustments were difficult. In the Jewish school the children could now feel more relaxed. Classes dwindled as families left. Teachers enquired whether a parent had been released from a concentration camp. There were bonds of sympathy and of a common fate, softening the traditional barriers between teacher and pupil. The return of a father was not a joyous affair. He came home, his head shaved, gaunt, clothes hanging off his body, often with bandages covering an injury. He had become hardly recognisable. Soon many left the country. But Jews did not experience uniform hostility. There were individual Germans who expressed sympathy and distanced themselves from what was happening. It was of little comfort as the Jews left in Germany now faced their future with foreboding.

Time to act

In Berlin, preparation for the coming war and the radical solution of the 'Jewish question' were forced forward at a frantic pace during the autumn and winter of 1938. Hitler left it to Göring to coordinate policies. In charge of the Four-Year Plan, Göring already had responsibilities for overseeing the economy and the build up of arms as well as for the final solution of the Jewish problem. He was intelligent, ruthless and loyal. On 12 November, in the aftermath of Crystal Night, he called a meeting of Nazi leaders to the Air Ministry to work out what was to be done to the Jews.[29] It was an extraordinary discussion even by Nazi standards. Problems were raised, so to speak, on the hoof. Göring, as was his custom, injected an air of black humour, addressing ministers with familiarity as *Kinder*, chums. It comes across as more like a gathering of Mafiosi, vying with each other to make useful suggestions. Time was spent on ridiculous detail. Goebbels, who was not in good odour with Göring, at one point suggested Jews should not be permitted to share compartments with Germans on trains. Goebbels next complained that the Jews in his *Gau* of Berlin were walking in the beautiful Grunewald forest on the outskirts, causing offence to good Germans. Göring ridiculed the propaganda minister; why not cordon off a part of the forest as a reservation for Jews only and populate it with animals with Jewish noses – elks, for instance?

What had made Göring furious was the destruction of property, of Jewish shops soon to be German, and the wholesale plundering that had occurred during the pogrom. The damage was done to the German economy, not the Jews. Goebbels kept quiet. Göring then got lost in a long discussion on the insurance aspect. A thousand million *Marks* in the form of an 'atonement fine' would be drained off the wealth the Jews had retained. Göring was out to grab all he could.

Heydrich was amazed at so much irrelevant discussion. Sight was being lost of the main policy objective of getting as many Jews as possible out of Germany. If no foreign currency was made available so they could emigrate, how could this be achieved? To clear them out of the Reich would take eight to ten years.

Göring now informed the ministers that the *Führer* had told him three days earlier that he would pressure foreign countries to take in the Jews in some colonial
territory like Madagascar, but if it came to war frustrating this solution, then
'there will be a great reckoning for the Jews'. Hitler on the last day of January
1939 spelt it out more precisely. 'If finance world Jewry in Europe and overseas
engulf the peoples in another world war, then the consequence will not be the
Bolshevisation of the world, and so the victory of Jewry, but the annihilation of
the Jewish race in Europe.' In preparing for war, he hoped to march eastwards
without having to fear attack from the West. The Jews, the 'wire pullers of power
in Washington and London', were thus warned that Hitler would have in his
hands millions of Jews as hostages. As he repeated his 'prophecy' several times,
it also served as an alibi, for whatever was done to the Jews would be not by his
hand but through the destiny the Jews had brought on themselves.

In response to demands that Jews be finally driven out of the 'German economy', Göring promised to issue an order that very day. It appeared at first as simple as that. It was agreed that the removal of the Jews from their shops and
businesses should happen as quickly as possible so as not to allow foreigners to
raise a new hue and cry. But Göring foresaw that haste could lead to temptation.
Aryanisation could only be achieved quickly if it was decentralised and decisions
were left to the local party, *Gauleiters* and heads of the state administration, like
Kaufmann's in Hamburg. The corruption that had occurred in the past, Göring
warned, would not be tolerated again. He threatened to reverse venal decisions.
He then pointed out the obvious. If the economy was not to be damaged, businesses to be Aryanised had to be taken over by new owners competent to run
them. Party applicants were only to be given preference all other qualifications
being equal. This proved an empty expectation; in the free for all it was good
party men and cronies who acquired valuable assets at knock-down prices.
Göring informed his colleagues that Hitler required all decrees to be passed on
the 'Jewish Question' should be scrutinised by him, but the *Führer* did not want
this to become publicly known, as in his present position he would be too com-
promised both at home and abroad. He added that he would rather not have
become involved in the 'Jewish Question', but as the head of the Four-Year Plan
this was unavoidable. What did he mean? What had the economic Four-Year
Plan and preparations for war to do with the 'Jewish Question'? Nobody asked.
Everyone understood the connection. The German Jews were to be robbed of
their capital and foreign holdings to keep the Germany economy on track, Göring
briefly explained. The ministers went on talking, meandering from one subject to
another. The Jews had become dehumanised objects.

I

A month after the meeting at the Air Ministry, Frick got in on the act.[30] He
invited party and state leaders from the regions, the finance minister, the police
president of Berlin and Heydrich on 16 December to the Ministry of the Interior.

Kaufmann sent Ahrens and Krogmann and, in a gesture of independence, stayed in Hamburg. Frick had gone to see the *Führer*. Power was based on being entrusted with his decisions.This meeting was important precisely because Hitler now made his views known. The racial issue was the 'most fundamental facing the Third Reich', Frick declared, opening the discussion. On that, he said, everyone was agreed. There had been conflicts between party and state which needed to be eliminated so they could all work together towards the objectives they were all agreed on. Hitler had made it clear with obvious emphasis that the *Mischlinge* were not to be equated with Jews and were to be excluded from the discriminatory measures against Jews. To the assembled ministers that was unwelcome news; Frick had to emphasise it was the *Führer*'s decision. The *Mischlinge* were even to be compensated for any damage done to their property during Crystal Night. Firms could employ them but could not be made to do so. Aryanisation did not apply to them but only to Jews. If a German was married to a Jew he or she remained a German. The definition of Jew, Frick explained, had to be narrow, as there were, with Austria included, 700,000. That number would be much greater if all the *Mischlinge* were added. The priority was to get rid of the 'full' Jews. The *Führer* expressly wished that emigration was to be furthered by all means and that no difficulties were to be placed in the way of Jews wishing to leave. Furthermore, there were plans to enable the Jews without means in Germany to emigrate. Every well-to-do Jew had to take with him four poor Jews and support them. The opposition of foreign countries to accepting Jews without means had to be overcome. To achieve this, a foreign loan based on Jewish capital in Germany would be raised, and for that reason Jewish capital had to be preserved and could not simply be confiscated. Hjalmar Schacht had been sent to London to negotiate a deal. Frick hoped that its success would provide the opportunity to get rid of the Jews. So far, 125,000 had left the old Reich and 50,000 Austria. Another 100,000 should be enabled to emigrate as soon as possible, but their total departure 'one has to expect would take several years'.

Schacht's efforts in London to secure a loan were taken seriously. Wholesale genocide of Germany's Jews would have 'solved' the problem quickly but was not yet considered. Frick admitted that there were many Germans who complained that Jews were still running shops, businesses and factories. Too little had been done. He assured everyone that would now change. Jews would be permitted to draw pensions. But exceptions would have to be made, especially in the vital area of exports. Much had already been achieved, but care had to be taken because of international conditions. The anger of the people the previous November was understandable, but attacks on Jews and their property were unlawful. No one had the right to be governed by passions. What was done had injured not only the Jews but the German people. The only positive outcome had been the push it had given the Jews to leave Germany; he hoped Germany would be rid of them in a few years.

Detailed plans were outlined: unemployed Jews would be forced to find work in groups; some Jewish businesses would be permitted to continue – the *Führer*

had personally ordered that a Jewish company should be formed to provide housing for Jews; the Jews would shortly lose their tenancy agreement rights; Jews
would not be placed in ghettos but would be concentrated in particular streets, so
the houses in these streets should remain in Jewish ownership. Hitler had also
rejected a number of proposals. One was to close whole streets to Jews. Instead
they could be curfewed on certain days. Hitler had also rejected the proposal that
Jews should be stigmatised by wearing a Yellow Star. He was learning from the
outrage expressed abroad over the events of Crystal Night. Signs saying 'Jews
not welcome' should only be shown in hotels and restaurants which the party fre-
quented, not everywhere. If Jewish welfare offices were no longer able to support applicants, state welfare payments should be made. The *Führer* had also
expressly declared that Jews may shop in German stores. One other suggestion
which Hitler also rejected was to deprive Jews who had been forcibly retired of
their pensions. This would have alarmed the civil service. Instead pensions
would be reduced. Party and civil servants now knew what was expected of
them.

On 28 December, Göring issued secret instructions throughout the Reich con-
veying 'Hitler's decisions on the Jewish question'.[31] They followed closely what
Frick had already reported at the earlier meeting. In Berlin and elsewhere Jews
were banned from theatres and cinemas. Blond Jewish children ignored such
prohibitions, as no one could tell they were not Aryan. There were a few more
detailed suggestions that were rejected by Hitler. No special compartments were
to be introduced on the railways, but Jews were no longer to be permitted in restaurant cars or sleeping carriages; they were not, however, to be forbidden from
using all forms of transport, buses and streetcars.

The most significant addition Hitler required was that Jews in mixed marriages were in future to be classified in several new categories. The classification
arose over the question of whether to force all Jews to move into Jewish quarters.
(The following April a law was passed depriving Jews of tenancy protection,
which incorporated the *Führer*'s decision of the previous December.) Marriages
between Aryans, now called of 'German blood', and Jews were redefined; there
was to be a new kind of mixed marriage called 'privileged'. This existed if there
were children not brought up as Jews. Then a distinction was to be made whether
the head of the household, the husband, was Jewish or of 'German blood'. If the
husband was of 'German blood' and the wife Jewish, such a mixed marriage
with children was in the most favoured position; the family could remain in their
home, the wealth of the Jewish wife and mother could be transferred to the
German husband or child. The same protection of 'privilege' was extended, however, only 'for the time being', to mixed marriages – such as the Solmitzes –
where the husband was Jewish and the wife German and their children were not
Jewish; the wealth of the Jewish father could, again, 'for the time being', be
transferred to the *Mischling* children but not to his wife. The concession, it was
explained, was granted as the sons could be called upon to serve in the army.
Mixed marriages where the husband was of 'German blood' and the wife Jewish

and there were no children were also 'privileged'. But if the husband was Jewish and the wife German, and the marriage was childless, then it was a 'non-privileged mixed marriage' and the husband was treated as a Jew; only the deportation was postponed. If the children were Jewish, then the whole family were to be treated as Jews (*Geltungsjuden*) and lost protection: their capital could not be transferred to the German partner, they could be moved into Jew houses, and they were to be included in the accelerated emigration movement. If the German wife divorced her husband, however, she would regain all her rights as a German. The state authorities, Göring declared, were to act strictly according to these clear decisions of the *Führer*, which remained the basis of future persecution until shortly before the end of the war. Only in 1944 and 1945, in a last effort to complete the 'final solution', did deportation of the Jewish partners of 'mixed marriages' begin. But it was too late: most of those deported or sent away to forced labour survived.

To prevent unrest, uncertainty, arbitrariness and corruption, the definitions had to be clear and made conditional only on establishing the religion of four grand-parents. They were not dependent on judgements of character or looks made by some official open to influence and bribery or personal whim. For a time, it is true, a process of reclassification was possible on appeal. But Hitler disliked this and put a stop to it. Later attempts by Heydrich to move Hitler away from strict classi-fication towards personal assessments of individuals all failed. Hitler the moderate seems out of character. But Hitler's preoccupation with such detail now and later was confined to *German* Jews, *German* mixed marriages and their descendants not out of concern for them but concern for the reaction of the rest of the German people and his international aims. Perhaps this need not have worried him as much as it did even during the war. He did not bother to issue such precise instructions when it came to Poles or Russians. Meantime, plenty of Germans had other con-cerns than what would happen to the Jews as they scrambled to profit from the robbery of Jewish possessions. What was planned and discussed in distant Berlin determined the fate of the Jews in Hamburg.

II

Wholesale Aryanisation or liquidation of businesses, the biggest opportunity to make gains, was practically completed in only a few months in Hamburg.[32] There was a rush after 10 November 1938. For every business there were three or four eager suitors. To speed the process, the selection and negotiations were conducted at short meetings with a minimum of paperwork. It was a recipe for corruption. In December 1938, the chamber of commerce drew up a list of some 800 businesses. Some were closed, reducing competition, their contents acquired at rock-bottom prices. Those that were Aryanised were considered of much lower value when in Jewish hands, the price their owners received, than the value once they were in Aryan ownership. The difference was the 'profit', part of which should have flowed into the coffers of the Reich, but not all of it did so. A Jewish business had no 'goodwill' that was taken into account when the valuer set the price. The valuers were picked party men and earned a good commission for their dishonest activities. Some new owners who had paid a better price before November 1938 now complained and even wanted some of their money back. The chamber of commerce was supposed to have a major role in the Aryanisation by proposing the valuers. In practice the economic adviser for the *Gau* of Hamburg, the 25-year-old Carl Otte, had the real say. Party members and cronies were preferred and protests from other applicants swept aside when they reached Kaufmann, who rewarded his friends. Of the 1,200 Jewish businesses still in existence in Hamburg before November 1938, only a few survived the following year. The Nazis wanted Aryanisation brought rapidly to a conclusion to forestall another outcry from abroad. The Jewish owners were left empty handed. Paul Berendsohn was refused permission to pass on the Köhlbrand dock to his 'half-Jewish' son. The purchase price was assessed at RM 400,000, from which a tax of RM 231,000 was deducted, which did not even leave enough to cover loans of RM 215,000. Forced to give up his valuable business, Paul Berendsohn was left penniless and in debt.

Cooperation between party, the chamber of commerce and the *Gau* economic adviser worked to the party's satisfaction. The honourable merchants of the elite Hamburg chamber of commerce, who did not miss out, were nevertheless concerned at what was going on. The whole process was outside the control of Hamburg's experienced businessmen and run by young party leaders like Otte and Kaufmann. The old elites were being pushed aside not only in politics, but now in the economic sphere as well. Kaufmann could choose to listen to their advice or ignore them. With a few honourable exceptions they were not particularly upset that the Jews were being cheated. Among these 'honourable' merchants there were many who profited. What worried them was that, if property could simply be taken from the Jews by passing a so-called law – that, is by the stroke of a pen – how safe were their own businesses from seizure by the party or the Reich if Hitler or Göring should one day decide it was in the interests of the Reich to kick them out? Would Kaufmann treat them any better then than he was now treating the Jews?

That there were such mutterings in Hamburg became clear from a speech Kaufmann delivered to the chamber of commerce in January 1939.[33] He said he understood that some honourable members were not happy at what had happened during the night of 9 and 10 November. He now wanted to reassure them, but the Jewish problem nevertheless had to be solved speedily; 'legal means' should be adopted. To lively applause, he declared: 'I am a decided opponent of those who believe that the problem, which does have to be solved positively, requires methods which normally are to be condemned.' Kaufmann claimed that in Hamburg he had tried to limit what had happened the previous November to the minimum that was necessary, and that this had won him the approval of Göring. 'It made no sense', he went on (to calls of 'Quite right!'), to ruin the goods of our nation; this destroyed not Jewish property but assets our nation needs. But I believe we have learnt our lesson; such things will not be repeated. We have to solve the [Jewish] problem in a restrained way, and quickly, so that the world accepts and does not raise its voice in loud complaint.

The reasonableness of the *Reichsstatthalter* was music to the ears of the assembled businessmen. Their *Gauleiter*, they thought, understood their needs. With his shameless belittling of the days of terror and vandalism, his distancing himself from them now, he had adjusted to current thinking in Berlin.

Aryanisation was supposed to progress in stages, according to Göring's directive. First of all came shops and businesses, factories and enterprises, such as tailors, the businesses of those Jews who came in direct contact with other Germans. Jewish ownership of property would come later. The Jews would not be moved to a ghetto but crowded into houses owned by Jews. That would free housing in the city for Germans. Wholesale businesses were not to be Aryanised immediately, but this did not save them for long. Their decline had, in any case, begun well before Göring's November and December 1938 decrees. The Hamburg chamber of commerce was well prepared. Lists in 1937 of all Jewish businesses and their financial state had been compiled in anticipation of measures to come, so all was now ready to earmark them. Where there were too many they were closed; where it was a good, well-established concern, a choice picking, the Jewish owner was forced to sell to a good party member at a knockdown price. Jews had not dominated any business but were significant in almost every branch of the economy. It became clear to Göring in 1938 that to drive out all the non-Aryan firms would cause irreparable damage. So his Four-Year Plan directives distinguished between 'Jewish' and other non-Aryan firms owned by *Mischlinge*. Businesses belonging to 'half-' or 'quarter-Jews' were deliberately excluded in the November 1938 decrees intended to 'free the German economy from Jews'.

Jewish wholesale businesses, large and especially small, had found it increasingly difficult to secure supplies and keep customers. The records of the Hamburg chamber of commerce provide the evidence.[34] Joel Rosenfelder owned a firm supplying animal feedstuffs. In 1937 he did business of over 11,000 RM, but in 1938 this had halved, and the following year his income had shrunk to just over 845 RM. Only a few personal customers had remained loyal and the business was now judged too small to warrant its continuing registration. Joel Rosenfelder was left penniless. Adolf Sachsenhaus, who dealt in timber supplies, did some RM 5,000 worth of business in 1937, just RM 3,000 in 1938 and only RM 1,500 in 1939; he relied on a few friendly customers in the end and occasionally supplied RM 300 or RM 400 worth of wood. Small though his income was, it was all the more vital to his family. He too was forcibly closed down. Günther Tradelius ran a foodstuff business and tried to sell his firm, but was ordered to liquidate it in 1939. Israel Cassuto had built up a specialised trade importing articles needed by hairdressers, but in 1939 he was refused an import licence and could no longer supply his customers. The well-known export business P. & A. Belmonte, Neuer Wall 54, ceased to exist; a note made by the chamber of commerce tersely explained the reason: its two owners, who had been arrested some time ago, were said to have committed suicide in prison. The owners, the three Belmonte brothers – 49-year-old Salomon, 45-year-old Paul and 43-year-old Alfred – were all strangled in Fuhlsbüttel on the same day in April 1939.[35] One way or another large and small wholesalers and factories were liquidated or Aryanised, while their owners emigrated, perished in concentration camps or were deported. That there were still survivors in 1940 comes as a surprise. They were meticulously listed, exempted and marked down for later take-over or liquidation.

The export of goods was so vital to the economy and rearmament that Jews engaged in the export trade were for a time allowed to carry on. The *Reichsstatthalter* accordingly, even after the outbreak of war, permitted a number of Jewish export and import firms to continue. L. Löwenthal and Ernst Alsberg exported medical drugs; Walter Behrend traded with Iran; A. L. Meyer's business was in corsets and bandages. Of the seventy-three Jewish wholesale export and import firms still registered, twenty-one were in business as late as the summer of 1940. Of the manufacturing concerns, only two remained in production – a paper manufacturer and a metal factory – both owned by Dutch Jews. Of twenty-eight export firms, two had survived, one with the unmistakable name Stapel & Israel, Hochallee 104. There appear to have been a handful even until 1941. Pressure had been constant from party organisations to drive them all out, hence the scrutiny of the listings even as late as 1942 noting there were no longer any Jewish businesses left. The delays illustrate too that local Nazi leaders could ignore Berlin's directives at least for a time, and sometimes altogether, as the treatment of businesses owned by *Mischlinge* in Hamburg shows. With few exceptions, driving the Jews out of the economy and robbing them destroyed their independence, but the Nazis did not stop at that: they enacted a blizzard of anti-Jewish decrees.

A new regulation required all Jews to 'sell' to the state at the state's valuation all artistic objects of value – anything made of silver or gold, as well as precious stones and pearls – by 31 March 1939.[36] They would be compensated 'according to weight' at a farcical few *Pfennige*. Jews were permitted to retain one wedding ring, one silver watch, two sets of used silver knives, forks and spoons per person, and 200 grams in weight of other silver objects. It was all very precise. This was to show how reasonable the Nazis were being. Compared to the true value of the precious objects as stated the previous April in the forms all Jews had to fill in, the valuation was now drastically reduced; one antique worth 10,000 *Reichsmark*, for instance, was now acquired by the state for 700. But many a silver tray, gold watch and antique candelabra found its way into the hands of corrupt dealers, who sold them on as profitable bargains. In Hamburg, the authorities had the good sense not to melt down the silver, thus enabling some surviving heirs after the war to recover family heirlooms.

There is a curious postscript to Aryanisation. Not every business was keen to lose former Jewish connections, although the party hounded firms to change to a 'German' trade name quickly. Most caved in to party pressure. A few held out. The Warburg bank was forced to change its name to Brinkmann, Wirtz & Co. only in the autumn of 1941. Another Jewish name which continued until the autumn was the well-known Jacobi brandy.[37] The new owners then tried, in an advertisement in the *Hamburger Tageblatt*, to make the best of the situation: 'A new name for an old concept', the advert read. 'The Jacobi distillery, under new management, has improved its already traditionally highly esteemed quality and now takes the name of its new owners, Deyle. The brand of Deyle too will be a guarantee of high quality and give exquisite enjoyment.' German Deyle, then, with the assurance of Jewish quality.

The Aryan owners of a well-known export firm in Hamburg in 1942 applied to keep its Jewish name. The chamber of commerce advised that no exceptions were any longer possible. They were sympathetic to the request, but it could not be denied that to make any exceptions to changing the names 'could in some cases disadvantage the economy'. Their advice was to delay this as long as possible in the hope that Berlin's instructions might still change. But why were these merchants so keen to preserve their Jewish identity after the Jews had been driven out of Hamburg? They were looking beyond the war, when they would resume trade with the foreign clients now fighting them. The good name the Jews had created was worth holding on to even though the business was no longer under Jewish ownership. Some survived right through the war. Kempinski on the Kurfürstendamm in Berlin remained Kempinski, without any Kempinskis, from the day of Nazi Aryanisation to the present.

In Hamburg, Kaufmann and the authorities paid no attention to what Berlin might want. Many enquiries reached the chamber of commerce as to whether business could be conducted with non-Aryan companies. The official response was pragmatic. In practice, Jewish commercial representatives abroad were kept on if no Aryan could be found.

The Hamburg state had already stopped buying from Jewish firms before 1938. In June of that year, Kaufmann on his own initiative extended this to firms owned by *Mischlinge* of the first degree – that is, Christians with two Jewish grandparents. But German sensibilities in 1938 meant people were still capable of protest.[38] The owner of a store selling typewriters and office equipment at Neuer Wall 103 challenged the practice and were backed by their lawyer, Dr Robert Kamisch. The owner in question was Arthur Lindemann of Lindemann & Sohn. The deceased father of Arthur Lindemann was classified a Jew and his mother was an Aryan, so Arthur Lindemann was a *Mischling*. Kamisch was outraged. 'Arthur Lindemann', he wrote,

> does not have to be ashamed of his ancestry. In his veins flows the Jewish blood of his father who had volunteered in 1914. Enclosed is a copy of his obituary from the *Hamburger Fremdenblatt*, 10 July 1918. It shows the

exemplary way Arthur Lindemann discharged his duties to the fatherland. As if it were not enough that Arthur Lindemann's father had volunteered in 1914, he also allowed his son to volunteer at the age of sixteen. The Lindemann family has without any doubt proved their patriotism to the fatherland, as neither father nor son were of an age where they had to serve .... I wish to add that in this matter what concerns my client is not the economic aspect ... state purchasing orders accounted only for one hundred Marks, but he believes he has a claim to continue to belong to the German *Volk* community; it is a question of personal honour.

In November, the application was rejected. Kamisch then registered a formal complaint. No response was sent for over a year. It was embarrassing because of Göring's orders. An internal minute reveals the cynical way the problem was resolved in 1940:

in view of the Reich instructions that *Mischlinge* of the first degree were not to be discriminated against, all firms in this position, including the Lindemanns, were to be told in a polite and appropriate way that there were no obstacles to their applying for state purchasing orders. On the other hand, the *Reichsstatthalter* does not wish that any official purchases should be made. If there were enquiries as to why they had not been successful, a reason should be given but without reference to their racial status as the cause.

There were still Germans like the lawyer Dr Kamisch, who as late as 1939 did not grasp the Nazi ideological obsession that all Jews were to be eliminated and thought a distinction should be made for 'good Jews'.

IV

In less than twelve months before the outbreak of war on 1 September 1939, 226 orders, ordinances and additions to laws were issued, making life ever more difficult for Jews. They ranged from the trivial to the devastating. On 12 November 1938 Jews were forbidden to go to theatres, cinemas, concerts, exhibitions and 'etc.', whatever that included; four days later, the right of veterans to wear army uniforms was 'withdrawn'; all Jews, *Mischlinge* and Aryans married to Jews had to register their addresses and personal details with the police; Jews were not permitted to keep carrier pigeons (29 November 1938); driving licences were no longer valid; Jews had to sell their cars to Germans; Jews could no longer be registered as midwives; Jews were no longer permitted to use restaurants and sleeping cars on the German railways (28 December 1938); if any 'half-Jewish' teachers were still employed in state or private schools, the minister was to be notified (10 February 1939); by order of the *Führer*, no new names of Jews on war memorials were to be added, but those already inscribed were not to be removed (Hitler had a head for minutiae: people would have wondered why names had been chiselled out, disfiguring the memorials in every town and village); Jews were permitted for medical reasons to visit a spa but were forbidden to walk in the parks of the spa or to attend any concert performances (16 June 1939); Jews were forbidden to participate in the Reich lottery (1 August 1939). And there were many more. Policemen could no longer marry Jewish *Mischlinge* of the second degree (8 December 1938); Jewish schools would no longer receive state aid (7 December 1938).

It also became intolerable for little Jewish orphan children in 'German' orphanages to live together with 'German' children.[39] In November 1938, the Youth Administration of Hamburg transferred them to Jewish orphanages. Particularly harrowing was the fate of little Edith Schiffmann. Just seven years old, she was removed by the police from a home run by the Hamburg authorities, first to an orphanage in Bergedorf and then to the Jewish orphanage in Hamburg, 'where', according to the official report, 'she belonged in the first place'. Nor did baptism make any difference. Catholic Anneliese Guhrauer, of Jewish parentage, was taken from a Catholic home. These children lost all that was familiar to them, all sense of security. A Jewish social worker who complained that the Jewish community could hardly be blamed for not looking after her and other children when all the leading officials were in a concentration camp was severely rebuked: 'It was not up to Jews to criticise government measures.' Families were torn apart. Jews, and racially defined Jewish parents, who had for years loved and cared for their adopted children had to give them up. Without a thought for anyone's feelings, the children were placed with 'German' mothers and fathers they had never met before. When it came to the bureaucratic application of racial considerations, those in charge lost human compassion.

Discrimination did not halt even in the face of death.[40] Hamburg's Health Administration wanted to exclude the corpses of the patients from the hospital mortuary chapels. A long correspondence ensued between the Health Authority and Hamburg's Legal Office, which advised that legal grounds were 'unfortunately' lacking to shut out Jewish corpses. After several weeks of toing and froing, a compromise was reached. To avoid Germans having to meet any Jews, Jewish corpses could be brought to the mortuary chapel but Jewish relatives were forbidden to pay their respects. Then it occurred to others that Jews and Aryans should no longer share the same burial grounds either. Kaufmann had to reach a decision about the already existing graves purchased by families in perpetuity. He ruled that, with the exception of long-established family graves, all newly deceased Jews should in future be interred in a separate part of the cemetery. The most distant plot was chosen so that German mourners would not be disturbed by passing Jewish gravestones. The practice of holding services in one of the chapels was also forbidden to Jews.

What applied to Jews in death was more relevant in life. There were no longer sufficient Jewish midwives to attend childbirths. The Nazi Association of Midwives, however, felt it intolerable that their members had to go into Jewish homes and the Jewish hospital to bring Jewish babies into the world. What all this shows is how normal human feelings had already become blunted well before the outbreak of the war. The Jews were regarded not only as different but were on the way to becoming outcasts. There were still unfortunate gaps in the exclusion of the living from public places. Goebbels was in control of theatres and cinemas and his ministry had forbidden Jews from attending them. But libraries, museums and botanic gardens fell under the control of the Education Ministry, which had issued no orders.[41] The Legal Office had to advise that there was no legal basis for excluding Jews. Though orders from Berlin forbade the wholesale use of signs saying 'Jews not wanted', it was not stopped. There were simply too many Germans who wished to prove their Nazi credentials. They reported any fellow countrymen who showed sympathy for Jews. Göring had to issue a special instruction condemning denunciation of shopkeepers who served Jews. With the liquidation of Jewish shops in 1939, the Jews had to shop somewhere.

Supine and ill-meaning Germans were making daily life for Jews difficult. Decent Germans, whose numbers were not insignificant, showed some solidarity with their Jewish neighbours but had to be careful. Germany in 1939 had become a very different place in just six short years. There were still Germans privately and in official positions who would try to be as helpful as was possible, and sometimes went beyond that, but they were isolated. From institutions in general, nothing good could any longer be expected. The identification of Jews in correspondence with authorities and other Germans became explicit by a decree on 17 August 1938 which came into force on 1 January 1939, when men had to add 'Israel' and women 'Sara' to their names. Jewish passports were taken from them to prevent departures abroad – possibly with valuables – without the knowledge of the Gestapo. Jews were issued instead with an identity card, which had to be produced whenever dealing in person with any official. Passports were granted again for emigration and stamped with a 'J', originally at the request of the Swiss. All appeals for exceptions on Hitler's instructions were to be refused. Even his favourite Wagner conductor at Bayreuth, Franz von Hoesslin, who was able to continue making music unhindered despite his wife being Jewish, could not win an exemption for her: she had to add 'Sara' to her name and have her passport stamped with a 'J' when she accompanied him abroad. There was no escape from the close meshes of the net. The Jews were branded. All that remained to be added was the Yellow Star which would identify them publicly. Meantime, Göring's decrees had deprived them of what was left of their livelihood.

Exodus

No time better exemplified the dedication, courage and tenacity of Jewish leaders in Germany than the year of 1939. With all the pillars of Jewish life crumbling, they did not lose their heads. Creating order out of the chaos as far as was possible, they rescued the lives of thousands and stayed at their posts, though they could have left and saved themselves. In dealings with the Gestapo, they were even able on a few occasions to negotiate by threatening to withdraw their cooperation. What little freedom of action was left they utilised. It is unjust to criticise them as collaborators.

The drastic changes had made it clear that resources would have to be centralised. Communities like Hamburg lost much of their independence. The Berlin community found this a hard pill to swallow. Although it raised the largest proportion of income, it would no longer have overriding say in the new *Reichsvereinigung der Juden in Deutschland*, established in February 1939 to replace the *Reichsvertretung*. The Gestapo now demanded that the new organisation should focus on only one task, emigration. The Jewish leadership resisted and the Gestapo gave way, not wanting to risk their collective resignation. Finally, as formalised in June 1939, the new *Reichsvereinigung* made itself responsible for welfare and education as well as for emigration. What the Jewish leaders could not escape was having to account for everything they did to the Gestapo headquarters in Berlin. Despite the threat of the concentration camp hanging over them, they did not hesitate to disagree and protest.

Emigration was the priority. The *Reichsvereinigung* hoped to ensure an orderly process with funds raised voluntarily from wealthier Jews, through taxation and with help from abroad. There was to be no panic departure. The plans envisaged an exodus over five years. The international Evian Conference the previous summer had opened only a few doors, but 70,000 Jews did manage to leave between January and July 1939, half from Austria and half from the old borders of Germany. One destination for a time without entry restrictions was the International Settlement of Shanghai, but the *Reichsvereinigung* resisted Gestapo efforts to hire ships and simply dump Jews there to starve. With hindsight, that was a mistake: anything was better than staying. Heinrich Stahl of the *Reichsvereinigung* told the Gestapo that driving Jews out of Germany by all means, fair and foul, would only lead to a backlash, with countries abroad shutting their doors even more tightly.

In the winter of 1938–9, an international emigration plan was drawn up[42] endorsed by Göring's Four-Year Plan and George Rublee, the chairman of the Inter-Governmental Committee on Political Refugees set up by the Evian Conference. Hjalmar Schacht, as has already been noted, initiated the talks in London and, following his dismissal as president of the *Reichsbank*, he was replaced by Helmut Wohltat, an official of the Economics Ministry. The plan applied only to Jews in Greater Germany, including Austria and the Sudetenland. About 600,000 Jews were still living in the Reich. The assumption was that 150,000 men and women who were between the ages of fifteen and forty-five would be able to earn a living and support 250,000 dependants. The 200,000 too old and infirm would stay in Germany and live out their lives. The project envisaged that the wage-earners would emigrate first, over the next three to five years, and once they had established themselves their dependants would follow. Those left behind were, according to the words of the plan, 'to live tranquilly unless some extraordinary circumstance should occur'. They would be financed by the sale of Jewish property and then by public relief. A trust fund would be established of not less than a quarter of Jewish wealth in Germany. Passage on German ships and equipment would be purchased in Germany for the departing wage-earners. If these contained imported raw material, it would be paid for by foreign funds. The *ha'avara* agreement was to continue for Palestine. It was also agreed that further indirect transfers from the trust fund abroad would be made available if German exports were bought in exchange. The Nazis hoped that the agreement would not only get rid of the Jews but also end the boycott of German goods. In July 1939 the draft regulations for the setting up of the trust fund were actually drawn up by the Gestapo. This was a seriously meant effort. With the outbreak of war, the scheme collapsed.

Did Hitler ever take it seriously? The German Jews were an embarrassment; emigration remained the priority. As late as the summer of 1939 Hitler thought Britain and France would not go to war. The emigration agreement, pointedly, was limited to Jews living in the Reich, not tying Hitler's hands as to how to deal with the 3 million Polish Jews and the millions living in Russia. Roosevelt called it an attempt to ransom Jews. Neville Chamberlain, Britain's prime minister, was more sympathetic, and the Warburgs in Hamburg and New York had seen it as the best chance to rescue German Jewry.

I

The trade in Jews before the war was profitable all round. Shipping lines German and foreign demanded extortionate fares. It was not only the outward passage that had to be paid but also the return journey, in case the landing was refused. First-class fares were good business too, as for a time they permitted passengers to land in some Latin American countries without visas. The passengers who purchased them were frequently crowded into third-class accommodation.

Hapag was not excluded from this bonanza. In May 1939 Hapag's directors were able to squeeze in an unscheduled extra journey transporting refugees on the pleasure liner *St Louis*, which had been booked for a lucrative cruise a month later by American passengers in New York.[43] There was just time enough to take 907 Jewish men, women and children to Cuba on the way across the Atlantic. They were all in possession of Cuban visas. For pleasure cruises the *St Louis* normally carried 500 passengers, so the refugee voyage meant a nice extra profit. Jews anxious to leave as soon as they could had no choice. They stood in long lines before the office of Hapag and those of other shipping lines, hoping to secure one of the scarce berths at any price.

The story of the voyage of the *St Louis* has been told in books and on film. Gustav Schröder was the ship's captain, reliable, experienced and long in Hapag's service. On 13 May 1939 the liner set sail. Bizarrely, the band on board struck up a farewell, the plaintive folk tune made popular at the time of emigration to America in the nineteenth century: 'must I then, must I then, leave for the wide world beyond …'. The captain and crew behaved impeccably, treating their Jewish passengers as valued guests. On 27 May, the *St Louis* dropped anchor in Havanna harbour. Now the trouble began. The Cuban dictator repudiated the visas. After six days of fruitless negotiations, the *St Louis* set sail once more. Captain Schröder received orders from Hapag to return to Hamburg with his passengers. There would then still just be time to sail to New York and pick up the American passengers, who had paid the company $45,000 for their pleasure cruise, a sum in precious foreign currency Hapag did not want to lose. Schröder had not before disregarded instructions from his employers. This time he did. The passengers, who included some 300 men who had been released from concentration camps, were terrified of being taken back. Captain Schröder telegraphed Hamburg, warning they would never allow themselves to be taken alive and would resort to desperate measures.

Schröder made slow progress, criss-crossing along the Florida coastline of the United States. Max Warburg and the Joint Distribution Committee in the United States appealed to President Roosevelt to permit the passengers entry, without success, despite sympathetic coverage of the dramatic story in the press all over the world. Only in Germany were reports forbidden. The behaviour of the Americans confirmed Hitler's views that no one wanted Jews. The fate of the *St Louis* was not unique. In other harbours and on the high seas overcrowded ships were waiting in limbo: in the Black Sea port of Sulina and Tulcea, 3,000 Jewish refugees were detained on board five ships; in Constanta, Mangalia and along the coastline of Palestine as well: human flotsam. When all else failed, some ships made their way to Shanghai.

The *St Louis*, running out of fuel, was eventually forced to head back to Europe. The American and European offices of the company frantically negotiated with European governments to take in the refugees between them. Finally on 13 June agreement was reached. Four days later the passengers landed in Antwerp and from there they travelled to their final destinations, in the Netherlands, Belgium, France and Great Britain. After they had landed in Antwerp they composed an illustrated scroll expressing their collective gratitude. It was handed to Captain Schröder by the Hapag office in New York, where he had arrived in time for the American cruise.

So much is well known. There is an unexpected ending. Captain Schröder, who had taken such exemplary care of his Jewish passengers, was a member of the Nazi Party, and not just a late opportunist; he was an *Altkämpfer*, one of Hitler's early supporters who had joined the party in the mid-1920s. When after the Second World War, on the occasion of receiving a decoration from the government for his humane behaviour, this was discovered, to his surprise, by a journalist, he asked Schröder how he could reconcile party membership with kindness to Jews. Schröder replied, 'The passengers were my responsibility as captain of the ship.' It shows that one can not easily categorise. Schröder's professional sense of duty took precedence over ideology; in the seafaring community there was a streak of independence, a tradition of saving lives. Schröder's attitude was not unique among Hamburg's sailors.[44]

II

The most unusual international rescue was the children's emigration movement, known by the prosaic title *Kindertransporte*.[45] It was organised by the *Reichsvertretung* in Berlin and a committee in London. Among the distinguished delegation which lobbied the home secretary after Crystal Night to plead for their admission was Max Warburg's daughter Lola Hahn-Warburg. The government agreed to waive the usual entry requirements. Humanitarian considerations played a part, a genuine horror at what was happening in Germany. The British government, which had restricted entry to Palestine, also felt a responsibility to provide an alternative refuge. Children attracted public sympathy and were no threat to the labour market at a time of continuing unemployment. But there were conditions. The incoming refugee children must not become a burden on the state; guarantors were required and additionally a payment for each child of £50. Before the outbreak of war almost 10,000 children, from babes in arms to adolescents of eighteen, reached safety. Nearly all were Jewish, but some were Christians racially defined by the Nazis as Jews. Organisations had to be built up from scratch in Berlin and London to make the arrangements. All finally depended on raising money and securing guarantees to maintain the children for unforseeable years to come.

The most remarkable aspect was the overwhelming public response, especially in Britain. Wealthy Jewish families like the Rothschilds issued guarantees for a hundred children and more; poor families took in a single child or clubbed together to provide the means to bring over children. Fund-raising was not confined to Jews. The archbishop of Canterbury and the Quakers launched appeals. One of the most successful was that of a former prime minister Lord Baldwin. *The Times* devoted its front page, usually reserved for advertising, to list the names of donors to the fund. Schoolchildren sent their pocket money. The contrast with the German churches and charitable institutions could not have been more stark. Not that Britain was immune to antisemitism. There was prejudice against Jews among all classes. Even Neville Chamberlain once remarked that he did not like them much, though he thought that this was no excuse to rob them. But Chamberlain was fully behind this humanitarian response. It was a British tradition to respond to human disasters. But, without the horrors of the November pogrom, the destruction, the looting, the burning of synagogues and reports about concentration camps, it is doubtful whether such a rescue effort could have been mounted. Britain was not alone. The Netherlands in particular also provided generous refuge, though for most of the children it proved tragically temporary.

At railway stations all over Germany there were heartbreaking scenes of parents waving goodbye, not knowing whether they would ever see their children again. The children set off in high spirits as if going on an exciting holiday. First came the railway journey on specially reserved trains. Each child was limited to taking one suitcase, whose measurements were exactly laid down, and 10 *Reichsmark*. The luggage was inspected, so that nothing of value could be smuggled out. Little Hans's violin was left behind. In his luggage his mother had placed some violin music in the hope that the new foster parent would find him another violin. None of the parents knew where their children would find a new home. The Gestapo supervised everything in the waiting room of the railway station, cordoned off for this purpose; as each child's name was called out by a Jewish community worker, the little ones slipped off their mother's lap; one last kiss, and they ran to join the other assembled children. In Berlin, where the trains passed through several stations, some parents rushed from one to the other for a last glimpse. How can words describe their anguish? Would they ever see their children again? But tears at parting had to be fought back for the children's sake.

First news was eagerly awaited.[46] Postcards arrived quickly. Passing through the Netherlands to the Hook of Holland, at every station there were volunteers handing out chocolate and offering to post the cards the children had hastily written.

> Dear Mummy, Auntie Olly, Uncles Albert and Edgar!
> We are now in Holland and I can hardly describe how we have been received. In Bentheim across the border we were given a cabbage and mutton meal and a sparkling drink. My companions in the compartment are nice and we are very cheerful. The Dutch people are extraordinarily kind to us; soon we will reach the boat at the Hook of Holland and we will set sail from there ....
> Affectionate greetings and kisses, with love,
> Yours, Anna

On 15 December another 300 children left Hamburg. One of these *Kindertransporte* was accompanied by Lotte, the wife of Rabbi Carlebach. The chief rabbi was sending his older children to safety; the younger ones would remain in the family nest. The Jewish adult escorts were heroes. After reaching freedom they had to return to Germany. If they failed to do so, the transports would be stopped. They all came back and most later perished. For the Gestapo the exodus of children was particularly welcome: they had many years of life before them and so presented more of a long-term problem than elderly Jews. Himmler issued special instructions that passports should be issued without delay. But not every child was so lucky. In January 1940 the *Reichsvereinigung*, in its sober annual report for the year 1939, simply provided the statistics without comment: more than 16,000 applications had been received and just over 5,000 had been successfully dealt with. The children who failed to get on a transport perished. In Berlin, the *Reichsvereinigung* was at pains to stick to German and foreign emigration laws, believing that this alone would allow the flow of emigrants to continue as they passed through the narrowing funnel of permitted entry.

III

In Hamburg, Max Plaut was put in sole charge by order of the Gestapo on 2 December 1938. He continued, however, to work with his senior associates as before. Thus finance was left in the hands of Leo Lippmann. Plaut could not evade Gestapo orders. He actually had many opportunities to leave Germany, as he paid visits abroad, to London before the outbreak of war and to Sweden after September. The Gestapo encouraged these journeys to facilitate further Jewish emigration and to solicit foreign currency transfers, ostensibly to assist Jewish welfare. His sense of duty and commitment to the Hamburg community brought him back.

Plaut was fearless, ready to break rules, and adroit at using contacts with sympathetic conservative senior civil servants, in order to secure favours and help. The most unusual aspect of his role in Hamburg was his relationship with Gestapo officer Göttsche. He used whatever influence he could exert to help some unfortunate members of the community, and many owed their lives to him. His dealings were always hazardous. If he overstepped the mark – and frequently he came close to doing so – Göttsche could have dispatched him to a concentration camp at the stroke of a pen.

Plaut endured several arrests but was released after short periods. For the Gestapo it made sense to leave the Jewish administration to the Jews, saving them trouble and time. That way overall control too was easier. It also made sense for Plaut and his senior associates to go along with this arrangement to secure as tolerable conditions as was possible. Plaut and Göttsche developed a partnership of inferior and superior, with Plaut never hesitating to speak his mind, manipulating situations to best advantage where possible. It helped that Göttsche had a German sense of gallows humour. Plaut was single, without a family to take care of apart from his widowed mother; the Warburgs had asked him to remain, and he relied on Fritz Warburg in neutral Sweden to get him out at the eleventh hour if necessary. Meantime there was work to be done.

Every Jew who could be brought out, legally or illegally, should be moved as quickly as possible. Jews in concentration camps were a priority. Delay could mean death or permanent injury. On one occasion, after a Latin American consul in Hamburg had run out of passports and visas, Plaut had them duplicated by a forger with the connivance of the Gestapo.[47] The ill-paid consuls became wealthy selling visas. Those of Haiti and Honduras were favourites. The recipients of unauthorised visas were told not to make any use of them but to present them to other countries with the request for a 'transit visa', supposedly to help them reach their ultimate destination. Once in the transit country they were instructed to go underground.

Plaut got into trouble with the Hamburg shipping authority responsible for preventing the exploitation of emigrants.[48] Now in Nazi Germany, with Jews in concentration camps and threatened daily, bureaucrats were applying the laws of an earlier century to protect Jewish passengers. The shipping authority had discovered that a middleman had taken money to secure entry visas to Paraguay. Plaut was involved and faced prosecution, but the Gestapo in Berlin ordered that the investigation started in Hamburg should be dropped. Plaut had taken a risk and this time had got away with it. The trade in visas continued in 1940. The foreign currency division of the Reich Ministry of Finance even permitted the transfer of RM 1,000 per visa from Plaut's special emigration slush fund to secure twenty each month from the Haitian consul in Hamburg. When the *Reichsvereinigung* in Berlin told him to end such illegal payments, Plaut replied it was the only way to secure the release of Jews from concentration camps and had the approval of the Hamburg Gestapo. The consuls of other countries were demanding even more for a visa, he explained – the Argentine consul five times as much; Haiti was relatively cheap.

Latin America, the United States and Shanghai could still be reached via neutral countries, Shanghai by boat or train across Russia and China, and Palestine clandestinely. Plaut knew he could approach old civil servants like the leading police administrator *Regierungsdirektor* Kempe and his successor Janssen to issue all the necessary passports. They first sent their underlings out of the office so they would not be overheard talking to Plaut, who would then be politely offered a chair. Payment for the passages had to be found in foreign currencies by relatives or friends abroad, or by contributions from charities such as the American Joint Distribution Committee. To solve the Jewish problem the Gestapo did not rely on securing financial help and international cooperation. They employed any means to get rid of Jews with or without valid visas. In Vienna, with the cooperation of the Jewish community, Adolf Eichmann organised a route down the international waterway of the Danube, across the Black Sea and the Mediterranean to a remote spot on the coastline of Palestine. The outbreak of war did not stop the traffic. A clandestine 'travel bureau' was opened by the Hamburg-America Line.

The voyages on ramshackle ships, adapted to cram in the passengers and with inadequate fuel and provisions, were an ordeal.[49] Only the good health and youth of the young Zionists, their high morale and discipline, overcame despair. Many sailings ended in tragedy and loss of life. The worst catastrophe befell the *Struma* in February 1942, which mysteriously sank in the Bosphorus with the loss of all but two of the 769 Jewish passengers. A different fate awaited the *Patria*, which managed to reach Tel Aviv in 1940 and was sunk by agents of the *Haganah*. The intention was to force the British authorities to permit the passengers to land. The explosion blew a larger hole in the ship than intended, and the *Patria* turned on its side and sank in ten minutes, drowning more than 250 people. But however great the risk, it was worth taking: 21,000 'illegal' immigrants reached Palestine before the outbreak of war. During the war another 17,500 set out in unseaworthy ships on the hazardous journey to *Eretz Israel*. One in five lost their life. Those who did reach safety were interned by the British. Nearly 40,000 Jews and thousands of their descendants owed their lives to the foresight of the Jewish leadership to allow nothing to stand in their way to rescue Jews, even if it meant supping with the devil.

What will happen now?

1 September 1939, a conflict like no other. That day in Poland the long planned racial war began and would end only with Hitler's suicide five years and eight months later. SS *Einsatzgruppen*, assisted by the *Wehrmacht*, unleashed terror, murdering at least 50,000 Poles and also several thousand Jews during the first few weeks of conquest in an orgy of lawlessness that shocked the army command in Poland, who feared the corruption of the young conscripts.[50] Any pretence to judicial process was abandoned. The murder squads were free to act unconstrained, despite their theoretical subordination to the army command. This marked the start of the 'final solution'.

As a theoretical concept, the 'final solution' had been debated before Hitler came to power. The fundamentals were clear. The healthy homogeneous *Volk* needed to eliminate all who were racially and biologically harmful to the gene pool, with the Jews being the most harmful of all. It was recognised that this could not be accomplished all at once. What had to be decided was how harmful the Jewish gene was when weakened by intermarriage, the number of 'infected' Germans, what was practicable in the light of these numbers, the timing and sequence of the necessary steps that would have to be taken, the implementation of how best to dispose of Jews and others, and how long this would take. During the years of peace, foreign repercussions needed to be taken into account. This was still true after the war started. While all Jews in the world remained the enemy to be eliminated, it was only prudent to deal with each group separately even after the war began. Hitler authorised the mass deportation of the Jews from the Reich, but not their systematic murder. He was cautious about the repercussions of other Germans, as the great majority of Jews were integrated in German society. This was especially true of those who had intermarried and of their descendants, together with their relatives – uncles, aunts and in-laws. Then there would be the problem of the Jews in the West. They could only be removed from Europe as part of negotiated peace settlements. So the final implementation of the 'final solution' would only become possible after the war. When Hitler realised in the autumn and winter of 1940 that he had failed to reach a peace with Britain, a change of policy once more became necessary.

Meantime, 50 million Poles and 1.7 million Jews in occupied Poland had created new immediate challenges foreseen well before the occupation. The speed with which Hitler during the first six weeks of the war transformed the first stage of his manic racial vision into reality still remains astonishing. He had not taken his closest associates fully into his confidence until the time for implementation of each step became imminent. What Hitler revealed during the month of September and early October 1939 was radical in scope. The records of four meetings of heads of Heydrich's security service, the SD, have survived and provide the evidence.[51]

By the time of the third meeting, on 21 September, Hitler had given clear guidance to Himmler, who passed this on to Heydrich. Heydrich informed his chiefs that the 'final solution' was the long-term aim but that it could be reached only in stages. What followed were instructions about the immediate stage. To start with, Jews would be concentrated in the larger towns in ghettos, where they could be controlled more easily. As many as possible would be allowed to cross or be driven across the demarcation line, but only gradually, so the Russians would not be upset by the sudden influx; 300,000 Jews would also be deported from the Reich, together with 30,000 gypsies. Instructions were sent by Heydrich the same day to the heads of the *Einsatzgruppen*, with copies to all the ministries involved in the 'Jewish question', thus asserting Himmler's and Heydrich's overall control. This message repeated what had been revealed at the SD meeting earlier and added further details. The measures, it was emphasised, were not the 'final solution'; that would take longer. The ghettos were a transitory step, and were to be situated in towns with good rail communications 'so that future measures may be accomplished more easily'.

Hitler reluctantly provided cover, with his signature backdated to 1 September 1939 for the mass programme to murder mentally handicapped Germans assessed as incurable. When the time was ripe, Hitler would clearly have had no compunction about the mass murder of Germany's Jews, who contributed an even greater danger to the *Volk*. In the autumn and winter of 1939, Jews in Poland were forced to wear a yellow star and were driven into overcrowded ghettos – the largest in Warsaw and Łódź. All adult males had to perform forced labour, while in unauthorised round-ups thousands perished. There was no organised genocide yet, such as Hitler ordered should be carried out against the political and spiritual Polish leadership. The very consciousness of a Polish nation was to be obliterated, the Poles becoming helots to serve their German masters. Large areas of Poland were annexed in the north-west to form the enlarged West Prussia and in the south-west to enlarge Silesia; central western Poland was renamed the Wartheland. What was left of Poland became a German colony, the General Government, whose governor, Hans Frank, was appointed early in October.

The Jews in the Reich were to be deported to a Jewish reservation under the control of the SS separated from the General Government. The German–Soviet treaty of 28 September 1939 had made additional territory available east of Warsaw and Lublin. If 3 million Jews had been forced to live in this swampy region they would not have survived long.[52]

The implementation of racial policies required more authority to be given to Himmler to combat interference from ministries and army commanders. On 7 October, Himmler's birthday, his appointment was announced as Reich commissioner for the consolidation of German nationhood. The appointment gave

Himmler additional responsibilties for 'eliminating foreign populations constitut-
ing a danger to the German Reich' – Jews, gypsies and Poles. Himmler's empire
was strengthened organisationally too by the fusion of Heydrich's security service, the SD, concerned principally with planning, and Heinrich Müller's secret
state police (Gestapo), carrying through implementation, into one organisation,
the Reich Main Security Office (*Reichssicherheitshauptamt*, RSHA).[53]

Adolf Eichmann was moved to the Gestapo with special responsibilities for
the implementation of deportation. In this capacity he consulted with the
Gauleiter of the Wartheland, who was keen to expel the Poles and Jews. In
October, Eichmann wanted to create a large Jewish holding camp on the border
of the demarcation line, using the railway station at Nisco as the destination,
before forcing as many as possible from there across into Soviet-occupied
Poland.[54] Two advance parties of several thousand were sent to build barracks.
But everything did not go smoothly. On orders from Heinrich Müller, chief of
the Gestapo, further transports were halted as Berlin insisted on central planning.
A month later, the Soviets blocked off the further influx of Jews. The 'reservation' never materialised. Now Jews could only be dumped into the towns of the
General Government, the ghettos in Warsaw and Łódź in the Wartheland.
Overcrowding threatened chaos. In the new year, Governor Frank successfully
lobbied Göring temporarily to halt further deportations of Poles and Jews.
While the intended deportation of hundreds of thousand Jews from Hamburg and
the Reich had to be postponed, the German Jews had gained no more than a
breathing space, while local Nazi leaders became increasingly frustrated by
the delays.

I

In Hamburg and throughout the *Altreich* (Germany within its 1937 borders),
Jews in September 1939 expected the worst. Had not Hitler threatened terrible
retribution nine months earlier in the *Reichstag*? But nothing much happened.
There was even the farce of conscription.[55] Jews of military age were called up
and required to report for duty. They lined up with all the Germans to be mus-
tered by an officer and were handed a blue pass stamped by the *Wehrmacht*,
'unworthy to serve'. They could now go home, envied by the less fortunate conscripts. But *Mischlinge* were fitted out with a uniform and deemed worthy to
fight. In this Hitler had reluctantly given in to *Wehrmacht* fears that the forces
would otherwise lose too many fighting men. It was anathema to him that racial
Germans and half-Jews should form bonds as comrades in arms. In the spring of
1940 he ordered that half-Jews be removed from the army, with just a few exceptions he might authorise for outstanding bravery. Dismissal in 1940 also applied
to German soldiers with Jewish wives. But the *Wehrmacht* dragged its feet and
responded only tardily to the Führer's order; 'quarter-Jews' remained in the ranks
until June 1944 and some beyond then.

The only immediate anti-Jewish measure announced during the first weeks of the war was to forbid Jews to leave their homes during the hours of darkness, from 8 p.m. to 6 a.m. Young Jewish males, it was feared, might molest German girls, who at night would not recognise their Jewish features. While atrocities were being committed in conquered Poland, life for the German Jews went on much as before, restricted but livable. Plaut too was surprised that nothing much had happened. Just before the war Göttsche had told him, 'Should war come, the Jews will be the first losers ... November 1938 was just a dress rehearsal.'[56] From other Gestapo contacts there was more disturbing news. Plaut heard that all the adult Jews would be arrested and placed in camps, where they would be put to forced labour. It did not happen. In Hamburg, the Jews were left alone. It was worse in the smaller towns and villages; here eager party leaders and officials, on their own initiative, inflicted discriminatory measures. They were soon ordered by the Gestapo to withdraw them. How Jews would be treated was not to be left to local whims. Jews at first received exactly the same ration cards and collected these in long queues, rubbing shoulders with the *Volksgenossen*. They used the same air-raid shelters and later carried with them gas masks issued in September 1940. One false and comforting conclusion drawn from this was that the Nazis had other worries now, and that German Jews would still be treated as Germans and not like Polish, Austrian or Czech Jews.

In Hamburg's free port, containers filled with furniture were still waiting after the outbreak of the war to be shipped to the emigrants abroad. Now they could no longer leave Hamburg by sea. Permission was given to transport them by way of a neutral port even to refugees in enemy countries. Containers were dispatched by rail from Hamburg and Bremen to Rotterdam. Jewish civil servants in receipt of pensions who had emigrated continued to receive them; they were meticulously paid into special accounts and dependants who were still living in Germany could draw out set amounts. In Hamburg payments of pensions into blocked accounts continued until 1941. The necessary annual proof that the Jewish pensioner was alive was transmitted by a neutral embassy if the retired civil servant or teacher lived in a country at war. That did not mean, however, that large sums could be withdrawn from the accounts. Only a meagre monthly allowance of RM 150 was permitted. On deportation, what was left fell into the hands of the Reich. When the refugees in Britain were interned on the Isle of Man in 1940, the *Wehrmacht* censors permitted the Red Cross to transmit short messages directly from Germany. Letters from parents and wives left behind and from other still neutral countries could also be sent by way of the United States until December 1941. The correspondence abruptly ceased on the day of deportation. These were islands of legal normality which survived because no other orders existed.

It still seemed that maybe it would not turn out so badly after all. There was no expectation that life would be easy, but one day the war would end and families would be reunited; meantime, despite increasing isolation, life would go on. One just had to make the best of difficult circumstances and not lose hope. Jews socialised among themselves; there were even a few Christians who continued some contact. When Fritz Warburg left his large house at Mittelweg 17 in May 1939, he placed it at the disposal of the Jewish community.[57] The *Sekretariat Warburg* provided offices and consulting rooms for the few remaining doctors, and a large room served as a library, an oasis of peace and calm. On the top floor Max Plaut had an apartment and office. It is to the credit of the Warburg bank that it continued its support of the *Sekretariat*, though it was technically financed from American resources. But at the Ferdinandstraße bank headquarters attitudes soon began to change.

II

It did not take the new owners of the bank long after Max Warburg's tearful departure to accommodate themselves to new circumstances. Earnings continued to flow for a time from the fees of money transfers to Palestine.[58] Palestine was not designated 'enemy territory'. But when in October 1939 German goods could no longer be exported there, the *ha'avara* indirect transfer agreement came to an end. It was quite a different matter, however, defending the interests of individual Jewish clients. When in November 1938 *Frau* Schocken asked the bank to administer her large capital of over 2 million *Reichsmark*, the partners agreed 'despite some doubt'. A few months later attitudes were hardening. When *Herr* Herz, a Jewish owner of three businesses, asked to be represented by the Warburg bank in the Aryanisation process, the partners agreed 'unanimously that it was not part of their business and they could not be expected to take it on'. Hans Israel, the owner of a factory, also received a negative reply when he asked the bank to deal with debtors who owed him RM 60,000. The partners recorded that '*Herr* Wirtz had decided that it was not in our [the bank's] interests to represent *Herr* Israel'.[59]

But the bank did do its best to look after its non-Aryan employees. Beatrice Pardo was a *Mischling* of the second degree. She worked as a cashier in the bank and so was in daily contact with clients. As she 'looked Jewish', it was thought advisable to move her to a back room. This was a traumatic shock for her. She began to feel insecure, afraid she might lose her job and be unable to find another, so she tried to alter her appearance by dying her hair blond and having surgery on her nose. She lost all confidence and aged forty-nine entered a Benedictine nunnery. She was just one of thousands of young *Mischlinge* fearful of what future was in store for them. 'Full Jews' could no longer count on Aryan employers to protect them. Most had lost their employment already.

III

The *Reichsvereinigung* had to make provision for the unemployed, for welfare, for beds for the infirm and sick and for children attending Jewish schools, and also to secure the necessary finances. In Hamburg, Kaufmann impatiently waited to take over the fine building of the *Talmud Tora Schule* in the Grindelhof. On 20 September

1939 the famous school was closed and the boys were crowded into the premises of the girls' school in the Karolinenstraße. The state subvention of 180,000 Marks was cut off, but Lippmann actually managed to obtain a final payment of 25,000 Marks to provide additional classrooms and equipment. The school in the Karolinenstraße was renamed 'Elementary and Secondary School for Jews'.[60]

Although German Jews faced increasing difficulties, as yet there seemed to be no need for despair. While men had spent time in concentration camps after their arrest in November 1938, even those who could not emigrate were released; women and children were not physically molested. But the Jews of Polish nationality who had lived in Hamburg for decades, and who were still in the city after they were supposed to have left, were incarcerated in a concentration camp. Plaut managed to secure the release of a few on arranging their emigration. But of those still in the camps only three survived.

The first malicious anti-Jewish wartime measure in October 1939 was to require Jews on the Jewish Day of Atonement (Yom Kippur) to give up their radio sets. The Gestapo, for their amusement, studied the Jewish calendar to identify the dates of the Jewish high holidays to force Jews to break religious traditions, so Jews became particularly apprehensive as such holidays approached.[61] They stood in long lines in their best clothes to hand over their wireless sets and received an official numbered receipt which they were told to keep carefully. It must not appear that anything had simply been stolen. They then returned to the synagogue. In Hamburg, the *Dammtor-Synagoge*, which had been demolished internally in November 1938 but was otherwise intact, had been fully restored from money privately raised. It now housed the Torah Rolls and silver from other Hamburg synagogues. The *Tempel* in the Oberstraße just stood empty but survived both the Nazis and Bomber Command.

The Jewish leaders in Berlin and Hamburg were facing mounting problems; expenditure was increasing hugely and resources were shrinking. An internal memorandum written for the leaders of the *Reichsvereinigung* just before the war graphically described the ongoing crisis:

> In consequence of the continuing emigration of younger Jews ... elderly Jews, often the oldest in a family, are left behind on their own and without any means. The same fate is experienced by those who are infirm and require nursing. They cannot hope to gain entry into foreign country ... the Jewish welfare organisation is left with the task of finding places for them to live and to be supported. The demand for old-age homes and nursing homes has increased enormously. By using every available space the homes have been able to increase their capacity ...[62]

The number of Jewish-owned houses had shrunk with Aryanisation, and the Jewish community was not permitted to acquire new housing. How bad the situation had become was evident from the statistics cited by the author of the paper. In Berlin, with thirteen old-age homes and 1,683 beds available, none were free and 3,000 elderly were waiting for a place. There were only two nursing homes providing 265 beds; every bed was filled and another 300 elderly sick people were waiting. Elsewhere there were four old-age homes, 111 beds – none free – and ninety elderly Jews needing urgent care; twenty infirm Jews could not be accommodated as the sixty-five beds had already been filled. In Hamburg, the new premises of the *Israelitsches Krankenhaus* in the Johnsallee were inadequate.

Finding somewhere for Jews to live became an ever increasing burden for the local branches of the *Reichsvereinigung*. Although Jewish property was supposed to be Aryanised last, the housing stock owned by Jews was rapidly falling. As in Hamburg there was a general housing shortage, Kaufmann ordered a listing of all Jewish tenants whose landlords were Aryans. Moving the Jews out of these would be a first step. The housing department of the Welfare Office would later become one of the driving forces urging the deportation of all Jews to the East. But from 1939 to the autumn of 1941 the world of the German Jews was still far removed from the horrors occurring in Poland and then in Russia.

STAATSRAT A.D.
DR. LEO LIPPMANN

DR · MAX PLAUT
VORSITZENDER DER GEMEINDE SEIT
ENDE 1938

DR · JOSEPH CARLEBACH

Leo Lippman, Max Plaut, Joseph Carlebach and Max Warburg, the four leaders of the Jewish community during the Third Reich. From 1937 onwards they were under the control of the Gestapo. They did all they could to ameliorate everyday life for the Jews left in Hamburg and for those about to be deported. The courtesy and dignity with which they corresponded with individual members of the Nazis is remarkable. Without their intercession, conditions would have been far worse – as they were, for example, in neighbouring Hannover.

The harbour: the Fairplay Tug Company, led by Lucy Borchardt, the only Jewish female ship owner, was 'Aryanized' on comparatively good terms and is today a leading global company.

A small shop in Hamburg after the November pogrom.

The Jewish fashion department store Hirschfeld was demolished internally in November 1938 but quickly renamed and reopened by its proud new owners.

The arrival of a *Kindertransport* in Harwich, December 1938.

June 1942: home from France.

Relaxing at the *Alsterpavillon*: all is well in Hamburg.

Gomorrha, three years later.

Platz der Jüdischen Deportierten

Im Jahre 1933 lebten in Hamburg 24.000 Juden.

Hier begann der Weg tausender jüdischer Bürger Hamburgs,
der in den Vernichtungslagern des Nazi-Regimes endete.

A plaque in remembrance of the Jewish deportees erected at the place where the deportations started. The translation of the inscription reads: Place of the Jewish deportees. In 1933, 24,000 Jews lived in Hamburg. Here the journey of thousands of Jewish citizens of Hamburg began which ended in the extermination camps of the Nazi regime.

After the war, memorial brass plaques were set into paving stones in front of the homes and apartments from which Jewish families had been deported. These are outside the villa in the Heimhuderstraße of my great-aunt Olga Misch and her brother Stanislaus Heller, who committed suicide together a few days after arriving in Theresienstadt.

6
HOLOCAUST

Dark reflections, plans, reports and cold statistics

Never in history has a community on the eve of its destruction left behind so precise a stock-taking as did the Jews of Germany, in the form of a statistical tabulation, a snapshot of conditions at the outset of the war.[1] In the *Altreich* there were still 185,242 Jews who lived in towns and cities. Now there were many more women than men – 107,627 as against 77,595. The incarceration in concentration camps of the men in 1938 and 1939 had made their needs seem more urgent, so more had been able to escape abroad. Would their wives and the elderly left behind be safe? Adult men had suffered physical abuse; the old, women and children would surely not be hurt. The age structure of the community was even more abnormal than before, with one in three over the age of sixty. No country had wanted to admit old people without means. Most Jews were out of work, and only one in five received an income from employment. This number included those on poverty pay, forced to work in separated groups in factories by the Nazi employment office in Hamburg under Gestapo control. The working conditions were atrocious, with rare humane exceptions, threats of the concentration camp hanging over anyone judged not to be performing adequately or arriving a few minutes late for work. When in 1940 Jews were forbidden to use public transport, this could mean a start from home at 4 a.m. and only few hours' sleep after a long day.

A quarter of the community were paupers, having used up their savings. They were dependent on welfare or were ordered into forced labour; others would soon join this group. The few with more substantial means had their accounts frozen and were able to draw only a small monthly amount. Their capital was earmarked by the Gestapo, which centrally from Berlin supervised the funds of the *Reichsvereinigung* and its branches; after accounting for every *Pfennig*, what was left ultimately fell into the hands of the Gestapo. Meantime it paid for their purposes, including sending Jews to their deaths.

I

Max Plaut was solely responsible to the Gestapo but continued to work closely with Leo Lippmann, Ludwig Löffler and Fanny David. He was not going to give up. The relationship he had established with Göttsche helped here and there to ameliorate conditions. Plaut also redoubled his efforts to secure visas and ship passages for Jews to enable them to leave. His activities, legal and illegal, saved several hundreds of lives. But Plaut knew time was running out: the great majority of the Jews under German rule, now more than 2.5 million, could not hope to emigrate. Should they just wait until Hitler decided what to do with them?

In the autumn of 1939 Plaut put forward a proposal, extraordinary at first glance.[2] He appeared to support the Gestapo's plans to deport the Jews and create an 'autonomous' Jewish reservation in the Lublin region. Plaut had obtained knowledge of these plans from the Gestapo, who urged him to use his Warburg connections to raise large funds abroad. His proposal is headed 'A contribution to the solution of the Jewish question in Greater Germany'. Plaut wanted a workable blueprint to be drawn up to settle 2.5 million Jews, including all the Jews still in the German Reich. He believed that agriculture and industry could provide tolerable living standards in this inhospitable region of Poland. Investment would come from the remaining wealth of the Jews in Germany. 'I am convinced', Plaut wrote, 'that one could also mobilise considerable resources abroad by showing that this would be the beginning of a solution, with the prospect of a happy future for the Jews of Central Europe.' He therefore urged that no more money should be spent on old-age homes and other institutions inside Germany. Leadership would be needed – the right people, of proven achievement, correctness, courage, discipline and staying power. From the tone of the paper, Plaut saw himself as one of these leaders.

It is today difficult to comprehend how Plaut could even have considered such a 'solution'. The Jews in Germany and occupied Poland were caught in a trap; emigration would now be possible only for a small number. In Poland 1.7 million co-religionists had been added to the approximately 350,000 to 400,000 Jews in Greater Germany. Plaut was as concerned for the future of Polish as of German Jewry. Unless the Jews themselves embraced a 'positive way out', he feared, much worse would befall them. Rather than wait, it appeared to make sense to seize the initiative and to try to escape the worst. Plaut was grasping at what at the time appeared possible, a solution which Hitler had hinted at in his *Reichstag* speech on 6 October 1939. By cooperating with the Nazis, the Jews might create for themselves a more tolerable future. The alternative of effective resistance in Germany was impossible. Anyone who took up arms would be caught, tortured and killed, together with their families and innocent members of the community taken as hostages. His initiative came to nothing. Meantime, in Berlin the Jewish leadership was putting together their annual account of the year.

II

There are few more moving documents than the official report of the work of the *Reichsvereinigung* in 1939, the *Arbeitsbericht*, completed in January 1940 and covering Hamburg and the whole Reich.[3] But how can anything be described as infused with feeling when it appears to be no more than a dry, factual, largely statistical account running to sixty-eight pages? The report describes unemotionally how German Jewry was expected to come to its end, the final stage of the dissolution of a once thriving cultural and religious community proud to be German. The end was not expected so quickly or in the way it came about. It was presumed the Jews would face gradual extinction in Germany when those too old or sick to leave ended their lives cared for by the remnants of Jewish welfare. What could have been more difficult for these courageous, able men and women who led the Jewish organisations and were steeped in German culture than to accept the responsibility of cutting ties with everything they had believed in and had worked for. A sense of duty kept them in Germany to care for those who could no longer help themselves while ensuring that a younger generation were prepared to earn a living in whatever foreign country would accept them. The only premise on which the Jewish leadership could still function was to believe that its own efforts of self-help with financial assistance from abroad would overcome the huge problems German Jewry was facing. The leadership thanked the organisations abroad who had provided financial assistance, especially the American Joint Distribution Committee, the Council for German Jewry in Britain and the Jewish Colonisation Association. The better-off German Jews had also made large sacrifices. Much more would still be needed.

The *Reichsvereinigung* in Berlin was headed in 1940 by Leo Baeck, Paul Eppstein, Moritz Henschel, Otto Hirsch, Philipp Kozower, Arthur Lilienthal, Julius Seligsohn and Heinrich Stahl. What was omitted from their report was that they were working under the immediate control of the Gestapo, on whom depended the degree of autonomy they could retain. The room for manoeuvre narrowed, but the Jewish leadership in 1939 and 1940 did not behave like supine underlings. Smaller communities were dissolved and amalgamated with larger ones as their membership shrank and their rabbis, employees and teachers became unemployed and needed assistance. In 1939, the financial needs of the *Reichsvereinigung* grew exponentially, having to fund emigration, training places, education and welfare for 70,602 of the Jews in Germany (without Austria) who had been pauperised and were old and sick.

The report also provides statistics of emigration. In all, 281,900 had left Germany by the close of 1939. The Jewish organisations could proudly look back on the fact that, from 1933 to 1939, more than half of German Jewry had been saved. Nor did efforts cease despite enormous obstacles after the outbreak of war, enabling another 6,000 to leave. To bring more Jews to safety was still the priority task.

There is an account in the report of the children's exodus, the *Kindertransport*. The figures are precise, every digit a young life: 16,328 children were registered with the *Reichsvertretung* by their parents to be found an unknown home abroad. The *Reichsvertretung* in the short time before the outbreak of war could enable only a third of them, 5,495, to escape; in December 1939, 10,833 were left waiting in Germany, of whom few survived. These were just some of the children trapped in Germany.

After the Jewish children were expelled from state schools in the winter of 1938, the *Reichsvereinigung* during the war still saw it as one of its most urgent tasks to create new places in Jewish schools. Overnight, books, desks and teachers had to be found, so that every Jewish child could receive a good education. A unified curriculum was drawn up. But as some communities were too small to support their own school, the children became boarders in the homes of larger communities. In the Guben province of Brandenburg there were now just four children; in Glogau in Silesia seven; in Göttingen, a famous university town, eight; in Hamburg 458. Altogether in Germany, without Austria, the *Reichvereinigung* located 9,550 children requiring schooling, all paid for from Jewish funds. Every child was provided with at least elementary education. The money available was insufficient for secondary education – two schools for Berlin's 2,907 children, one school in Breslau, one in Cologne and one in Frankfurt, all cities with larger Jewish populations. As yet no one could imagine that these children would never reach adulthood. In Hamburg, there was now only one *Judenschule*, the former girls' school in the Karolinenstraße, teaching all the children. Two boys were still able to sit the highest state leaving examination, the *Abitur*, in 1940, but, for most, education no longer continued after sixteen years of age. The Jewish community set great store on continuing to provide an excellent education, and teachers and the children worked hard to obtain good results. Attendance was compulsory, and, until all Jewish education was forbidden on 30 June 1942, if a child failed to turn up, a welfare officer was sent to enquire the reason. Even then, teaching was provided secretly in rooms of the community. It was stoic and tragic. There had to be a future for the children.

Equipping younger men and women for emigration by training them in manual skills did not slacken either but was severely limited by lack of funds. There were many more applicants than could be accommodated. Some would make it still to Palestine. A number of German towns had permitted camps to be set up and local employers took advantage of cheap labour. A special agreement with the Nazi farmers' association provided work for another 1,200 men and women to bring in the harvest. They had to labour under most primitive conditions and needed help with clothing and essentials. Other placements, again not enough, were supported to train men and women in a great variety of skills – metalwork, carpentry, tailoring, corset-making, hairdressing, optic and colour photography, domestic and nursery training. All those efforts in the end would help only a few hundred.

By December 1939, a quarter of German Jewry had become totally dependent on support from the *Reichsvereinigung*. The state of provision for special needs was catastrophic. Between 2,500 and 3,000 mentally handicapped patients required closed institutional care, and the 190 beds in the only Jewish mental hospital at Sayn could not accommodate them. The remainder were sent to German state or Christian religiously affiliated mental hospitals, where they lived together with Aryans. But for how much longer would this be the case?

What expectations were there for the future? When everyone capable of emigrating had gone, only those too young, too old or too sick were expected to be left in three years' time. The report ended with this dignified conclusion:

> We have now worked for seven years. To complete our work, important tasks still face the *Reichsvereinigung*. Large funds are necessary for the main work, the support of emigration, training, education, welfare and caring for the sick. The dissolution of German Jewry is continuing. Nearly two-thirds have already left Germany. A further two-thirds of the 240,000 remaining in Greater Germany are potentially able to emigrate. An estimated 160,000 of these will require some support from the *Reichsvereinigung*. Preparations for emigration and training add to the costs. More than half of those not able to emigrate will require support in the next few years. To achieve this in three years, a sum exceeding RM 100 million will be needed. The capital of the *Reichsvereinigung*, of the communities, charitable foundations, the number of members who still possess capital, cannot nearly cover even this amount. We continue to count on the help of those who have emigrated and hope also that the great organisations abroad who have helped so far will not deny their support in this the last phase in the dissolution of German Jewry.

The leaders of German Jewry still believed in December 1939 that Nazi intentions could be met by an orderly process of self-help, by the sacrifices and dedication of Jews still inside Germany and assistance from abroad. Given time, and a minimum of cooperation from the Nazi state, they might indeed have completed the task; instead they too would become the victims of physical annihilation. There existed two worlds: that of the racial and biological victims and that of all the other Germans. Among the general population, the mood of depression when war began turned to euphoria nine months later. For the Jews there was no such relief. Hitler's 'Thousand-Year Reich' in the summer of 1940 appeared more firmly established than ever before.

When the war is won

Had Hitler been right all along? Paris falls after a lightning campaign of six weeks; the humiliation of capitulation after the First World War is erased. Even former staunch opponents, such as the historian Friedrich Meinecke, began to question whether they had been wrong about the *Führer*. Hitler made a triumphant tour on his return from France. The flame of national pride burnt so brightly that there were even persecuted families like the Solmitzes who joined in the general fervour. Luise Solmitz cast her troubles momentarily aside, but not for long, as the reality of life in Nazi Germany and fears of the future filled her with foreboding.

> 7 August 1940. How we too would like to enjoy everyday living.
> 7 September 1940. There will never be peace for us. When it does come, who will still be alive?
> 5 October 1940. ... children evacuated from Hamburg.
> 10 October 1940. Invited L. to Hamburg, but who wants to come to a city destined to die? Whoever can, flees.[4]

The Solmitzes were more concerned for their daughter than themselves. Gisela could only marry another *Mischling* of the first degree or a Jew. That she was baptised and attended church regularly did not alter anything. Love for an Aryan was forbidden. The young man who asked Major Solmitz for her hand had to be enlightened. Luise chronicled her despair. Gisela was young and fell in love again, this time with a Belgian engineer working in Hamburg. The town hall gave the Solmitzes good advice. Why not marry in Brussels? Major Solmitz's record as a war hero now not only protected him but no doubt could assist Gisela in gaining permission to move to Belgium. But times were far from easy. Fredy Solmitz was still a racial Jew. The Solmitzes lived in daily dread that one day the exemptions he enjoyed in a 'privileged' mixed marriage would be cancelled and he would then suffer the fate of all the Jews. His was a wretched existence, shunned by neighbours. Few remained loyal. Nor could the Solmitzes close their ears to rumours all around – terrible rumours about what awaited Jews deported to the East. But what was happening in Poland surely would not happen here in Hamburg! Jews looked for any good signs. When the rations for Jews began to be curtailed, wounded Jewish war veterans like Major Solmitz received them in full. Aryan husbands, despite their Jewish wives, were serving in the *Wehrmacht* and their wives received full allowances. The Nazis had no record of brutalising women, children and the old. Surely Germans would never stoop so low? Most Jews knew a friendly baker, butcher or greengrocer who would put something aside to supplement the meagre rations Jews were allowed. As long as Jews still had some money or could sell their possessions, they, like everyone else, could turn to the thriving black market, where most things were available. One day the war would end.

I

In February 1940, there was a rude shock for Germany's Jews.[5] At short notice 1,200 Jews were deported from Stettin to Lublin with only what they could carry. Everything left behind was confiscated by the Nazi welfare service, the NSV. The very old and sick were left behind with no one to care for them. Plaut was visiting Berlin at the time and had gone to the offices of the *Reichsvereinigung* in the Kantstraße. What was to be done? Someone would have to go to Stettin and deal with the Gestapo and look after the old and sick. Rabbi Baeck turned to Plaut. 'Why me?', Plaut asked. 'Stettin on the Baltic is not in my region of responsibility.' 'You are the only one without a family', Baeck explained.

Having arrived in Stettin, with his usual skill Plaut negotiated with the Gestapo. The *Reichsvereinigung*, he offered, would 'buy back' the stolen goods for a payment of RM 90,000 to the NSV. The Gestapo agreed. Beddings, linen, medicines and other necessities were then sent on to Lublin. Even more remarkable was Plaut's exploit in stopping another deportation, this time from East Friesland, which was in his region of responsibilities. The Gestapo consented provided the Jews were found new homes in Berlin, Hamburg and other cities. These early deportations, the Gestapo assured the *Reichsvereinigung*, were one-off affairs to free accommodation for war workers.

Then, in the summer of 1940, the *Reichsvereinigung* was told by the Gestapo to make plans for the Jews to live in Madagascar.[6] With the victory in the West, this opportunity to solve the Jewish question in Western Europe had been seized on by Himmler. He suggested to Hitler that the Jews be dispatched to somewhere in Africa; the Bolshevik method of physically exterminating a people was 'un-German and impossible'. Ribbentrop's Foreign Ministry now took up the running and produced the 'Madagascar Plan'. For Hitler, the Madagascar Plan held one attraction, at a time when he was still hoping to make peace in Western Europe: it would camouflage his intention to destroy the Jews over time by disease and maltreatment. But it could never have solved the problem of the Jews in the East. Heydrich from the start in all probability regarded it as a hairbrained scheme. He did not have long to wait. Ribbentrop had appointed experts to advise him, and they poured cold water on the plan just two months later. An international shipping fleet would be needed, costs would be enormous, and it would take at least four years to transport the Jews. The final blow was that Britain did not sue for peace in the summer of 1940, and so the Royal Navy blocked the way. Heydrich had already concluded by the end of June, in writing to Ribbentrop, that 3.25 million Jews would not be able to emigrate and that only a 'territorial solution' was possible.[7] That clearly pointed to Eastern Europe, where the majority of the Jews lived already.

In October 1940, another shock was in store for the Jewish community. Suddenly the Jews from the west of Germany, the Palatinate and Baden were expelled to unoccupied France. The two *Gauleiters* of Baden and the Palatinate had taken the initiative. They had earlier been given orders by Hitler to clear Alsace-Lorraine, annexed by Germany, of all non-German peoples within ten years. They now thought, why not extend the expulsions to Jews in their own *Gaus* in the Reich? Trains took some 7,000 Jews to a camp in western France. The French were powerless to resist. The overall policy of getting *German* Jews out of the Reich by all and any means possible remained still in place. That is why on 25 October 1940 a ban was issued forbidding the emigration of (Polish) Jews from the General Government, so that they should not block openings still available abroad for German Jews. But what does this show? It reveals Hitler's continued anxiety over the reaction of other Germans to simply murdering the *German* Jews somewhere in the East. It would take another year before that too became acceptable. When the *Reichsvereinigung* got news of these latest depor- tations, they had sent warnings to their provincial branches advising Jews to hide.[8] Otto Hirsch, the director, was among the most courageous of the Jewish leaders. Once a senior civil servant in Württemberg, he miscalculated that he and his colleagues were not without power. They protested to the Gestapo and asked for prayers for the deportees to be said in synagogues. Hirsch paid for his resistance with his life.[9] Sent to the Mauthausen concentration camp in February 1941, he died from maltreatment only four weeks later. To be a Jew was danger- ous; to be a prominent Jew in 1940 was even more dangerous.

II

The technique of disposing of people by poison gas was first employed in the 'euthanasia' killings.[10] In July 1940, 200 Jewish victims were taken from a Berlin asylum to the Brandenberg killing centre. In September, it was Hamburg's turn. Plaut received a sudden notification from the Langenhorn Institution that Lilli Lehmann, whose guardian he was, would be transferred to another hospital.[11] 'On whose authority?', Plaut asked. At first he was told that there could be no discus- sion. Plaut went immediately to the hospital to find out more and to see whether anything could be done. He learnt that the orders came from the Gestapo. One hundred patients would be moved. Plaut managed to arrange the release to their families of a few and a visit to the others by their families to say goodbye.

The following day, the day of transportation, an elaborate camouflage exercise was staged. At the Hamburg goods station stood a train marked with red crosses attended by doctors and nurses in white uniforms. This was supposedly all orga- nised by the 'Columbus Transport Company', which would take the patients to the 'hospital' in Cholm, described as a modern state institution in Poland. Why the deception? To reassure the Jews or other Germans?

The Gestapo told Plaut he could remain in touch with the patients once they were in Cholm. He could also write to the Jewish elders of the ghetto in Lublin, encouraging them to visit the patients. The Gestapo in all likelihood knew better. From Lublin later came disturbing news. There was no mental hospital in Cholm. When a death certificate was sent from Cholm for a patient who at the last moment had been released before boarding the train and found himself in the best of health, the conclusion was inescapable. The patients had never reached Poland, but had been murdered in a German euthanasia centre.[12] Plaut concluded:

> From that time on we knew that the concentration camp meant death in the worst way; we now recognised that the most important point of Hitler's party programme, the solution of the Jewish question, aimed at the

extermination of all Jews within the territories under German control. We all realised that. Our reaction could not be despair, but a really heroic steadfastness.

Another 'special group' to be deported from Hamburg, less noted and written about, were the 'gypsies'.[13] Their racial classification was far more hit and miss than that of the Jews. Anyone whose lifestyle was unsettled, including Roma and Sinti, could be called a gypsy. There was a great deal of intermarriage, but distinctions between 'half-' and 'quarter-gypsies' were haphazard. Most were poor, many known to welfare officers. Their disappearance raised even less public disapproval than did that of the Jews.

III

The general population of Hamburg was not entirely ignorant about what was going on in Poland. People did not only have to rely on rumours or the graphic reports of returning soldiers on leave. Hamburg was twinned with Łódź, now Litzmannstaadt. The authorities encouraged visits of teachers and administrators to help Łódź catch up with German civilisation. The ghetto was on many a sightseeing tour. One German social worker, thanks to an acquaintance in the SS, was escorted through its streets. In a letter written to a friend there is no hint of sympathy.

> I was not able to feel the slightest pity for the thousands of Jews behind the barbed wire. Although I have feelings for Jews and have done my utmost to help them whenever I had the opportunity, I was overcome by disgust and aversion such as I have never felt before. When one sees the Jews the determination to exterminate them becomes understandable.

Frau Frieda Schmidt, a tailoress and the recipient, showed more understanding.[14]

> Jews only take advantage and have enslaved those who have had too close a relationship with them, which is their own fault. I think it is much worse that a whole defenceless and innocent people are robbed and enslaved by the National Socialists ... *Frau* B. throws out the baby with the bathwater when she believes that the Jews must be destroyed ... I can well imagine that I too would have felt revulsion at the sight of these Jews who have been herded together. But they would have had no opportunity to buy decent clothing. I still feel pity for the Jews.

Frau Schmidt wrote in her diary that one treated animals better than Jews: 'such hatred and malevolence'. It would get worse, as she discovered when visited by a young *Wehrmacht* soldier on leave from Poland, who told her how Jews 'were hanged, shot, dragged through dirt ... beards cut off the orthodox, beaten, their homes plundered'. Thousands of returning soldiers recounted similar experiences.

IV

For the Jews left in Hamburg, life became harder every passing month. Ominous were the constant questionnaires. Every possession had to be listed. Bank accounts were blocked. Soon nothing could be sold or disposed of without the Gestapo's permission. The slightest transgression could lead to a concentration camp or beatings in a Gestapo cell. Rations were constantly curtailed. Jews received no clothing coupons and had to rely on mending their wardrobe. Shoes were a problem, especially for growing children. The community's second-hand clothing store provided for the needy. There were too few Jewish doctors, nurses and hospital beds.

In the summer of 1941 the Jews were still living all over the city, many in their old apartments surrounded by the comfort of family furniture. At least once you closed your front door you were still 'at home'. The better-off Jews occupied large apartments, some with four or five bedrooms. They were eyed jealously by the less favoured. Hamburg had for years suffered from a housing shortage, made worse by the air raids.[15] Not surprisingly, the Nazi Welfare Office discussed ways and means of removing the Jews. In April 1940 there was a meeting of senior administrators, who demanded that all Jews should be forced to move into the available housing stock owned by Jews. One participant at the meeting, a high-ranking storm trooper, *Obersturmbannführer* Plander, had a better idea: send them packing to Poland. Oskar Martini, head of the welfare services during the Weimar years, who had adjusted well to the Nazis and continued to head Hamburg's Welfare Office, recorded their views. He felt no particular sympathy for Jews; but the problem with Plander's suggestion was, he said, that Göring had forbidden such local initiatives. Plander was not satisfied. Martini should put the suggestion to Kaufmann. Martini promised he would. Plander had to wait another year before he found the reply more to his liking.

The flourishing Jewish community had shrunk to no more than 7,500 souls. Six weeks later, half would be gone. Any last illusions that they were Germans, not Poles or Russians, were shattered. The new assault began in the month of September 1941 with a decree that all Jews over six years old had to fix a yellow star on their outer garments. The size and cost, 10 *Pfennige*, was prescribed, and nineteen days were allowed for their manufacture. There was no hint of what was to follow. That was being decided in secret elsewhere.

On 18 September 1941 Himmler sent a message to the *Reichsstatthalter* of the *Wartheland*.

> It is the *Führer*'s wish that the *Altreich* and the Protectorate should be emptied of and liberated from the Jews from west to east as soon as possible. I am thus endeavouring to ensure that the deportation of the Jews from the *Altreich* and the Protectorate to the territories incorporated into the Reich

during the past two years is completed during this year as a first step preparatory to their being sent further east in the spring. During the winter,
I intend to send some 60,000 Jews from the *Altreich* and the Protectorate to
the Litzmannstadt ghetto, which, as I understand, is just able to accommodate them ...

The tone of the letter is still vague about their ultimate fate.[16]

There were uncertainties. Hitler had intended to complete the 'final solution'
after the war was won.[17] But would that be soon? With the expected early victory
in Russia, would the war come to an end on the continent of Europe to all intents
and purposes by the spring? Or would Britain continue to hold out, strengthened
by the United States, drawn into a 'world war' by the Jewish wire-pullers in
Washington? There was still no fixed timetable to implement the final solution.
The systematic murder of Jews under German control, except for the Jews of
Russia, had not yet been authorised by Hitler.

The three months of September, October and November 1941 were critical in
the evolution of the final solution. Policy intentions hardened from week to week.
Himmler's order on 18 October, a month after his message to Greiser putting a
stop to the further emigration of Jews, pointed to another now preferred outcome –
their destruction. The door of escape was closed for Jews in the West, allowing
only a few exceptions. Topf & Söhne of Erfurt received *urgent* orders for some
twenty-five gas chambers, destined for the creation of industrial human extermination factories at Majdanek, Chelmno, Belzec, Sobibor, Treblinka and Auschwitz.
Blueprints for crematoria II, a gas chamber and anteroom to be constructed at
Auschwitz-Birkenau, also date from the autumn of 1941.[18] All this evidence shows
that earlier suppositions that mass murders were first started simply on local initiatives, and that central planning in Berlin came later, require modification.

Besides constructing the facilities for extermination, which would not be
ready for several months, a series of administrative organisational issues also
had to be addressed. On 29 November Heydrich sent out invitations to the principal bureaucrats and SS commanders involved in the implementation of the final
solution for a meeting to take place in Wannsee on 9 December. Their coordination was an important link in the chain.

The first step was to organise the deportations to the East. The Gestapo offices
in Hamburg and the Reich were ready to make a start in mid-October. The summons went out by registered mail.[19]

    Gestapo Hamburg   Hamburg, [date]

Evacuation order

Your evacuation from Greater Hamburg is ordered forthwith. The order
also applies to your relatives as follows ...

Transportation will be carried out without delay. You and your relatives, from today for the duration of the transport, are subject to exceptional regulations. Your property and possessions and those of your relatives count as confiscated. You must appear at the Moorweidenstraße 36, at the following time […], with your [Jewish] identification card, passport, labour book, receipts of invalid or Reich Insurance and ration cards.

Every person may bring with them

1.   a suitcase with necessities up to the weight of 50 kg
2.   a complete set of clothing
3.   bedding with a blanket
4.   provisions for three days (food for the transport will be supplied by the Jewish committee)
5.   money up to RM 200. Any sum beyond this has to be given over at the control.

The following is forbidden to be taken with you.

1.   share certificates, foreign money, savings books, etc.
2.   any valuables made of gold, silver or platinum, with the exception of a wedding ring
3.   anything live, ration cards, goods which are not permitted.

The enclosed questionnaire has to be filled in by every person being evacuated and has to be handed in at the control. The pages are to be filled in with a typewriter as soon as possible. The Jewish Committee has been asked to assist with this. For any pages that cannot be read or have been badly filled in, RM 20 will be deducted from the currency you are permitted to take with you.

After you have left your apartment you are required to lock it and to hand the key to your local police station. The police station will certify receipt of the key. You are responsible for the orderly condition of your apartment and the appearance of your relatives when they report. Damage to goods or attempted flight will be dealt with by special measures. Enclosed is a key ring for the apartment key.

A 'key ring': the Gestapo thought of everything.

Exit from Hamburg

A day like any other. The postman rings and you sign for a registered letter. You open the envelope. The shock on reading the contents defies imagination. You have done nothing wrong, but the Gestapo is placing you under arrest. The envelope contains detailed instructions. From that moment on, life has irrevocably changed. You have just forty-eight hours to decide what to take with you; you can only take what you can carry. You have to make list after list of everything you have to leave behind, and you will never see your possessions again. There are a few treasured mementos. If photographs of your children and parents – images reminding you of happier times – are taken out of their frame they do not weigh much. The Jewish community office urges you to pack essentials – warm clothing, bedding, blankets, pots and pans – and sufficient food to last three days. That leaves little else to take with you within the weight you are allowed. Some Jews had hidden jewellery and now agonise whether they dared sew it into the lining of a coat. A few still knew loyal German neighbours and friends who rushed to help.

Frau Flügge, a Hamburg school teacher, was among the few who kept up close relations with Jewish children and friends. She helped amid tears a Jewish husband and wife to pack their suitcases and fill in the inventory of all their possessions. 'Imagine the barbarity', she wrote to her daughter. 'They received the "order" through the mail; in two days they will have to leave Hamburg. Where to? Russia? Poland? With certainty, to destruction and death.'[20] She accompanied them to the Moorweidenstraße on 24 October 1941 as far as she was allowed to go before the final parting. They were deported, although the husband had secured a medical certificate saying that he was too ill to travel. He had gone with it to the Gestapo, only to be pushed out of the door. 'Only the dead will stay here', they called after him. They were just two people of the more than a thousand who were deported to the ghetto in Łódź. Once *Frau* Flügge had obtained their postal address she began sending them parcels, until one day they too were moved 'to an unknown address' – that is, to their death. It took courage to show open friendship for Jews. *Frau* Flügge's punishment was to be transferred by the authorities to a school considered inferior, but she survived the war.

A greengrocer was very upset when she saw elderly women having to leave a Jewish old-age home: 'such a little group of misery'. 'It's a good thing that this pack is being cleared out', said another onlooker. 'Are you talking to me?', she replied. 'Just keep quiet.'[21] A few belongings were found in a dustbin. In less than three months, half of Hamburg's remaining Jewish population had gone in four large transports to Łódź, Minsk (twice) and, on 6 December 1941, Riga. Kaufmann had hoped to speed things up and remove the remainder quickly. He urged Hitler that the housing shortage in Hamburg would be alleviated by their departure. But Kaufmann had not been responsible for the timing of the deportations. Hitler had decided to implement this stage of the final solution, the deportation of all Jews not married to Germans. The last stages, the *endgültige Lösung*, the *final* solution, would have to wait until the war was won. But even the removal of those Jews whose fate had been decided ran into delays, as the setback before Moscow in the winter of 1941 necessitated the use of all available trains for the *Wehrmacht*. Deportations from Hamburg did not resume until 1 July 1942.

The news of the deportations spread like wildfire through the community. Everyone now feared for their future. Some took refuge in suicide. Dr Bauer, a Jewish lawyer, before taking this ultimate step wrote a letter to his little daughter – a letter which could not be sent, but which he hoped would survive and be read by her after the war was over.[22]

> My dearly beloved daughter,
>
> I parted from you more than two years ago and, despite all the terrible things that have happened since then, 11th March 1939 was the most tragic day of my life. I can still see you before me, how with a doll in your arms, holding the hand of Aunt Dorothy, you entered the plane which took you, my sweetest most treasured one, away from me. I have often had doubts whether I did the right thing to send you away to strangers, however loving. I did it out of love for you. This was the only way I could make sure that you would grow up a free human being, receive a good education and be well brought up by your Uncle Gordon and Aunt Dorothy ...
>
> Today the first transport of Jews leaves Hamburg ... there are said to be 2,000 out of 7,000 Jews still left here in Hamburg. I am not on the list, but it is certain that more transports will follow until all the Jews have been taken out of Hamburg and the rest of Germany. So your mother and I will soon follow. No one knows what will happen to us, but what is certain is that only a small number of those sent away will survive the hunger and cold, dirt and disease. I don't know what I will do when it is my turn, but I thank the good God that I had the strength to save my beloved child from this fate.
>
> I have not seen you for a year and a half. Whether you will receive this first and last letter I don't know. But you are already a different girl to the six-year-old child that was torn from my heart ... even your language is no longer the same as mine.
>
> But I hope my words will show you how great a love I feel for you. I had meant you to inherit everything I had received from the family, but once I am sent away I shall have nothing ...

Just over two months later, Dr Bauer wrote a second letter. He had tried to save his own life and that of his wife by proving that his wife was Aryan and that theirs was a mixed marriage. But his application was rejected. Deportation was now certain.

> Hamburg, 8 January 1942
>
> Four transports of 3,000 Jews left Hamburg in October and December 1941. We only know from the first that it arrived in Łódź. About the others, which are said to have gone to Minsk and Riga, one knows nothing definite, but terrible rumours are circulating. In any case, I have made up my mind that I will not submit myself to the terrible humiliation, hunger, cold,

dirt and disease only to suffer a tortured death in the end. My strength is gone. I hope that your mother's and my suffering was a sacrifice for you so that you can lead a better and happier life. Of the few happy hours and days allowed us, we have to thank you for most of them. You did not bring us a single day of sorrow. For that I thank you from all my heart. If later you should think of us, then be proud of me. I have never done any harm to anyone and suffer innocently. You, my dear daughter, must become strong and happy. Perhaps your mother will find a way out if I am no longer. I wish to give up my heart to save you both ...

I

The final deportation of 1941, to Riga in December, was notable for including Joseph Carlebach and his family.[23] Carlebach had been *persona grata* with the Gestapo in Hamburg. He would not have been deported so soon but for his Jewish New Year message to members of the congregation in concentration camps, which instilled the hope in them that they would one day be free and that the sun would shine again. Was he forecasting the destruction of the Nazi state? When a copy fell into the hands of Heinrich Müller, Gestapo chief in Berlin, he ordered Göttsche to send Carlebach to Auschwitz, where he was to be 'finished off' in not more than a week. Auschwitz was not yet the death factory where more than 1 million Jews would perish. It had been set up for Poles and Russian prisoners of war. But others were sent there already in 1940. The camp was the most feared, and Jews sent as punishment there were condemned to early sadistic murder.

Plaut, on hearing from Göttsche that he had received this order from Berlin, appealed to the Gestapo chief to send Carlebach to Riga instead, as a deportation transport for Riga was about to be assembled.[24] Göttsche felt sorry for Carlebach – 'The stupid idiot, why did he have to do that?' – but added that he could not go against orders from Berlin. Plaut telephoned Carlebach to come at once to try to change Göttsche's mind. Göttsche relented. He would tell Müller that, amid all the work of preparing the Riga transport, he had not had time to read his message. It was a rare show of independence. Holding his head high, Joseph Carlebach, his wife Lotte and their four children boarded the train with some 800 fellow Jews on 6 December as if going on a holiday. Only one son, Salomon (Peter) would survive. Joseph Carlebach, Lotte, fifteen-year-old Ruth, fourteen-year-old Noemi and thirteen-year-old Sara, Hindenburg's godchild, were all shot in the woods outside the camp. The *Hamburger Tageblatt* reported Carlebach's death belatedly in the spring of 1943 as having occurred 'from natural causes'. It was strange that they bothered with news of the death of a Jew.

The Nazis were anxious to persuade the people that, despite the war, life could still go on as before. The theatres, the opera and the concert halls were open. In Hamburg, on the day of the first deportation, a well-loved comic actor, Heinz

Rühmann, was playing the lead in *The Gentleman in Furnished Rooms*, and the *Hamburger Tageblatt* reported that the whole of Hamburg was laughing. As the last transport of 1941 left, it was Mozart week.

II

What awaited the deported Jews from Hamburg? A few survivors have left accounts. One of the most graphic was written after the war by Henry Rosenberg.[25] The Rosenberg family, husband, wife and children, was deported on 8 November 1941. As the train sped from Hamburg's goods station past the well-kept houses in the suburbs, they saw their city for the last time. Only Henry Rosenberg would survive the Nazi death camps. Here is his account.

> The carriages were not heated. With so many people and so much luggage it was not possible to settle down, let alone sleep. With all the tension and nervousness amongst us the merest trifle could result in quarrels and disputes. And under these difficult conditions our journey took us via Berlin and Warsaw to the Russian border, arriving at the railway station of Minsk on the evening of 11 November 1941. The first night we stayed in our carriages, because the SS did not want to take us off the train during darkness.
>
> On the opposite platform stood a train, its open carriages crammed with Russian prisoners of war, almost all of them without coats despite the severe cold. A guard shouted at them that they were about to be given some food, but if they began fighting with each other the guards would make use of their firearms. An interpreter translated, then it all started. The guard threw two or three loaves into the railway carriage, and it was obvious that the starved prisoners would be fighting for them. As soon as the guards saw this they opened fire on the prisoners with their machine-guns. We heard the screams of the prisoners. Later on the many dead were thrown out of the carriages, the guards claiming that 'they acted under orders', since lawlessness had broken out among the prisoners. That was to be our first sight of Minsk. During the night more and more SS men armed with rifles and machine-guns approached our train, and on the morning of 12 November we were taken off the train.
>
> Minsk ghetto, 12 November 1941
>
> At 5 o'clock in the morning an SS major turned up to give the SS and us his orders. We had to leave the train and assemble with our hand luggage in front of each carriage in order to be counted. Then we – that is, the transport leader and the twenty of us who were responsible for each of the carriages – were taken to the ghetto and told: 'Anyone who runs away or refuses to obey orders will be shot. A hundred people will be shot for every one who runs away.' We further received the order to clear up the 'Red House', an unfinished school building, by 8 o'clock in the evening, as

anyone found out in the street after 8 o'clock would be shot. We were taken through the building, which earlier had accommodated hundreds of fellow sufferers. The stoves were still burning, everything was strewn about, and the floor was covered with hundreds of corpses. It was a horrible sight – the second impression of Minsk. After we had left the house, one lorry after another came carrying people guarded by Ukrainian SS. Then two hours later almost all of our 1,000 people assembled in the square. A lot of searching, calling and screaming started; everyone wanted to know what was in that large house, and everyone returned aghast at what they had seen. When things had settled somewhat, the men and women started to clean it. The dead were taken out to the square; their soiled and infested belongings, thought to be unusable, were just thrown out of the window to be burnt on the square. Later we realised and regretted the mistake we had made, for all these things, once cleaned, could have been used.

The Russian Jews who tried to come over to us to talk were driven away by the SS. Only a few of them managed to reach us, and what they told us was for us unbelievable. They cried and screamed and searched for their relatives among the dead. That is how we got to know that, in Minsk on 9 November 1941, 30,000 Jews had been murdered. During that day nobody thought of eating. We were just very thirsty, but water was not available, because we were not allowed to go to the only available well. Only in the evening were we allowed to fetch water, and some of us then began to eat.

At 5 o'clock it turned dark, yet there was no light, water, windows or heating, nor chairs, beds or tables in the house. But after all we had gone through, we were at least glad to have a roof over our heads, and for a start were able to sit on the floor. Thus after a while a thousand people shared the thirty halls, which were no larger than ordinary classrooms. No sooner had all settled than the SS major turned up and asked for Dr Frank, the Jewish leader. He received the immediate order for all the men to be divided into two groups, the first group to go to the station to empty the carriages and to carry the suitcases and other luggage to the lorries, and the second group to stay in the camp to unload them and to take the food and provisions to the house. It was understandable that fatigue had made people very tired, but it was an order that it was impossible to refuse, let alone demonstrate against. The SS, with five large lorries and guards, took the first group to the station.

The railwaymen had simply thrown everything onto the tracks; the carriages had already gone except for five cattle trucks filled with various goods. The SS could think of nothing better to do than to examine every piece of luggage, throwing out all the contents; at best, only half was put back. The luggage considered worthless was loaded onto the lorries to be driven to the ghetto; worthwhile possessions were placed in another lorry and driven to the SS barracks. What happened to them there we got to know only later. The luggage destined for the ghetto was taken to a large square near the building and unloaded there. Later on, the five carriages, which contained sewing machines, agricultural tools, mattresses, bicycles and food, were unloaded. All of this was immediately confiscated, and only some essential provisions – flour, bread, barley, a little sugar and substitute coffee – were permitted to be taken to the ghetto. The cheque that had been made out by the Hamburg Gestapo for the deported Jews was confiscated by the SS in Minsk in settlement for their 'expenses'.

Only a few days earlier, despite restrictions, they had lived near normal lives in familiar surroundings. The sights that greeted them were unimaginable, even in their worst nightmares. Somehow until now they had still held on to the belief that the Germans were a civilised people. The shock of the reality was overwhelming.

III

In Minsk, the problem of finding enough room for the Jews from Germany had been solved for the time being. No need in Russia to worry about open massacres. The situation in Łódź was different, belonging as it now did to the Reich; with frequent visitors from Hamburg, large-scale massacres inside the ghetto were avoided.

The first transport from Hamburg, which had left on 25 October 1941, had not known what to expect.[26] People had put on their most serviceable clothing as protection against the cold. The Jewish community authorities had provided them with food and the kind of equipment they believed to be of greatest use – cooking pots, spades and shovels – for the motley crowd of young and old, lawyers and professional men for the most part, their wives and children and grandfathers and grandmothers. We know more about the short life of the Jews in Łódź than of those in Minsk. The Jewish authorities there wrote a secret chronicle of events, hidden when the ghetto was liquidated in 1944 and discovered after the war. Only a few of Hamburg's Jews remained in the ghetto six months after their arrival. Most had been rounded up and taken away. No one in the ghetto knew where they had gone or what fate awaited the departed. In fact they had been taken to Chelmno where they were murdered. Trains left punctually at 7 a.m. and returned empty in the evening.

Erwin Baehr was one of some eighteen survivors from that first deportation of 1,034 men, women and children from Hamburg.[27] But cold statistics as stoically recorded by the Jewish authorities in Hamburg do not begin to convey the horror of what was happening: 3,163 'racial' Jews were deported between October and December 1941 of whom fewer than seventy survived. With killings on such a scale, even meticulous German records do not enable us to be completely accurate. The chances of survival from mass deportation in 1941 and 1942 were minuscule and for children non-existent. Just before the deportations began, 7,547 Jews were registered with the Jewish authorities as living in Hamburg. While the deportations in 1941 were in progress, 150 people were recorded as dying, many of them suicides. During October and November 1941, another 121 Jews still managed to emigrate. By the end of that year there were 4,051 Jews left in Hamburg.

IV

Until final decisions were reached, the Jews from Hamburg and the Reich were held in ghettos in the Wartheland, Lithuania, Poland and Ukraine; the euphemism was that they were being 'resettled'. In overcrowded, disease-ridden quarters on starvation rations, the able-bodied were forced to work in factories for the *Wehrmacht*. They were imprisoned by walls and fences and shot if they attempted to escape. The ghettos were administered by Jewish elders, *Judenräte*, under the whips of the Gestapo. In the Łódź ghetto in the Wartheland the existence of postal services created the illusion of normality for those left behind. After all, 'Litzmannstadt', was now a German town. It is not difficult to imagine the shock of the first Hamburg deportees to reach Łódź, in October 1941. Soon they too, like earlier deportees, struggled to survive, Hamburg a distant memory, another lifetime.[28] After three more transports, deportations temporarily came to a halt. Glimmers of hope revived the Jewish community as winter turned to spring and early summer in 1942 and no more deportations occurred. What the Jews did not know was that their fate had already been sealed at the start of the year.

On 20 January 1942, the meeting previously postponed took place in Am Großen Wannsee, just outside Berlin.[29] Here Heydrich explained to the assembled bureaucrats and SS commanders from the East that the fate awaiting 12 million Jews was extermination. At the meeting Heydrich secured the acquiescence of the Nazi bureaucracy that he and Himmler would take overall charge of implementing and coordinating the 'final solution'. That was an important administrative step forward. Only one other issue affecting a small percentage of Jews caused any difficulties. Who were they? Why just them?

Some thousand such Jews lived in Hamburg and about 19,000 in the Reich. These were the racial Jews, like Friedrich Solmitz, married to an Aryan spouse. Heydrich would have liked for such marriages to be dissolved so that the Jewish spouse could be deported. Nor was there unanimity about the treatment of their *Mischling* children. The Ministry of the Interior and the Ministry of Justice found Heydrich's proposals unacceptable. But their concern was only about those who were German. No such fine tuning would be necessary for Poles or Russians. For Heydrich, it was anathema to exclude any Jews. How could there be a final solution as long as Jews and part-Jews defiled the already less than perfect German genetic pool? But on this question, despite all the power of the Gestapo, he was unable to cross the red line Hitler had drawn in 1939.

V

It was shortly after the Wannsee meeting that Himmler and his staff began to finalise the organisational preparations for the final solution of more than 2 million Polish Jews in the General Government. The operation to kill them all was named *Aktion Reinhard* – mass murder in honour of Heydrich. Odilo Globocnik, the higher SS and police commander of the Lublin District in the General Government, was Himmler's choice to implement the unprecedented undertaking.

By July 1942 the extermination camps were ready; from the first planning stages in the autumn of 1941, they had become operational in less than a year. It needed the fanatical drive and coordination of the Gestapo headquarters in Berlin to accomplish this. Himmler and his cohorts did not just respond piecemeal to local pressures; the initiative came from Berlin. Nor could Himmler simply have acted on his own on so huge a murder enterprise without the approval of Hitler. In Chelmno, gassing in special vans had already begun in December 1941. The first Jewish victims were transported there from the surrounding areas of the Warthegau. They were followed mid-January 1942 by Jews and Gypsies from the Łódź (Litzmannstadt) ghetto. The trains left in the morning, and returned in the evening carrying the belongings which the victims were supposed to have needed at their new destination. That left little to the imagination. Some 145,000 men, women and children, mainly Jews, but also Poles, Gypsies and Russians, were murdered until the final liquidation of the Łódź ghetto. The SS obliterated the camp in the spring of 1943 to destroy the evidence and landscaped the area back into peaceful countryside. Chelmno had served its purpose to make now German Warthegau *judeurein*, free of Jews.

Chelmno was not, however, one of the new centres planned through *Aktion Reinhard*. Something more efficient than gas vans and open-air shootings was ideally needed to accomplish the task in the year that was planned to complete it. So work began on the construction of more extermination centres.

The first, Belzec, where building had already started on 1 November 1941, was transformed into a pure killing centre. Gas chambers and crematoria were designed, ordered and installed. In mid-March 1942 the new facilities began to kill Jews. That summer even larger facilities were installed. Before the machinery of death was halted in December 1942, the SS guards had turned 550,000 human beings to ash. Belzec was then also demolished.

It was soon realised that Belzec alone could not murder all the Jews. At a second extermination centre, Sobibor, from April 1942 to October 1943, 200,000 Jews became its victims. The end was nevertheless remarkable when the remnant rose to kill some of their captors and escaped. Most were recaptured and put to death, but some reached the partisans in the forests and about fifty survived until liberation.

Treblinka was an existing concentration camp. Here a new killing centre, Treblinka II, was built. Between July and the end of August 1942, 215,000 Jews from the Warsaw ghetto met their deaths in its gas chambers. With the help of superior designed crematoria and gas chambers, before it ceased operations, it is estimated that at least 750,000 Jews were killed. Treblinka too witnessed a revolt of the last victims in August 1943. At most a third of those who got away, a hundred prisoners, reached temporary safety, the rest were recaptured and, together with the remaining prisoners, all killed. Treblinka had done its work by the summer of that year. It was then demolished in an attempt to hide the evidence.

Belzec, Sobibor and Treblinka were the three *Aktion Reinhard* camps which between them had murdered at least 1.5 million Jews. Yet it was not these three extermination centres that symbolise the Holocaust, but the largest of all the camps – Auschwitz. Auschwitz was a vast complex of camps: the concentration camp, where few of even the most fit survived for long; the industrial camp, with its own horrendous death toll; and the extermination Birkenau centre, with its gas chambers and crematoria, to which the weak, the old and the children were assigned on arrival and the weakened and sick were transferred from other camps.

Auschwitz had begun as a concentration camp for Poles. In early 1941 there were plans for a large extension employing labour in a second camp for the benefit of the IG Farben chemical concern and the state. With the start of Barbarossa, thought was given to incarcerating Russian prisoners in Auschwitz. In early September 1941, according to commandant Hoess's memoirs (which are not entirely reliable on dating, though on this occasion collaborated by another witness), Russian prisoners of war were gassed experimentally using Cyclon B gas. That foreshadowed a more sinister future for the new camp, Auschwitz II, Auschwitz-Birkenau. Instead of Russians, Jews were now targeted for extermination. At Auschwitz II a small farmhouse, known as Bunker 1, was equipped with gas chambers capable of killing 800 at a time, and here Jews were gassed from March until December 1942. Bunker II took over with three gas chambers from the summer of 1942 until the autumn of 1944. A large new complex of anterooms, gas chambers and crematoria was completed in the spring of 1943. There was now an oversupply of facilities until in the summer of 1944 when the Hungarian Jews arrived. In a few weeks more than half a million Jews were gassed. By now Auschwitz's death toll surpassed even that of Treblinka. The gas chambers of Majdanek, meantime, were disposing of the Jews of Lublin. It was no longer only the Jews in Poland who met their deaths, but the Jews of Germany, the occupied West and Eastern and Central Europe.[30]

V

On 11 July 1942, when the deportations resumed in Hamburg, the first train took 300 old and young people straight to Auschwitz. Among them were the children from the Jewish orphanage.[31] They stand out because of their age and because they were not accompanied by their parents. Bela Anschlawski was aged not quite three; a stranger would have had to cradle ten-month-old Uri Becker; Rescha Fischer had been born just seven months earlier. Older boys and girls would experience the full horror: there was sixteen-year-old Irmgard Horn and the two Rothschild sisters, Miriam, aged nine, and Regina, thirteen. On the ramp the finger pointed to the gas chamber. The terror of the children requires little imagination. Some were transported with a parent – Ella Feldheim, alone with her baby. There were also a few older people in their seventies on this transport instead of the one leaving four days later for Terezín. A few prominent names can be identified, such as 65-year-old Helene Burchardt, of the well-known Altona branch of the Warburgs. All that is left are lists of names, each one once a life lived or barely begun.

A week later Dr Heinrich Wohlwill, once a distinguished member of the elite Hamburg chamber of commerce, was deported to Terezín, the make-believe pleasant Theresienstadt.[32] Heinrich Wohlwill was a descendant of the well-known nineteenth century Wohlwills. He loved the city in which he had played such an important industrial role. He had invented in 1903 a process for the recovery of copper that remained in use down to the Second World War. His patent became the basis for the growth of an industrial concern in Hamburg, the world-class Norddeutsche Affinerie, of which he was technical director from 1913 to 1933 and a member of the board. After all the Jewish board members had been removed in 1933, he continued to assist the company in a less exposed position.

A man of culture, widely read, and a talented musician, he had led a fulfilled family life surrounded by his four children and his grandchildren. His son, a daughter, his sister and one brother had all left Germany in time. Parted from their children and grandchildren, Heinrich Wohlwill and his wife were now virtually alone. Few relatives remained. An elder sister, Sophie, was still living in Hamburg, as was one other daughter, Margarete, who had married an Aryan; their children were baptised. Margarete's marriage and her Christian children saved her from deportation. Another survivor was Paul Wohlwill, a cousin, also because of his Christian spouse. Once the musical evenings in Heinrich Wohlwill's home at Hindenburgstraße 111 had been attended by friends and family – happy social gatherings. Now, 'Many people no longer come to us. We live on an island. Just now and then our friends visit us.' He nevertheless kept himself useful and active, helping in the small hospital allocated to the Jews, soliciting donations for impoverished Jewish musicians, spending time socially in the Jewish community rooms, and tending his garden and playing his violin.

On 17 July 1942 the dreaded deportation order arrived. The evening was spent playing Brahms and Beethoven sonatas accompanied by a close non-Aryan family friend. As they made music together they were able to put out of their minds what the next day would bring. The following morning, near to despair, Heinrich tearfully said goodbye to his sister Sophie. He tried to take his old Tyrolean violin with him, but the Gestapo routinely deprived the deportees of anything of value. A faithful elderly maid, Johanna, a member of their household for nineteen years, accompanied Dr Heinrich and *Frau* Hedwig Wohlwill to the Moorweide assembly point, insisting on carrying their luggage as far as the Gestapo would permit her. Eight years after coming to power, the Nazis had not succeeded in breaking all attachments between Christians and Jews. After the war, Hedwig Wohlwill, who survived Theresienstadt, described their tearful parting for her grandson.

The transport left for Terezín on 19 July. Wohlwill's 71-year-old sister Sophie followed a few months later, arriving in the ghetto in March 1943. To the terrible experience of the deportation for an old lady was now added what she described as the hardest blow of her entire life, when she learnt that her beloved brother Heinrich had died. Only two months before the privations of the ghetto also claimed her own life, she wrote an affectionate memoir of him that survived the war.

By the autumn of 1942, 58,000 people were herded together in the space where 7,000 had previously lived. Internal life was regulated by the Jewish elders under Gestapo control. 'Theresienstadt' was a German lie, a fiction for the outside world that the Jews had been 'resettled' in a healthy and reasonable environment to live out the rest of their lives. During 1942 and 1943, more than 2,115, mostly the elderly, from Hamburg were dumped there. Altogether more than 115,000 Czech and German Jews were deported to Terezín. Neither water nor food, neither sanitation nor space could support that number. About a third of the 42,124 German Jews, after an interim stay, were dispatched to the Auschwitz extermination camp. Even so, there would have been no room in Terezín for the remainder had they not so quickly succumbed to a 'natural death'.

Remarkably, the quest for scientific knowledge and culture proved unquenchable even in such surroundings. It gave life a purpose. The doctors drew charts which monitored diseases and the life and death of the inmates in weekly graphs. The Jewish 'self-administration' developed into a bureaucracy, though the real masters were the Gestapo. Distinguished professors delivered lectures on philosophy and German literature. There were even concerts, which for a brief time transported audiences to another world. Only the physical destruction of the people themselves, the fate of the great majority, could extinguish their spirit.

The Jews have gone

What did Germans in the Reich really know and believe? The Wannsee meeting was held in secret, but Hitler's speeches which threatened the extermination of Jews were broadcast and printed in the newspapers with banner headlines. *Frau* Schmidt, one 'ordinary' German, a tailoress, did not interpret Hitler's rantings as mere hate-filled rhetoric. In October 1942 an entry in her diary reflects her abhorrence:

> Hitler spoke in the same old way … I only listened to the end of his speech, but that was enough to become aware how he is motivated by evil and the basest impulses. There was so much hatred in the sentences he devoted to the Jews, 'And even if today they have not stopped laughing, they will soon not laugh any more.' Now, thanks to him, they have gone. They can no longer laugh. And the few who are left have had all their human right taken away and no longer need to laugh. I have never seen him before convulsed with such hatred and will to destroy. If I were to imagine how he looks,

he would have blood-rimmed eyes, a foaming mouth and hair matted with sweat.

'What could be the reason for so much hatred?', she wondered. There was a widespread rumour that Hitler was of Jewish descent! 'That thought', *Frau* Schmidt confided to her diary, 'struck me like lightning when I met a lady travelling from Frankfurt.' One can only imagine the scene: a crowded railway carriage in wartime Germany, two elderly ladies sitting side by side, and *Frau* Schmidt instigating a conversation. It is striking that a rumour probably started abroad by Hitler's enemies, which had no foundation, was also circulating in Germany. Had her companion heard that Hitler was half Jewish? Her companion responded that 'this was not just a rumour, it really was a fact. Hitler was born out of wedlock and was really called Schickelgruber. I have heard this several times.'[33] It was careless conversation, and they were lucky not to be reported. There was a good deal of such subversive talk even among strangers, especially after Stalingrad. Hitler was now mockingly called *Gröfaz* (*grösster Feldherr aller Zeiten*) – greatest military genius of all time.

I

News of massacres was filtering through in 1942 and 1943 from BBC broadcasts, soldiers on leave, the party network and visitors on business who had travelled east.[34] Cut off from its overseas markets, Hamburg's chamber of commerce in November 1939 had been quick off the mark to exploit opportunities in Poland. Later representatives were sent to the General Government and Ukraine, where they could not have avoided witnessing what was happening. In the records just one laconic observation is recorded, dated 12 November 1943: 'The willingness of the farmers to deliver [their produce] is good, but the treatment of the Poles unfortunately is not as one would wish' – something of an understatement.[35] When taken together with what Nazi leaders said and wrote, Germans who did not close their eyes were aware that terrible crimes were being committed in the East. A report in the *Hamburger Tageblatt* early in 1942 even spoke of extermination: 'We have experienced Jewry in its purest cultural form and we are happy that the Jewish pest has been exterminated by National Socialism.'[36] Then, more explicitly, on 7 January 1943, reporting that, in Russia, the security forces, the SS, police units, the SD, the security service and *Einsatzgruppen* were fighting a cowardly, brutal enemy behind the front: 'There are also considerable numbers of Jews who are members of these criminal bands; we do not wish them a better existence.'[37]

With good contacts, those in positions of authority did not have to interpret what the Propaganda Ministry chose to reveal. They had more precise information of what was happening in the East. The contemporary journal of an officer in the *Wehrmacht* stationed in Hamburg provides graphic confirmation.

Colonel Ernst Ebeling was a career officer, a veteran of the First World War. When Hitler in 1935 repudiated the Versailles Treaty, new opportunities opened for experienced officers. Although he was forty-eight years old, Ebeling was able to join and contribute to the build-up of the *Wehrmacht*. He could reconcile this with repudiation of the Nazis, as the *Wehrmacht*, despite its loyalty oath to the *Führer*, still regarded itself as separate and independent from the Nazis. When war broke out, Ebeling fought in Poland and France. In April 1941, at the age of fifty-one, he was promoted to the rank of colonel and sent to Hamburg. He served there as chief of staff of the Tenth Military District, responsible for conscripton and training. This was an important posting. *Wehrkreis X* sent reinforcements, several hundred thousand men, to the Russian front.

Ebeling, who had begun despising the Nazis, ended hating them. He wrote to his wife in December 1939, 'Those to whom the German people have given their trust are a disgrace.' Later he wrote in his journal, 'Hitler is the most despicable criminal in the history of Germany ... the price of war is blood.'[38] Ebeling records his growing alienation from the crimes the Nazi war machine was committing. This war was for him a totally different experience from the First World War. He chronicled the relapse into barbarity and the inevitability of retribution to relieve his impotence and guilt.

> 2 February 1942. Now Germany suffers the revenge for the inhumane way it is treating Russian prisoners of war ... when the first prisoners were taken, the fanatical rage against these 'beasts' expressed itself in the most outrageous ways ... a Russian only had to bend down, then he would be shot on the pretext that he was about to pick up a stone to throw at his guard ... everywhere the attitude is, let the beasts perish ... in one camp in Wietzendorf, of the 55,000 Russians, 21,500 have died ...
>
> 22 March 1942. ... The best qualities of the German people have been undermined, religion despite all promises is persecuted, the morality of the young people has reached a low never seen before, ... to kill people, even sadistic torture is tolerated when the victims are Jews, Poles, Serbs or Russians. What for instance has happened to the deported Jews from Hamburg who were supposed to be sent to a ghetto in the East? 8 kilometres outside Smolensk they were shot en masse by Latvian soldiers. In comparison a clean shot in the back of the neck, as with the Russians, is the highest form of humanity. [The Jews] are shot and wounded, lose consciousness and are then buried alive in mass graves ...

An entry in Ebeling's journal at the time of the Stalingrad catastrophe is particularly revealing. Ebeling declined an invitation to a farewell dinner in honour of Police General Becker, who was leaving the General Government.

> 29 December 1942. Becker cannot stomach the shooting of Jews; the thought that these massacres have already reached 3 million, and that a further 1 million are to be liquidated, grips one with cold horror ...
>
> 3 January 1943. ... Deeply troubled, I take refuge again in my journal ...

31 January 1943. In Stalingrad the Germans are bleeding to death for their rulers. Those in power have risen out of the slime and are enriching themselves from the people's wealth and possessions of the Jews, avoiding serving at the front line. To make the German people even more helpless, every effort is made to involve them in sharing responsibility for the crimes committed during the war – Jews – Poles – Czechs, crimes which cry to heaven. If in the case of the last two nations one can possibly cite sabotage as an excuse, it is impossible to do so for the Jews. Their fate is the cruelest known to history. The German people really are innocent and not capable of committing such infamy. Rumours circulate how the killings are carried out. Even if only half of such cruelty were true, one would have to lose all one's faith in Providence if not only those who are responsible but also the murderers [who carry out their commands] are not called to account.

Ebeling still hoped for a miracle. Would the Western Allies help Germany stem the Bolshevik advance? – though he realised this was not possible with Hitler and the Nazis in power. 'The criminal instincts of the Russian and our leaders', he wrote,

> are too closely similar. Our youth, especially the women, are being systematically corrupted; our young men with false notions of belonging to the master race are taught to 'accept' the slaughter of Jews, Poles and Russians, even wounded Russian prisoners, as completely in order. The *Wehrmacht* joins in …
> 11 April 1943. The work of the SS. Mass murders of Jews, Poles and Czechs – alcohol no longer necessary, those who do the shooting are not unwilling accomplices but, to enjoy it more, refine what they do.
> 17 April 1943. We are marked with the sign of Cain for the murder of millions of Jews, Poles and Czechs – as far as the Jews are concerned, women and children are not spared …

That summer, city after city was bombed into ruins and ashes. It was Hamburg's turn in August 1943. Ebeling now expected the *Wehrmacht* would call a halt and seize power from the criminal regime. He noted briefly in his journal the failed attempt to kill Hitler on 20 July 1944. Then his journal falls silent. It had become too dangerous to leave evidence of sympathy with the plotters. Hidden, it survived the war, as did Ebeling. There were thousands of decent Ebelings who, despite knowledge of the atrocities committed not only by SS death squads but by the young conscripts of the *Wehrmacht*, could see no way out but to continue to serve the regime to the bitter end.

Hamburg had made its own notorious contribution to the mass killings, which were perpetrated by the Reserve Police Battalion 101, some 500 strong. It was recruited mainly from middle-aged men, largely of lower-middle-class social background, who accompanied the *Wehrmacht* into Poland at the outbreak of war, their first taste of cruelty and worse. Later they assisted in the brutal so-called resettlement of some 40,000 Jews and Roma and Sinti from the annexed Polish territory, renamed the Wharteland, with shootings and violence. Back in Hamburg, they guarded the Jews assembled for deportation in the autumn of 1941. They then returned to Poland, where they committed mass kill-ings soon after their arrival. On 13 July 1942 they rounded up the Jews of the village of Jozefow, some 1,500 women and children and the old, of no value as forced labourers, who were shot and buried in mass graves. Reinforced, and reconstituted more than once, this small police battalion murdered 38,000, mainly Jews. Except superficially, Hamburg was no different to anywhere else.[39]

On the home front, Goebbels skilfully exploited the dread of revenge: 'Behind the onrushing Soviet divisions we can see the Jewish liquidation squads.' His *Sports-Palast* speech in Berlin on 18 February 1943, which was broadcast all over Germany, ended with ten rhetorical questions to the hand-picked audience to whether the people's confidence in the *Führer* and victory was unshaken. To stormy applause, Goebbels demanded 'total war'. The new propaganda line of arousing fear from the vengeful Jews and Russians proved effective.

II

Fear at home of the Gestapo was pervasive. But the majority of Germans were in no danger of arrest. Those who did not approve took refuge in 'internal' dis-sent, like Colonel Ebeling and *Frau* Schmidt; a few actively resisted, while oth-ers sought religious guidance as husbands and sons fell at the front for Hitler and the fatherland. Cities now had charred bodies lying in the street, and there was carnage everywhere. Was there a God in heaven?

Where could people turn for spiritual support? Hamburg was overwhelmingly Lutheran, but one in six of the population no longer identified with any church. Even of those who did, probably no more than half attended church regularly. The trend of secularisation had been hastened by the regime. But what could be offered by bishops and pastors who, with few exceptions, had at best passed over the persecution of the Jews in silence? At least there were fewer reminders of their persecution, as they were rapidly disappearing.

With the election of Franz Tügel as *Landesbischof* in March 1934, Hamburg's Protestants had a spiritual leader who had addressed the synod that had elected him in party uniform with a swastika armband, vowing his loyalty to Adolf Hitler and Martin Luther. Church politics were complicated in the Third Reich. There was no unified Protestant Church which, unlike the Catholic Church, could speak with one authoritative voice. There were twenty-eight provincial *Landeskirchen*, which did not all coincide with state boundaries. These were also split internally between the German Christians, who sought to fuse National Socialism with Christianity, the Confessing Church, and a middle group. There was one thing besides patriotic fervour on which they agreed. The Lutheran clergy of all persua-sions was deeply conservative and as such welcomed Hitler as a bulwark against the threat of godless Marxism.[40] They saw Hitler returning Germany to stability, and even hoped that his popular appeal would stem the drift away from the churches. Those who publicly opposed the discrimination and persecution of Jews were a small minority; most welcomed limiting Jewish influence in 'German' society.

In Hamburg too there was division. Bishop Tügel had at first identified with the German Christians but then had left them, rejecting their view of the Old Testament as a Jewish book. For Tügel, the Old Testament remained a revered part of the Holy Bible. The Jews he condemned were the 'modern Jews' of the Christian era. He attacked them as viciously as any Nazi, claiming they corrupted every facet of life. The treatment of the Jews was a matter for the state, he said, and the Church should take care not to interfere. But Tügel was not a craven opportunist; his beliefs were based on conviction. In curious contradiction, though, he could be helpful to a pastor deprived of his calling because of his marriage to a Jewess. For converted Jews he showed little sympathy, believing that most of the conversions were not genuine; for the deported Jews he exhibited a callous disregard. Although in 1945 he could assert that he had stood up to the Nazis, had distanced himself from the German Christians and had brought peace to divided Hamburg, he was pressured to step down. Many theologians managed to save themselves despite unsavoury pasts, but Tügel had gone too far.

There were few Protestant theologians and lay congregants who saw where Nazi policies were heading. One member of the laity of the Confessing Church, Elisabeth Schmitz, as early as 1934 appealed to the synod of the Confessing Church to assist Christian 'non-Aryans'.[41] With every passing month, as Nazi persecution increased, she became more deeply involved and appalled at the silence of the Churches and their refusal to follow their Christian duty. She now became aware that this extended to the unbaptised Jews as much as to the converted and their descendants. It was not enough for isolated pastors to speak out; it was the duty of the Church leaders to provide guidance. That is why she took a new step, writing an account of the plight of German non-Aryans, 'Zur Lage der deutschen Nichtarier', and handed it over in time for the third meeting of the Prussian branch of the Confessing Church, which was meeting in Berlin-Steglitz for four days from 23 September 1935. It was never brought to the attention of the assembly, and so her impassioned plea with its many examples of injustices was not heard. The Church leaders confined themselves to what they themselves called 'the minimum' of opposition, only standing by the validity of baptism and the continuing right of Christians to convert Jews who sought Christianity, and taking care not to challenge the state on their treatment of Jews.

Elisabeth Schmitz had written her *Denkschrift* before the Nuremberg Laws were made public. She then wrote a supplementary account detailing, with examples, their impact on the lives of Jews and other non-Aryans whose livelihoods and existence were threatened. She duplicated her appeal, and in May 1936 sent 200 copies to leading members of the Confessing Church. Again there was no echo.

Worse followed, step by step, until the shock two years later of the November pogrom. Now appalled by what she was witnessing, Elisabeth Schmitz sent a letter and visited the pastor of the Confessing Church congregation of Dahlem, Helmut Gollwitzer. She urged that the Day of Penance, *Bußtag*, could not be allowed to pass that November without prayers for the Jews and prayers of forgiveness. Gollwitzer responded with a fiery sermon, one of the few protests in Germany following 'Crystal Night', damning the 'caution of the Church' and condemning the cowardice of Christians, all of whom, he said, shared the guilt of the atrocities occurring. And what needed to be done now?, he asked. 'God wishes to see deeds', 'Open your mouths for the dumb', 'Protect your innocent hunted neighbour'. The congregation reacted in shocked silence.

Elisabeth Schmitz's letter to the pastor was also remarkable for a prophetic warning:

> When one begins marking property [with the star of David], it may end with marking people, and then a consequence becomes likely I do not wish to specify. Orders would be willingly followed sadistically and without conscience, just as they are today. I am convinced – if it should come to that – that, with the last Jew disappearing from Germany, Christianity will cease to exist.

That same year she took a personal stand, resigning her position as a schoolteacher, saying she could not reconcile her teaching with the requirements of Nazi ideology. Characteristic of the ambiguities of the regime, those immediately responsible for her granted her a pension. Miraculously, she escaped the attentions of the Gestapo when she hid Jews in her apartment. She survived the war unsung for her courage. The post-1945 Berlin Protestant Church did not recall her; independent spirits like her were unwelcome.

An effort was made at least to help the 'Jew' Christians. The Pastor Grüber Office, opened after the November pogrom to assist Protestant 'Jews' to emigrate, functioned for just two years and was closed by the Gestapo in December 1940. Pastor Heinrich Grüber survived a concentration camp, but his assistants perished.

During the war, Bishop Theophil Wurm in Württemberg was the most outspoken senior cleric. In letters to the Reich Chancellery he pleaded for converted Jews and their descendants.[42] Not until December 1943, however, did he privately condemn 'the extermination policy of Jewry'; by then it was too late. He too avoided any public challenge. A few individual pastors in Germany did speak up, but in Hamburg, after the closure of the *Jerusalem Kirche*, Jews received no support. When in December 1941 the German Evangelical Church Council requested that the *Landeskirchen* should exclude Jew-Christians from participating in services with Germans, Bishop Tügel complied.[43] Pastor Auerbach, who was not of pure Aryan descent, was charged to look after their spiritual needs. Pastors in the Hamburg *Landeskirche* were not even supposed to hold burial services for converted Jews. For Pastor Kohlschmidt of the *Christuskirche* in

Eimsbüttel-Hamburg, this went too far: 'No one can prevent me from accompanying a member of the Christian confession on their last journey.'

III

The Catholic congregation in Hamburg was small, just 63,000 strong in a city-state of over a million – too small to be headed by a bishop. It therefore came under the bishopric of Osnabrück, whose bishop in the 1930s, Wilhelm Berning, was sympathetic to National Socialism. In Hamburg, the congregation was headed by Bernhard Wintermann, who had also welcomed the National Socialists. Unlike elsewhere in Germany, the Catholics had little to complain of in Hamburg. *Reichsstatthalter* Kaufmann, son of a faithful Catholic mother, spared them any conflict. In Hamburg there were no martyrs. Wintermann survived the war and was honoured both by the Vatican and the Federal Republic.

The voice of the Catholic Church, as a unified church based on a hierarchy, did matter to the regime. But no condemnation came from the German Catholic Church of atrocities until far too late, and then only in a veiled form. Even at that point there was silence about the Jews, just dark hints from bishops and clergy that what befell them was God's will. Only a few individual priests prayed for them. Those who did, such as Bernhard Lichtenberg, the provost of Berlin's St Hedwig Cathedral, were taken into Gestapo custody and did not survive. Pope Pius XII was a distant figure; the Vatican kept its silence in public. Catholic Poles were abandoned in 1939, so what hope was there for Jews?[44]

In Germany, the head of the Catholic Church was Cardinal Adolf Bertram, archbishop of Breslau. Of his opposition to the Nazis before 1933 there can be no doubt.[45] Priests then were forbidden to have any dealings with the Nazis. He saw with clarity that Nazi ideology could not be reconciled with Christianity. Yet, when Hitler came to power, Bertram too bowed to the necessity of finding an accommodation that set the Church on a slippery slope of moral decline. Troubled by the persecution of 'racial' Catholic 'Jews', he did take some steps to assist them, but acted quietly and without challenging Nazi injustices. The St Raphael Association, with headquarters in Hamburg, helped 10,000 Catholic 'Jews' to emigrate with the regime's full approval until it was closed and further emigration was forbidden.[46] Through the Caritas Welfare League, Catholic 'Jews' without means or work were assisted. But Bertram judged it to be useless to try to influence Hitler on the fate of the Jews. The most he felt might be achieved was to try to save the converted and the descendants of mixed marriages and to keep mixed marriages inviolate.

The most formidable public attack on the Nazis in the history of the Third Reich came from Bishop Clemens August Graf von Galen in the summer of 1941 and spread like wild fire throughout Germany. Galen denounced the killing of 'unproductive lives', so-called euthanasia. Euthanasia did not end but was pursued with more secrecy. A few weeks after Galen's famous sermons, the Jews of Münster began to be deported. Galen remained silent. It was not that the Church was ignorant: many reports reached the hierarchy through a network of priests. A remarkable channel of information was also created by one brave woman who established direct contact with the *Reichsvereinigung*. In Berlin, a Bishop's Office of Assistance and Help for Catholic Jews and half Jews, *Hilfswerk beim Bischöflichen Ordinariat Seelsorge- und Fürsorgestelle für katholische Juden und Halbjuden*, had been set up under the authority first of Provost Bernhard Lichtenberg and, after his arrest in October 1941, of Bishop Konrad Graf von Preysing. It was run by Margarete Sommer. Although forbidden to do so, and so risking being sent to a concentration camp, she paid frequent visits to Martha Mosse, a Jewess in charge of the housing department of the *Reichsvereinigung*, which unbeknown to applicants, provided lists of Jews to the Gestapo to be deported. Armed with information, Margarete Sommer tried to get Cardinal Bertram to act, but without success. She did not give up. She sent reports to the church authorities, providing them with detailed accounts of the deportations, at least one of which reached the Vatican in August 1942. When in February 1943 the Jewish partners of mixed marriages were arrested and incarcerated in the Rosenstraße in Berlin and Jews so far protected by war work in factories were rounded up for deportation, she hurried to Breslau to speak to Cardinal Bertram in person and handed him a detailed report of arrests and deportations.[47]

Margarete Sommer wished to go much further. She wanted the Church to know where the non-Aryans were being held and that a commission should be permitted to visit the camps, but Bertram and other bishops thought that to make such demands would be unwise. Then, on the eve of the annual meeting of Catholic bishops in Fulda, Bertram on 30 August 1943 received a letter several pages long.[48] It has lain buried ever since amid thousands of printed documents published in many volumes after the war under the auspices of the Catholic Church. It was dated 24 August 1943 and was conveyed by hand to 'His Eminence the Cardinal and Archbishop Dr Bertram in Breslau'. This is what the anonymous correspondent told him.

> As can be gathered from newspapers, you will not be participating in the meeting at Fulda. My intention was to send this letter to Fulda, to inform the conference about the crimes committed in the past four years in the General Government by the German people against the Jews. As I am a Jew I will limit myself to the crimes against the Jews. Up to the present time 4,000,000 (four million) Jews have been murdered. Are you aware of that? ... I swear by the Almighty that what I am putting to paper is based on the absolute truth, so help me God.

The letter described the occupation of Poland; Jews were driven from their homes, they were without shelter, their possessions taken away.

> Globocnik, SS and police chief in Lublin, in charge of the mass murder of Jewry, was able to report to the *Führer* that Lublin was free of Jews. Every

town had its mass graves. I do not wish to exceed your patience by describing the murders ... the first destruction of Warsaw resulted in 330,000 victims ... as the murder of all Jews could not be accomplished, two places were created for mass extermination, for Lublin and Galicia, Belzec was set up. [A description of murders ...] Cracow's Jews were murdered ... about 8,000 Jews in camps are still alive ... children no longer exist ...

The writer ended his letter not with an appeal for help – it was too late for that – but with damnation.

I wish to close my report, with its brief descriptions, on the assumption that, *Herr* Cardinal, you will yourself agree that a people capable of such crimes have no right to live under the sun. Every German, and you as well, is guilty of the mass crimes. May God the Almighty not leave this people unpunished. I firmly believe that the punishment will come. The Jewish people who gave the world Revelation will survive this ruin. The German people who gave birth to a devil will meet its ruin through him.

Finally, Bertram was moved to try to intercede not only for the Catholic 'Jews', but cautiously, indirectly included Jews in letters to the Gestapo headquarters, the main Reich Security Office and the Reich Chancellery.[49] He still avoided speaking of Jews by name, but referred to

8,000 non-Aryans, including many who are Christians, some in racial mixed marriages and others who are not ... such marriages cannot later be torn apart for racial reasons by the state where there is no guilt ... such actions harm the blessed working together of state and Church, which has never been so important as in the present.

The emphasis was only on the inviolability of marriage. Bertram received no reply.

That year, as every year, Bertram sent Hitler fulsome birthday wishes: 'Your worries are our worries and the worries of the whole of Catholic Germany.' The following year, in April 1944, Bertram again conveyed his good wishes and prayers for victory. A year on, the Russians were in Breslau and Hitler could no longer be reached in Berlin.

And those who stayed behind

A new and terrible task had faced Plaut and the leaders of the Jewish community after September 1941 – to care for Hamburg's Jews while carrying out orders to prepare for their deportation. Lists for each transport have survived, with more than a thousand names on some. Was their composition in Jewish hands or those of the Gestapo?[50] In Berlin, under the guise of the housing department, Dr Martha Mosse returned the forms from which the Gestapo made up the transport.

In Hamburg, what happened is more obscure. Plaut after the war insisted the community office in Hamburg did not make the choice of who would be transported. The officials could not avoid Gestapo orders to make returns providing details of marriage, children, nationality, age, former profession, and so on, for every Jew in Hamburg. The community office did sometimes succeed in securing Gestapo agreement to postpone someone's deportation, and such places were made up from the 'reserves'. The practice of sending the elderly to Terezín did not begin until the summer of 1942. By then tens of thousands of old people had already been sent to the East to ghettos, waiting rooms on the way to death camps or to their immediate death. There were a few Jews, besides the workers in the community office, whose services to Hamburg may have won the respect of the Gestapo. That may be the reason why they were deported later. Invalided and decorated war veterans also were not among the early deportees. Much more than that cannot be gleaned from studying these lists. Uncertainty remains. Not all transports were organised in the same way.

Plaut took personal charge of trying to provide, as best as the community could, supplies of medicines and other necessities to accompany each train.[51] Whether the deportees received any of them on arrival in the East was up to the whims of the Gestapo, who could help themselves to whatever they wished. At the assembly point in Hamburg, community volunteers provided warm food and straw mattresses, trying to make the deportees' last night's stay as tolerable as possible. In Hamburg the Gestapo did not resort to open violence such as occurred in Hannover and elsewhere. Once the deportees had been loaded onto the trains they were beyond the control of the community. If they were dispatched to the Łódź ghetto or Terezín, contacts could again be established for a time.

The Jewish community leaders knew that their work was now split into two quite separate functions: they continued to care to the best of their ability for the Jews still left in Germany, but they had also become an arm of the Gestapo. Hannah Karminski, working for the *Reichsvereinigung* in Berlin, summed up their agony: 'It is so difficult to be here – the morphine of our work helps.' The few survivors who had worked in the *Reichsvereinigung* or its branches faced accusations after the war that they had collaborated and knowingly sent Jews to their death. This does them an injustice. Most of the Jews sent east in 1941 to ghettos were not killed that year. One could at least hope if the war did not last too long that they would survive. All but two of the transports in 1942 when they resumed from Hamburg went to Terezín.

As long as the offices of the Jewish organisation in Germany remained in existence, they could not halt the deportations, but it was possible to maintain postal communications and to send parcels of food to Terezín. These Plaut organised on a large scale. Donations from well-wishers – Baron Berenberg-Gössler was one large benefactor – enabled Plaut to organise at their peak 300 packets a week from outlying Hamburg post offices. A family in Terezín was permitted to receive one parcel a month. Much of the content had been obtained on the black market. On one occasion the Hamburg Gestapo gave Plaut permission to send a grand piano. He filled it with medicines. Receipt of parcels was gratefully acknowledged. Messages were reassuring, giving a false picture of normality. No one dared tell the truth about conditions in mail open to the Gestapo to read. From Terezín the transports rolled on to Auschwitz.

What at first became known in Hamburg did not indicate that Jews were being sent to their certain death, but that conditions in the ghettos were so bad that it was a race against time. Survival over several years would be unlikely for most. That became clear to Plaut when news secretly reached him from Minsk.

> Early in 1942 *Herr* Valentin Burchard, who had been deported to Minsk on 8 November 1941, succeeded in getting a letter to me in which he described the catastrophic conditions under which people had to live. This made it clear that if the war was prolonged people could not survive. Actually, just a few survived from every transport. Auschwitz was known about soon after it was established. When other camps were full or closed because of epidemics, people were sent to Auschwitz, where they were categorised into three groups for treatment. Category 1 meant that after one week their death would be announced. I received information about the inmates every three months; packets could be sent there. [Plaut was referring to the slave labour complex.] None of the Burchard family of five survived. The slave labour camps were set up around the extermination camp to service factory complexes like the synthetic oil and rubber plant at Monowitz. Here there was a slim chance of survival, unlike in the main camp.[52]

Plaut, on frequent visits to the *Reichsvereinigung* in Berlin, was able to gain a better overview than if his responsibilities had been confined simply to Hamburg and North-West Germany. The Hamburg Gestapo followed Göttsche's orders not to maltreat the Jews during the process of deporting them. His motive was to avoid difficulties and problems and isolated public protests, but some remaining feelings of decency may have also played a part. It was unnecessary to behave as the Gestapo was behaving in neighbouring Hannover or on occasion in Berlin. But his humanitarian feelings did not go so far as to stop those under him from beating arrested Jews in one of the Gestapo cells or trying to counter orders he received from Berlin. He took pride in the fact that making Hamburg *judenrein*, free of Jews, went smoothly. The ultimate fate of the Jews was out of Göttsche's hands and did not seem to trouble his conscience.

At the top of the SS structure in the Reich and occupied territories were the personal representatives of Himmler, the higher SS and police commanders (Höhere SS- und Polizeiführer, HSSPF), responsible for hundreds of thousands or murders. Rudolf Querner was the HSSPF in Hamburg for *Wehrkreis* 10, Nordsee, which included Northern Germany from May 1941 to January 1943, and was Göttsche's superior. His forebears were minor aristocrats and his father served as an officer in the First World War. Rudolf Querner joined the party in 1933 and the Hamburg order police in 1936, becoming its commander at the outbreak of war. His personal responsibilities included the deportation of the Jews.

Deportation was dreaded. People lived from day to day. Those who anxiously enquired in the Beneckestraße about what lay in store were reassured that life in 'Theresienstadt' would be tolerable. A few children were allowed to accompany a parent or grandparent. For the Gestapo there was one problem. The Protectorate did not count as foreign soil and the assets of Jews sent there could not simply be confiscated according to the law. In the crazy world of the Third Reich, legal formalities had to be observed for Germans even if they were Jews. A way out was found. Elderly and infirm Jews were forced to buy their care and accommodation in a home in Terezín for life before they left. The money was paid into an account controlled by the Gestapo. The long years of life on which the calculations were based ensured a good return, as death in Terezín was rapid. News from Terezín would suddenly end as families disappeared.

I

The Jews still in Hamburg had to obey every new directive.[53] Ignorance could have fatal consequences. Directives were posted on the walls of the community office each week and sometimes twice a week.

No. 1. 13 January 1942

Jews are required to hand over furs, skis, ski clothes and woollens on the instructions of our supervisory authority [euphemism for the Gestapo]. The following guidelines apply:

1. The people affected are those who are Jews according to the Nuremberg Law of 14 November 1935, but the order does not apply to:
   a. the Jewish spouse in a mixed marriage where there are children, also if the marriage no longer exists, and also if the only son has fallen in the war.
   b. the Jewish wife of a mixed marriage without children.
   c. Jews of foreign nationality when of a nationality of an occupied country.
2. Detailed items to be handed over include fur-lined gloves, male boots, woollens of all kinds, as long as not absolutely necessary for personal use. The strictest criteria will be applied.

No. 2. Membership Contributions 1942, 13 January 1942

… Those members of the Jewish community organisation who expect to join an evacuation transport are requested to pay their dues for the whole year in one instalment.

No. 7. Medical Provision for Hamburg's Jews, 10 February 1942

From the Organisation of Pharmacies in the Nordmark the following information:

1. Jews may only purchase medicines in pharmacies between 9 and 10 o'clock.

2. Only prescriptions marked urgent by the doctor will be dealt with at other times.

No. 11. Relations with Foreigners, 25 February 1942

All contacts between Jews and foreigners who are not Jews is in principle undesirable and is to be avoided.

In such cases where for reasons of employment or other reasons contact is necessary, this has to be notified by the Jew to the *Reichsvereinigung* in Berlin under reference JA.

To all Jews of Hamburg, 27 February 1942

1. Jews should only use public transport for the most necessary reasons (to and from work).
2. When using public transport, the greatest reserve is to be observed and no seats should be occupied. In the case of streetcars, the platform in front is to be occupied.
3. No conversations should be conducted.

No. 12. Distribution of Mazzoth for Passover, 1942/5702

1½ kg per person will be distributed … on receipt, the following declaration on oath which has to be signed.

'The undersigned declares on oath that he/she and those with them who have received Mazzoth will not consume any kind of bread.

I undertake immediately on receipt of the ration coupons to give up the bread coupons …'

No. 21. Jews are required to move to houses of the Jewish community (no date)

All Jews (except those in mixed marriages) who do not live in a house administered by the Jewish community, or have not received notification to do so, are immediately to report to the Jewish community office, Beneckestraße 2, room 18.

Jewish Identification to be Attached to Apartments, 15 April 1942

Jews required to wear the Jewish Star are to affix a Yellow Star of David to be clearly visible to the outside door of their apartment.

Signs are not to be attached to the outside of the buildings but inside the main door.

No. 29. Postal Communication with Persons who have been Deported, 10 April 1942

It is still at present not possible to communicate by post with those deported to the East.

The interruption of postal communication with Litzmannstadt ghetto continues.

Domestic Animals, 15 May 1942

1. Jews required to wear the Jewish Star are as from today forbidden to own domestic animals (dogs, cats, birds).
2. Jews have to notify the Jewish community office what animals they have.
3. Animal inspectors will be notified by the Jewish community office to collect the animals.

It is forbidden to give the animals to third parties to take care of them.
Any attempt not to carry out this order will be prosecuted by the police.
This order does not apply to foreign Jews not required to wear the Yellow Star.

No. 37. Use of Hairdressers, 17 June 1942
Jews required to wear the Jewish Star are forbidden to make use of hairdressers with the exception of Jewish hairdressers.

17 June 1942
Electrical equipment – record players and records, including heaters, sunray lamps, heated cushions, pots and pans, vacuum cleaners, irons, etc., are to be delivered up.

17 June 1942
Typewriters, bicycles, cameras, binoculars to be delivered up.

No 42. 22 June 1942
Transfer of money to Litzmannstadt is no longer permitted.

No date
Jews are no longer permitted to purchase books in bookshops.
They may only purchase books held by the *Reichsvereinigung*.

No 2. 20 February 1943, Order for Men and Women to Report for Work to Defend the Reich
All Jews not in work or not fully in work, namely:
Jewish men aged 14–65
Jewish women aged 15–55
are ordered by 1 March 1943 personally to report for work at the Employment Office, Sägerplatz 10, Hamburg.

The Jews still remaining fell into a kind of apathy and acceptance of one restriction after another, proliferating week by week. Most were absorbed as yet another pin prick. Expectations were now so low that it was enough if you escaped being sent East. But some directives hurt more than others. It was devastating to have to give up a much loved pet. The Nazi authorities thought of everything. You could not have dogs, cats and birds left behind, starving, or roaming the streets when their guardians were deported. But why were Jews not allowed to find other homes for them? Perhaps to avoid tearful public farewells or to save on food consumption – who knows?

For Plaut and his co-workers, it was an immense relief that all the remaining transports, except one, were sent to Terezín. By 1 August 1942 only some 500 racially defined Jews who did not belong to the group of about 1,000 protected by marriage to an Aryan spouse were left in Hamburg. Hamburg had shown zeal.

II

Plaut's office at Beneckestraße 2 became a centre of information for enquiries about the deported. The effusive thanks for the parcels received with basic items of food and other essentials told their own tale.[54] There is no mention of the epidemics, the overcrowding, the dirt and lice, the brutality of SS guards, and the fear of arrest and punishment. Attached to the Terezín ghetto was a compound known as the Little Fortress, which housed Austrian SS. From there no one returned. Correspondence with the East and Terezín was sparse and the recipient of a card in Hamburg would pass messages around. All communications sounded as if they were sent from a normal stay abroad, with only glimpses of reality between the lines.

> My dear Dr Hannes,
> Many thanks for your card and the parcel, which gave me much pleasure. I was very interested in your news about your daughter. I am well and I am content. My closest relative unfortunately succumbed to an old heart ailment. Füchschen and Hannes are now together with my brother. I hope you are well. How are Sachs in the Rabenstraße? Greetings to all friends and acquaintances. To you and family especially warm greetings. I very much long for a sign of life from all.
> Your Franz Rappolt
> Theresienstadt 28/9/43
> Hauptstraße 25[55]

> Dear Friends,   16 June 1943
> I am very happy to be able to send you news. I am well and I am in good health. I was a helper in an old-age home during the first months here. Now I am working in a branch of art which really satisfies me. My aunt is together with her sisters. Please send my warm greetings to my nieces. I hope they are all well. Letters and parcels always arrive punctually. I see my brother Max every day; he too works diligently.
> Elfriede Höniger,
> Theresienstadt, H V.

A card also reached Plaut from Rabbi Leo Baeck, a member of the council of elders in Terezín, who survived. That he did not pass on information that transport from Terezín led to the death camps of Auschwitz later caused controversy. He wanted his fellow Jews to live in peace as long as this was possible, as he could not change their fate. In Terezín, he worked heroically, teaching and holding services. Plaut replied that he was pleased to have his good news. 'As for myself, I am working again fully [Plaut had suffered a serious leg infection for some weeks] and look after the one area left to me, social assistance. That has become a great task as a result of enemy activity [the devastating air raids on Hamburg].'

Among his correspondents was a German 'Aryan' who desperately sought information.

Dear Dr Plaut,   20 June 1943

More than five weeks have passed since my poor dear wife has left Hamburg without having received from her any sign of life. I therefore most respectfully would like to ask you personally whether meantime you have been able to discover where my wife is. If you are not able to give me any information where my loved one might be, I have the intention to seek information directly from the Gestapo. Do you think this is advisable and do you think it would lead to success?

Dear Dr Plaut,   27 June 1943

Last Sunday I wrote to you to find out where my dear wife is. I have been without news for more than six weeks. I also wrote that if you did not have her address I would turn to the Gestapo. Last Monday I just could no longer rest and I went to the Gestapo, where I met our acquaintance *Herr* Kuhn. He was surprised at my coming to see him and I expected to hear nothing favourable. I told him I wanted to have the address of my wife. He told me he did not know it, but added, 'you can have your wife back again, new favourable regulations have been introduced regarding mixed marriages.' I should therefore immediately write a request for her release to the Gestapo headquarters in Berlin giving as the reason I needed the nursing care of my wife. I should send it off at once. Monday midday I sent the request off. Now I live in hope soon to have my wife back with me. What is your opinion about that?

In August he wrote again that he lived in hope now that his wife would shortly return. He had sent an application to the Gestapo and he was encouraged that they had asked for more information. Meantime he had received news that his wife was in Birkenau and he wanted to know whether he could send her parcels there. Plaut replied that they could be sent through the *Reichsvereinigung* in Berlin. Then, in mid-September, another anxious letter:

Dear Dr Plaut,   15 September 1943

For your letter I am very grateful. It is splendid that you were able to save your house [a bomb had set it alight] … The main reason for this letter is the following. Yesterday *Herr* Kuhn from the Gestapo came to me and told me that I should let you know that Robert Meyer had died [in Fuhlsbüttel concentration camp]. When I asked for the cause of death, he said from infection, more he could not say ... what do you think about that? ... From my wife I have not heard anything for four weeks. I would like to know, *Herr* Dr Plaut, what kind of a camp Birkenau is. Is it under Jewish administration or is it under the Gestapo: is it a concentration camp? How often can my wife and I write? After receiving your letter I immediately sent a parcel of food. How frequently may I do this? When I asked *Herr* Kuhn whether my wife would be released, he replied he was certain of it but it could take three months. When do you think she will be released?

Plaut replied, 'The camp in which your wife is, is a work camp under the direction of our supervisory authority. Mostly Jews are there. As far as I know you may write and send a parcel at least once a month ... I hope your wife will return at the time *Herr* Kuhn indicated'. Two weeks later he received one more letter.

> Dear Dr Plaut,   30 September 1943
> I have just received the information from the Auschwitz camp organisation that my wife died on 12 September and that she was cremated on 16 September. Just imagine how I feel, and what do you think about this –
> P.S. I received a death certificate. Do I have to report her death to the authorities here?

> Dear *Herr* Schüsselburg,   5 October 1943
> I was deeply affected by your letter of 30 September. After your previous letter I had not expected that you would receive such sad news so soon. In any event I wish to express my deep condolences at your heavy loss. May you be spared from such heavy blows in the future. If you have the intention to bury the urn in Celle I am happy to advise you. A separate report of her death to the authorities is not necessary in my view ...
> Yours,
> Max Plaut

III

In Hamburg, 'social activity' meant looking after the shrinking community, providing everyone with shelter, deciding on priorities, filling the far too few beds available for hospital and nursing care, paying out minimal support to those without any means, collecting rents and following the orders of the Gestapo, fitting out to the extent possible the carriages in which the deportees were sent out of Germany, maintaining morale and having to account for all they did to the Gestapo. Every *Pfennig* spent had to be justified, as the Gestapo expected to confiscate the lion's share of the large sums left in the community accounts when the Jews had finally been liquidated.

The devotion of the workers in the Jewish community office who did their best in awful circumstances comes through from the correspondence that has survived. They were unwilling 'tools of the Gestapo'; they were the last humane interface between the individual Jew and the Nazi state, though powerless to alter anyone's ultimate fate.

Among the onerous tasks beginning in early April 1942 was the mass relocation of Hamburg's Jews into *Judenhäuser*, Jew-houses, on the orders of the Gestapo – always referred to as 'our supervisory authority'.[56] The available houses were in bad shape, but it was impossible to make major repairs, let alone renovations. Jews were crowded into less and less space, sharing kitchens and bathrooms. First came instructions to report to the community office, and a date was set when the apartment occupied had to be vacated. Rarely could the permission of the Gestapo be secured to postpone moving because of special circumstances. An 'application' had to be made for housing in a Jew-house, and a tenancy agreement was drawn up which included the rent to be paid. Anger and frustration was understandably directed against the Jews who had to administer all this. For most the stay in a *Judenhaus*, nursing home or hospital was temporary until their deportation day. They had come from well-appointed apartments with family furniture. Crowded into one or two rooms, they tried to keep a few of their prized possessions, but most of the furniture had to go. First they needed permission to sell. That alerted the Gestapo where some good pieces might be obtained cheaply.

The forty-five Hamburg Jew-houses in 1942 were crowded to capacity, one room per couple, with toilet and kitchen facilities shared by several couples. Couples in mixed marriages were placed in separate houses. The 'Aryan' partners were all 'ordinary' Germans from all social classes, husbands and wives who loyally stood by their spouses and families through all hardship and danger. With the forcible removal of these Aryan partners from their homes to Jew-houses, the Gestapo now had a new lever to separate the couples by persuading the non-Jewish spouse to divorce their partner. Divorce was made easy. The Aryan wives or husbands could then stay in their apartments and all restrictions would immediately fall away. A few elderly people, pressured by their children, fell into this trap.

Anna S. was seventy-four years old.[57] Widowed with two children, she had married Manuel, now classified a racial Jew, in 1910. He cared for the two 'Aryan' children of the first marriage, ensuring they received a good education.The couple had no children of their own. In 1925 Manuel S. joined the Lutheran Church. After Hitler came to power, the growing children began to distance themselves from their stepfather. Anna's son Max was a member of the SS early on and served in the Gestapo headquarters in Berlin during the war. Her daughter was married to a dentist, also an early party member. *Frau* Anna S. explained in a letter she sent to the authorities that, from her own family's service to the Nazi cause, it was clear that her husband had not tried to influence her children. She appealed to Plaut in August 1942 that her husband should be left in peace in their apartment. A week later she received a negative reply from Plaut: the 'supervisory authority' had rejected her plea. For her children a Jewish stepfather was an embarrassment, and Anna S. gave in to their pressure. Writing to the Jewish community officers, she said: 'I have up to now shared the difficult life and destiny of my husband, but I cannot share his fate any longer if it entails separation from my children.' After friends of the family had spoken to *Herr* Stephan at the Gestapo offices, Anna S. was persuaded to ask for a divorce. Now her husband had to leave their home. She wrote again to the Jewish community office: 'I am very concerned that my husband is provided with good accommo- dation … above all with meals. He previously owned a factory in Altona. He is very polite, a large man, and would be very unhappy in a small room.' As the divorce had not been finalised, it was possible to put him in a Jew-house for mixed marriages, the Pension Derenberg, Rutschbahn 11. When the divorce became final in October, he was told to move out. His stepdaughter obviously had feelings for him and intervened, and Göttsche allowed him to stay. In January 1943, the Gestapo was once more forthcoming, permitting him to share a room in another mixed-marriage Jew-house, Schäferkampsallee 29.

So much can be gleaned from contemporary records. *Frau* S. continued to look after her divorced husband and regularly sent her cleaning lady to him to tidy his room, do his washing and bring him food. But no longer protected by his marriage, Manuel S. was deported to Terezín on 1 February 1943 and died there three months later. Anna, who had been unaware that divorce was as good as a death sentence for her husband – the Gestapo had not explained the consequence of the divorce – took her own life on 2 August.

Hertha Kassel, when ordered to leave her flat for a Jew-house or divorce her husband, replied, 'I will never voluntarily agree to a divorce because my hus- band fought four years for Germany and so also for me.' There were 'ordinary' Germans from all walks of life caught up in the insane racial persecution, who when they married were not conscious of 'a problem'. Then there were tragic cases: a Jewish husband would initiate the divorce or even commit suicide to ease the plight of his family.

Not all divorces were innocent.[58] One husband desperately appealed in vain to his wife, who was under the influence of her family, not to divorce him until after the war as it would sign his death warrant. A baker divorced his wife because her Jewish appearance put off his customers and damaged his business. Typical of the pleas made on behalf of Aryan spouses was the submission of *Frau* J. Her lawyer had a problem. She had knowingly married her Jewish husband in 1934 after the Nazis came to power. He managed to put together for her a kind of logi- cal case. At the time she had mistakenly thought that the aim of the party was only to exclude Jews from political participation. It was reasonable for her to assume that, had world Jewry not caused Germany to be plunged into a new world war, the fate of the Jews would have been better. She had been mistaken. She realised now that the aim was to isolate Jews completely and to remove them from the Reich. The measures against Jews now no longer made it possible for her to live with her husband.

It really did not matter how flimsy the case, divorces were readily granted. It is all the more remarkable that, despite all pressures, the great majority of wives and husbands remained true. They fought like tigers for their spouses and for

their *Mischling* children and so saved their lives. These 'Aryan' wives and husbands who stood by their persecuted partners were 'ordinary' Germans too.[59]

IV

We catch glimpses of life in the *Judenhäuser* from correspondence between
aggrieved tenants and the Jewish community officials.[60] In Benekestraße 4,
Herr Goldschmidt complained that the walls were so damp that the wallpaper
was peeling off and that the toilet floor was covered with water. *Herr* Soldin, a
well-known artist whose portraits had once hung in Hamburg's official buildings,
was seventy-seven years old; his family on the paternal side had lived for 200
years in Hamburg. He was looked after by 'Sister Dora', and accommodated in
the care home at Laufgraben 37; Aryan relatives sent some support. Tired of life,
he was deported in June 1943 to Terezín and did not survive.

Tactful mediation generally conciliated neighbours who complained about
each other's habits and lack of cleanliness. The gross overcrowding was bound
to create such problems. Ella Czapla had been assigned one room for herself and
her two daughters; her grown-up son, twenty-year-old Bruno, was to share a
room with two others; he never appeared and there is a note that 'he had gone to
sea' – presumably he had escaped on a ship as a sailor. The two younger children
missed school frequently, a Jewish social worker reported, because the mother
worked all day to supplement her widow's pension. Bruno was caught. They
were all deported, their fate unknown. The Jewish community officials had no
alternative but to carry out the orders of the 'supervisory authority', but they did
so with endless patience and courtesy.

Beneckestraße 2 housed the offices of the community administration, repair
shops and the so essential second-hand clothes store. In Beneckestraße 6 the
Jews who could not care for themselves were housed. In Beneckestraße 4, there
was a hairdresser and a prayer room that was also used for social purposes. The
community leaders did their best to give some shape and meaning to life in the
Jew-houses. Bizarrely, it is a tenant's complaint that brings a scene to life.

Lissy shared a room with her 66-year-old mother, Jenny von Halle. They
asked that the door of their room should be better soundproofed as they were
next door to room 20.

> That room is used from morning until night without pause … the first visi-
> tors arrive at 7 o'clock to prepare the room for a religious service half an
> hour later. Throughout the morning the room is used for lessons or music
> practice; in the afternoon there is another religious service; in the evening
> the young people socialise. There are also plans in preparation to hold lec-
> tures and similar events in the room.

The Halles did not wish to spoil the youngsters' time of relaxation, but asked for
a little peace at night. The social room was obviously once full of life; all that

remains now are the ghostly echoes. Mother and daughter were deported to Terezín eleven weeks after writing their letter, and perished, as did those whose presence in the next-door room had disturbed them. As the Jews were transported east to begin a journey of suffering which for most ended only with death, there were other Germans who benefited from their plight.

The final chapter

The deportation of the Jews produced a golden shower of desirables for the Gestapo, who had first pick before the less privileged *Volksgenossen*. Few could resist bargains. Hundreds of containers belonging to the Jews who had emigrated were stranded in Hamburg's port. They were broken open and the contents distributed or sold at auction. Occasionally there was a bonus when, with the connivance of sympathetic customs officials, valuables had been smuggled into the containers; these did not appear on any inventory, so now they simply disappeared. Those who were in the good books of high Nazi officials sent in their wish lists. In a shameless letter to Kaufmann's henchman in Hamburg, Heinz Horn, one of Hitler's devoted secretaries at the *Führer*'s headquarters reminded him that he had promised to look out for two refrigerators. So far, Horn replied, five auctioneers, despite instructions from Kaufmann, had not located any, 'but you will receive the first two which are unpacked before any other requests are met'.[61]

Auctions were held of the possessions left by the deported Jews. The public could bid after the Gestapo and other favoured servants of the state or party had acquired most things worth having. The auctioneers dependent on the Gestapo for their appointments did not hesitate to join in the corruption. A list of the possessions of Professor Siegfried Korach, once a much-loved doctor of the *Israelitisches Krankenhaus*, has survived.[62] Eighty-eight years old, he was deported in June 1943; his deportation was not even postponed by the death of his wife four days earlier, and Professor Korach was taken from his lovely apartment in the Hartung Straße to the hell of the ghetto. The old did not survive long. His valuable medical library of 600 books was acquired by a Hamburg doctor for just 121 *Reichsmark*, an average of 20 *Pfennige* per volume; a Meissner porcelain figure went to *Herr* G. for 41 *Reichsmark*; another buyer was eager for his top hat and paid 2 *Reichsmark*; medical instruments fetched 8 *Reichsmark*; his wife's handbag and a pair of boots 7. The names of the lucky bidders are all preserved. Korach's considerable wealth was confiscated by the Reich. Nothing was left; nothing was too small not to find a happy buyer. That was one way the Nazis implicated 'ordinary' Germans in the crimes committed against the Jews. Behn, a civil servant in Hamburg's branch of the Reich Finance Ministry, acquired Lippmann's valuable furniture for a song. But this was different. Plaut had arranged this so that relatives after the war could make a claim.

There was profit, too, to be made from live humans. During the early months of the war surprisingly few Jews had been conscripted into forced labour. The SS had made plans for large labour camps before the war, but Hitler would not sanction them. Later, with labour scarce, Jewish men and women between the ages of sixteen and sixty-five were ordered into factories, road-making and other heavy labour. A corrupt official, Willibald Schallert, was responsible to the Gestapo for assigning Jews to workplaces.[63] He was a particularly unsavoury and brutal character. If he decided Jews were not working well enough, he labelled them as saboteurs and had them sent to their death in concentration camps. But he could be bribed – something Plaut was able to take advantage of. The Jews received the lowest wages, no holidays or extra rations for heavy work, and in addition to all the usual taxes had to pay another 15 per cent special Jew tax. Still, at least they thought by contributing to the war effort they were safe – a sad illusion, as it turned out: 40,000 were employed at one time in Germany, but they too were deported in 1943.

After the summer of 1943 only the Jews in mixed marriages and their children remained working in Hamburg and Germany. As long as the war lasted the so-called half-Jews were relatively safe provided the Gestapo did not pin some transgression on them. Some *Mischlinge* escaped persecution altogether. That the need for doctors in Hamburg was so dire is possibly the reason the *Mischlinge* were allowed to practise. Among them were the three sons of the celebrated dermatologist at the *Israelitisches Krankenhaus* Paul Gerson Unna.[64] After his death in 1929, his sons continued to run the clinic he founded in the Osterstraße. Until 1935, the Hamburg authorities classified the Unna clinic as a private Jewish hospital, as the Unnas were half-Jews. The clinic continued to treat Aryan patients. After 1935 the categorisation 'Jewish hospital' was dropped, and under the supervision of the Unnas the clinic remained much in demand until bombs destroyed it in 1943. No harm came to the three Unna doctors, but one grandson, Karl Unna, though only a quarter-Jew, was dismissed from the Eppendorf university hospital in 1933 as non-Aryan, in accordance with the law of 7 April 1933. He emigrated to the United States and became there a distinguished professor, while his brother was conscripted into the *Wehrmacht* during the war – just one example how the racial legislation affected one family in a crazy and arbitrary way.

Michael Hauptmann was a *Mischling* who did not have valuable professional services to offer. In 1940, at the age of twenty, he was lucky to find a position in a bank, where he remained for four years. During the last year of the war Kaltenbrunner, the Security Police chief in Berlin, ordered a rigorous registration of all Jews in mixed marriages and *Mischlinge* not in war work. They were sent to camps of the notorious Todt organisation and employed in heavy labour building fortifications. Those living in Hamburg were more fortunate in that most were not herded into camps; they cleared rubble and snow in groups. Many were too old and sick to stand up to the rigours for long. Michael was still young enough to come through without physical damage.[65]

Michael's mother, Eva Hauptmann, as a Jewess, was also conscripted to do forced labour. A talented violinist, and before 1933 professor at Hamburg's conservatory, she now had to work in a tailor's shop repairing *Wehrmacht* uniforms. With fellow Jewesses she was assigned to a separate room and forbidden to speak to the other employees. For the week's work she was paid just 9 *Reichsmark* – insufficient to live on. Eva and Michael were wife and offspring of a mixed marriage. Claus, the husband and father, was an Aryan. Eva was spared deportation since she lived in a 'privileged' mixed marriage, and the family survived the hardships of war, one of hundreds of such families in the Third Reich with similar histories. However, there is one difference to their story. Claus Hauptmann was the son of Germany's most celebrated literary figure, the Nobel Laureate Gerhart Hauptmann. Before 1933, Gerhart Hauptmann had cultivated close associations with Jews, having a devoted Jewish secretary, a Jewish publisher, the S. Fischer Verlag, and a Jewish daughter-in-law. Like so many intellectuals, however, he accommodated to the new regime. Did he try to do anything for his blighted family? We do not know. If so, it did them no good.

I

On the morning of 10 June 1943, Göttsche appeared with the Gestapo at the community offices in the Beneckestraße 2. He told the assembled employees and voluntary workers that he had orders to close the office of the *Reichsvereinigung* and that they would all be deported on the next transport, which, to their relief would go to Terezín – perhaps a reward for services rendered. Max Plaut was not deported but placed under house arrest.[66]

Most of the others perished. But there were still Jews in mixed marriages living in Hamburg, Berlin and other cities. Who would take care of them now after the closure of the *Reichsvereinigung*? Himmler realised it was necessary to create a shadowy successor so that the Gestapo could continue to control their capital.[67] The successor organisation was also useful in handling the Jews. Local offices functioned as arms of the Gestapo run by 'protected' Jews in mixed marriages until the end of the war.

Staatsrat Leo Lippman was among the functionaries to receive the deportation order. He had worked for the community to the last. From fragments of surviving correspondence emerges a man who never ceased to deal courteously and sympathetically with the many complaints and cries for help that reached him. He was also stiff-necked and determined to ignore Nazi restrictions in his personal life. The Gestapo left him alone. He was useful to them, running the finances of the Jewish organisation meticulously, and perhaps there was still just a residue of respect for the once principal civil servant in charge of Hamburg's finances. Lippmann, unlike Plaut, though a proud Jew, had lost faith in religious observance. In his will he asked to be cremated without the presence of a rabbi.

The Lippmanns continued to live in the Sierichstraße in a ten-room apartment furnished with exquisite antiques and Persian carpets until it was destroyed in an air raid in June 1943.[68] They then moved in with Plaut, who lived in a villa, Böttgerstraße 5, in the elegant Pöseldorf district of Hamburg. In his old apartment Lippmann had kept his Aryan maid. On his many trips abroad before the war he had indulged in photography and had in his possession a beautiful photographic collection. On Saturday afternoons he gave illustrated talks to invited guests, who included Aryan friends and former colleagues. Among those not afraid to come was Garvens, the former head of Hamburg's Audit Office. A number of old colleagues also kept the Lippmanns supplied with food. As far as possible, life went on as normal, and there was plenty of work to occupy the day. Clearly, the Gestapo allowed Lippmann privileges for a limited time in acknowledgement of his valuable services – one of many ambiguities in Nazi Germany.

Leo Lippmann and his wife, in their seventies now and no longer in good health, were not prepared to exchange their civilised existence for the pestilence and dirt of a ghetto.[69] They knew that one day the deportation order would arrive, and when it did they had decided they would together go to their death in their own bed. On the day Göttsche informed the assembled officials in the Beneckestraße that they would be sent on the next train to Terezín, the Lippmanns resolved the time had come. That afternoon Lippmann invited Plaut and his 'Aryan' friend Theodor Boë, of the coal business Boë & Fetelsen, for afternoon coffee; that evening he wrote a farewell letter warmly thanking all his colleagues. He wished them a good future in time of peace, which he hoped would not be long delayed. In accordance with his wishes, no attempt was made to resuscitate them when they were found the following morning, and the police were to be notified only after their deaths. Theodor Boë saved some of Lippmann's valuable possessions for his brother Arthur Lippmann, who had emigrated in time. So ended, unsung, the life of one of Hamburg's most loyal servants, who had navigated the city-state's finances through the most difficult years of its existence, and had been applauded and respected until his summary dismissal with Hitler's coming. But during the last decade of his life he had not remained idle, his wealth of experience benefiting Hamburg's Jewish community.

II

1943 was different from the earlier years of the war. The dream of victory faded. People now thought about their survival and prayed for the return of fathers and sons. The social services in Hamburg described the mood of the people, working long hours, their nights disturbed by air alarms, as apathetic: the cheering had long gone.[70]

The depression had increased among the working population after the fall of Stalingrad, a social worker reported in February 1943; there was a general fear of poison gas; mail from the encircled troops no longer reached anxious relatives from the eastern front. Another report spoke of war-weariness and that many families expressed doubt whether the war would end well. The mood of defeatism was strengthened by the soldiers on leave from Russia. One retreat after another: the surrender of the Afrika Korps in Tunisia in May followed two months later by Italy's desertion. The question increasingly asked was when the war would end. There was dread that Hamburg would suffer the same fate as other cities and be destroyed by devastating air raids. When it happened, it proved to be the destruction of a city such as had never before been experienced in so short a space of time.

On 25 July 1943 the sirens sounded at 0.19 hours.[71] The RAF mounted one of the heaviest raids of the war, with 700 Lancaster bombers. The result was 10,000 dead and 154,000 made homeless. The following day the American Flying Fortresses dropped their bombs over industrial Hamburg, with the ship-builders Blohm & Voss on the Elbe a prime target. Hamburg had hardly been restored to even a minimum of order when the second British night attack, on 27–8 July, targeted the residential districts, where 427,000 people lived. Panic set in: 900,000 fled the city, disregarding the appeals of Kaufmann, who on 28 July had ordered the evacuation of only women and children. Many had not waited for Kaufmann's permission. During the night of 29–30 July came the third British night attack. The working-class districts of Rothenburgsort, Hammerbrook, St Georg, Hohenfelde, Hamm and Eilbek, with their dense hous-ing, were the worst affected. The firestorms suffocated those sheltering in the cellars. The last raid was mounted on 3 August and completed 'Operation Gomorrah'. Had the city been punished for its sins?

Statistics cannot reflect the horror of those ten days. Charred corpses lay in the streets. The ruins of Hamburg were covered by a cloud of dust through which the sun did not penetrate, and 21,000 soldiers and firemen were over-whelmed by the onslaught. The death toll of 37,000 can only be estimated. Total casualties probably reached 125,000. A wall was built to surround the 'dead dis-tricts' of Hammerbrook, Rothenburgsort and Hamm-Süd. Few rescue services attempted to enter some of the worst affected districts and the badly injured, who could not drag themselves out, perished where they lay. The railway sta-tions were gutted, industry was heavily damaged, hospitals and schools were not spared. A city of a million was without running water until mid-August; gas was restored in early September and electricity only later that month. Yet the experiences of those who had left Hamburg to find shelter in emergency accom-modation was so dispiriting that, despite orders for them to stay away, the non-working population drifted back. By the end of November more than 1 mil-lion lived precariously once more in the devastated city. For a time the authority of the state was weakened.

There was little feeling of gratitude for the emergency services and supplies rushed to the city. But it could have been even worse. The catastrophe had been anticipated. Shelters were built and cellars reinforced; the Hamburg fire services as early as 1940 had studied the lessons to be learnt from the destruction of Rotterdam. The emergency services supplied tanks of drinking water, and public food distribution centres were set up; the aid train *Bavaria* arrived with extra rations. Goebbels was admired for being plucky enough to come to the city, while Göring came late to a chilly reception. War production surprisingly did recover but not to the levels before Gomorrah. In September social services described public feelings: although the worst had been overcome, there was renewed apathy, anxiety and anger that the 'better' districts like Harvestehude had not been damaged as badly as the working-class ones. The high-ranking Nazis with houses in Blankenese, a pretty suburb on the Elbe, had come through unscathed.

Given so much suffering and need in the city, few people thought much about the few Jews still in their midst. Most of them were in mixed marriages and so did not have to wear the yellow star. As for those who were required to display the star, they just took it off. The Gestapo held back. They did not want to rouse the agitated population further. Jews stood in line with other Germans to receive free food at the public soup kitchen on the Moorweide.[72] No one cared any longer. There were not enough Jews now to be assigned to special shops; they could secure their sparse rations anywhere, though their coupons were marked with a large 'J'. As one German city after another was turned to ashes, people thought that the war surely could not be waged for much longer. The more canny Germans prepared cautiously for the time after Hitler's Reich and quietly helped a Jew here and there. Doctors treated them, as did local opticians. After the war, a good Jewish testimony, which became known as a *Persil-Schein*, a 'Persil coupon', might stand them in good stead. Nothing very brave or forbidden needed to be attempted. The Jews had nearly all gone by 1943: at least you would be unlikely to meet any when celebrating the birth of the Jewish saviour that Christmas.

III

Max Plaut was a law to himself. He was still living in the Böttgerstraße with his mother early in 1943. When an incendiary fell on the roof he managed to extinguish it before the whole house burnt down. During air raids the Jews were allowed to use the large bunker built between the Grindel and the Rothenbaumchaussee close to where the Bornplatz Synagogue had once stood. The Jews were assigned the two lower levels, which were the safest, the Aryans the upper storeys. There were smaller shelters in the Böttgerstraße and on the Mittelweg. After the devastating raids during July and August, Plaut took in twenty-two Jews made homeless after the destruction of their Jew-house. Kaufmann's air-raid shelter was close by, so they all went to the *Reichsstathalter*'s which was the only one where there was still running water. When the all-clear sounded they could take some water home.

It was just luck that few Jews lost their lives. Plaut thought not more than ten. Some joined those leaving Hamburg and, with the loss of official records, were able to blend in with the refugees. Beneckestraße 2, holding the records of the Jewish organisation, was also destroyed. For just a few persecuted Jews, Gomorrah had a silver lining. For others, there was now a new crisis; they were without shelter and had lost the last of their belongings. In overcrowded rooms they slept on the floor. Beds were unobtainable. How to replace lost clothes? The second-hand community clothing store had earlier been closed by the

Gestapo. As always, the Jewish officials had had to produce an inventory. The list of the few confiscated shirts, coats, shoes and trousers, so carefully husbanded up to then, makes pathetic reading but would have met desparate needs. Now people had only what they stood up in. Plaut sent a plea to the successor Jewish organisation in Berlin, which dispatched from their store what fifty bombed-out families in Hamburg most urgently needed, as the Nazi social welfare, the NSV, certainly would have given them nothing.[73] There was enough to supply one shirt for each male, but not underpants or pairs of trousers, four brassieres, twenty-five nightshirts for children and sixty handkerchiefs; shoes were a particular problem – twenty-five pairs in assorted sizes for men, twenty-five pairs for children and seventy-five for women were dispatched; bedding was in short supply, too, except for one hundred pillowcases, and only fifty sheets made up the rest of the consignment. A few beds were still available for the badly injured and sick in a house in the Schäferkampsallee, the last premises of the once famed *Israelitisches Krankenhaus*. Plaut did what he could during the weeks he was still in Hamburg.

Plaut was able to leave on 24 January 1944.[74] Fritz Warburg in Sweden had at the last minute secured for him an exchange for Germans interned in Palestine. Himmler had sanctioned the idea of allowing foreign Jewish nationals in Germany, those with prominent connections, as well as others with relatives in Palestine who could secure certificates, to leave. Departures to Switzerland against a payment to the Gestapo of 100,000 Swiss francs were also possible. In exchange, Germans would be enabled to come home and Gestapo coffers would benefit. The Jews intended for these exchanges were brought together in a camp specially created in the spring of 1943 – the later notorious Bergen-Belsen, not far from Hamburg. In 1943 Himmler thought 10,000 Jews could be exchanged or, as in the case of Spanish and Portuguese Jews, were sent home from Bergen-Belsen. In fact, only 358 left Bergen-Belsen under exchange agreements.

Plaut was first sent to a camp in Bavaria, then to a camp in France, where he joined some 270 other fortunate Jews of all ages allowed to leave. Some had come directly from concentration camps, including Auschwitz. Plaut then travelled across the Balkans and the Middle East until, with his mother, he reached Haifa early in July after a twelve-day journey.

IV

There was pitifully little provision for the seriously ill Jews still in Hamburg when once they had enjoyed the best facilities in the city.[75] The former Jewish old-age home in the Schäferkampsallee after the pensioners had been deported served as the last refuge. Here there was no shelter from air raids and the sick were moved into corridors with one nursing assistant; when the siren sounded the remainder spent the time of the raids in holes dug in the garden. There were no longer enough nurses available, so that the five doctors still in Hamburg took on night duty in addition to their daily work. As the premises were no longer a 'hospital' but the 'Jewish dispensary', the Jewish doctors still allowed to practise were called sickness attendants. They were all in mixed marriages, which is why they had not been deported. Many beds were filled with patients who had tried to commit suicide. The Gestapo made frequent visits and tried to discover how drugs such as Veronal had been obtained. Attempted suicide did not save anyone from deportation; patients were taken from the hospital at the first opportunity, in a removal van so as not to attract the attention of passers-by.

Hamburg's health administration showed decency in its treatment of the hospital, closing its eyes to medication, skimmed milk and other essentials being delivered. Connections with a fish wholesaler and a horse slaughterer provided badly needed fresh food. Some old suppliers of the hospital from better days remained loyal. The *Germania Apotheke* in the Fröbelstraße kept the hospital adequately stocked with medical supplies. A grocer at the end of the Rothenbaumchaussee heaped a cart filled with vegetables and pushed it to the hospital while it was still in the Johnsallee. Unfortunately he was spotted as he passed the former Jewish community premises at Rothenbaumchaussee 38, which had been taken over by the Gestapo. The Gestapo took reprisals and the supply ceased. A baker sent over white bread to the Schäferkampsallee for patients suffering from ulcers. Some neighbours nervously provided small parcels of food, overcoming the anxiety of being found out. The inclination to blame all Germans as a people for the crimes against the Jews breaks down as we discover the not insignificant number who stand out for their courage and committment to help. In Hamburg, Friedrich Petersen was one of the righteous Germans.

The Petersens lived in a flat at Hansastraße 35. The rest of the house was occupied by Jewish tenants with whom the Petersens had little contact – that is, until the Nuremberg Laws in 1935. Petersen was employed as a senior civil servant and his neighbours came to ask his advice. Petersen was no Nazi. He hung such a small swastika flag from the balcony on obligatory days that it provoked zealots to break his windows. In 1939, though of retirement age, he rejoined the administration and became the assistant of Dr Ziegler, a fervent Nazi and former mayor of Wandsbek. Petersen was responsible for authorising allowances to special groups such as disabled veterans. Ziegler either was not aware of Petersen's activities or preferred not to know about them. Petersen provided transport to bedridden Jews, telling Ziegler the vans were needed by the Gestapo. He used false names to send drugs to the Jewish hospital and food not allowed to Jews; when a colleague discovered the subterfuge he told him this was done with Ziegler's approval.

The Jews could not be left to starve and die of disease in German cities. This provided opportunities for Germans who wished to help. Another benefactor was Professor Dr Lorenz Treplin, in charge of the surgical department of the district hospital in Barmbeck.[76] Politically he had been a conservative member of the German People's Party (DVP) before 1933. Though he had reached the retirement age of sixty-five in 1940, he continued working as a surgeon throughout the war. In 1943, he responded to a desperate plea from the Jewish hospital to undertake surgery there as well, as no surgeon was any longer available for complicated cases. The Hamburg health authority probably knew, though Treplin's official record makes no mention of his work in the Jewish hospital, for which he sought no payment. He died in 1952, aged seventy-eight. Dr Hannes, the director of the Jewish hospital after the war, gave the funeral oration honouring a man

> who, at a time of severe persecution of the Jews, a time of desperate needs, had the courage without a second thought or question to act as surgeon in this hospital as soon as he was approached. He spread hope and comfort as, with a kindly face, he moved through the corridors, You enabled us to retain faith in the goodness of humanity.

Treplin was a German who also deserves to be counted among 'the righteous'. Like so many, he was confused by the dangers that appeared to confront Germany. He only became a member of the Nazi Party in 1937 to retain his position, but shared none of Hitler's hatred and responded to the high ethical demands of his profession with simple goodness. How can we categorise such a German? What degree of guilt should he share?

V

During the last two years of the war there was no let-up in persecution. The Gestapo's obsession only grew as the number of Jews fell to just a few. In the spring and summer of 1943, another 450 Jews were deported from Hamburg. In July there were just 1,250 'racial Jews' still left, the overwhelming majority in mixed marriages. After Gomorrha, the Gestapo could no longer obtain accurate figures, as the records of the Jewish community in the Beneckestraße had been destroyed. For the Gestapo this was a disaster. How could they now ensure that not a single Jew would be left in Hamburg? Plaut had reported in October that 357 Jews could not be accounted for. Most had probably fled with the other 900,000 Germans.

In January 1944 the Gestapo ordered Max Plaut, shortly before his departure, to collect more Jews for deportation within twenty-four hours, and sixty-one were dispatched; of these late deportees to Terezín only fourteen are certain to have survived. There were now hardly any Jews left not living in mixed marriages, and the Hamburg Gestapo began separating families and deporting the Jewish racial spouses. The category 'privileged mixed marriages' no longer counted. On 30 January 1945 nineteen were taken, and on 14 February 198 men and women were deported. Four died in Terezín, but the remainder returned after liberation. Among these was Alice Kruse.

Although she was living in a 'privileged mixed marriage' with a son, Alice Kruse had had a hard time during the war years.[77] She had watched the deportation of her father, mother and sisters. She herself had only escaped by a hair's breath when denounced for going to the cinema. What saved her when she had been summoned to the Gestapo was that her husband was serving in the *Wehrmacht*. She was let go with a warning. Her little son became severely disturbed by the taunts of other children; no nursery school would admit him. Then, in February 1945, Alice received the summons to assemble in the Grindelhof for deportation. She despaired and contemplated suicide, knowing that no one had ever returned. Her husband, who meantime had been dismissed from the *Wehrmacht* as unworthy to serve, managed to persuade her to obey the Gestapo order. The worst moment for her was the realisation that she would be parted from her child. When the time came the boy had disappeared, unable to bear what was happening.

The Jews in mixed marriages still awaiting deportation were assigned to heavy forced labour.[78] One hundred were housed in barracks in the Ohlsdorf cemetery in terrible conditions during the winter of 1944–5. There is a list, dated 14 February 1945, of 128 men – the oldest Gustav Haurwitz, aged eighty, and the youngest Rudolf Teich, twenty-four – forced to undertake heavy labour clearing Hamburg's streets. From concentration camps, in prisoners' clothing providing inadequate protection from the cold, more could be seen at work. Hungarian Jewish women had also been brought back to the concentration camp Neuengamme and sent out to factories in a pitiful state of health. None of this was hidden from the eyes of the passers-by.

During the last few weeks of the Nazi Reich the Hamburg administration lived in a world of unreality. Desperate attempts were made to secure an answer from Berlin as to whether a worker who was employed in the gasworks and was discovered belatedly to have one Jewish grandfather could continue in state employment – a strange priority with the enemy at the door. From Dr Berkowitz, the Jewish trustee responsible for the Jews still in Hannover, came an urgent request to Hamburg for more yellow stars, as supplies had run out.

Rudolf Querner had been replaced as higher SS and police commander by Georg Henning Graf von Bassewitz-Behr, whose record as a mass murderer in the East was second to none. From 1943 to the end of the war he ruthlessly exercised Gestapo and SS powers in Hamburg. Thousands of innocents were murdered in camps during the last weeks of the war, 15,000 gypsies in Mauthausen alone. As the Red Army drove west, evacuations from Estonia had begun already in August 1944. In September 3,000 women from Auschwitz reached the Neuengamme concentration camp near Hamburg. A flotsam of inmates from the camps was moved from one to another, thousands dying on the way; those unable to walk were shot.

One destination was Bergen-Belsen, set amid the beautiful Lüneburger Heide, not far from Hamburg, which was originally constructed for Russian prisoners of war. In April 1943 a separate compound housed the thousands of Jews who were intended to be exchanged for Germans in enemy hands. Its character changed after March 1944, as more and more prisoners were dumped there: 8,000 women were transferred from Auschwitz in November 1944 and by the end of the year the camp housed over 15,000. Bergen-Belsen then ceased to be regarded as a work or temporary camp for exchanges and under the SS took on the functions of a concentration camp. The horror of the last four months were chronicled in film following its liberation by British troops on 15 April 1945.[79] Thousands of Jews, including a young girl by the name of Anne Frank, were crowded in from other camps. The number of inmates rose to 60,000. Neglect, starvation and disease accounts for the huge death rate during the last weeks of the war: 34,000 corpses lay in heaps around the camp. When the war was over, the people of Hamburg were forced to come face to face with just this small corner of Nazi genocide. Bergen-Belsen, with Neuengamme, was one of the main camps. There were also dozens of smaller satellite camps, housing thousands of slave labourers, where the death rates shot up to catastrophic levels. Hundreds of Germans lived in close proximity to the camps.

In Hamburg, Gestapo sadism plumbed new depths during the last days.[80] For just a little longer, their power remained unchallenged. Soon, they knew, it would be all over. Although there were not many victims, one of the most heartrending atrocities occurred in a school on the Bullenhuser Damm in the very heart of Hamburg. The building had been taken over by the SS. Medical experiments were conducted there on twenty-four Russian prisoners of war and twenty Jewish children, all of whom were murdered two weeks before the entry of the British troops in order to obliterate the evidence. Another tragedy at the end of war was the sinking of the *Cap Arcona* in the Baltic Sea in the Bay of Lübeck, on board prisoners transferred from Neuengamme concentration camp.

On 30 April, only three days before the arrival of British troops, the Gestapo demanded a final tabulation of Jews. Hamburg had not been completely cleansed. Of the 674 Jews still in the city, 631 were in mixed marriages. It was too late for them to be sent to Terezín, as the Russians had cut rail communications. There were also thirteen single Jews – why they had survived and who they were has not been clarified. Finally, there were five foreign Jews. The Gestapo could take satisfaction from the fact that 5,880 Jews had been deported. As best as can be ascertained, at most 552 survived the camps, nearly half of them the late deportees in 1945 to Terezín. Of the 3,162 Jews first deported in 1941, only some sixty may have survived (it is not possible to establish precisely the statistics). With the end of the Third Reich, the final solution remained incomplete, but not by much.

As the war drew to a close and the Jews had all but disappeared from their midst, people began to think about them with feelings of dread. Not everyone was as well informed as Colonel Ebeling, who had learnt through his contacts that millions of innocent people – innocent Jewish women, children, men, old and young – had been sadistically murdered. The general population did not have precise details but knew enough to fear what soldiers entering Germany with justified hatred would now in turn do to them.

VI

During the early evening of 3 May, the Eighth Army entered Hamburg. For the few surviving Jews and the *Mischlinge*, the nightmare of deadly danger was over.[81] Now began a new struggle for existence and the effort to secure some compensation in the war-ravaged occupied country. Of the half million Jews by religion who had lived in Germany in 1933, about 210,000 had emigrated, some of whom, in France and the Low Countries fell into Nazi hands again. No more than 20,000 were still alive in Germany, more than half of them owing their survival to their loyal Christian spouses.

Kaufmann was arrested on 4 May. In charge now was Carl Vincent Krogmann, who received his orders from the British. The Nazi senate was made responsible for the preservation of law and order and for providing more than a million people with basic food and shelter. Uncertain of their role, they behaved as if still owing a duty to Hitler's Reich. At their meeting on 8 May, five days after the British occupation, Friedrich Ofterdinger, still heading social services, enquired whether Nazi laws should be applied or whether Jews should be given the same support as those 'of German blood'. Senator Martini, combining callousness with pragmatism, advised they should not be treated differently, 'as there were so few cases', but the senate could reach no agreement and left it to the British to decide.[82] Happily that was the last time the Nazi senate functioned. On 7 May, Germany surrendered on all fronts.

A week later Krogmann was replaced by Rudolf Petersen, brother of the last democratic mayor of Hamburg, and a new senate was appointed. Petersen proved to be a good choice and took prompt steps to provide the most immediate assistance – food, financial support and shelter – to Jewish survivors, helped by a sympathetic young British officer. Stragglers from the camps gradually got back to Hamburg. Buses were sent to Terezín in June to collect 150 'racial' Hamburg Jews. Among them was Alice Kruse, who on 29 June was received by her loving husband and son. She could not find adequate words to describe the joy of her return. It took her a long time to recover in health and spirit and resume normal relations with her fellow Germans.

What, meanwhile, happened to the leading Nazis?

The head of the Gestapo Regional Office in Hamburg from 1940 to 1941 was Heinz Seetzen, who later commanded *Einsatzgruppe* D and B in Russia. He hid under a false name in Blankenese, was arrested in September 1945 and committed suicide. His successor, Josef Kreuzer, was chief of the Hamburg Gestapo until 1944, when he led *Einsatzgruppe G* in Romania; convicted as a war criminal, he died in 1958. The record shows that the heads of the Hamburg Gestapo were sadistic, ruthless killers second to none. Jews, Roma and Sinti had nothing to hope for, either from them or from the Security Main Office in Berlin.

Claus Göttsche, as the war drew to its end, attempted to hide under a false name. He also provided himself with plenty of funds, having, in a final example of corruption, transferred close to a quarter of a million *Reichsmark* of ill-gotten Gestapo capital secured from Jewish victims from the Norddeutsche Bank to his own account. Göttsche's hideout was discovered by British soldiers; he escaped arrest by biting into a cyanide capsule. His subordinate Walter Wohlers disappeared; the case against him was suspended in 1964.

Rudolf Querner was arrested in May 1945 and escaped trial by committing suicide in prison; among his decorations was the Cross of Merit of the German Red Cross. Hans Stephan, who took over from Göttsche in September 1943, was arrested but not prosecuted for lack of evidence and was released in 1949. Hermann Kühn, the 'bloodhound', was held in 1945, convicted in 1950 and released in 1951. Astonishingly, Bruno Streckenbach, who had headed the Gestapo in Hamburg from 1933 to 1939, escaped trial and punishment in Germany. In 1939 he organised the *Einsatzgruppen* in Poland and later took over in Russia. He was responsible for the deaths of hundreds of thousands of Poles, Jews and Russians. A general in the *Waffen* SS, he was captured by the Russians and sentenced to twenty-five years imprisonment but amnestied in 1955 on the occasion of Chancellor Adenauer's visit to Moscow. Streckenbach returned to Hamburg and secured an appointment as a company secretary and retired with a good pension. The first attempt to try him was abandoned in 1974 and he avoided a second trial on grounds of ill health. He died in 1977 in his early seventies.

Karl Kaufmann was another survivor. He embellished his image as the 'good *Gauleiter*', humane to the Jews and, in defiance of Hitler and the high command, solely responsible for the surrender of Hamburg to the British Army without a fight. Arrested on 4 May 1945, he was interned. On his way to court in Nuremberg later, the car taking him overturned and he was declared unfit to be tried. Incorrigibly, he flirted with reviving an extreme right-wing political movement and was once more put behind bars. In 1953, duly 'denazified', he was released. Taking advantage of his 'former good contacts', he founded a lucrative insurance business with his old *Gau* economic adviser and until his death in 1969 ended his days in comfort.

Georg Ahrens, Uncle Baldrian, tried to offer his services as an expert adviser to the first post-war senate; the offer was declined. Interned, he was brought to trial in 1948. A six-year prison sentence, reduced on appeal, led to his release in 1949. He lived on unremarkably until his death in 1974.

Oskar Martini, once a senior civil servant in Weimar, then smoothly serving Nazi Hamburg, managed the best transition of all from the old Nazi leadership. He actually retained ministerial office in Petersen's new senate until October 1945. He was then absolved of any guilt by the denazification proceedings. Held in high esteem for his welfare reforms, he received many honours from his grateful countrymen. There was little danger of denunciation from colleagues themselves implicated in wrong-doing; only recent research has dented his image and uncovered his Nazi past.

Of the Jewish survivors, Max Plaut returned to Germany, married and settled in Bremen. He had not been happy in Palestine, where he had been exposed to bitter and unjust accusations. He died in Hamburg in 1974. Ludwig Loeffler, one of the senior members of *Reichsvereinigung* in Hamburg, survived Terezín and Auschwitz and returned to Hamburg, where he was appointed as head of the restitution administration. A lawyer, he played a leading role in re-establishing the

Jewish religious community. Oswald Lassally, who had survived the assassination attempt, emigrated and returned after the war to a senior position in Hamburg's police force.

Luise Solmitz and 'Fredy' were survivors. *Frau* Solmitz, not entirely cured of robust patriotism, now directed her anger at the British occupation. Their house, Kippingstraße 12, also survived. The small garden Luise Solmitz tended remains a peaceful oasis to the present day. The children of neighbours still remember the Solmitzes. The *Herr Major* after the war was a conspicuous figure who had lost none of his military bearing. Gisela did not return to Germany but settled in France. Fewer than 200 Jews straggled back from abroad, many too old and sick to survive elsewhere; the largest single group returned from Shanghai.

Victims of Nazi persecution organised themselves into a number of self-help associations. The largest was the *Notgemeinschaft der durch die Nürnberger Gesetze Betroffenen* (Emergency Association of those Aggrieved by the Nuremberg Laws), which represented Jews, *Mischlinge*, and the *Jüdischversippte* ('Germans' with Jewish spouses). Partners in so-called wild marriages, unable to marry formally because of the Nuremberg Laws, now applied to have their children legitimised. It took years to secure even the semblance of justice.

Religious life was revived predominantly by surviving German Jews. But as the older German generation died they were supplanted in Hamburg by new generations of Jews from Iran and Eastern Europe. Links with German-Jewish culture weakened until today it has all but disappeared. The flourishing pre-war culture of German Jewry is no more. It took new root in the West and Israel, undergoing yet another transformation. Today, in the Federal Republic, museums and memorials are silent reminders of that once vibrant past.

7

REFLECTIONS

Does the Holocaust have to remain beyond rational understanding, as is so often asserted? What we call civilisation is not proof against barbarity when a society falls into the hands of ideologically driven ruthless dictators. Difficult as it is to accept, the range of human nature includes at its extremes the perpetrators of genocide.

*

The enemies of civilisation gained strength in Germany and Europe before the 1914 war, but there were high barriers of resistance. It seemed unthinkable they would succeed in breaking through. That is why German Jews felt secure and were rational in their expectations. They were ready to face their enemies and, with like-minded allies, to take them on. Prejudice and discrimination, they believed, would in time be overcome. They were Germans and Germany was their home.

*

The rise and fall of German fortunes closely mirrors the growth and ebbing of extremist agitation against the country's Jewish citizens. That was evident during the First World War and becomes clear too during the life of the Weimar Republic. The difficult early years were marked by extremist threats until, during the final disastrous two years, they achieved their breakthrough. Out of the fourteen years, only four years of comparative good and stable times were experienced by the people. All the more remarkable, then, were the achievements in social progress and the world of culture. What is often overlooked is the political stability of the regional states, Prussia in the forefront, the small city-state of Hamburg a model where democratic decency was maintained for a short time even beyond 30 January 1933.

*

Seventy-four years before the republic failed, the English philosopher John Stuart Mill, in his essay *On Liberty* (1859), wrote, 'A civilisation that can succumb to its [once] vanquished enemy [the barbarians] must first have become so degenerate that its appointed priests and teachers, nor anybody else, has the capacity or will to stand up for it.' Weimar did not quite end like that. There was strong resistance by a minority of several million; yet there is insight too in what Mill foretold. During the last two years of the republic, its appointed ministers began to think of authoritarian alternatives to escape the seemingly insoluble parliamentary stalemate. In the depth of the Depression, with living conditions on a seemingly endless downward spiral, the majority of the people were also giving up on parliamentary democracy. Two extremist parties, the Nazis and the communists, weakened support for the governing middle, whose leaders in the Reich shunned supporting Jewish citizens openly for fear of losing the supporters they had left.

As for the 'priests' and 'teachers', the rot set in well before 30 January 1933, leaving German Jews without adequate protection. In Hamburg, traditions were a little stronger, the governing political elite more robust, but the tide sweeping against it could not be turned back. Only a reversal of economic conditions – a leadership infusing hope, the adoption of Keynesian financial counter-policies – might have changed the condition the country was in. It was Hitler who adopted that course.

*

It is striking how quickly the authoritarian state was established. The great national political parties could be abolished without causing any major unrest. The Centre Party, which had retained its supporters, disappeared meekly with the signature of the Concordat. The leaders of the once great Social Democratic Party went into exile. Sporadic local underground activities posed no serious threat. Neither the Social Democrats nor the communist rank and file, as long as they did not openly act against the regime, were in any personal danger. The leaders of the Social Democratic Party even received pensions in Hamburg. And why was the destruction of the major political parties possible? Because the majority of the people did not mourn their demise.

*

Institutions once pillars of a civilised modern state collapsed under the pressure of the Nazis, just like the political parties. The independent judiciary, with a tradition going back to the early days of the Prussian monarchy, surrendered its independence when it accepted the removal of 'non-Aryan' judges and lawyers from the courts. Inevitably Hitler became the final judge and jury. Curt Rothenberger, heading the Nazi judiciary in Hamburg, exemplified the transformation.

Moral leadership would have been expected from the two Christian churches. The Catholic German hierarchy struck a Faustian bargain which set it on the path of moral decline, with its most senior cleric, Cardinal Adolf Bertram, assuring Hitler of his support until the end of the war. Old and weak, with the Red Army at the door, he placed his remaining hopes of halting the Godless floodtide in Hitler's retention of his grip over *Volk* and *Wehrmacht* – beyond lay chaos. The Protestant bishops showed no more moral strength. Catholic and Protestant resistance from the courageous few pastors and priests and members of the laity, lacking the support of their superiors, was all the more remarkable.

The persecution of the Jews was passed over in silence by Lutheran synods. The belief that Christianity superseded Judaism was general. Even Dietrich Bonhoeffer, one of the most courageous Protestant theologians, who joined the resistance during the war, struggled with this concept early on. For Bishop Tügel, in Hamburg, it presented no problem. He took pride in declaring that he was an antisemite of long standing. The anti-Judaism of both churches made legitimacy of Nazi persecution plausible.

*

No country can be governed without an able bureaucracy doing its job. Once the non-Aryans are deducted from all those who were dismissed, one would have expected more to have been forced to leave for other reasons. The majority carried on administering laws in a 'professional' manner without sensitivity of the impact on lives.

The educators showed no more spine. In the schools, especially at secondary level, the Nazis were quick to appoint the right headmasters and remove teachers who opposed them. In Hamburg, earlier headmasters of the elite *Johanneum*, a place of learning that had taught Hamburg's Jewish elite for generations, would have turned in their graves to witness how quickly their famous school had adjusted. The universities lost some of their most distinguished professors. Their colleagues debated whether to thank them for their contributions. Few showed solidarity, fearing it could threaten their own positions. Hamburg was no exception.

*

Goebbels showered the stars of the stage and concert hall with monetary rewards. A little more licence was allowed to protect an actor or musician unfortunately not purely Aryan or married to a Jewess. When you remove from the lists of famous actors, musicians, writers and academics all those who were not blighted by racial laws or political associations, only a few were left.

Compliance was so widespread that 'terror' cannot explain the readiness to conform or make whatever compromise the regime required. Luise Solmitz, commenting on the behaviour of some of her compatriots, bitterly observed that 'there was no need to crawl on all fours'.

*

For the Jews to feel themselves to be without any protection, it was not necessary for rabid racists to form the majority in the civil administration, the professions or the churches. Those with a conscience allayed their misgivings by finding good reasons for the discrimination and injustice. There were also Germans who sympathised with Jews and in small ways wanted to help, but they were outnumbered by those ready to profit from the misery of the Jews and the willing helpers of the regime. Between the poles of the extremes, the majority lived in a moral void. The Third Reich opened new opportunities. People supported the regime because of its astounding success abroad, the success in overcoming mass unemployment at home, and ideological persuasion, social

Darwinism, when linked to race science, lending credibility to propaganda. And everyone who wanted to do so could now wear a uniform in one or other of the Nazi organisations with the prospects of a whole ladder of advancement. You could pick and choose as long as you showed at least token support for the party. The Third *Reich* offered something to the many. Hatred of Jews was not at the top of the people's agenda.

*

Were the German Jews in part themselves to blame for the discrimination and persecution? Had they been too successful in private banking, commerce and the professions, as newspaper owners, musicians and actors? There were Jewish academics who agreed with the view that the spread of occupations among Jews was 'unnatural' and 'unhealthy', and that Jews should follow occupations in proportion to the rest of the population. It sounds plausible as long as individual choice is not considered a human right and merit a measure of judgement. The antisemites accused Jews of reaching the higher social strata by insidious means, infiltrating what should be a purely 'German' sphere. But the Jews were Germans! The antisemites turned reality on its head. Germany's Jews were making a contribution to the country's prosperity and culture out of proportion to their number. They were no longer a 'separate', 'alien' community model for a 'multicultural society' – an umbrella term for a society that can take quite different forms. There were also Jewish villains, just as there were Christian ones. The Jews, too, were 'ordinary' Germans.

*

It was not only the ill-educated who harboured common prejudices against Jews, but also well-educated, decent and moral Germans like Luise Solmitz, even though her husband was of Jewish parentage. Jews were stigmatised as a group with common negative characteristics. Yet most people came into contact with Jews who did not conform to these stereotypes when they shopped at the local bakery, called the doctor to attend to their sick child or worked for a Jewish employer. The contradiction was obvious but dismissed: the Jews you actually knew were always the exception. The mental trick that allowed you to retain your prejudices was not peculiar to Germans but prevalent throughout the Western world. Centuries of misinformation, abuse, and even hatred, propagated principally by the Church, conditioned people to accept the negative image.

*

The issue of the so-called Jewish question was not high on people's agenda in 1933 or later, despite all the Nazi propaganda. If anyone had said during the early Nazi years that his Jewish neighbours would soon end up in special camps, to be murdered by state of the art equipment made in Germany, he would have been thought insane. Hitler was careful to disclaim any such intention early on.

*

How should we interpret the elections of 5 March 1933 confirming Hitler in power? Some writers stress that more than half the electorate did not vote for the Nazis, that the elections were neither open nor fair, that the subsequent Enabling Law was juridically flawed. All this is true. But at least as important is the need to highlight other facts. The Nazi Party secured more than twice as many votes as the Social Democratic Party, the next largest party. In a system of proportional representation, with three other main parties competing, the NSDAP achieved a stunning victory. The supporters of democratic parliamentary government had shrunk to a minority.

In 1933 there were nevertheless millions who recorded their opposition to the Nazis. What happened to make this sizeable opposition so ineffective in subsequent years? Terror is not the principal explanation. How many opponents were left when the swastika was raised over the Eiffel Tower?

*

Misunderstanding what Hitler was capable of lingered even down to the early years of the war. Directives distinguished between the 'patriotic German Jew', who had fought for the fatherland, and the rest. Jewish disabled veterans of the First World War were granted at first the same rations as the rest of the population. German-Jewish leaders still thought after the outbreak of war that the liquidation of the German-Jewish community would be achieved by emigration over the years and by the natural death of the elderly. German Jews did not expect to be treated like Poles and Russians.

*

Human behaviour is dependent on external circumstances, which changed rapidly for Germans, Jews and gentiles who passed through wholly different eras – the prosperous years of *Kaiser* Wilhelm, the First World War, Weimar, the Third *Reich* and the Second World War, the Allied occupation and post-war reconstruction. During each of the five discontinuous decades, outlooks and motivations adjusted to the drastic changes of their world. The gap between generations widened. Older values eroded. Could it all have turned out differently?

Police Commissioner Claus Göttsche, head of the section dealing with Jews in the Hamburg Gestapo, would have ended his career normally had the Nazis not come to power; Oskar Martini, heading welfare in Hamburg, did conclude his with high praise, as in his lifetime no one discovered his vicious Nazi past. Curt Rothenberger was a highly regarded young judge with an intimate Jewish friend; his friend became a well-known publisher in the United States, while Rothenberger ended up in prison.

*

Is not the survival in 1945 of some 20,000 Jews evidence that there were Germans ready to risk their lives to save Jews? Actually there were far fewer righteous Germans than there were Polish, French and Dutch people who rescued Jews. The majority of the remnants in Germany survived in part thanks to Hitler, who wished to avoid conflicts where Jews by marriage were closely embedded in German society. Their fate, the last phase of the 'final solution', he had decided was to be postponed until after the war. The majority of Jewish survivors in Germany owed their lives not to being hidden but to their steadfast Christian wives or husbands.

*

A question often asked is why Jews did not leave Germany sooner. Two reasons stand out. The first is that it was not all that bad to begin with in the cities, where most Jews lived. The abyss did not open all at once. Another is that it meant giving up home and possessions for an uncertain future. This was easier for the younger than the older generation. Those with transferable skills, such as doctors, had more of a chance to start a new life than, for example, lawyers, whose knowledge counted for nothing in a foreign land. In any case, until the flare-up of persecution in the autumn of 1938 opened doors a little wider, the decade of high unemployment and antisemitism did not make German Jews welcome abroad. If the whole community had tried to leave during the first four years, countries of refuge would have closed their doors even more tightly than they did.

*

The experience of German Jews was overwhelmingly positive before the advent of the Nazis and extrememists. Prejudice existed everywhere, but did not halt their increasing integration in Western national societies. The Hamburg senate for more than a hundred years developed cordial and supportive relations with the representatives of the Jewish community. Not a few of its officials provided outstanding help, reflecting their personal commitment.

The spread of hate was the work of a significant minority before the Nazi breakthrough in 1930, but their later success has led to unbalanced judgements about earlier times. The positive past also explains why the majority of German Jews during the early years of the Third *Reich* did not foresee the murderous dimensions of the later years.

*

As Jews were faced with exile, they were assailed by doubts as to whether they and their forebears had been wrong to feel complete as Jews and Germans. The debate about the place of Judaism in German society had gone on since the Enlightenment and with it a positive upsurge of interest in Jewish culture and ethics. German Jewry resolved its questioning along a variety of paths. Some it took to conversion. The majority found ways to embrace both cultures, were comfortable to be Germans and Jews, while differing in their religious orientation. This multifaceted attitude to culture contrasted starkly with the barren conformist Nazi ideology. But were German-Jewish attitudes utopian? Actually contemporary Jewry in the Western world shares the same conviction.

*

The German-Jewish leadership during the years of the Third *Reich* showed courage and enterprise and saved two-thirds of the community. They are blamed for 'cooperating' with the Nazis, but what options did they have? They could not prevent the deportations or the Holocaust. The real issue is whether their presence helped or worsened the lives of the Jewish community. Max Plaut, like the other leaders who remained serving the community after the outbreak of war, could have emigrated. He too would have been deported from Hamburg had it not been for Fritz Warburg's last-minute successful intervention, when he arranged his inclusion in an exchange with the German Templars in Palestine.

*

The Jewish leadership was the interface between the Gestapo and the Jewish community. They could do nothing to avert the Holocaust. They struggled with some success to make Jewish life possible while Jews still remained in Germany. The leaders of Jewish organisations did not try to hide the fact that the decisions affecting the lives of individuals were not their own but those of their 'supervisory authority' – a euphemism for the Gestapo.

*

Hamburg is rebuilt. The neo-Renaissance *Rathaus* dominates the skyline across the Binnen-Alster, along whose banks are imposing façades and villas. But for a mosque the scene has hardly changed; life has returned to normal were it not for an invisible black hole, the missing German Jews.

*

It was not just a Jewish civilisation that the Nazis destroyed in Germany but German civilisation, of which it was also a part. New Jewish communities now live in Hamburg and the rest of Germany, a quarter the size of the old, not German in origin, bringing with them varied traditions from their former homes. Jews migrated to the German lands through the centuries; this migration, however, is different. The newcomers are not being absorbed by a larger, well-established German-Jewish community steeped since the eighteenth century in German culture and absorbed into German society. Those Jews have gone. There exists no longer a Jewish community proud of its German past and contribution to German culture. The curtain of the Holocaust lies between the past and the present, impeding easy relationships. What has gone, the death of a civilisation, cannot be replaced. A new civilisation has to be rebuilt on the foundations of understanding the past.

REFERENCES AND SOURCES

Over the years I have had the good fortune to have worked in a large number of archives. Without the assistance of their conscientious and helpful staff, the collection of the evidence would simply have been impossible. In Hamburg, the Staatsarchiv/Hamburg State Archive (St A H), Forschungsstelle für Zeitgeschichte (FZH), Institut für die Geschichte der Deutschen Juden, Handelskammer/Hamburg Chamber of Commerce, Warburg Bank, Jerusalem-Gemeinde and Christianeum Hamburg-Blankenese; in Berlin, the Bundesarchiv/National Archives and Evangelisches Zentralarchiv/Protestant Central Archive; in Hannover, the Stadtarchiv/City Archive; in London, the Wiener Library Archive and the Public Record Office (now the British National Archives); in Jerusalem, Yad Vashem and the Central Archives for the History of the Jewish People; in New York, the Leo Baeck Institute Archive; in Washington, DC, the Holocaust Memorial Museum Archive and the National Archives, State Department; in Waltham, Massachusetts, the Brandeis University Archive; and in Stanford, California, the Hoover Institution of War, Revolution and Peace Archive at Stanford University.

Prologue

1 Luise Solmitz, in her Journal, 24 October 1941, recorded what her daughter Gisela told her about the first deportation that evening, Forschungsstelle für Zeitgeschichte in Hamburg (hereafter, FZH), 11 S 13.
2 Erwin Baehr, letter recounting his experiences, 14 August 1954, FZH, 626-2.
3 Luise Solmitz, Journal, 7 November 1941, FZH, 11 S 13. This transport was sent to Minsk; *Gedenkbuch für die jüdischen Opfer des Nationalsozialismus in Hamburg* (Hamburg: Staatsarchiv, 1965; rev. ed., comp. Jürgen Sielemann and Peter Flamme, 1995), pp. 15–28.
4 Henry Rosenberg's manuscript memoir written after the war, FZH, 626-2.
5 Statistics based on *Gedenkbuch für die jüdischen Opfer des Nationalsozialismus in Hamburg*.

1 Earlier times

1 Günter Böhm, 'Die Sephardim in Hamburg', in *Die Juden in Hamburg 1590 bis 1990*, ed. Arno Herzig and Saskia Rohde (Hamburg: Dölling & Galitz, 1991), pp. 21–40. See also Jutta Braden, *Hamburger Judenpolitik im Zeitalter lutherischer Orthodoxie 1590–1710* (Hamburg: Christians, 2001).

2 Günter Marwedel, 'Die aschkenasischen Juden im Hamburger Raum (bis 1780)', in *Die Juden in Hamburg 1590 bis 1990*, pp. 41–60. Oskar Wolfsberg-Aviad, *Die Drei-Gemeinde: Aus der Geschichte der jüdischen Gemeinden Altona, Hamburg, Wandsbek* (Munich: Ner-Tamid Verlag, 1960).
3 Irmgard Stein, *Jüdische Baudenkmäler in Hamburg* (Hamburg: Christians, 1984). Saskia Rohde, 'Synagogen im Hamburger Raum', in *Die Juden in Hamburg 1590 bis 1990*, pp. 143–85.
4 The history of the Wohlwill family is told in the Wohlwill family collection, Leo Baeck Institute Archive, New York, AR 2672–2675, which contains the account of Immanuel Wohlwill (1799–1848) written by Sophie Wohlwill, the granddaughter of Immanuel and second daughter of Emil Wohlwill (1835–1912), Immanuel Wohlwill's son. Sophie Wohlwill and her brother Heinrich perished in Terezín (Theresienstadt).
5 Henri Soussan, *The Science of Judaism: From Leopold Zunz to Leopold Lucas* (Research paper 3, University of Sussex, Centre for German-Jewish Studies, 1999). On the Christian side, in a brochure from a generation earlier, entitled 'Concerning the Civic Improvement of the Jews' (1781), a senior Prussian civil servant, Christian Wilhelm Dohm, blamed persecution of the 'degraded' Jew on the Christians. Jews by nature were no different to others, and the state should bring about their emancipation and become responsible for their 'moral improvement'. Another thirty years would pass before, in 1812, Jews became citizens of Prussia, well ahead of Hamburg. Robert Liberles, 'Dohm's Treatise on the Jews: A Defence of Enlightenment', *Leo Baeck Institute Year Book*, 33 (1988), pp. 29–42.
6 Ismar Schorsch (quoting S. Rubaschoff, 'Erstlinge der Entjudung', in *Der jüdische Wille*, 1 (1918–19)), in 'Breakthrough into the Past: The Verein für Cultur und Wissenschaft der Juden', *Leo Baeck Institute Year Book*, 33 (1988), pp. 3–28.
7 Ludwig Philippson, cited by Amos Elon, *The Pity of It All: A History of the Jews in Germany 1743–1933* (New York: Henry Holt, 2002), p. 159. The translation from the German here differs in style but not in meaning.
8 The best account is Helga Krohn, *Die Juden in Hamburg 1800–1850: Ihre soziale, kulturelle und politische Entwicklung während der Emanzipationszeit* (Frankfurt: Europäische Verlagsanstalt, 1967). An excellent overview is David Sorkin, *The Transformation of German Jewry, 1780–1840* (Oxford: Oxford University Press, 1987). An excellent account of the structure of the Hamburg Jewish community, relations with the senate, the appointment of Isaak Bernays as *chachan* and the dispute with the *Tempel* congregation can be found in Stephen M. Poppel, 'The Politics of Religious Leadership: The Rabbinate in Nineteenth-Century Hamburg', *Leo Baeck Institute Year Book*, 28 (1983), pp. 439–70.
9 Sophie Wohlwill, account of Immanuel Wohlwill, Wohlwill family collection, Leo Baeck Institute Archive, New York. Immanuel Wohlwill was chosen in 1822.
10 Manuscript, Immanuel Wohlwill, 'Notizen auf einer Spazierfahrt von Hamburg nach Kiel im October 1829', Wohlwill family collection, Leo Baeck Institute Archive, New York, pp. 22ff.
11 Krohn, *Die Juden in Hamburg 1800–1850*, pp. 30ff.
12 Werner Jochmann and Hans-Dieter Loose, eds, *Hamburg: Geschichte der Stadt und ihrer Bewohner*, vol. 1 (Hamburg: Hoffmann & Campe, 1982).
13 Helga Krohn, *Die Juden in Hamburg: Die politische, soziale und kulturelle Entwicklung einer jüdischen Großstadtgemeinde nach der Emanzipation, 1848–1918* (Hamburg: Christians, 1974). The standard overview is Werner Mosse, Arnold Paucker and Reinhard Rürup, eds, *Revolution and Evolution: 1848 in German-Jewish History* (Tübingen: Mohr, 1981). In 1851 the constitutional separation theoretically made marriage possible between Jews and Christians, but marriage was impossible in a church unless the Jewish spouse converted, and no synagogue would marry a religiously mixed couple. That barrier was only removed ten years later with the introduction of civil marriages.

14 Friedrich Wohlwill, his son, wrote a brief account of his life: 'Emil Wohlwill', Wohlwill family collection, Leo Baeck Institute Archive, New York. From Emil Wohlwill's letters and journals, with extensive quotations from an unpublished account written by his daughter Sophie, ibid.

15 Emil Wohlwill to Betty Lehmann, née Wolff, 24 March 1853, in Sophie Wohlwill, 'Emil Wohlwill', p. 10.

16 Emil Wohlwill to Betty Wolff, no date – 1853 or early 1854 – ibid., p. 14.

17 Emil Wohlwill to Fanny Wohlwill, 11 November and 30 November 1856, ibid., pp. 63–5.

18 Ibid., pp. 185ff; pp. 216ff, his declaration of leaving the Jewish community and his citizenship of Hamburg.

19 Friedrich Wohlwill's account of his father's work, Wohlwill family collection, Leo Baeck Institute Archive, New York.

20 *100 Jahre Beiersdorf: 1882–1982* (Hamburg: Beiersdorf, 1982). Ekkehard Kaum, *Oscar Troplowitz* (Hamburg: Wesche, 1982).

21 Ernst Hamburger, *Juden im öffentlichen Leben Deutschlands* (Tübingen: Mohr, 1968), p. 39. Leo Lippmann, *Mein Leben und meine amtliche Tätigkeit: Erinnerungen und ein Beitrag zur Finanzgeschichte Hamburgs*, ed. Werner Jochmann (Hamburg: Christians, 1964). The Lippmanns had lived for generations in Germany: Joseph, Leo's father, moved to Hamburg in 1870. Conversion was rare in the nineteenth century and converts took pride generally in their Jewish ancestry. For the best overview, written by leading scholars, see *German-Jewish History in Modern Times*, 4 vols, ed. Michael A. Meyer and Michael Brenner (New York: Columbia University Press, 1986–8).

22 Ina S. Lorenz, 'Zehn Jahre Kampf um das Hamburger System (1864–1873)', in *Die Hamburger Juden in der Emanzipationsphase (1780–1870)*, ed. Peter Freimark and Arno Herzig (Hamburg: Christians, 1989), pp. 41–82. Arno Herzig, 'Die Juden in Hamburg 1780–1860', and Ina S. Lorenz, 'Die jüdische Gemeinde Hamburg 1860–1943', in *Die Juden in Hamburg 1590 bis 1990*, pp. 61–100. A general overview is Jacob Toury, *Soziale und politische Geschichte der Juden in Deutschland, 1847–1871: Zwischen Revolution, Reaktion und Emanzipation* (Düsseldorf: Droste, 1977).

23 Based on a manuscript kindly made available to me by Professor Walter Elkan.

24 Ties to Judaism were weakened. Fears that the Jews in Germany would disappear altogether or be reduced to an insignificant small number were widespread. The first serious scientific study of the phenomenon is Felix Theilhaber, *Der Untergang der Deutschen Juden* (Munich: Reinhardt, 1911; 2nd ed., 1921, repr. Munich: Kraus, 1980). Also the lecture by his son Adin Talbar, 'About my Father Felix Theilhaber', lecture at the fifth congress of the European Federation of Sexology, 29 June–2 July 2000, www2.hu-berlin.de/sexology/GESUND/ARCHIV/P_TALBAR.HTM.

25 For an overview, the standard work is Werner Mosse and Arnold Paucker, eds, *Juden im Wilhelminischen Deutschland, 1890–1914* (Tübingen: Mohr, 1976). Krohn, *Die Juden in Hamburg 1848–1918*, p. 124.

26 For a history of the bank and the Warburg family, see Ron Chernow, *The Warburgs: The Twentieth Century Odyssey of a Remarkable Jewish Family* (New York: Random House, 1993); Eduard Rosenbaum and Ari Joshua Sherman, *Das Bankhaus M. M. Warburg & Co., 1798–1938* (Hamburg: Christians, 1976), Eng. trans. as *M. M. Warburg & Co., 1798–1938, Merchant Bankers of Hamburg* (London: Hurst, 1979). The Altona Warburg branch is less well known. Gentiles in Altona elected Moritz Warburg to the Prussian parliament in 1867 and Albert Warburg to preside over the Altona chamber of commerce.

27 Werner E. Mosse, 'Drei Juden in der Wirtschaft Hamburgs: Heine – Ballin – Warburg', in *Die Juden in Hamburg 1590–1990*, pp. 431–46; Werner E. Mosse, *Jews in the German Economy: The German-Jewish Economic Elite, 1820–1935* (Oxford: Clarendon Press, 1987); Bernhard Huldermann, *Albert Ballin* (London: Cassell, 1922); Lamar Cecil, *Albert Ballin: Business and Politics in Imperial Germany, 1888–1918* (Princeton, NJ: Princeton University Press, 1967).

28 An excellent overview is Peter Pulzer, *The Rise of Political Anti-Semitism in Germany & Austria* (rev. ed., London: Halban, 1988); Reinhard Rürup, *Emanzipation und Antisemitismus: Studien zur 'Judenfrage' der bürgerlichen Gesellschaft* (Göttingen: Vandenhoeck & Ruprecht, 1975), pp. 74–114; Annegret Ehmann, 'From Colonial Racism to Nazi Population Policy: The Role of the So-Called Mischlinge', in *The Holocaust and History: The Known, the Unknown, the Disputed, and the Reexamined*, ed. Michael Berenbaum and Abraham J. Peck (Bloomington: Indiana University Press, 1998), pp. 115–33. In 1905 and 1906, mixed marriages were banned in Germany's African colonies.

29 Pauline M. H. Mazumdar, in *Eugenics, Human Genetics and Human Failings* (London: Routledge, 1992), describes the origins of the Eugenic Society and its critics in Britain.

30 Robert Proctor, *Racial Hygiene: Medicine under the Nazis* (Cambridge, MA: Harvard University Press, 1988), pp. 14–17.

31 Mazumdar, *Eugenics*, pp. 89–95.

32 Among a large literature, a good discussion is in George L. Mosse, *The Crisis of German Ideology: Intellectual Origins of the Third Reich* (New York: Grosset, Dunlap, 1964), pp. 93–7.

33 Proctor, *Racial Hygiene*, pp. 59–94.

34 Ibid., pp. 39–43, 217–22.

35 Uriel Tal, *Christians and Jews in Germany: Religion, Politics and Ideology in the Second Reich* (Ithaca, NY: Cornell University Press, 1975), pp. 223–89; H. S. Chamberlain, *The Foundations of the Nineteenth Century* (London: John Lane, 1911); Arthur J. De Gobineau, *Versuch über die Ungleichheit der Menschenrassen*, 4 vols (Stuttgart: Fromann, 1902–4); Fritz Stern, *The Politics of Cultural Despair: A Study in the Rise of the Germanic Ideology* (Berkeley: University of California Press, 1961).

36 Moshe Zimmermann, *Wilhelm Marr: The Patriarch of Anti-Semitism* (Oxford: Oxford University Press, 1986); Donald L. Niewyck, 'Solving the "Jewish Problem": Continuity and Change in German Antisemitism, 1871–1945', *Leo Baeck Institute Year Book*, 35 (1990), pp. 335–70.

37 Tal, *Christians and Jews in Germany*, p. 277. It was a problem for Hitler, too. In the *Table Talk* (*Hitler's Table Talk 1941–44*, 2nd ed., London: Weidenfeld & Nicolson, 1973) he said he believed the father of Jesus was a Roman soldier; the mother had to be Jewish, which, by Nazi definition, made Jesus a *Mischling* (hybrid).

38 Donald L Niewyck, 'Solving the "Jewish Problem"', p. 343; Moshe Zimmerman, 'Two Generations in the History of German Antisemitism: The Letters of Theodor Fritsch to Wilhelm Marr', *Leo Baeck Institute Year Book*, 23 (1978), pp. 89–99.

39 Günter Brakelmann, Martin Greshat and Werner Jochmann, *Protestantismus und Politik: Werk und Wirkung Adolf Stoeckers* (Hamburg: Christians, 1982).

40 Werner Jochmann, *Gesellschaftskrise und Judenfeindschaft in Deutschland 1870–1945* (Hamburg: Christians, 1989); Pulzer, *The Rise of Political Anti-Semitism in Germany & Austria*.

41 Iris Hamel, *Völkischer Verband und nationale Gewerkschaft: Der Deutschnationale Handlungsgehilfen-Verband 1893–1933* (Frankfurt: Europäische Verlagsanstalt, 1967). The association attracted 75,000 members.

42 Uwe Lohalm, *Völkischer Radikalismus: Die Geschichte des Deutschvölkischen Schutz- und Trutz-Bundes 1919–1923* (Hamburg: Leibniz, 1970), pp. 27–71.

43 Jochmann and Loose, *Hamburg: Geschichte der Stadt und ihrer Bewohner*, vol. 2, pp. 81ff.; in 1910 there were more Jews than gentiles living in Hamburg who had been born in the city.

44 Albert Wolffson was a member of one of Hamburg's best-known Jewish families. His brother Dr Isaac Wolffson had been a contributor to the revised edition of the *Bürgerliches Gesetzbuch* (Civil Code). His daughter Agnes introduced the teaching of domestic science to Hamburg's elementary schools, later expanded to all schools by the education department. The progressive social initiatives of Jews were typical of

those who were better placed in Hamburg, who also helped to develop cooperatives and trade unions and introduced German literature and art to working people. Jewish publishers produced books by young avant-garde authors who were supported by a Jewish Maezenas. Obituary of Agnes Wolffson, 18 March 1936, *Gemeinde-Blatt der Deutsch-Israelitischen Gemeinde.*

45 Jochmann and Loose, *Hamburg: Geschichte der Stadt und ihre Bewohner,* vol. 2, pp. 54–8; Ernst Hamburger, *Juden im öffentlichen Leben Deutschlands* (Tübingen: Mohr, 1968), p. 247.

46 Richard J. Evans, *Death in Hamburg: Society and Politics in the Cholera Years 1830– 1910* (Oxford: Oxford University Press, 1987). An article reporting on Dr Reincke's investigation was also published by the *British Medical Journal,* no. 1678, 25 February 1893, pp. 429–30.

47 Arnold Paucker, *Der jüdische Abwehrkampf gegen Antisemitismus und Nationalsozialismus in den letzten Jahren der Weimarer Republik* (Hamburg: Leibniz, 1968), pp. 26–44. There were cultured Christian Germans too who fought anti-Semitism: see, especially, Barbara Suchy, 'The Verein zur Abwehr des Antisemitismus (I): From its Beginnings to the First World War', *Leo Baeck Institute Year Book,* 28 (1983), pp. 205–39. William II's father, Frederick III, was also a determined opponent of anti-Semitism. His tragic death from cancer in 1888 after reign of only ninety days altered the course of German history.

48 There is an overview in the standard work, Werner Mosse and Arnold Paucker, eds, *Deutsches Judentum in Krieg und Revolution, 1916–1923* (Tübingen: Mohr, 1971). See also Paul Mendes-Flohr, 'Im Schatten des Weltkrieges, 1918–1945', in Avraham Barkai, Paul Mendes-Flohr and Steven M Lowenstein, eds, *Deutsch-jüdische Geschichte in der Neuzeit,* vol. 4 (Munich: Beck, 1997), Eng. trans. as *German-Jewish History in Modern Times* (New York: Columbia University Press, 1998); George L. Mosse, 'The Jews and the German War Experience 1914–1918', Leo Baeck Memorial Lecture, New York, 1977.

49 Luise Solmitz, Journal, 6 August 1914, FZH, 11 S 1.

50 Ibid., 23 March 1915.

51 Ibid., 22 August 1914.

52 Of the 96,000 Jews, over 11,000 were under-age volunteers, 84,000 fought at the front and just under 30,000 were decorated. *Deutsche jüdische Soldaten, 1914–1945,* ed. Heinrich Walle for Militärgeschichtliches Forschungsamt (Herford: Mittler, 1984, 3rd ed., 1987), p. 107. The date 1945 in the title is an error; apart from fewer than a dozen Jews who had hidden themselves among the troops, *no Jews* served in Hitler's armies. The *Mischlinge* by definition did not belong to the Jewish community or they would have been counted as Jews.

53 Ernst Loewenberg, 'Mein Leben in Deutschland vor und nach dem 30. Januar 1933', manuscript, Harvard History Prize Competition, March 1940, Leo Baeck Institute Archive, New York, p. 3: 'In dem Tagebuch, das mein Vater seit dem ersten Kriegstag führte, finden sich schon im September 1914 Bemerkungen über Angriffe gegen jüdische Drückeberger.'

54 Ibid., p. 5.

55 The standard work is Egmont Zechlin, *Die deutsche Politik und die Juden im Ersten Weltkrieg* (Göttingen: Vandenhoeck & Ruprecht, 1969). See also Werner T. Angress, 'The German Army's "Judenzählung" of 1916: Genesis – Consequences – Significance', in *Leo Baeck Institute Year Book,* 23 (1978), pp. 117–38.

56 Ian Kershaw, *Hitler 1889–1936: Hubris* (Harmondsworth: Penguin, 1998), p. 96; Adolf Hitler, *Monologe im Führer-Hauptquartier, 1941–1944,* ed. Werner Jochmann (Hamburg: A. Knaus, 1980), p. 132.

57 Loewenberg, 'Mein Leben in Deutschland', p. 6.

58 The standard work is Trude Maurer, *Ostjuden in Deutschland 1918–1933* (Hamburg: Christians, 1986).

59 Luise Solmitz, Journal, 31 January 1916, FZH, 11 S 1.
60 Steven E. Aschheim, *Brothers and Strangers: The East European Jew in German and German Jewish Consciousness, 1800–1923* (Madison: University of Wisconsin Press, 1982). According to the census of 1 December 1885, there were 473,000 Jews of German birth and 90,000 of foreign birth. Children of assimilated Jews like myself were told not to copy 'Eastern' Jewish mannerisms in dress, not to talk with their hands (*mauscheln*) and to speak high German – though a few Yiddish expressions were common, such as *meschugge* (nuts) and *nebbich* (pitiable).
61 *Kriegsbriefe deutscher und österreichischer Juden*, ed. Eugen Tannenbaum (Berlin: Neuer Verlag, 1915). Nearly a million Jews fought on all sides, including 300,000 in the Russian armies.
62 Volker Ullrich, 'Massenbewegungeu in der Hamburger Arbeiterschaft im Ersten Weltkrieg', in *Arbeiter in Hamburg*, ed. Arno Herzig, Dieter Langewische and Arnold Sywottek (Hamburg: Verlag Erziehung und Wissenschaft, 1983), pp. 407–18.
63 One of many good overviews is Hans Mommsen, *The Rise and Fall of Weimar Democracy* (Chapel Hill: University of North Carolina Press, 1989), pp. 1–50. The best survey, with a critical discussion of the academic literature, is Ursula Büttner, *Weimar: Die überforderte Republik, 1918–1933* (Stuttgart: Klett-Cotta, 2008). See also Richard J. Evans, *The Coming of the Third Reich* (Harmondsworth: Penguin, 2003), the first volume of a trilogy.

2 The shadow of the Nazis

1 Luise Solmitz, Journal, 6 November 1918, FZH, 11 S 4.
2 This section on Weimar is based on Ursula Büttner, 'Der Stadtstaat als demokratische Republik', in *Hamburg: Geschichte der Stadt und ihrer Bewohner*, ed. Werner Jochmann and Hans-Dieter Loose, vol. 2 (Hamburg: Hoffmann & Campe, 1986), pp. 131–48. An excellent comprehensive history of Weimar Hamburg is Ursula Büttner, *Politische Gerechtigkeit und sozialer Geist: Hamburg zur Zeit der Weimarer Republik* (Hamburg: Christians, 1985) – the years of unrest to 1924, pp. 13–190. See also Ursula Büttner, *Weimar: Die überforderte Republik 1918–1933* (Stuttgart: Klett-Cotta, 2008), pp. 33–64.
3 The turbulent history from 1919 to 1920 can be followed in Hans Mommsen's third chapter, 'Founding a Democracy', in *The Rise and Fall of Weimar Democracy* (Chapel Hill: University of North Carolina Press, 1989), pp. 51–88.
4 Richard A. Comfort, *Revolutionary Hamburg: Labor Politics in the Early Weimar Republic* (Stanford, CA: Stanford University Press, 1966); Ursula Büttner, *Politische Gerechtigkeit und sozialer Geist*, pp. 13–46; Angelika Voss, Ursula Büttner and Hermann Weber, *Vom Hamburger Aufstand zur politischen Isolierung: Kommunistische Politik 1923–1933 in Hamburg und im Deutschen Reich* (Hamburg: Landeszentrale für politische Bildung, 1983), pp. 9–45. Also Ursula Büttner, 'Der Stadtstaat als demokratische Republik', in *Hamburg: Geschichte der Stadt und ihrer Bewohner*, vol. 2, pp. 135ff. For Jewish politicians, see Martin Liepach, *Das Wahlverhalten der jüdischen Bevölkerung* (Tübingen: Mohr, 1996), pp. 16–26.
5 Thomas Krause, *Hamburg wird braun: Der Aufstieg der NSDAP von 1921–1933* (Hamburg: Ergebnisse-Verlag, 1987), pp. 17–50; Werner Jochmann, *Nationalsozialismus und Revolution: Ursprung und Geschichte der NSDAP in Hamburg, 1922–1933* (Frankfurt: Europäische Verlagsanstalt, 1983).
6 The definitive study is Uwe Lohalm, *Völkischer Radikalismus: Die Geschichte des Deutschvölkischen Schutz- und Trutz-Bundes, 1919–1923* (Hamburg: Leibniz, 1970). Their membership in 1919 was 30,000 and in 1920, 110,000.
7 Arnold Paucker, *Der jüdische Abwehrkampf gegen Antisemitismus und Nationalsozialismus in den letzten Jahren der Weimarer Republik* (Hamburg: Leibniz, 1968). Avraham Barkai, 'Politische Orientierung und Krisenbewußtsein', in Avraham Barkai,

Paul Mendes-Flohr and Steven M. Lowenstein, eds, *Deutsch-jüdische Geschichte in der Neuzeit*, vol. 4 (Munich: Beck, 1997), pp. 102–22, Eng. trans. as *German-Jewish History in Modern Times* (New York: Columbia University Press, 1998). Ulrich Dunker, *Der Reichsbund jüdischer Frontsoldaten, 1919–1938* (Düsseldorf: Droste, 1977). In 1924 the *Stahlhelm* excluded Jewish veterans.

8 Luise Solmitz, Journal, 24 May 1920, FZH, 11 S 7.

9 Max Warburg, 'Aus meinen Aufzeichnungen'; part of Warburg's memoirs were privately printed in 1952, but the whole manuscript is in the Warburg Archives at the bank in Hamburg. This account of his meeting with Rathenau is in the unpublished part of the manuscript, vol. 2, as was his attempt 'to rally influential people in Hamburg'.

10 Ron Chernow, *The Warburgs: The Twentieth Century Odyssey of a Remarkable Jewish Family* (New York: Random House, 1993), pp. 228–30.

11 Ursula Büttner, *Politische Gerechtigkeit und sozialer Geist*, pp. 171–232.

12 Martin Liepach, *Das Wahlverhalten der jüdischen Bevölkerung* (Tübingen: Mohr, 1996).

13 Max Warburg, 'Aus meinen Aufzeichnungen', pp. 127–8.

14 Leo Lippmann, *Mein Leben und meine amtliche Tätigkeit: Erinnerungen und ein Beitrag zur Finanzgeschichte Hamburgs*, ed. Werner Jochmann (Hamburg: Christians, 1964), pp. 298–9, 590, 656–77.

15 There is now a definitive study of the University of Hamburg, *Hochschulalltag im 'Dritten Reich': Die Hamburger Universität 1933–1945*, ed. Eckart Krause, Ludwig Huber and Holger Fischer, 3 vols (Berlin and Hamburg: Reimer, 1991).

16 *Enge Zeit: Spuren Vertriebener und Verfolgter der Hamburg Universität*, a volume accompanying an exhibition at the University of Hamburg in 1991, compiled by Angela Bottin and Rainer Nicolaysen (Berlin and Hamburg: Reimer, 1991), p. 16. This incident took place in 1919.

17 Toni Cassirer, 'Aus meinem Leben mit Ernst Cassirer' (the citations here are from the manuscript in the Leo Baeck Institute Archive, New York), p. 110. There are several book editions: New York (1950); Hildesheim (Gerstenberg, 1981); Hamburg (Meiner, 2003).

18 Eckart Krause et al., *Hochschulalltag im 'Dritten Reich'*, p. 137.

19 There is an interesting number of essays in *Jews in the Weimar Republic*, ed. Wolfgang Benz, Arnold Paucker and Peter Pulzer (Tübingen: Mohr Siebeck, 1998).

20 Toni Cassirer, 'Aus meinem Leben mit Ernst Cassirer'.

21 Helmut Fangmann, Udo Reifner and Norbert Steinborn, *Parteisoldaten: Die Hamburger Polizei im '3. Reich'* (Hamburg: VSA, 1987), pp. 26ff.

22 Erwin Garvens, Tagebuch, 13 and 16 March 1931, Staatsarchiv, Hamburg (hereafter St A H), 622-1 Garvens.

23 Luise Solmitz, Journal, 16 March 1931, FZH, 11 S 10.

24 Ina Lorenz, *Die Juden in Hamburg zur Zeit der Weimarer Republik* (Hamburg: Christians, 1987), vol. 2, pp. 1048–9. Max Warburg, 'Appell an die evangelische Kirche', 7 January 1932, and reply, 9 January 1932, ibid., pp. 1058–60.

25 Arnold Paucker, *Der Jüdische Abwehrkampf*, pp. 217–32.

26 Henning Timpke, *Dokumente zur Gleichschaltung des Landes Hamburg 1933* (Frankfurt: Europäische Verlagsanstalt, 1964), pp. 15ff.

27 Ursula Büttner, 'Das Ende der Weimarer Republik und der Aufstieg des Nationalsozialismus in Hamburg', in Ursula Büttner and Werner Jochmann, *Hamburg auf dem Weg ins Dritte Reich* (Hamburg: Landeszentrale für politische Bildung, 1983), pp. 7–38. In the *Reichstag* election in Hamburg on 6 November 1932, the vote for the Nazi Party dropped from 33.7 per cent to 27.2 per cent; the SPD also lost votes, from 31.7 per cent to 28.6 per cent, and the parties of the centre declined even further, scarcely holding 6 per cent between them; the communists increased their share from 17.7 per cent to 21.9 per cent, and the right-wing conservatives also gained, from 5.2 per cent to 9.3 per cent.

28 The standard work, with abundant detail and statistics, is Ursula Büttner, *Hamburg in der Staats- und Wirtschaftskrise 1928–1931* (Hamburg: Christians, 1982), especially pp. 109–15, 139–40, 539–42, 548–50, 676–85. For a balanced portrayal of

achievements and deficits of the Weimar years in Hamburg, see also Ursula Büttner, *Politische Gerechtigkeit und sozialer Geist*, pp. 190–287. Unemployment rose from 50,000 in December 1928 to 164,000 in December 1932. Unemployment benefits were wholly inadequate, little more than half the low wage, later reduced to a third.

29 Wolfgang Kopitzsch, 'Der Altoner Blutsontag', in *Arbeiter in Hamburg*, ed. Arno Herzig, Dieter Langewiesche and Arnold Sywottek (Hamburg: Verlag Erziehung und Wissenschaft, 1983), pp. 509–16. To gain Nazi support, Papen lifted the April 1932 ban on uniformed Nazis.

30 According to Kaufmann (Thomas Krause, *Hamburg wird braun*, p. 192), in the summer of 1932, of the 10,000 to 12,000 party members, 6,000 were unemployed. We have more accurate statistics for storm troopers: in September 1932, 2,600 of the 4,500 were unemployed. However, these were not mainly workers but the sons of skilled artisans (*Handwerkersöhne*) conscious of the lower-middle-class status from which they had fallen. The Nazi Party before 1933 was not predominantly a party of the proletariat. There is a good analysis in Thomas Krause, *Hamburg wird braun*, pp. 192–4.

31 Werner Jochmann, *Im Kampf um die Macht: Hitlers Rede vor dem Hamberger Nationalklub von 1919* (Frankfurt: Europäische Verlagsanstalt, 1960); Werner Johe, *Hitler in Hamburg* (Hamburg: Ergebnisse-Verlag, 1996), pp. 43–76.

32 Garvens, Tagebuch, 1 December 1930 and 15 February 1932, St A H, 622-1 Garvens.

33 Ursula Büttner and Martin Greschat, *Die verlassenen Kinder der Kirche* (Göttingen: Vandenhoeck & Ruprecht, 1998), p. 35. In this book Professor Büttner deals with the attitude of the Protestant Church to the persecution of the Jews and converted Jews, pp. 31–69.

34 Ina Lorenz, *Die Juden in Hamburg zur Zeit der Weimarer Republik*, vol. 2, pp. 1045–60.

35 Rabbi Posner to DEKB-Amt (*Deutsches Evangelisches Kirchenbundesamt*), received 5 August 1932; *Evangelisch-Lutherisches Landeskirchenamt* (for Schleswig-Holstein) to Posner, 9 August 1932; DEKB-Amt to Posner, 8 September 1932; Posner to DEKB-Amt, 9 October 1932; *Evangelisches Presseamt für Deutschland* to DEKB-Amt, 19 October 1932, Evangelisches Zentrala Archiv, Berlin.

36 Garvens, Tagebuch, 25 April 1932, St A H, 622-1 Garvens.

37 Thomas Krause, *Hamburg wird braun*, pp. 192ff.

38 Leo Lippmann, *Mein Leben und meine amtliche Tätigkeit*, pp. 619–20.

39 *Hamburger Anzeiger*, 26 May 1931.

40 Manuscript, Warburg Bank Archives, Hamburg; *Israelitisches Familienblatt*, January 1933.

41 For Germany as a whole, see Theodore Abel, *Why Hitler Came to Power* (Cambridge, MA: Harvard University Press, 1986), and Jürgen Falter, *Hitlers Wähler* (Munich: Beck, 1991). The events in Hamburg on which the interpretations in Luise Solmitz's Journal are based are recounted in Ursula Büttner and Werner Jochmann, *Hamburg auf dem Weg ins Dritte Reich*.

42 All the quotations are from Luise Solmitz's Journal: 30 December 1928, 6 September 1930, 11–12 September 1930, 14 September 1930, 22 October 1930, 16 January 1931, 25 February 1931, 22 October 1931, 4 February 1932, 24 March 1932, 30 January 1933, FZH, 11 S 8-11.

3 How will it end?

1 It is not clearly established whether Baeck actually used this frequently quoted phrase. It seems, however, probable, as contemporaries later vouched for the fact.

2 Ursula Büttner, 'Das Ende der Weimar Republik' (pp. 7, 32–3), Werner Jochmann, 'Die Errichtung der nationalsozialistischen Herrschaft in Hamburg' (pp. 39–73) and documents, in Ursula Büttner and Werner Jochmann, *Hamburg auf dem Weg ins Dritte Reich* (Hamburg: Landeszentrale für politische Bildung, 1983). The crisis of the governing parties in the Hamburg senate after they had lost the majority in the local state *Bürgerschaft* elections of 27 September 1931 is detailed in Büttner, *Politische Gerechtigkeit und sozialer Geist* (Hamburg: Christians, 1985), pp. 274–87.

3 *CV Zeitung*, 17 March 1933.
4 Luise Solmitz, Journal, 2 February 1933, 6 February 1933, 19 February 1933, FZH, 11 S 11.
5 Ibid., 21 February 1933, 25 February 1933.
6 Ibid., 1 March 1933.
7 Ibid., 3 March 1933, 5 March 1933.
8 Henning Timpke, ed., *Dokumente zur Gleichschaltung des Landes Hamburg 1933* (Frankfurt: Europäische Verlagsanstalt, 1964).
9 There is a huge literature on the Nazi takeover. Excellent overviews with large bibliographies are Ian Kershaw, *Hitler 1889–1936: Hubris* (Harmondsworth: Penguin, 1998), pp. 431–95; and Michael Burleigh, *The Third Reich: A New History* (London: Macmillan, 2000), the Weimar period, pp. 27–145, and the first months of the Nazis in power, pp. 149–97. A judicious account by a German historian is Bernd-Jürgen Wendt, *Deutschland 1933–1945: Das 'Dritte' Reich: Handbuch zur Geschichte* (Hannover: Fackelträger, 1995), pp. 1–125. A more recent publication, stressing the violence of the early weeks and months, is Richard J. Evans, *The Third Reich in Power*, volume 2 of a trilogy (Harmondsworth: Penguin, 2005). The best account is in German: Ursula Büttner's *Weimar* (Stuttgart: Klett-Cotta, 2008) convincingly demonstrates how too many burdens were placed on the Weimar Republic – '*die überforderte Republik*'.
10 Copies of the election pamphlets of the *Deutsch-Nationale Volkspartei*, in author's private possession.
11 Results of the *Reichstag* elections of 5 March 1933

For Germany			For Hamburg		
NSDAP	17,277,328	43.9%	NSDAP	318,747	38.8%
National allies	3,136,979	8.0%	National allies	65,540	8.0%
SDP	7,181,273	18.3%	SDP	220,748	26.9%
KPD	4,847,939	12.3%	KPD	144,333	17.6%
Centre Party	4,425,000	11.2%	Centre Party	15,714	1.9%
BVP	1,073,551	2.7%	DVP	19,724	2.4%
DVP	432,255	1.1%			
DStP	334,315	0.8%	DStP	28,470	3.5%
Participation	88.8%		Participation	88.95%	
Spoilt votes	0.8%		Spoilt votes	1.1%	
	(315,008)			(9,168)	
Population:	65,200,000		Population	1,230,838	

Results of the *Reichstag* elections of 6 November 1932

For Germany			For Hamburg		
NSDAP	11,737,021	33.1%	NSDAP	207,057	27.2%
DNVP	2,959,053	8.3%	DNVP	71,067	9.3%
SPD	7,247,901	20.4%	SPD	218.078	28.6%
KPD	5,980,239	16.9%	KPD	166,748	21.9%
Centre Party	4,230,545	11.9%	Centre Party	13,316	1.7%
BVP	1,094,597	3.1%			
DVP	660,889	1.9%	DVP	25,199	3.3%
DStP	336,447	0.9%	DDP/StP	41,136	5.4%
Participation	80.6%		Participation	83.0%	
Spoilt votes	0.8%		Spoilt votes	1.4%	
	(287,471)			(10,543)	

Source: Wahlen in Deutschland; www.wahlen-in-deutschland.de.

Historians have discussed the question of who voted for the Nazis. The problem is that the composition of the party membership cannot be equated with that of the general voters. There is agreement that their success was due to a higher voter turnout and that they drew voters from all classes. In 'red' Hamburg, the SPD and KPD were much stronger than in the rest of Germany, together, despite persecution and harassment, polling on 5 March 1933 44.5 per cent, only just behind the NSDAP and DNVP on 46.8 per cent. The weaker showing of the NSDAP in Hamburg obliged them to form a coalition government, but not for long before assuming sole power. In Hamburg, as elsewhere, the one-party state evolved within a few weeks. Parliamentary democracy was dead.

12 Timpke, *Dokumente zur Gleichschaltung des Landes Hamburg 1933* is still the best account of the Nazi takeover in Hamburg in 1933; see pp. 15–94, 147–50, 169–94 and 227–35. For details of arrests and executions in Hamburg, St A H, 113–2 Innere Verwaltung (Department of the Interior), A II 4b. For a recent multi-authored history of Hamburg with nineteen researched contributions, published for the Forschungsstelle für Zeitgeschichte in Hamburg, *Hamburg im Dritten Reich*, ed. Josef Schmid (Göttingen: Wallstein, 2005).

13 Records of the NSDAP in Hamburg, November 1933, St A H, 614-2/5.

14 *Gauverordnungsblatt* no. 13, 16 November 1933; *Rundschreiben* (circular) 164 of NSDAP, *Gauleitung Hamburg*, 15 December 1933. Also *Bericht über die Ergebnisse in den einzelnen Kreisen am 12 November 1933*, St A H, 614-2/5, A4, vol. 1. The comparable figures for Germany including Hamburg: 95.1 per cent voted to leave the League of Nations in the plebiscite and 92.1 per cent in the *Reichstag* elections; Kershaw, *Hitler 1889–1996: Hubris*, p. 495. The referendum in Hamburg showed that most opposition was recorded in the working-class districts – Billwärder Ausschlag (25 per cent), Hammerbrook (22.8 per cent), Neustadt (19.4 per cent) and St Pauli (18.7 per cent) – and the least in the well-to-do districts – Rotherbaum (8.1 per cent) and Harvestehude (7.5 per cent).

15 Luise Solmitz, Journal, 10 November 1933, FZH, 11 S 11.

16 Frank Bajohr, 'Hamburgs "Führer"': Zur Person und Tätigkeit des Hamburger NSDAP-Gauleiters, Karl Kaufmann (1900–1969)', in *Hamburg in der NS-Zeit: Ergebnisse neuerer Forschungen*, ed. Frank Bajohr and Joachim Szodrzynski (Hamburg: Ergebnisse-Verlag, 1995), pp. 59–91. This report is also based on the documents of the party relating to Kaufmann, at the time kept in the Berlin Document Centre, now in the Bundesarchiv Berlin (National Archives).

17 The conclusion is based on my analysis of the records of the *Senatskanzlei-Personalabteilung*, St A H, 131-10. The best treatment of the issue is Uwe Lohalm, '… *anständig und aufopferungsbereit': Öffentlicher Dienst und Nationalsozialismus in Hamburg 1933 bis 1945* (Hamburg: Ergebnisse Verlag, 2001), pp. 11–25.

Hamburg	Higher civil servants	Lower ranks	Workers
Employed 1 Jan 1933	17,251	12,042	13,480
Employed 1 Apr 1934	17,114	12,701	12,518
Dismissed by 31 Jan 1934		574	
Dismissed by 30 Apr 1934		1,651	

Source: Lohalm, ibid., p. 71.

Although in the lower ranks of the police many had supported the Social Democrats, only 160 were removed. For a detailed analysis, Uwe Lohalm's study is essential.

18 There is a file in the *Forschungsstelle*, FZH, 12-1/A, on Georg Ahrens, based on his legal trial in April 1948, recording the statements of witnesses Erich Lüth, W. Schiedemann, Professor Ipsen and Dr Paul Lindemann. The reference Ahrens gave to Dr Friedrich Wohlwill, lecturer in pathology, 13 April 1934, St A H, 131-10 *Senatskanzlei-Personalabteilung*, 1934 Ja I 9. For Friedrich Wohlwill, see Anna von

Villiez, *Mit aller Kraft verdrängt: Entrechtung und Verfolgung 'nicht arischer' Ärzte in Hamburg 1933 bis 1945* (Munich and Hamburg: Dölling & Galitz, 2009), pp. 429f.

19 For the terror against political opponents, see Gertrud Meyer, *Nacht über Hamburg: Berichte und Dokumente 1933–1945* (Frankfurt: Röderberg, 1971), pp. 9–51 and 174–5.

20 Details about the lives of Eggers, Deutschmann and Jansen is based on their post-war trials in Hamburg.

21 *Stadthaus in Hamburg: Gestapo-Hauptquartier 1933 bis 1943*, ed. Reinhard Buff (Hamburg: Wartenberg, 1981).

22 Reported in *Hamburger Fremdenblatt*, 26 May 1933. See also Timpke, *Dokumente zur Gleichschaltung des Landes Hamburg 1933*, pp. 227–35.

23 For Rothenberger's career and administration of justice, see Werner Johe, *Die gleichgeschaltete Justiz* (Frankfurt: Europäische Verlagsanstalt, 1967), pp. 58ff.

24 Erwin Garvens, Tagebuch, 20 July and 19 August 1933, St A H, 622-1 Garvens.

25 Timpke, *Dokumente zur Gleichschaltung des Landes Hamburg 1933*, pp. 176–7.

26 *Hamburgischer Correspondent*, 31 March 1933. Frank Bajohr, *'Arisierung' in Hamburg* (Hamburg: Christians, 1997), pp. 44–54; Eng. trans. as *'Aryanisation' in Hamburg: The Economic Exclusion of Jews and the Confiscation of their Property in Nazi Germany* (Oxford: Berghahn, 2001), pp. 28–34.

27 John E. Kehl, US consul general at the American embassy in Berlin, 31 March 1933 and April 1933, State Department Records, National Archives, Washington, DC.
    The US administration took no such benevolent attitude to the persecution of the Jews. See especially Leon Dominian, consul general, to the Secretary of State, 21 April 1933; memorandum of Secretary of State Cordell Hull of a discussion with Hans Luther, German ambassador, on 'Mistreatment of Jews in Germany', 3 May 1933. Cordell Hull represented US views and expectations of a return to normal conditions, and Luther responded with assurances that the situation was constantly improving.

28 Max Plaut, interview recorded by Dr Schottelius, 3 July 1954, FZH, 12 Plaut.

29 Ibid., 19 September 1955.

30 A fascinating guide is Harald Vieth, *Von der Hallerstraße 6/8 zum Isebek und Dammtor: Jüdische Schicksale und Alltägliches aus Harvestehude-Rotherbaum in Hamburg seit der Jahrhundertwende* (Hamburg: H. Vieth, 1991), here, Café Timpe, p. 97. A lavishly illustrated multi-authored account of Jewish life is *Eine verschwundene Welt: Jüdisches Leben am Grindel*, ed. Ursula Wamser and Wilfried Weinke (Springe: Klampen, 2006).

31 Luise Solmitz, Journal, 11 March, 1 April, 5 April, 15 April 1933, FZH, 11 S 11.

32 Ibid., 1 April, 5 April, 15 April 1933, FZH, 11 S 11.

33 Eberhard Röhm and Jörg Thierfelder, *Juden, Christen, Deutsche*, vol. 1: *1933–1935* (Stuttgart: Calwer, 1990), pp. 141–66.

34 For a listing of Jewish businesses, see Frank Bajohr, *'Aryanisation' in Hamburg*, pp. 292–305: 625 were Aryanised in 1938–9; in 1938 in Greater Hamburg (including Altona, Wandsbek and Harburg) there were still 1,201 businesses before Aryanisation; between 1933 and 1938 many businesses were closed. We can only estimate Jewish businesses in 1933; there must have been well over 1,200.

35 Ibid., pp. 22–6. For the boycott in Hamburg, pp. 28–34.

36 Until 1934 the Tietz department store remained in Jewish ownership.

37 Deputation für Handel, Schiffahrt und Gewerbe (Department of Trade) to Finanzdeputation, 19 September 1933, St A H, 313-5 Steuerverwaltung, A 50b.

38 Report in St A H, 132-1 Senatskommission für die Reichs- und Auswärtigen Angelegenheiten, III A1 a1 Band 3.

39 One copy of the senate circular of 18 March 1933 is in St A H, 321-2 Baudeputation, B 17.

40 Ron Chernow, *The Warburgs: The Twentieth Century Odyssey of a Remarkable Jewish Family* (New York: Random House, 1993), pp. 325ff; also the foundation of

the Kara Corporation, funding the emigration of Jewish psychiatrists from interest accumulating on the US brothers' loan to the Warburg bank as a consequence of the Karstadt loan, p. 439. There is further material on relations with Karstadt in the Warburg Bank Archives.

41 Minutes of the meetings of the Hamburg Chamber of Commerce, 11 April, 12 April, 21 April, 12 June 1933, Archive of the Hamburg Chamber of Commerce. See also Hans Bielfeldt, *Staat und Wirtschaft: Beiträge zur Geschichte der Handelskammer Hamburg* (Hamburg: Christians, 1980).

42 Max Warburg, 'Aus meinen Aufzeichnungen', pp. 149–50, Warburg Bank Archives; Chernow, *The Warburgs*, p. 380.

43 Chernow, *The Warburgs*, pp. 429ff. In the bank's archives are preserved the names of the firms that continued to do business with the bank. The archives are very voluminous and when I examined them were uncatalogued, on shelf after shelf, and had evidently not been used by researchers. I was able to focus only on a few in the account I have given here.

44 See the article by Annegret Ehmann about Euler in the *Bensheim Zeitung*, 11 November 1993. On the status of the *Mischlinge*, see Ursula Büttner, *Die Not der Juden teilen: Christlich-jüdische Familien im Dritten Reich: Beispiel und Zeugnis des Schriftstellers Robert Brendel* (Hamburg: Christians, 1988); the introduction is the most reliable treatment of Nazi legislation on the changing definitions of 'non-Aryans', the *Mischlinge* and Jews. See also Jeremy Noakes, 'Wohin gehören die "Judenmischlinge"? Die Entstehung der ersten Durchführungsverordnungen zu den Nürnberger Gesetzen', and John A. S. Grenville, 'Die "Endlösung" und die "Judenmischlinge" im Dritten Reich', in *Das Unrechtsregime: Internationale Forschung über den Nationalsozialismus*, vol. 2: *Verfolgung – Exil – Belasteter Neubeginn*, ed. Ursula Büttner (Hamburg: Christians, 1986), pp. 69– 89 and 91–121 respectively. Statistics can only be estimated. Professor Büttner's authoritative figures (*Die Not der Juden teilen*, pp. 14f.) are based on those of Leo Lippmann, a good authority, calculated in 1941.

45 Ursula Büttner and Martin Greschat, *Die verlassenen Kinder der Kirche* (Göttingen: Vandenhoeck & Ruprecht, 1998), pp. 220 and 127; also Jeremy Noakes, 'The Development of Nazi Policy towards the German-Jewish "Mischlinge", 1933–1945', *Leo Baeck Institute Year Book*, 34 (1989), pp. 291–354.

46 The documents were kindly made available to me after a lecture in Berlin by a group of young scholars who remained anonymous. The quotations are from the records of the Evangelisches Zentralarchiv, Küsteramt Zehlendorf, 1934.

47 *Nationalsozialistiche Monatshefte*, October 1930.

48 Uwe Lohalm, *'… anständig und aufopferungsbereit': Öffentlicher Dienst und Nationalsozialismus 1933 bis 1945* (Hamburg: Ergebnisse-Verlag, 2001), pp. 11–25; see pp. 71–3 for detailed tables. On 1 January 1933 the Hamburg civil service consisted of 42,773 persons, and by January 1935 there were 40,854; some state civil servants had become employed by the Reich and vice versa, so the figures are not strictly comparable, but they show only a small decline.

49 The new senate confirmed his appointment on 11 March 1933, three days after the appointment of the new senate. Leo Lippmann, *Mein Leben und meine amtliche Tätigkeit: Erinnerungen und ein Beitrag zur Finanzgeschichte Hamburgs*, ed. Werner Jochmann (Hamburg: Christians, 1964), pp. 612, 620, 623ff. Leo Lippmann, *'… daß Ich wie ein guter Deutscher empfinde und handele': Zur Geschichte der Deutsch-Israelitischen Gemeinde in Hamburg in der Zeit vom Herbst 1935 bis zum Ende 1942* (Hamburg: Dölling & Galitz, 1993), introduction by Ina S. Lorenz, 'Dr. Leo Lippmann: Zwei Berichte', pp. 7–9. For the Nazi takeover in Hamburg, see also Werner Johe, 'Im Dritten Reich 1933–45', in *Hamburg: Geschichte der Stadt und ihrer Bewohner*, ed. Werner Jochmann and Hans-Dieter Loose, vol. 2 (Hamburg: Hoffmann & Campe, 1986), pp. 265–320. A detailed analysis is in Henning Timpke, *Dokumente zur Gleichschaltung des Landes Hamburg 1933*, pp. 75–91, 129–50.

50 Lippmann's funeral oration, 13 October 1933, St A H, 622-1 Familie Lippmann, A4, vol 2, p. 51.
51 For an excellent general treatment, see *Medizinische Wissenschaft im 'Dritten Reich': Kontinuität, Anpassung und Opposition an der Hamburger Medizinischen Fakultät*, ed. Hendrik van den Bussche and Angela Bottin (Berlin and Hamburg: Dietrich Reimer, 1987); for Hamburg, see the thoroughly researched study by Anna von Villiez, *Mit aller Kraft verdrängt*.
52 Matthias Andrae, 'Die Vertreibung der jüdischen Ärzte des Allgemeinen Krankenhauses Hamburg-St. Georg im Nationalsozialismus' (diss., Universität Hamburg, 1997, microfiche; rev. ed., Norderstedt: Books on Demand, 2003). Also family papers of Arthur Lippmann, St A H, 622-1 Familie Lippman A4.
53 John A. S. Grenville, 'Juden, "Nichtarier" und "Deutsche Ärzte": Die Anpassung der Ärzte im Dritten Reich', in *Die Deutschen und die Judenverfolgung im Dritten Reich*, ed. Ursula Büttner (Hamburg: Christians, 1992), pp. 191–206.
54 *Deutsches Ärzteblatt*, 21 May 1932, p. 207. See also John A. S. Grenville, 'Juden, "Nichtarier" und "Deutsche Ärzte"'; Susanne Hahn, 'Revolution der Heilkunst: Ausweg aus der Krise?', in *Der Wert des Menschen: Medizin in Deutschland 1918– 1945*, ed. Christian Pross and Götz Aly (Berlin: Hentrich, 1989), pp. 71–99.
55 Accurate statistics are difficult to establish, especially distinguishing Jews (four or three Jewish grandparents) and non-Aryans (two or one Jewish grandparents), as they were not differentiated until 1935. On 20 November 1934 the *Hamburger Tageblatt* cites 267 Jewish and 73 other non-Aryans. The *Ärzteblatt* statistic for Hamburg illustrates the plight of all doctors: in 1934 there were 1,511 doctors, or one doctor for every 806 people, whereas in 1913 the proportion was one doctor for every 1,359 people (*Ärzteblatt für Hamburg und Schleswig-Holstein*, 1 December 1935).
    A list of Jewish doctors: *Jüdische Ärzte im Bereich der Reichsärztekammer*, 13 November 1936, St A H, A 832/1 (library), box 1. The list was marked 'confidential' (*nur für den Dienstgebrauch*). There is now quite a large literature on doctors in Nazi Germany.
56 Toni Cassirer, 'Aus meinem Leben mit Ernst Cassirer', manuscript, Leo Baeck Institute, New York; the whole of this account is based on pp. 175–186. Rektor Leo Raape to Cassirer, 8 April 1933, St A H, 364-5 I Universität I, A 1.6. His letter is printed in the 1950 edition of Toni Cassirer's memoirs, pp. 176f.
57 Even professors who should have been exempt from dismissal under the Hindenburg exceptions were pensioned off, such as Professor Walter Berendsohn (17 July 1933), also honorary professors Ernst Delbanco (17 July 1933) and Fritz Saxl (13 July 1933) and Professor Erwin Panofsky, despite faculty attempts to retain him. St A H, 364-5 I Universität I, A 1.6.
    The splendid comprehensive history of the University of Hamburg during the Nazi years has no equal in Germany. It was a huge project in three volumes, with fifty-six contributors examining general issues, each faculty and each department: Eckart Krause, Ludwig Huber and Holger Fischer, eds, *Hochschulalltag im 'Dritten Reich': Die Hamburger Universität 1933–1945* (Berlin and Hamburg: Reimer, 1991). For the facts here cited, particularly, Eckart Krause, 'Wie es dazu kam', pp. xxi–xlix; Barbara Vogel, 'Anpassung und Widerstand', pp. 3–83; Peter Freimark, 'Juden an der Hamburger Universität', pp. 125–49; Rainer Hering, 'Der "unpolitische" Professor', pp. 85–111; Geoffrey J. Giles, 'Professor und Partei', pp. 113–24; Peter Borowsky, 'Die Philosophische Fakultät 1933 bis 1945', pp. 441–58.
    For Albrecht Mendelssohn Bartholdy, Moritz Liepman, Gerhard Lassar, Kurt Perels and Magdalena Schoch (Mendelssohn Bartholdy's assistant), see Norman Paech and Ulrich Krampe, 'Die Rechts- und Staatswissenschaft', in *Hochschulalltag im 'Dritten Reich'*, pp. 867–901; Rainer Nicolaysen, 'Für Recht und Gerechtigkeit: Über das couragierte Leben der Juristin Magdalena Schoch (1897–1987)', in *Zeitschrift des Vereins für hamburgische Geschichte*, 92 (2006), pp. 113–43. Professor Mendelssohn Bartholdy was the honorary director of the famous *Institut für Auswärtige Politik*. For its history, see

Gisela Gantzel-Kress, 'Das Institut für Auswärtige Politik ...', in *Hochschulalltag im 'Dritten Reich'*, pp. 913–38. For another exiled scholar, then assistant at the Institute for Social Economy, see the splendid biography by Rainer Nicolaysen, *Siegfried Landshut: Die Wiederentdeckung der Politik: Eine Biographie* (Frankfurt: Jüdischer Verlag, 1997). Sixty-one university teachers, Jews and non-Aryans, were dismissed or retired in 1933 and a few later – a 'cleansing' more radical than among other professions.

For Professor Otto Stern's achievements in physical chemistry, see Wolfgang Walter, 'Otto Stern, Leistung und Schicksal', in *Hochschulalltag im 'Dritten Reich'*, pp. 1142–54.

58 *Hochschulalltag im Dritten Reich*, pp. 1123–5.
59 Peter Freimark, 'Juden an der Hamburger Universität', ibid., pp. 133–42. On the students of the university, Michael Grüttner, 'Die Studentenschaft 1930 bis 1945', ibid., pp. 201–36.

Statistics in St A H, Universität I, 364-5 I, N 20.1, reveal the rapid decline in 1933 of 'non-Aryan' students. Among registered students for the summer semester 1933 were 110 full 'racial' Jews; of these, the fathers of 62 were war veterans. There were 36 *Mischlinge* first degree (two Jewish grandparents) and second degree (one Jewish grandparent). In the winter semester 1933, there were 26 full racial Jews and 25 *Mischlinge* registered; 29 communist students were also excluded (Hamburg University report 12 October and 8 December 1933). In the summer semester 1934 there were so few 'racial' Jews and 'non-Aryans' attending that the number was within its 'legal' quota.
60 Luise Solmitz, Journal, 20 May 1933, FZH 11 S 11.

4 Courage in adversity

1 Ernst Loewenberg, 'Mein Leben in Deutschland vor und nach dem 30 Januar 1933' (Harvard History Prize Competition, March 1940), manuscript, Leo Baeck Institute Archive, New York, pp. 12–17.
2 The correspondence and file on Ida Eberhardt is in St A H, 361-3 Schulwesen Personalakten, Lichtwarkschule 6.
3 Hildegard Milberg, Schulpolitik in der pluralistischen Gesellschaft: Die politischen und sozialen Aspekte der Schulreform in Hamburg, 1890–1935 (Hamburg: Leibniz, 1970), for the statistics, pp. 370f. See also Uwe Lohalm, '... anständig und aufopfer-ungsbereit': Öffentlicher Dienst und Nationalsozialismus in Hamburg 1933 bis 1945 (Hamburg: Ergebnisse-Verlag, 2001), p. 73; Hans-Peter de Lorent, 'Personalpolitik', in 'Die Fahne Hoch': Schulpolitik und Schulalltag in Hamburg unterm Hakenkreuz, ed. Reiner Lehberger and Hans-Peter de Lorent (Hamburg: Ergebnisse-Verlag, 1986), pp. 203–12. In August 1933, Senator Witt appointed 315 new headmasters and deputy headmasters; by 1935 more than half of the old headmasters had been replaced. In 1933, 204 teachers were moved to different schools. On the basis of the 7 April 1933 law, 637 teachers had been dismissed or pensioned by 1935 – nearly all the older teachers and those who had supported the socialist parties, but generally with full pensions (only older teachers benefited from this ruling, as pensions started only after ten years in office and with very small sums which increased only slowly); 468 new young teachers were appointed to replace them.
4 Dr W. Unna to Dr Zindler, 11 September 1935; Zindler to *Landesunterrichtsbehörde*, 11 September 1935; St A H, 361-2 II, Oberschulbehörde II, Lichtwarkschule.
5 The *Paulsenstift*, named after Charlotte Paulsen, was founded in 1849 for the poor and moved to new buildings in 1866. Anna Wohlwill, chosen by colleagues as head-mistress, developed the school according to the model of Friedrich Froebel; child self-activity was encouraged so that children grew up in harmony.
6 Hanna Glinzer to Carl Melchior, 15 April 1933; Melchior to Glinzer, 18 April 1933; complaint by a parent to Kaufmann, 4 June 1934; Hanna Glinzer's reply, 18 June 1934, St AH, 361-3, Schulwesen Personalakten, Paulsenstift, 52.

7 From Ralph Giordano's semi-autobiography, *Die Bertinis*, quoted by Reiner Lehberger, 'Als unsichtbare Mauern wuchsen', in *'Die Fahne Hoch'*, pp. 309–12.
8 Puttfarken, 'Report on Jews at the *Johanneum*', 14 February 1938, St A H, 361-2 II Oberschulbehörde II, Johanneum, A1 no. 50; see also a contribution by one of the students, Gerd-Michael Lackmann, 'Die Aufstellung einer Hitlerbüste in meiner Schule – 20 September 1935', in *Das Johanneum: Mitteilungen des Vereins ehemaliger Schüler*, no. 1 (1981), pp. 2–19. Before 1938 there was no requirement to isolate Jewish children at their desks; Puttfarken took the step on his own.
9 *Wilhelm-Gymnasium Hamburg 1881–1981: Eine Dokumentation über 100 Jahre Wilhelm-Gymnasium*, ed. Peter-Rudolf Schultz (Hamburg: Hower, 1981), pp. 140–93; Rudolf Heymann is quoted on p. 173. It is interesting to note the inconsistencies in Nazi Germany. Herbert Spiro was a Jewish boy. In 1935, a year early at the age of ten, he passed the entrance examination to both the *Wilhelm-Gymnasium* and the *Johanneum* with such high marks that the latter, despite its Nazi enthusiasm, competed with the former to have him. Dr Lundius, headmaster of the *Wilhelm-Gymnasium*, was not a rabid Nazi, though occasionally he appeared in SA uniform.
10 Not every teacher was Jewish; German literature was generally taught by a Christian even in the Nazi years. Double that number of young Jews attended German state schools in 1936. Ursula Randt, *Die Talmud-Tora-Schule in Hamburg, 1805 bis 1842* (Munich: Dölling & Galitz, 2005).
11 Finanzsenator to Krogmann, 29 August 1935, St AH, 131-4, *Senatskanzlei-Präsidialabteilung*, 1934 A11/9.
12 Arthur Spier's account is in letter to Dr Grosthoff, 30 April 1980, Institut für die Geschichte der deutschen Juden Archive, 14-002 Arthur Spier.
13 The account is based in part on 'Claus Göttsche, 1899–1945', at www.rrz.uni-hamburg.de/rz3a035//goettsche.html. Göttsche's official rank in 1938 was Kriminalkommissar and SS Hauptsturmführer. The division of the Gestapo dealing with Jews, Freemasons and Sects, 1935–1938, was Dezernat II B and that with Jews alone the Judendezernat II B 2. The regional Gestapo Office was housed in Hamburg, 8 Stadthausbrücke; the Dezernat II B and II B2 at 2 Düsternstraße until 1942 and at 38 Rothenbaumchaussee, the former Jewish community offices, after 1942. Göttsche was transferred in 1943 to the Gestapo Dezernat II N dealing with news.
14 File in St A H, 361-2 II, Oberschulbehörde II, *Israelitische Töchterschule*, B263. For its history, see Ursula Randt, *Carolinenstraße 35: Geschichte der Mädchenschule der Deutsch-Israelitischen Gemeinde in Hamburg* (Hamburg: Verein für Hamburgische Geschichte, 1984).
15 *Gemeindeblatt der Deutsch-Israelitschen Gemeinde zu Hamburg*, 17 October 1930, FZH, 624-3. In May 1933, 620 pupils attended the girls' school, which increased to 710, but emigration reduced their number after 1937.
16 For this account of Wilhelm Oberdörffer I am indebted to Dr Randt for material she placed generously at my disposal.
17 *Versammlungsprotokolle* (minutes of meetings), 20 March 1930–14 May 1935, St A H, 614-2/4 *Bürgerverein für Harvestehude-Rotherbaum*, 1 vol. 4.
18 Wilfried Weinke, 'The Persecution of Jewish Lawyers in Hamburg: A Case Study: Max Eichholz and Herbert Michaelis', *Leo Baeck Institute Year Book*, 42 (1997), pp. 221–37.
19 *Mitteilungsblatt des Centralausschusses Hamburgischer Bürgervereine*, 6 April 1933.
20 *Versammlungsprotokoll*, 13 May 1933, St A H, 614-2/4 *Bürgerverein für Harvestehude-Rotherbaum*, 1 vol. 4.
21 For all the new regulations affecting Jews in 1933, see *Das Schwarzbuch: Tatsachen und Dokumente: Die Lage der Juden in Deutschland 1933* (Frankfurt: Ullstein, 1983); also, for the later years, Joseph Walk, ed., *Das Sonderrecht für die Juden im NS-Staat* (Heidelberg: Müller, 1981) — an invaluable citation of laws and ordinances affecting the 'racial Jews'.

22 A good overview is Herbert A. Strauss, 'Jewish Autonomy within the Limits of National Socialist Policy: The Communities and the Reichsvertretung', in *Die Juden im nationalsozialistischen Deutschland 1933–1943*, ed. Arnold Paucker, Sylvia Gilchrist and Barbara Suchy (Tübingen: Mohr, 1986), pp. 125–52. Another valuable study is by Avraham Barkai, *'Wehr Dich': Der Centralverein deutscher Staatsbürger jüdischen Glaubens 1893–1938* (Munich: Beck, 2002).

23 'Berufsumschichtung und Auswanderung', by Herbert Wiesenthal, printed manuscript issued by the *Jüdischer Zentral-Verein E.V.*, 1936, private collection. Jewish Agency statistics of Jews emigrating to Palestine (note: more mainly from Central Europe than from Germany)

	From Germany	*From elsewhere, mainly Central Europe*
1933	7,200	23,117
1934	9,429	32,930
1935	7,860	53,994

24 Ina Lorenz, 'Seefahrt-Hachschara in Hamburg (1935–1938): Lucy Borchardt: Die einzige jüdische Reederin der Welt', *Zeitschrift des Vereins für Hamburgische Geschichte*, 83/1 (1997), pp. 445–72. Fairplay is today one of the leading companies offering these services in ports throughout the world.

25 Avraham Barkai, 'German Interests in the ha'avara Transfer Agreement, 1933–1939', *Leo Baeck Institute Year Book*, 35 (1990), pp. 245–66. There are a few records of transactions also in the archives of the Warburg bank. The Reich Ministry of Finance Circular 54/1933, *Palestina Treuhandstelle* (Haavara Agreement), can be found on the internet.

26 Alan E. Steinweis, 'Hans Hinkel and German Jewry', *Leo Baeck Institute Year Book*, 38 (1993), pp. 209–19. The standard work on the Kulturbund is Volker Dahm, *Geschlossene Vorstellung: Der Jüdische Kulturbund in Deutschland, 1933–1941* (Berlin: Hentrich, 1992). There is a collection of memories and photographs, ed. Eike Geisel and Henryk M. Broder, *Premiere und Pogrom: Der Jüdische Kulturbund 1933–1941* (Berlin: Siedler, 1992). By August 1936, the Kulturbund had sold 5,800 seats. It enjoyed much more success and support in Hamburg than in Berlin.

27 The meeting on 27 and 28 April 1935 is recorded in a *Protokoll der Tagung* in the Alfred Hirschberg collection, Leo Baeck Institute Archive, New York, AR 3975; in the Hamburg collection in the archives, AR 2590, there is an almost complete collection of programmes and circulars of the Hamburg *Kulturbund* from 1934 to 1938. Finally, Heydrich to Gestapo in all German states, 13 August 1935, *Richtlinien*, ordered that assimilationist tendencies were to be suppressed and leaders of local *Kulturbünde* should as far as possible be Zionists; Bundesarchiv, Koblenz/Berlin, R 58/276.

28 Statistics in Herbert Freeden, *The Jewish Press in the Third Reich* (Oxford: Berg, 1993). In 1934, the circulation of *C.V.- Zeitung* was 50,000; *Jüdische Rundschau*, 37,000; the (Hamburg) *Israelitisches Familienblatt*, 36,500; of the newspapers published by the communities (*Gemeinden*), the circulation was, in Berlin, 46,000; Frankfurt, 7,200; Breslau, 5,300; Munich, 4,500 – the total amounting to 205,850. Few Jewish families were without one of these papers. See also Katrin Diehl, *Die jüdische Presse im Dritten Reich: Zwischen Selbstbehauptung und Fremdbestimmung* (Tübingen: Niemeyer, 1997).

29 *C.V.- Zeitung*, 15 June, 17 August and 20 September 1933; reference to *Nationalsozialistische Monatshefte*, no. 38, May 1933.

30 *Jüdische Rundschau*, 13 April, 29 August, 20 October 1933, quoted by Freeden, *The Jewish Press in the Third Reich*, p. 51. The 'yellow badge' was introduced eight years

later. Weltsch's comment was not a 'prophecy'; his reference was to medieval times. Jews should hold their heads high and not hide their religion. He expected in 1933 the majority to go on living in Germany, which is probably why he later regretted having made his clarion call to German Jewry.

31 Birgit Wulff, *Arbeitslosigkeit und Arbeitsbeschaffungsmaßnahmen in Hamburg 1933– 1939: Eine Untersuchung zur nationalsozialistischen Wirtschafts- und Sozialpolitik* (Frankfurt: Lang, 1987). Temporary work was provided for twenty-six weeks, then unemployment pay; 9,000 permanent jobs were created. By the end of 1934, unemployment in Hamburg fell by only a quarter, from 167,000 to 112,000; this was much less than in other German cities. The high proportion of 'blue-collar' unemployed in Hamburg is noticeable. See also Werner Johe, 'Im Dritten Reich 1933–45', in *Hamburg: Geschichte der Stadt und ihrer Bewohner*, pp. 299–313, and Frank Bajohr, *'Aryanisation' in Hamburg: The Economic Exclusion of Jews and the Confiscation of their Property in Nazi Germany* (Oxford: Berghahn, 2001), pp. 87f.

32 *Jüdische Gemeinde, Vorstandsprotokolle* (minutes of board meetings), 3 December 1935, St A H, 522-1 Jüdische Gemeinden, 297, vol. 22.

33 Of the total income tax in 1935 of RM 421,000, more than half – RM 234,000 – was paid by a small number of wealthier Jews. The Reich tax rate on income for the higher income groups was between 35 and 40 per cent. The Jewish tax rates were 23 per cent on top of the Reich rate, thus raising the total tax by almost a quarter above the Reich tax. In Hamburg, the State Finance Department collected the taxes for the Jewish, Lutheran and Catholic churches and passed it on. The Lutherans and Catholics paid only a quarter of the amount the Jews paid. In 1936, there were 40,000 Jewish unemployed in Germany. *Gemeindeblatt*, 15 May 1936. In 1939, 52,000 Jews were assisted by welfare – that is, 26 per cent of the Jewish population at a time of full employment. There was little prospect of balancing the budget in 1937.

34 *Repräsentanten-Kollegium* der *Jüdischen Gemeinde*, 17 December 1934, St A H, 522-1 Jüdische Gemeinden.

35 *Protokoll Vorstandssitzung*, 1 October 1935, St A H, 522-1 Jüdische Gemeinden, 297, vol. 22.

36 Werner Cohn, 'Bearers of a Common Fate?: The "Non-Aryan" Christian "Fate Comrades" of the Paulus-Bund, 1933–1939', *Leo Baeck Institute Year Book*, 33 (1988), pp. 327–66.

37 The most thorough account of the legislation in Ursula Büttner, *Die Not der Juden teilen: Christlich-jüdische Familien im Dritten Reich: Beispiel und Zeugnis des Schriftstellers Robert Brendel* (Hamburg: Christians, 1988), pp. 11–71.

38 Bernd Nellessen, 'Die schweigende Kirche: Katholiken und Judenverfolgung', in *Die Deutschen und die Judenverfolgung im Dritten Reich*, ed. Ursula Büttner (Hamburg: Christians 1992), pp. 259–71; 2nd ed. (Frankfurt: Fischer, 2003), pp. 305–19; Lutz-Eugen Reutter, *Katholische Kirche als Fluchthelfer im Dritten Reich: Die Betreuung von Auswanderern durch den St. Raphaels-Verein* (Hamburg: Paulus Verlag, 1971), pp. 45ff.

39 The archives of the Jerusalem-*Gemeinde* have not survived. This account is based on *Jerusalem-Brief*, no. 71, August/September 1986, copies of *Zions Freund* preserved at the Jerusalem-*Gemeinde* in Hamburg, and an interview with a survivor, the late Werner Steinberg, a *Mischling* member. The Jerusalem-*Gemeinde* was founded by the Belfast Presbyterian Church in 1844; its heyday was in the 1880s and 1890s. Pastor Frank, a Jewish convert, joined in 1883, and had to leave with Pastor Moser in 1937, when they escaped from the Gestapo after a tip-off. *Zions Freund*, with a circulation of 45,000, was read far beyond Hamburg, and after appearing since 1900 was shut down in 1936. For a fascinating history, see Harald Jenner, *150 Jahre Jerusalem-Arbeit in Hamburg* (Hamburg: Jerusalem-Gemeinde, 2003). My great-aunt Olga Misch, a faithful Christian of Jewish descent, a victim of the Holocaust, was a member of the Jerusalem-*Gemeinde*.

40 The account is based on the almost complete set of the *Mitteilungsblatt* of the *Paulus-Bund* from 1933 to 1939, FZH, 623-8. In the autumn of 1933, Günther Katz, at the opening press reception, claimed 'millions' of non-Aryans could not be ignored.

41 John A. S. Grenville, 'Die "Endlösung" und die "Judenmischlinge" im Dritten Reich', in *Das Unrechtsregime: Internationale Forschung über den Nationalsozialismus*, vol. 2: *Verfolgung – Exil – Belasteter Neubeginn*, ed. Ursula Büttner (Hamburg: Christians, 1986), pp. 91–121, here 102–3.

42 Circumcision was advocated primarily for hygienic reasons in Britain and the United States in the 1860s and 1870s and became more widespread in the first half of the twentieth century, when it gained ground also among the secular and reform Jewish community. It was first condemned in Germany by the small Frankfurt reform movement in 1843 as cruel and unnecessary. For the debate, see John M. Ephron, *Medicine and the German Jews* (New Haven, CT: Yale University Press, 2001).

43 Max Warburg, 'Aus meinen Aufzeichnungen', vol. 3, Warburg Bank Archives. Warburg's letter to Emil Helfferich is also in the bank's archives.

44 Only extracts of the Lösener memorandum of 27 August 1935 have ever been published; it is in the Bundesarchiv, Berlin, R 18/5513. Present at the meeting were the following ministers: Hjalmar Schacht, Schwerin von Krosigk (Finance), Bernhard Rust (Education), Franz Gürtner (Justice), Wilhelm Frick (Interior), Reinhard Heydrich (Security) and Adolf Wagner (Hitler's representative). Heydrich sent a detailed memorandum to all the participants. For antecedents, see Frick to Lammers, 22 May 1935 and enclosure. Lammers noted a report was made to Hitler on 7 June 1935, Kreutzberger collection, Leo Baeck Institute Archive, New York, Box 9, f 3.

45 Heydrich, 9 September, to participants of 20 August meeting. See *Die Judenpolitik des SD 1935 bis 1938: Eine Dokumentation*, ed. Michael Wildt (Munich: Oldenbourg, 1995), pp. 70–73.

46 There are by now many good accounts of the Nuremberg rally, for example, Ian Kershaw, *Hitler 1889–1936: Hubris* (Harmondworth: Penguin, 1998), pp. 561–73, and Michael Burleigh, *The Third Reich: A New History* (London: Macmillan, 2000), pp. 294–8. A convenient collection of the Blood Law and Citizenship Law of 15 September 1935 and the decrees that followed on 14 November 1935, with the complete texts, is *Gesetze des NS-Staates*, ed. Ingo von Münch and Uwe Brodersen (Paderborn: Schöningh, 1994), pp. 119–25. Bernhard Lösener and a colleague arrived on 13 September and presented four drafts to Hitler, who struck out that the blood laws applied only to Jews.

47 Note by Hans Pfundtner, 24 January 1936, on receiving communication from Hans Heinrich Lammers, Reich Chancellery, Bundesarchiv, Berlin, R 18/5508. Lowering the age from forty-five to thirty-five, thus remaining a child-bearing age, angered Hitler, but it was too late to change it once more. There is much confusion in the literature regarding the racial legislation. Jews defined racially could be Jews or Christians by religion (four or three Jewish grandparents). *Mischlinge* (one or two Jewish grandparents) could never be Jews by religion; if they belonged to the Jewish community they were dealt with as Jews and were then *Geltungsjuden*. Jews by conversion from Christianity – there were a few in Germany – with four Christian grandparents were Aryans. The Hindenburg concessions applying to non-Aryans were rescinded; a few 'quarter-Jew' *Mischlinge* of the second degree remained in the state service until the autumn of 1944.

48 Luise Solmitz, Journal, 9 September, 15 September, 25 September, 30 September, 13 October, 28 October, 6 November, 15 November, 18 December 1935, 17 September 1936, 20 September 1937, FZH, 11 S 11.

49 Wulff, *Arbeitslosigkeit und Arbeitsbeschaffungsmaßnahmen in Hamburg 1933–1939*.

50 Confidential reports, 1934–1936, St A H, 113-3 *Verwaltung für Wirtschaft, Technik und Arbeit*, III.9.

51 Reports to Welfare Office, 3 April, 7 April, 9 April, 14 April, 19 April 1936, St A H, 351-10 I *Sozialbehörde I*, VG 30.70.

52 German News Agency statement, 17 September 1935, www.jewishvirtuallibrary.org/jsource/Holocaust/newnurm.html. Kershaw, *Hitler 1889–1936: Hubris*, p. 570.

53 Declaration of the *Reichsvertretung*, in *Jüdische Rundschau*, 24 September 1935.

54 On the career of Rudi Ball (1910–1975), see www.sihss.se/RudiBallbiography.htm.

55 Michael Burleigh, *The Third Reich: A New History*, p. 324.

56 Despite the protests of the US consul, the president of the International Olympic Committee, Henri de Baillet-Latour, sanctioned Berlin. A good account is by Duff Hart-Davis, *Hitler's Games: The 1936 Olympics* (London: Century, 1986).

57 Hitler's *Denkschrift für den Vierjahresplan 1936* was read out to ministers on 4 September 1936; see the discussion in Kershaw, *Hitler 1889–1936: Hubris*, pp.19ff. The memorandum was drawn up by Hitler late in August.

58 Wilhelm Stuckart, secret note on a conference in the Ministry of the Interior, 29 September 1936, Bundesarchiv, Berlin, R 18/5514.

59 An important account of the build-up of the *Sicherheitsdienst*, SD, is in the introduction to Michael Wildt, *Die Judenpolitik des SD 1935 bis 1938: Eine Dokumentation*.

60 For example, *Lagebericht, April bis Mai 1936*, Bundesarchiv, Berlin, R 58/991, and Theodor Dannecker's memorandum on Jewish organisations: *Das innerdeutsche Judentum: Organisation, sachliche und personelle Veränderungen, geistiges Leben und die Methodik seiner Behandlung*, no date, between May and 'winter 1937/38', both in Wildt, *Die Judenpolitik des SD 1935 bis 1938*, pp. 84–94 and 142–50.

61 The SD produced an unsigned memorandum in January 1937 on freeing Germany from Jews. The suggestion was ignored that Jews should be sent to 'low' cultural countries in Latin America where their influence could not harm Germany. *Zum Judenproblem*, January 1937, may have been a collaborative effort or written by Eichmann alone. Bundesarchiv, Berlin, R 58/956; see also Wildt, *Die Judenpolitik des SD 1935 bis 1938*, pp. 95–105.

62 *Lagebericht für den Monat September 1935, Staatpolizeistelle Erfurt*, 5 October 1935; *Lagebericht für den Monat September 1935, Bielefeld*, 3 October 1935, Kreutzberger collection, Leo Baeck Institute Archive, New York, Box 9, f1. *Lagebericht für den Monat October, Hannover*, 4 November 1935, Bundesarchiv, Berlin, R 58/552.

63 Hans Robinsohn, *Justiz als politische Verfolgung: Die Rechtsprechung in 'Rassenschandefällen' beim Landgericht Hamburg, 1936–1943* (Stuttgart: Deutsche Verlags-Anstalt, 1973). On Max Eichholz, see Wilfried Weinke, 'The Persecution of Jewish Lawyers in Hamburg', *Leo Baeck Institute Year Book*, 42 (1997), pp. 221–37; 'Hamburgs Kampf gegen Rassenschande', in *Hamburger Tageblatt*, 25 March 1939, FZH. The *Hambuger Tageblatt* reported on the 'exemplary struggle', which had secured 119 convictions in 1938.

64 Hamburg became a model of a Nazi region when it came to sterilisation. Andrea Brücks, Jan Gross, Friedemann Pfäfflin and Christiane Rothmaler, 'Sterilisation nach dem Gesetz zur Verhütung erbkranken Nachwuchses in Hamburg', in *1933 in Gesellschaft und Wissenschaft* (Hamburg: Hamburg University Press, 1984), vol. 2, pp. 157–84. *Ratsherrenberatung, Durchführung des Erbgesundheitsgesetzes in Hamburg*, 8 February 1939, St A H, 122-5 Ratsherrenkanzlei, 20.

65 But *Der Stürmer* (Julius Streicher), the *Völkischer Beobachter* (party paper, Alfred Rosenberg), *Der Angriff* (Joseph Goebels) and *Das Schwarze Korps* (SS), which made no secret of the intention to eliminate Jews, were read by many Germans.

66 A collection of papers on the treatment of non-Aryans in public welfare is in St A H, 351-10 I Sozialbehörde I, VT 12.25. This collection was assembled in preparation for a meeting of the welfare experts of the *Deutscher Gemeindetag* on 10 June 1937. Among the papers are: *'Behandlung der Juden in der öffentlichen Fürsorge in Hamburg'* (Treatment of the Jews in public welfare at Hamburg); unsigned memorandum, *'Stellung der Juden in der Gesetzgebung'* (Position of Jews in the Legislation), Hamburg; report, *'Fürsorgerische Betreuung von Nichtariern'*, Munich ('Care of Non-Aryans'); Dr Plank's report from Nuremberg; and a comprehensive list with handwritten

annotations. Concerning this subject I have gained many insights from discussions with Dr Lohalm; see especially his *Fürsorge und Verfolgung: Öffentliche Wohlfahrtsverwaltung und nationalsozialistische Judenpolitik in Hamburg 1933 bis 1942* (Hamburg: Ergebnisse-Verlag, 1998); and his *Völkische Wohlfahrtsdiktatur: Öffentliche Wohlfahrtspolitik im nationalsozialistischen Hamburg* (Munich and Hamburg: Dölling & Galitz, 2010).

67 Sister C. T. to the president of the *Gesundheits- und Fürsorgebehörde*, Oskar Martini, 2 June 1937, St A H, 351-10 I *Sozialbehörde* I, VT 12.25.

68 Sister E. H. to Oskar Martini, 2 June 1937, ibid.

69 The *Gemeinde* (community) was a public corporation and could raise taxes collected for it by the State Finance Office; the Hamburg state supervised Jewish schools, teachers and rabbis, who held a status comparable to *Beamte*, civil servants. Community decisions were reached democratically and, contrary to orthodox tradition, women had the vote. On the organisation of the Jewish community in Hamburg, see Ina Lorenz, *Die Juden in Hamburg zur Zeit der Weimarer Republik* (Hamburg: Christians, 1987), vol. 1, pp. lxxvff. The account (p. 375) is based on the Plaut papers in the Hamburg State Archives. Plaut's papers (interviews, reports, memoranda) are to be found at St A H, 622-1, Familie Plaut, D38–39; the Leo Baeck Institute Archive, New York, Kreutzberger collection; and FZH, 12 Plaut.

70 St A H, 622-1, Familie Plaut, D39/5.

71 Jewish (racial) population in Germany, excluding Austria

	Total	*Emigrated*	*Excess of deaths over births*
1933a	525,000	37,000	5,500
1934	482,500	23,000	5,500
1935	454,000	21,000	5,500
1936	423,000	25,000	6,000
1937	393,000	23,000	7,000
1938	345,000	40,000	8,000
1939	257,000	78,000	10,000
1940	224,000	15,000	8,000 10,000 deported
1941 1 May	169,000		
1 Oct	164,000	8,000	4,000 25,000 deported

Note: aEstimate: no 'racial' statistics available.

Financial assistance to emigrate was given in 1936 to 25,000, in 1937 to 23,000, and altogether since 1933 to 129,000.

72 Frank Bajohr, in *'Aryanisation' in Hamburg*, p. 314, has worked out significant statistics for Hamburg. Examining a sample of 310 firms, he found only 8.7 per cent were 'Aryanised' during the years from 1934 to 1937, 54.2 per cent in 1938 and 36.8 per cent in 1939, which would indicate strong survival before 1938. However, since this is only a 'sample', caution is necessary; nor does it indicate how many businesses simply closed down. Another significant statistic, on pp. 312f., shows how some of the larger Jewish wholesale and export businesses increased their turnover despite Nazi discrimination (see table on p. 291).

   Our knowledge of the decline of Jewish economic enterprises between 1933 and the end of 1938 is still incomplete. Peter Hayes ('State Policy and Corporate Involvement in the Holocaust', in *The Holocaust and History*, ed. Michael Berenbaum and Abraham J. Peck (Bloomington: Indiana University Press, 1998), pp. 197–218) estimates that there were about 100,000 Jewish businesses altogether and that the smaller enterprises and Jews in the professions suffered the most dismissals, shop closures or sales, with a loss of 60 per cent before the end of 1937. The larger concerns showed remarkable resilience, as no more than 30 per cent changed hands. Jews were

Value of trade in *Reichsmark*

	1931	1933	1935	1936	1937
A. Krause & Co.overseas export	522,190	322,134	442,275	924,513	
Gold-Schmidt & Mindus radios, musical instruments, bicycles	1563,000	198,1000	1,900.000		
Maaβ & Riege South American imports coffee, cocoa, rubber		384,000	480,000	869,000	1,054,000
Ostindienhaus H. Colm clothing store	346,000	472,000	635,000	735,000	776,000
Bottina Shuh GMBH Shoe shops	1,330,283a	1,149,317	1,060,940	1,031,194	1,094,945
Campbell & Co.optical store			601,200	737,200	790,700

Note: ^a1932

still active after the Nuremberg Laws as directors or on managing supervisory boards at Mannesmann, I. G. Farben, Rheinstahl, AEG, Waldhof Feldmühle and the Berliner Handelsgesellschaft as late as the end of 1937; even the Nazified Dresdner Bank retained a hundred Jewish employees in Berlin and five directors until early 1938. Loyalty to Jewish colleagues, however, weakened as these firms and banks became increasingly dependent on the state and then came under pressure from the party. Commercial self-interest and expediency then dominated, with few exceptions. That some Jews before 1938 saw reassuring signs for the future, however, becomes more understandable.

These conclusions are generally confirmed by Ingo Köhler's study *Die Arisierung der Privatbanken im Dritten Reich: Verfolgung, Ausschaltung und die Frage der Wiedergutmachung* (Munich: Beck, 2008). With Heinrich Hunke as Berlin's *Gauwirtschaftsberater* and since 1938 president of the *Verein Berliner Kaufleute*, Aryanisation was speedily radicalised. In 1933, 160,000 Jews owned some 28,000 to 30,000 enterprises; close to three-quarters of private banks were Jewish and Jewish department stores employed thousands of Aryan employees. They were generally able to hold on longest.

73 Leo Lippmann's manuscript memoir of his life, 'Mein Leben und meine amtliche Tätigkeit', was secretly deposited in the Hamburg State Archives. After the war Werner Jochmann published this important self-testimony of his work and the record of Hamburg's financial management during the years of the Weimar Republic. It is sparse for the Nazi years, obviously, in case of its discovery by the Gestapo. A manuscript account of the *Gemeinde* during the years after 1935 to 1942 was among the records found in the Hamburg State Archives and was later published in an excellent edition with commentaries by Ina Lorenz, Wolfgang Curilla *et al.*, in Leo Lippmann, '... *daβ Ich wie ein guter Deutscher empfinde und handele': Zur Geschichte der Deutsch-Israelitischen Gemeinde in Hamburg in der Zeit vom Herbst 1935 bis zum Ende 1942* (Hamburg: Dölling & Galitz, 1993), pp. 85–118.

74 In 1936, taxes were increased to 23 per cent on top of the Reich tax. Three-fifths of the income was contributed by a small number of members and one-fifth from members with incomes of RM 18,000 to RM 30,000 a year. In 1939 the community's capital was over RM 7 million and the annual budget 1.5 million. In November 1942, RM 5 million was transferred to Berlin. St A H, 522-1 Jüdische Gemeindn, Film Sa. 1052, and file 433, Gemeindesteuer Allgemeines, 1936–1938.

75 For a history, see Mary Lindemann, *140 Jahre Israelitisches Krankenhaus in Hamburg: Vorgeschichte und Entwicklung* (Hamburg: Israelitisches Krankenhaus, 1981). Despite generous contributions from the Warburgs and others, the deficits could no longer be covered in 1939; the hospital, 'for the duration of the war', was turned over to the army. *Protokoll Vorstandsitzung*, 2 April 1935, St A H, 522-1 Jüdische Gemeinden, 297, vol. 22.

76 *'Behandlung von Forderungen der Hansestadt Hamburg gegen das Israelitische Krankenhaus in Hamburg'*, 1938, St A H, 113-5 Staatsverwaltung E IV B 2. In 1929 modernisation had cost RM 1,700,000; RM 450,000 was privately raised and the state of Hamburg had provided a loan of RM 1,250,000. The agreement of 1840 stipulated the land and buildings would revert to the state if no longer used as a hospital.

77 Minute *'Sitzung des Beirats der Sozialverwaltung'*, 22 December 1938, St A H, 351-10 I, Sozialbehörde I, StA 26.19b, Bd I. The six taken over were the Heimann-Stift, the Rée-Stift, the Vaterstädtische Stiftung, the Hartwig Hesse Witwen Stift, the Leja-Stift and the Betty-Stift. The three remaining to the community were the Mendelssohn and Israel-Stift, the Warburg-Stift and the Martin Brunn-Stift. The figure 'fewer than ninety-one' is arrived at because some were occupied by elderly couples.

78 There were 2,900 welfare recipients in the winter of 1935–6 and 3,700 in winter 1938–9. Uwe Lohalm, *Fürsorge und Verfolgung*, pp. 49–58.

79 The Nazi computation was as follows: the building's pre-1914 value, RM 90,459, less the cost of demolition RM 25,000, minus a welfare bill of close to RM 100,000; the Jewish community would have received no compensation and have been left to pay RM 34,000. Negotiations concerning the Bornplatz Synagogue, 9 March to 6 July 1939, St A H, 311-2 IV Finanzdeputation IV, SuL IV D1a XXXVI 1b CVIII.

80 Between 1918 and 1933, 545 left the community. In 1926, thirty-eight Jewish men and forty Jewish women married Christians; about eight out of ten of their children and practically all the grandchildren were baptised. That same year there were eighty-six marriages between Jewish partners.

81 On Carlebach's life, with documents, see Miriam Gillis-Carlebach, *Jüdischer Alltag als humaner Widerstand: Dokumente des Hamburger Oberrabbiners Dr. Joseph Carlebach aus den Jahren 1939–1941* (Hamburg: Verein für Hamburgische Geschichte, 1990), pp. 9–118; Eng. trans. as *Jewish Everyday Life as Human Resistance 1939–1941: Chief Rabbi Dr. Joseph Zvi Carlebach and the Hamburg-Altona Jewish Communities: Documents of Dr. Joseph Zvi Carlebach, 1939–1941* (Frankfurt: Lang, 2008).

82 The *Tempel*, founded in 1817, introduced a regular order of service, prayers in German, a prayerbook in German and Hebrew, a choir, hymns and an organ. But the Torah and circumcision remained central. However, the dietary laws were no longer strictly adhered to. In 1926 there were 1,179 members. For a recent excellent history, see Andreas Brämer, *Judentum und religiöse Reform: Der Hamburger Tempel 1817–1938* (Hamburg: Dölling & Galitz, 2000).
    The Neue Dammtor synagogue was built in 1895 and was attended mainly by better-off Jews; it followed a more moderate orthodoxy after splitting in 1912 from the orthodox *Synagogenverband*, with 1,183 members in 1926. The *Synagogenverband* provided the chief rabbi, and in 1926 its congregation was the largest, with 5,300 members. Jewish law was observed. It played a distinguished role in Jewish life. In 1821, Isaak Bernays, a reforming rabbi who called himself not 'rabbi' but *chacham*, 'wise one', according to Sephardic custom, had followed traditional studies in the Würzburg Yeshiva and secular university studies. He adopted an order of service and a sermon in German, but no organ. His pupil Rabbi Raphael Samuel Hirsch in Frankfurt developed modern orthodoxy. There was also a small ultra-orthodox *Austrittsgemeinde*, which did not accept the chief rabbi. Dr Schottelius, interview with Max Plaut, 25 January 1954, FZH, 12 Plaut.

83 Joseph Carlebach's father, Dr Salomon Carlebach, was rabbi of Lübeck, a Talmudic scholar and well versed in German literature. Joseph was the eighth of twelve children and

fathered nine himself. His mother was the daughter of Julius Preuss, a Talmudic scholar and doctor. Gillis-Carlebach, *Jüdischer Alltag als humaner Widerstand*, pp. 9–44.

84 '*Feier zur Einführung Sr. Ehrwürden des Herrn Oberrabiners Dr. Joseph Carlebach, 22 April 1936 (30 Nissan 5696)*', Central Archives for the History of the Jewish People, Jerusalem.

85 *Gemeindeblatt* (Hamburg), 19 April 1934, FZH, 624-3.

86 Ron Chernow, *The Warburgs* (New York: Random House, 1993), pp. 436–9. *Protokolle Chef-Besprechungen*, 25 August 1936, Warburg Bank Archives, Hamburg.

87 *Gemeindeblatt* (Hamburg), 18 June 1937, FZH, 624-3.

88 To supervise and transfer money for emigration to countries other than Palestine, *Altreu* and the Bank of International Settlement were set up, but with only one-tenth of the capital hoped for. *Gemeindeblatt* (Hamburg), 9 February 1937, FZH, 624-3. For this account I have used the published (New York, 1952) and unprinted manuscript portions of Max Warburg's 'Aus meinen Aufzeichnungen', his memoirs, in the Warburg Bank Archives.

89 This period is perceptively covered by Ron Chernow in chapter 32 ('The Twilight Dynasty') of *The Warburgs*, pp. 460–86. Also illuminating is Eric M. Warburg's chapter on the Nazi years and the efforts, from 1930 to 1933, by a small group to keep the Nazis out under the slogan 'Hold Open the Door', referring to trade. *Times and Tides*, privately printed in Hamburg, 1983, pp. 97–125.

90 The Warburg Bank Archives, when I had access, were being organised and catalogued. I was able to examine them in a 'raw state'. Much remains to be fully researched. I have consulted the files on Max Warburg's relations with Schacht and a number of financial accounts of German firms who banked with the Warburgs. These could only be sampled. I wish to express my thanks to the present partners for access to the vaults of the bank. At the stage when I consulted the papers, precise locations with reference numbers could not be given.

5 Save yourself if you can

1 Dr Velden to Senator Nieland, 3 August 1935, St A H, 313-4 I *Steuerverwaltung* I, II A1 b, I N.

2 Details about the situation in Austria and the Jewish *Kultusgemeinde*: Berichte, May 1938, 29 November 1938, December 1938, in *Eyewitness Reports: Jews in Germany, 1938–1939*, Wiener Library Archive, London, B 210, B 218, B 95, K4b. See especially *Novemberpogrom 1938: Die Augenzeugenberichte der Wiener Library, London*, ed. Ben Barkow, Raphael Gross and Michael Lenarz (Frankfurt: Jüdischer Verlag im Suhrkamp Verlag, 2008), and Peter Longerich, *Holocaust: The Nazi Persecution and Murder of the Jews* (Oxford: Oxford University Press, 2010), pp. 117–20. Of the large amount of available literature, Ian Kershaw, *Hitler: 1936–1945 Nemesis* (London: Allen Lane, 2000), is an excellent introduction, pp. 69–86. For a personal account of events in Vienna, see George Clare, *Last Waltz in Vienna: The Destruction of a Family, 1842–1942* (London: Macmillan, 1982). Dr Cäcilie Friedmann, the sister of the dynamic official of the Wiener Kultusgemeinde, recorded a memoir in Prague, 5 December 1945, Leo Baeck Institute Archive, New York; Friedman was later murdered by the Nazis. On the work of the security service, see report of the Abteilung II 112, April to May 1938; Hagen's account of the work of the Zentralstelle für jüdische Auswanderung, November 1938; and report of the Abteilung II 112 for the year 1938, all in Michael Wildt, *Die Judenpolitik des SD 1935 bis 1938: Eine Dokumentation* (Munich: Oldenbourg, 1995), pp. 186–90, 190–93, 193–4 and 194–205. On the persecution of 11,000 Sinti and Roma, see Guenter Lewy, *The Nazi Persecution of the Gypsies* (Oxford: Oxford University Press, 2001), pp. 56–62.

3 The original questionnaire I found in the *Oberfinanzbehörde* records in the Magdalenenstraße, Hamburg, now St A H, 314-15 Oberfinanzpräsident (Devisenstelle

und Vermögensverwertungsstelle); Frank Bajohr, *'Aryanisation' in Hamburg: The Economic Exclusion of Jews and the Confiscation of their Property in Nazi Germany* (Oxford: Berghahn, 2001), pp. 106–9. For a perceptive analysis of the years 1933 to 1939, see Avraham Barkai, *From Boycott to Annihilation: The Economic Struggle of German Jews, 1933–1943*, trans. William Templer (London: University Press of New England, 1989).

4 Plenary meeting of the *Handelskammer* (Hamburg Chamber of Commerce), 11 March 1938; memorandum by General Georg Thomas, chief of the armaments staff of the OKW over the 'fundamentals' for a history of the years 1933–1939, written in 1944, in Werner Jochmann and Hans-Adolf Jacobsen, *Ausgewählte Dokumente zur Geschichte des Nationalsozialismus 1933–1945* (Bielefeld: Verlag Neue Gesellschaft, 1966), vol. 3, document; Bernd-Jürgen Wendt, *Deutschland 1933–1945: Das Dritte Reich: Handbuch zur Geschichte* (Hannover: Fackelträger, 1995), pp. 423–68.

5 Half of the Jewish businesses were small concerns selling clothes, furs, etc., small workshops, tailors, milliners and decorators. Estimates vary widely as to what proportion survived in 1938 since 1933, from a quarter to two-thirds; 9,000 Jews were still in business in Germany mid-1938.

6 Friedrich Lütjohann, Notiz, 2 August 1938, St A H, 311-2 IV Finanzdeputation IV, SuL 10b 9.

7 Max Warburg, 'Aus meinen Aufzeichnungen', vol. 3, p. 444, Warburg Bank Archives, Hamburg.

8 Frank Bajohr, *'Aryanisation' in Hamburg*, pp. 206–9 and p. 245. Ron Chernow, *The Warburgs: The Twentieth Century Odyssey of a Remarkable Jewish Family* (New York: Random House, 1993). 'Compensation' received left Max Warburg with a deficit of over RM 2 million. The Nazi computation was as follows: total value, including Amsterdam branch, RM 11.6 million, less Amsterdam branch RM 6.4 million; RM 3 million sleeping capital retained in the bank was later confiscated. That left RM 2.2 million. From this amount, RM 1 million was deducted for permission to Aryanise (!), RM 1.08 million for permission to keep the Amsterdam bank, RM 1.221 million Jewish property levy after Rath's assassination, RM 850,000 Reich flight tax, and RM 450,000 emigration levy, leaving a deficit.

9 Max Warburg, correspondence, Warburg Bank Archives.

10 Max Warburg to James P. Warburg, 2 June 1938, Warburg Bank Archives.

11 This extraordinary effort has come to light in the Warburg Bank Archives: Max and Fritz Warburg to *Reichsstatthalter*, 18 August 1938.

12 Ron Chernow, *The Warburgs*, pp. 473–6.

13 Lists of non-Aryan doctors who continued practising were drawn up in 1936 and then removed from circulation. Well known was the Unna family, children of the celebrated Paul Gerson Unna and Maria Unna, who continued to practise in their private clinic. Friedrich Ofterdinger, *Verzeichnis jüdischer Ärzte*, 13 November 1936, St A H, A 832/1, box 1; Anna von Villiez, *Mit aller Kraft verdrängt: Entrechtung und Verfolgung 'nicht arischer' Ärzte in Hamburg 1933 bis 1945* (Munich and Hamburg: Dölling & Galitz, 2009), pp. 104–6.

14 Georg Ahrens to mayors of Altona, Wandsbek and Harburg-Wilhelmsburg, 28 April 1938; *Reichsstatthalter* to Minister of the Interior, 13 August 1938; Minister of the Interior to *Reichsstatthalter*, 13 October 1938, 10 July 1939; Lindemann to *Reichsstatthalter*, 27 June 1939; *Gemeindeverwaltung*, 31 October 1938, 19 December 1941, 3 January 1942, all in St A H, 131-4 Senatskanzlei-Präsidialabteilung, 1934, A 77 vol. II.

For the changes in Hamburg's administration, see Uwe Lohalm, *Hamburgs nationalsozialistische Diktatur: Verfassung und Verwaltung 1933 bis 1945* (Hamburg: Landeszentrale für politische Bildung, 1997). Among Jewish street names changed were those of Anna Wohlwill, Gabriel Riesser, Anton Rée, and Paul Gerson Unna, and, among those of Jewish descent or connection, the Hallers, Felix Mendelssohn, Heinrich Heine and Richard Dehmel, the well-known dramatist married to a Jewess.

15 Personal experience: I was in a cinema in Berlin at the time.

16 A good account is Trude Maurer, 'Abschiebung und Attentat: Die Auswanderung der polnischen Juden und der Vorwand für die Kristallnacht', in Walter H. Pehle, ed., *Der Judenpogrom 1938: Von der 'Reichskristallnacht' zum Völkermord* (Frankfurt: Fischer, 1988), pp. 52–73.

17 Based on an account by *Herr* and *Frau* Friedfertig, Tel Aviv, November 1944, in the Central Archives of the Jewish People, Jerusalem, 01/35. Max Plaut's recollections are in St A H, 622-1, Familie Plaut, D39.

18 Uwe Dietrich Adam, 'Wie Spontan war der Judenpogrom 1938', in Walter H. Pehle, *Der Judenpogrom 1938: Von der 'Reichskristallnacht' zum Völkermord*, pp. 74–93. Ian Kershaw, *Hitler, the Germans, and the Final Solution* (New Haven, CT: Yale University Press, 2008), p. 251.

19 Of the many accounts, a good analysis is Ian Kershaw, *Hitler: 1936–1945 Nemesis*, pp. 135–53; also Michael Burleigh's account, *The Third Reich: A New History* (London: Macmillan, 2000), pp. 325–34.

20 For the pogrom in Hamburg, a good overview is Uwe Lohalm, *Die nationalsozialistische Judenverfolgung, 1933 bis 1945* (Hamburg: Landeszentrale für politische Bildung, 1999), pp. 29–33. Kaufmann's role, and a destruction of the legend that he stopped the pogrom in Hamburg, is examined by Jürgen Sielemann, 'Fragen und Antworten zur Reichskristallnacht in Hamburg', *Zeitschrift des Vereins für Hamburgische Geschichte*, 83 (1997), pp. 473–501.

21 This account is based on the report in the *Daily Telegraph*, 11 November 1938.

22 Luise Solmitz, Journal, 7 November, 9 and 10 November, 11 and 12 November, 14 November 1938, FZH, 11 S 12.

23 Margarete Frick, Tagebuch, 5 December 1938, private access.

24 Entry by Cardinal Faulhaber, 12 November 1938, *Akten Kardinal Michael von Faulhabers*, vol. 2: *1935–1945*, ed. Ludwig Volk (Mainz: Matthias Grünewald, 1978, 2nd ed., 1984), p. 604. Decision of the Synod of the Confessing Church, 10–12 December 1938, quoted in confidential report 8/38 of the *Bund für Deutsches Christentum*, 25 December 1938, St A H, 113-5 Staatsverwaltung, E IV B 2.

25 Elisabeth Schmitz, a Berlin schoolteacher and a member of the Confessing Church, berated the leaders for not standing up for the Jews, writing that it was 'no exaggeration to speak of the attempt to annihilate Jewry in Germany'. Quotation in a memorandum of September 1935: *Elisabeth Schmitz und ihre Denkschrift gegen die Judenverfolgung: Konturen einer vergessenen Biographie (1893–1977)*, ed. Manfred Gailus (Berlin: Wichern, 2008), p. 206. See also her biography by Manfred Gailus, *Mir aber zerriß es das Herz: Der stille Widerstand der Elisabeth Schmitz* (Göttingen: Vandenhoeck & Ruprecht, 2010).

26 Max Plaut, discussion with Dr Schottelius, 19 June 1960, FZH, 12 Plaut.

27 Author's experience.

28 *Sitzungsprotokolle des Gemeindevorstands*, 12 June 1934, 29 January, 6 August, 27 August, 3 September, 17 September 1935, St A H, 522-1 Jüdische Gemeinden, 297, vol. 22. Education imposed a heavy drain on community funds.

29 The conference of 12 November 1938 has frequently been quoted. Full texts are in *Der Prozeß gegen die Hauptkriegsverbrecher vor dem Internationalen Militärgerichtshof*, 42 vols (Nuremberg, 1947–9), vol. 28, pp. 499–540; *The Trial of the Major War Criminals before the International Military Tribunal* (London: HMSO, 1947–9). Leading civil servants, Göring, Funk, Gürtner and Heydrich attended. For discussion by the judicial authorities in Hamburg, see report on *Präsidentenbesprechung*, 1 February 1939, St A H, 213-1 Oberlandesgericht, 3131E-10/7; copy in FZH, 333-22. Those who had injured Jews in Hamburg were not to be prosecuted, the senior judges decided, as they had acted on superior orders.

30 Memorandum of guidelines for the meeting of the *Regierungspräsidenten*, 16 December 1938, Bundesarchiv Berlin, R 18/5519; report from Peter Ernst Eiffe,

Hamburg's minister in Berlin, of meeting at the Reich Interior Ministry, 16 December 1938, *Beilage zum Tagebuch Krogmann*, FZH, 6263.

31 *Schnellbrief*, secret, Göring to *Reichsminister des Innern, Reichswirtschaftsminister*, and other Reich ministers, 28 December 1938, Bundesarchiv, Berlin, R 18/5519.

32 See Bajohr, '*Aryanisation in Hamburg*', pp. 292–305. In Hamburg, 395 businesses were closed and 405 Aryanised.

33 Speech by Kaufmann to the Hamburg Chamber of Commerce, 6 January 1939, in H. Hassbargen, '*Der ehemalige Gauleiter Kaufmann im Spiegel seiner eigenen Worte*', manuscript, 13 August 1951, FZH, 12-1 / K. Kaufmann.

34 The Hamburg Chamber of Commerce lists of Jewish concerns were regularly updated; in 1937 there were 39 wholesalers, 10 coffee importers, 28 in the fur trade, 14 food importers from overseas, 4 metal firms, 5 oil importers, as well as manufacturers of footwear, corsets, chemicals and cigarettes and a tugboat company.

The accounts of Joel Rosenfelder, Adolf Sachsenhaus, Günther Tradelius and Paul A. Belmonte are all in 'Entjudung des Großhandels', Hamburg Chamber of Commerce Archive, 100 B1 37.

35 The murder of the Belmonte brothers is in *Gedenkbuch für die jüdischen Opfer des Nationalsozialismus in Hamburg* (Hamburg: Staatsarchiv, 1965; rev. ed., comp. Jürgen Sielemann and Peter Flamme, 1995), p. 88.

36 Special 'purchase offices' were set up on 25 January 1939. Letter of *Reichswirtschaftsminister* (Reich Minister for Economics), '*Errichtung öffentlicher Ankaufsstellen nach § 14 der Verordnung über den Einsatz des jüdischen Vermögens vom 3. 12. 1938*', 1 March 1939. Alf Krüger, *Die Lösung der Judenfrage in der deutschen Wirtschaft* (Berlin, 1940), pp.184–85; Joseph Walk, ed., *Das Sonderrecht für die Juden im NS-Staat* (Heidelberg: Müller, 1981), p. 276.

37 *Hamburger Tageblatt*, 25 September 1941, FZH. The decree of 27 March 1941 required names to be changed but permitted a transitional period until the end of 1942. Correspondence, Hamburg Chamber of Commerce to M.J.E, 6 May 1942; to its Berlin representative, 3 July 1942; to Amtsgericht supporting Rappolt und Söhne Nachfolger to retain trademark 'Eres' for its internationally known clothes, all in Hamburg Chamber of Commerce Archive, 100 B1/31. Enquiries as to whether business could be conducted with non-Aryan firms, 8 March 1938; 5 April 1938; 19 July 1939, ibid., 100 B1 39.

38 An extensive correspondence between the responsible authorities, Arthur Lindemann and Dr Kamisch can be found in St A H, 311-2 IV Finanzdeputation IV, BV SuL 1 G: letters to *Hamburgische Vermögens- und Liegenschaftsverwaltung*, 11 February 1938, 17 February 1938, 27 October 1938, 30 January 1939; reply to Kamisch, 3 November 1938; confidential memorandum, 12 March 1940.

39 Report 'Überführung volljüdicher Kinder aus Heimen des Landesjugendamt in das Jüdische Waisenhaus', November 1938, St A H, 354-5 I Jugendbehörde I, 359c.

40 Correspondence in *Gesundheitsverwaltung*, Senator Ofterdinger, 4 April 1939, *Rechtsamt*, 17 April 1939, 3 June 1939, 12 July 1939, St A H.

41 *Garten- und Friedhofsamt* to *Bauverwaltung*, 6 May 1939, giving decision of *Reichsstatthalter*, St A H.

42 George Rublee to Helmut Wohltat, 1 and 17 February 1939; chief of the Gestapo to Göring and other ministers, 7 July 1939. Leo Baeck Institute Archive, New York, Kreutzberger collection, Box 17, f 7.

43 Hans Herlin, *Die Reise der Verdammten: Die Tragödie der St. Louis* (Hamburg: Kabel, 1984); Georg J. E. Mautner Markhof, *Das St. Louis-Drama: Hintergrund und Rätsel einer mysteriösen Aktion des Dritten Reiches* (Graz and Stuttgart: Leopold Stocker, 2001); Georg Reinfelder, *MS "St. Louis": Die Irrfahrt nach Kuba – Frühjahr 1939* (Teetz: Hentrich & Hentrich, 2002).

44 A report and other documents on a similar journey of Captain Alfred Leidig are in FZH, 11 L 6.

45 Karen Gershon, *We came as Children: A Collective Autobiography* (London: Victor Gollancz, 1966); John A. Presland, *A Great Adventure: The Story of the Refugee Children's Movement* (London, 1944), London Metropolitan Archives.

46 The children's letters are in *Eyewitness Reports: Jews in Germany 1938–39*, Wiener Library Archive, London, B135. The newsreels reported the arrival of the first 196 children in Harwich on 2 December 1938.

47 Memo of a talk by Max Plaut in Tel-Aviv, 26 December 1946, 'Die Gemeinde Hamburg in den Jahren von 1933 bis 1943', recorded by Dr Kurt Ball, St A H, 622-1, Familie Plaut, D39/5.

48 Interview, Plaut with Schottelius, 25 January 1954, FZH, 12 Plaut.

49 Chenan Benhar, '107 Days on the SH-7: Experiences and Events of the Last Large Refugee Transport from the Reichsgebiet', *Leo Baeck Institute Year Book*, 46 (2001), pp. 305–32.

50 On conditions in Poland, Martin Gilbert, *The Holocaust: Jewish Tragedy* (London: Collins, 1986), pp. 84–108.

51 *Reichssicherheitshauptamt, Amtsbesprechungen*, 8 September, 13 September, 21 September, 29 September 1939, Bundesarchiv, Berlin, R 58/954.

52 On the German–Soviet Friendship Treaty, see John A. S. Grenville, *The Major International Treaties, 1914–1945* (London: Methuen, 1987), p. 199.

53 Overlapping functions and responsibilities were complex. The *Reichssicherheitshauptamt* (RSHA) in 1939 became the headquarters combining all the police forces with the Gestapo and the SD. While these had up to then been distinct organisations, there had already been some cooperation, and a personal link had been established in June 1936 when Heydrich, chief of the SD, was additionally appointed chief of security police, with the Gestapo under him. After his assassination in Prague in May 1942, there was a delay of several months before Ernst Kaltenbrunner succeeded him, in January 1943. Over and above the RSHA was Himmler as *Reichsführer* SS, responsible to Hitler alone. See Louis Snyder, *Encyclopaedia of the Third Reich* (New York, 1976), p. 286.

54 Richard Breitmann, *The Architect of Genocide: Himmler and the Final Solution* (London: Bodley Head, 1991), pp. 35–45, 66–84; Kershaw, *Hitler: 1936–1945 Nemesis*, pp. 233–52; Claudia Steur, *Theodor Dannecker: Ein Funktionär der 'Endlösung'* (Essen: Klartext Verlag, 1997), pp. 25–34; Peter Padfield, *Himmler: Reichsführer SS* (London: Macmillan, 1990), pp. 266–281. There are numerous discussions of the origins of the Holocaust. Among the detailed analysts for the period 1939–1941 is Peter Longerich, *Politik der Vernichtung* (Munich: Piper, 1998), pp. 250ff. For a detailed and carefully reconstructed analysis of the phases leading to the 'final solution', see Yaacov Lozowick, *Hitler's Bureaucrats: The Nazi Security Police and the Banality of Evil* (London: Continuum, 2002). Clearly German Jews and *Mischlinge*, as well as Western Jews for a time, were regarded differently; there was much discussion and confusion from 1941 to 1945. The book clarifies Eichmann's central role in the Holocaust as a leading functionary who was consumed with hatred of Jews and who, together with bureaucratic colleagues, carried through the genocide, fully aware it went against all civilised moral tenets. Lozowick thus rejects Hannah Arendt's mass murderer as a mere bureaucrat following orders.

55 Max Plaut, 'Aufzeichnung', not dated (post-war), St A H, 622-1, Familie Plaut, D39/3.

56 Ibid.

57 Ron Chernow, *The Warburgs*, pp. 503–5; Robert Solmitz, 'Das Sekretariat Warburg' and 'Meine Erinnerungen an Dr Max Plaut', Leo Baeck Institute Archive, New York.

58 Transfers to Palestine, *Chef-Besprechungen*, 22 September, 20 October 1939, 22 January, 20 March 1940; transfers from the American Jewish Joint Distribution Committee, 22 September 1939, Warburg Bank Archives, Hamburg.

59 *Frau* Schocken's request, *Herr* Herz's request, Hans Israel's request, *Chef-Besprechungen*, 19 November 1938, 31 May 1939, 23 May 1939, respectively, Warburg Bank Archives, Hamburg.
60 Ursula Randt, *Carolinenstraße 35: Geschichte der Mädchenschule der Deutsch-Israelitischen Gemeinde in Hamburg* (Hamburg: Verein für Hamburgische Geschichte, 1984).
61 Max Plaut, in answer to questions by E. G. Loewenthal, 14 June 1968 – a lengthy account of great value. Loewenthal sent a copy to Max Kreutzberger in a letter dated 14 November 1968. Kreutzberger collection, Leo Baeck Institute Archive, New York, AR 7183.
62 Memorandum for Paul Epstein, 7 July 1939, *Reichsvereinigung*, Epstein Akten, Yad Vashem, Jerusalem. Removal of tenancy protection, *Reichsgesetzblatt*, vol. 1, 1939, part 1, p. 864.

6 Holocaust

1 At the outbreak of war there were only a relatively few Jews in forced labour – 6,722, according to Plaut; another 6,000 were employed by Jewish organisations and 4,707 were in training organised by Jewish organisations, mainly in agriculture. Only 2,272 were still in paid employment or self-employed. The Jewish population of Hamburg numbered 14,244, of Berlin 72,452, and of Frankfurt 21,874. St A H, 622–1, Familie Plaut.

According to Gruner, the standard work, the total Jewish population in the *Altreich* in September 1939 was 185,000. Wolf Gruner, *Der geschlossene Arbeitseinsatz deutscher Juden: Zur Zwangsarbeit als Element der Verfolgung 1938–1943* (Berlin: Metropol, 1997), p. 350. There were between 51,000 and 53,000 Jews in forced labour out of a still remaining Jewish population of 167,245 in July 1941, shortly before the deportations began. In September 1939, Gruner, unlike Plaut, estimated 20,000 Jewish forced labourers. The statistics for the *Kindertransporte* did not include the number privately arranged. The overall total reached around 10,000.
2 Max Plaut, 'Ein Beitrag zur Lösung der Judenfrage im grossdeutschen Raum', undated. ST A H, 622-1 Familie Plaut.
3 'Arbeitsbericht der Reichsvereinigung der Juden in Deutschland für das Jahr 1939, Reichsvertretung der Juden', Leo Baeck Institute Archive, New York, ARZ 105/362. Statistics as to the precise number of Jews still in Germany after the outbreak of the war are difficult to arrive at, since in 1939 'racial Jews' included some Christians, and some of the statistics would have added *Mischlinge*. The official statistics of the May 1939 census counted 233,676 racial Jews and 213,930 by religion. Statistics of the Gestapo census of 20 October 1939, in the Plaut papers, give 185,222 in nine major cities of the *Altreich*. To these one might add another 20 to 30 per cent living outside of them, so about 246,000 plus the Austrian Jews. The *Arbeitsbericht* of the *Reichsvereinigung* for December 1939 calculated 240,000 Jews for the *Altreich* on 31 December 1939. Emigration statistics are cited as follows: 1933, 51,700; 1938, 46,000; 1939, 68,000 – a total up to December 1939 of 281,900.
4 Luise Solmitz, Journal, FZH, 11 S 12.
5 Plaut, memoir, St A H, 622-1 Familie Plaut, D39/3; Plaut, interview with Schottelius, 11 July 1953, FZH, 12 Plaut.
6 *Reichsvereinigung*, Aktennotiz: 'Vorladung im Geheimen Staatspolizeiamt', 25 June 1940, Yad Vashem, Jerusalem.
7 Peter Longerich, *Holocaust: The Nazi Persecution and Murder of the Jews* (Oxford: Oxford University Press, 2010), pp. 160–64.
8 Otto Dov Kulka, 'The *Reichsvereinigung* and the Fate of the German Jews, 1938/9–1943', in *The Jews in Nazi Germany, 1933–1943*, ed. Arnold Paucker, Sylvia Gilchrist and Barbara Suchy (Tübingen: Mohr, 1986). Paul Sauer, 'Otto Hirsch

(1885–1941): Director of the Reichsvertretung', *Leo Baeck Institute Year Book*, 32 (1987), pp. 341–68. See also Longerich, *Holocaust*, p.172.

9 The leading functionaries of the *Reichsvereinigung* were always in greater danger. See Max Plaut's account in St A H, 622-1 Familie Plaut, D39/3. For a history and documentation of the *Reichsvereinigung* and its predecessor, the *Reichsvertretung*, see *Deutsches Judentum unter dem Nationalsozialismus*, vol. 1: *Dokumente zur Geschichte der Reichsvertretung der deutschen Juden, 1933–1939*, ed. Otto Dov Kulka (Tübingen: Mohr Siebeck, 1997); Esriel Hildesheimer, *Jüdische Selbstverwaltung unter dem NS-Regime: Der Existenzkampf der Reichsvertretung und Reichsvereinigung der Juden in Deutschland* (Tübingen: Mohr,1994). On Otto Hirsch, see Sauer, 'Otto Hirsch (1885–1941): Director of the Reichvertretung'.

10 More than 150,000 Germans were murdered in the so-called euthanasia programme. The killings continued in 1941. From Hamburg's state mental hospital Langenhorn, of the 3,755 patients sent to killing centres, only 488 were alive in 1945. *Wege in den Tod: Hamburgs Anstalt Langenhorn und die Euthanasie in der Zeit des Nationalsozialismus*, ed. Klaus Böhme and Uwe Lohalm (Hamburg: Ergebnisse-Verlag, 1993). There is a file of euthanasia reports in the Forschungsstelle für Zeigeschichte, Hamburg, no. 3512. See also Henry Friedländer, *The Origins of Nazi Genocide: From Euthanasia to the Final Solution* (Chapel Hill: University of North Carolina Press, 1995).

11 Plaut, 'Aufzeichnung', St A H, 622-1 Familie Plaut, D 39/3.

12 For the charges of the supposed patients in Cholm, *Pflegekosten der Irrenanstalt Cholm*, 6 May 1941, records of the *Reichsvereinigung*, Yad Vashem. The daily costs were RM 3 and burial costs RM 65. By March 1941, the *Reichsvereinigung* had been sent bills for RM 100,000. On 2 October 1941 a note listed 1,100 patients, of whom 1,050 had died. This bill was for RM 478,574 and 71 *Pfennige*. Typical of death certificates was Dr Keller's, from the Landes-Pflegeanstalt (state mental hospital) at Grafeneck, to Moritz Israel Fleischer, 5 June 1940, whose son had supposedly 'unexpectedly died of the swelling of his brain. With his serious and incurable disease, death was for him a deliverance.'

13 Yaron Matras, *Roma und Cinti in Hamburg*, published by the Senate of Hamburg (1992). See also John A. S. Grenville, 'Neglected Holocaust Victims: The Mischlinge, the Jüdischversippte and the Gypsies', in *The Holocaust and History: The Known, the Unknown, the Disputed, and the Reexamined*, ed. Michael Berenbaum and Abraham J. Peck (Bloomington: Indiana University Press, 1998), pp. 315–26; Vivianne Wünsche, Uwe Lohalm and Michael Zimmermann, *Die nationalsozialistische Verfolgung Hamburger Roma und Sinti* (Hamburg: Landeszentrale für politische Bildung, 2002); Linde Apel, ed., *In den Tod geschickt: Die Deportationen von Juden, Roma und Sinti aus Hamburg 1940 bis 1945* (Berlin: Metropol, 2009).

14 *Frau* Schmidt, Tagebuch, 17 November 1938, 29 October 1939, 16 March 1941, and 4 October 1942, Hoover Institution on War, Revolution and Peace, Stanford, California.

15 'Über die Tätigkeit des Wohnungspflegeamts', 1 April 1940–31 März 1941, Report no. 1, July 1941, St A H, 353-2 II Wohnungsamt II, 309; minutes of meetings of *Beiräte für Sozialangelegenheiten*, 11 April 1940, 9 October 1941, 13 November 1941, St A H, 351-10 I Sozialbehörde I, StA 26.19b, vols II and III.

16 Jeremy Noakes and Geoffrey Pridham, *Nazism, 1919–1945*, vol. 3: *Foreign Policy, War and Racial Extermination* (Exeter: University of Exeter Press, 1988), p. 1113.

17 There is a large literature on the question of when Hitler decided on the murder of the *German* Jews and different interpretations, largely on account of different questions being answered. My contribution, 'Die "Endlösung" und die "Judenmischlinge" im Dritten Reich', in *Das Unrechtsregime*, ed. Ursula Büttner, (Hamburg: Christians, 1986), vol. 2, pp. 91–121, drew attention to the importance of distinguishing between *German* and Russian and Polish Jews. Peter Longerich's *Politik der Vernichtung: Eine Gesamtdarstellung der nationalsozialistischen Judenverfolgung* (Munich: Piper,

1998) emphasises the difference between general planning and the actual decision to start the killings. Also see his *Der ungeschriebene Befehl: Hitler und der Weg zur 'Endlösung'* (Munich: Piper, 2001). Important contributions are Yaacov Lozowick, *Hitler's Bureaucrats: The Nazi Security Police and the Banality of Evil* (London: Continuum, 2002), and Ian Kershaw, *Hitler, the Germans and the Final Solution* (New Haven, CT: Yale University Press, 2008), pp. 237–81.

18 Michael Thad Allen, 'Not just a "Dating Game": Origins of the Holocaust at Auschwitz in the Light of Witness Testimony', *German History*, 25/2 (2007), pp. 162–91.

19 The Hamburg Gestapo deportation orders are in St A H, 314-15 Oberfinanzpräsident (Devisenstelle und Vermögensverwertungsstelle). I found them before their delivery to the Hamburg State Archives in the cellar of the finance office at Magdalenenstraße. A different version, sent out in Württemberg not directly by the Gestapo but by the Jewish organisation, is less peremptory in tone and is printed in Noakes and Pridham, *Nazism, 1919–1945*, vol. 3, pp. 1117–18.

20 Elisabeth Flügge, letter to her daughter, 24 October 1941, private access. See Elisabeth Flügge, *Wie wird es weitergehen ...: Zeitungsartikel und Notizen aus den Jahren 1933 und 1934*, ed. Rita Bake (Hamburg: Landeszentrale für politische Bildung, 2001).

21 Luise Solmitz, Journal, 5 December 1941, FZH, 11 S 13.

22 Dr Otto Bauer's letters in FZH, 6262. He perished in Mauthausen concentration camp.

23 Max Plaut, 'Aufzeichnung', 14 June 1968, for E. G. Loewenthal, who passed it on to Max Kreutzberger, Leo Baeck Institute Archive, New York, Kreutzberger collection, AR 7183.

24 Max Plaut, 'Aufzeichnung', 14 June 1968, Leo Baeck Institute Archive, New York, Kreutzberger collection, AR 7183.

25 Henry Rosenberg's account, FZH, 6262. The Minsk transport actually left on 8 November 1941, a day after assembly in the Logenheim.

26 *The Chronicle of the Lodz Ghetto 1941–1944*, ed. Lucjan Dobroszycki (New Haven, CT: Yale University Press, 1984), pp. 164–7.

27 The calculations are based on *Gedenkbuch für die jüdischen Opfer des Nationalsozialismus in Hamburg* (Hamburg: Staatsarchiv, 1965; rev. ed., comp. Jürgen Sielemann and Peter Flamme, 1995); a manuscript, 'Der jüdische Religionsverband Hamburg im Jahre 1942: Die Liquidation der jüdischen Stiftungen und Vereine in Hamburg', which Leo Lippmann compiled before committing suicide on 11 June 1943, published as '... daß Ich wie ein guter Deutscher empfinde und handele': Zur Geschichte der Deutsch-Israelitischen Gemeinde in Hamburg in der Zeit vom Herbst 1935 bis zum Ende 1942* (Hamburg: Dölling & Galitz, 1993), pp. 85–127; and a document entitled 'Vertrauensmann der Reichsvereinigung der Juden in Deutschland für den Bezirk Hamburg to the Gestapo', 15 April 1945, microfilmed from the archives in Moscow, Reichsvereinigung, no. 35, Yad Vashem Archives, Jerusalem.

28 Dobroszycki, *The Chronicle of the Lodz Ghetto 1941–1944*, pp. 164ff.

29 There is plenty of literature on the Wannsee meeting. Eichmann's record is translated in Noakes and Pridham, *Nazism*, vol. 3, pp. 1125–36. See also Christian Gerlach, 'The Wannsee Conference, the Fate of German Jews, and Hitler's Decision in Principle to Exterminate All European Jews', *Journal of Modern History*, 70/4 (1998), pp. 759–812; Kershaw, *Hitler: 1936–1945 Nemesis*, pp. 487–95, for a brief and judicious overview; John A. S. Grenville, 'Neglected Holocaust Victims: The Mischlinge, the Jüdischversippte, and the Gypsies'; Peter Longerich, *Die Wannsee-Konferenz vom 20 Januar 1942: Planung und Beginn des Genozids an den europäischen Juden* (Berlin: Hentrich, 1998). Goebbels wrote in his journal on 15 February 1942, three weeks after the Wannsee Conference,

> The Führer expressed his view once more that he is determined ruthlessly to finish [*aufzuräumen*] with the Jews in Europe. One can have no sentimental attitudes about this. The Jews have earned the catastrophe which they are now

experiencing. They will experience their own destruction together with that of our enemies. We must accelerate this process with cold ruthlessness, and we will have done mankind a great service to free tortured mankind from thousands of years of Jewry ...

This passage (my translation), published in Louis Lochner's edition of *The Goebbels Diaries, 1942–1943* (London: Hamish Hamilton, 1948), is well known. When I consulted the microfilmed original in the Hoover Institution Archive in Stanford, I found an earlier, then unpublished, portion of significance; Goebbels wrote that, while in Berlin, he had spoken not only to Hitler but also to Heydrich. It would seem highly probable that Heydrich had also spoken to Hitler about the outcome of the Wannsee Conference. The whole entry of 15 February 1942 and a more complete version of Goebbels's diaries have subsequently been published: *Die Tagebücher von Joseph Goebbels*, ed. Elke Fröhlich, 32 vols (Munich: Saur, 1998–2008), Part II: *Diktate 1941–1945*, vol. 3: *January–March 1942* (1994). Himmler saw Hitler on 18 December 1941 and made an entry in his official appointment book: 'Jewish question/extermination as partisan'. Special Archive, Moscow, 1372-5-23, quoted by Peter Witte, Michael Wildt and Martin Voigt, *Der Dienstkalender Heinrich Himmlers 1941/42* (Hamburg: Christians, 1999). 'Partisan' suggests the reference is to killing Jews in Russia while the war is still continuing. The files of the Ministry of Justice read in their full context dispose of David Irving's controversial claim that, even at the time of the Wannsee meeting, Hitler wished to postpone the final solution until after the war. Hitler was especially sensitive to the treatment of German Jews in mixed religious marriages and their descendants, not wishing to upset the 'German' close relatives during the war. His concern did not extend to Polish or Russian Jews. The final solution had to be handled differently, depending on Germany's relationship with a country in Eastern or Central Europe or in the West, whether ally, neutral or occupied territory.

Heydrich was frustrated on the issue of the *Mischlinge*, though pleased in general that the meeting had gone so smoothly. When Franz Schlegelberger, acting minister of justice, received the record of the Wannsee meeting and that of the subsequent one, held on 6 March 1942, he wrote to Hans Heinrich Lammers, Hitler's state secretary at the Reich Chancellery, that he found Heydrich's proposals, which were intended to 'form the basis of the plan to be submitted to Hitler', 'completely unacceptable'. He asked to meet and discuss this with Lammers. The two men conferred in March 1942. Roland Freisler, state secretary at the Ministry of Justice (later the notorious judge of the People's Court), initialled a brief note of their conversation. It recorded Lammers telling Schlegelberger that the Führer had repeatedly told him that he wished the solution of the Jewish question, the 'final solution', to be postponed until after the war. Did this mean Hitler wished to postpone the genocide of Europe's Jews? What was being discussed on 20 January, however, was a specific problem, not genocide of Jewry in general, already taken for granted, but the 'difficult' issue of German Jews closely related to Germans (Aryans). The genocide was proceeding with Hitler's full approval, but the fate of the German *Mischlinge* and Jews married to Germans he intended to settle after the war. Lammers promised to draw Hitler's attention to Heydrich's proposals so that he would not be taken unawares when plans were put to him. No plan was submitted by Heydrich, as he was assassinated in Prague four months after Wannsee, and further meetings could not reach any agreement. Franz Schlegelberger to Lammers, 12 March 1942; Lammers to Schlegelberger, 18 March 1942; Freisler's minute of Schlegelberger's meeting with Lammers, undated; Schlegelberger's own proposals, 'concerning the final solution of the Jewish question', 5 April 1942; Bundesarchiv, Berlin, Reichsjustizministerium R 22/53.

30 There is a huge literature discussing and disagreeing about the precise timing of the end phases of the decision to murder the Jews of Europe *en masse*. The most

accessible translation of critical documents is to be found in Noakes and Pridham, *Nazism*, vol. 3, pp.1086–208, here also on the *Einsatzgruppen*, pp. 1086–102; Heydrich's own brief, signed by Göring and dated 31 July 1941, pp. 1103–4; Himmler to Greiser, 18 September 1941, pp. 1113–14; the death camps, pp. 1137–208. See also Heinz Höhne, *The Order of the Death's Head* (London: Pan, 1972), pp. 357–69; Lozowick, *Hitler's Bureaucrats*; and Ian Kershaw's discussion in *Hitler, the Germans and the Final Solution*, pp. 29–116. The *Aktion Reinhard* is discussed in detail by Longerich, *Holocaust*, pp. 280, 282, 288, 295–6, 332–4, 339–41, 378–9.

31 *Gedenkbuch für die jüdischen Opfer des Nationalsozialismus in Hamburg*, pp. 46ff.

32 Hedwig Wohlwill's account, 'For Albrecht Max Brandis on the Occasion of your Confirmation, 23 March 1947: A Memoir of Dr Heinrich Wohlwill by your Grandmother' (in German, private collection).

33 *Frau* Schmidt, diary entry, 4 October 1942, Hoover Institute Archive, Stanford, California.

34 On the German people more generally and their reactions to the persecution and genocide of the Jews, studies of particular importance are Werner Jochmann, *Gesellschaftskrise und Judenfeindschaft in Deutschland, 1870–1945* (Hamburg: Christians, 1988); Ian Kershaw, *Popular Opinion and Political Dissent in the Third Reich* (Oxford: Clarendon Press, 1983); David Bankier, *The Germans and the Final Solution* (Oxford: Blackwell, 1992); Sarah Gordon, *Hitler, Germans and the Jewish Question* (Princeton, NJ: Princeton University Press, 1984); Ursula Büttner, ed., *Die Deutschen und die Judenverfolgung im Dritten Reich* (2nd ed., Frankfurt: Fischer, 2003), with a perceptive overview by the editor, 'Die deutsche Gesellschaft und die Judenverfolgung: Ein Bericht über Forschungserträge und ungelöste Fragen', citing several hundred books and articles. In May 1942 a report from Erfurt told of 'extraordinary rumours circulating of mass shootings and the victims having to dig their graves first'. *Die Juden in den geheimen NS-Stimmungsberichten, 1933–1945*, ed. Otto Dov Kulka and Eberhard Jäckel (Düsseldorf: Droste, 2004), p. 491. See also Eric Johnson and Karl-Heinz Reuband, *What We Knew: Terror, Mass Murder, and Everyday Life in Nazi Germany* (London: John Murray, 2005), and Ian Kershaw, *Hitler, the Germans and the Final Solution* (New Haven, CT: Yale University Press, 2008), pp. 119–234.

35 Minute of the assembly of the Hamburg Chamber of Commerce, 12 November 1943, in its archives

36 'Wir sind froh, dass die jüdische Pest durch den Nationalsozialismus ausgerottet wurde', *Hamburger Tageblatt*, 12 February 1942, FZH.

37 *Hamburger Tageblatt*, 7 January 1943, FZH.

38 Diary of Colonel Ernst Ebeling, entries 2 February, 22 March, 29 December 1942, 3 January, 31 January, 14 February, 11 April and 17 April 1943, FZH, 11 E 1.

39 The activities of Reserve Police Battalion 101 were brilliantly reconstructed by Christopher R. Browning in *Ordinary Men: Reserve Battalion 101 and the Final Solution in Poland* (London: HarperCollins, 1992). The issue which attracted controversy was his analysis of some members of the force, which led him to the conclusion that ordinary people can be turned into killers in the right circumstances and after conditioning. However, some members, a minority, refused to shoot innocent Jews. This conclusion was challenged by Daniel Goldhagen in 'Ordinary Men or Ordinary Germans', a contribution to *The Holocaust and History*, pp. 301–7, as well as later in his *Hitler's Willing Executioners: Ordinary Germans and the Holocaust* (New York: Alfred A. Knopf, 1996), chapters 6–9 and 15. Browning argues that these men, as far as can be gleaned from the limited information available on their backgrounds, came from one of the least Nazified cities in Germany and that their lower-class backgrounds in Weimar disposed them to support the parties of the left. My own research suggests that, after 1933, there was not a great deal of difference between Hamburg and other cities. As Christopher Browning has shown, the battalion's membership

frequently changed; it is also striking that the sadistic henchmen recruited by the Gestapo in Hamburg came from all social strata. The Third Reich knew how to attract those it needed, only occasionally making mistakes, but it is not clear whether the members of this force were volunteers or conscripted at different times. The members of the police battalions were not civilian policemen but belonged to the militarised order police that had originated in Hamburg in the early Weimar Republic to protect it against revolution; they remained in continuous existence until 1933, when they were reorganised by the Nazis. While any answer must be conjectural, it does seem clear at least that previous political allegiances, age or class did not necessarily make individuals immune to the blandishments of the Nazis. But perhaps Goldhagen and Browning are not all that far apart: it is always necessary to distinguish between individuals in a group, as Browning does; hopefully the majority of ordinary people cannot be conditioned into becoming sadistic killers who enjoy their work, but some can. Human nature spans a wide arc, from saint to darkest evil-doer.

40 Martin Greschat, 'Die Haltung der deutschen evangelischen Kirchen zur Verfolgung der Juden im Dritten Reich', in Büttner, ed., *Die Deutschen und die Judenverfolgung im Dritten Reich*, pp. 273–292, 2nd ed., 320–341.

41 *Elisabeth Schmitz und ihre Denkschrift gegen die Judenverfolgung: Konturen einer vergessenen Biographie (1893–1977)*, ed. Manfred Gailus (Berlin: Wichern, 2008); Manfred Gailus, *Mir aber zerriss es das Herz: Der stille Widerstand der Elisabeth Schmitz* (Göttingen: Vandenhoeck & Ruprecht, 2010). Marga Meusel, for many years a welfare worker of the Berlin Confessional Church, was thought to be the author. Martin Greschat, '"Gegen den Gott der Deutschen"': Marga Meusels Kampf für die Rettung der Juden', in Ursula Büttner and Martin Greschat, *Die verlassenen Kinder der Kirche: Der Umgang mit Christen jüdischer Herkunft im 'Dritten Reich'* (Göttingen: Vandenhoeck & Ruprecht, 1998), pp. 70–85. An important early study is Richard Gutteridge, *'Open thy Mouth for the Dumb!': The German Evangelical Church and the Jews, 1879–1950* (Oxford: Blackwell, 1976); Further, for the Nazi years, Wolfgang Gerlach, *Als die Zeugen schwiegen: Bekennende Kirche und die Juden* (Berlin: Institut Kirche und Judentum, 1987).

42 Martin Greschat, 'Die Haltung der deutschen evangelischen Kirchen zur Verfolgung der Juden im Dritten Reich', p. 283, 2nd ed., p. 332; also Ursula Büttner, 'Von der Kirche verlassen: Die deutschen Protestanten und die Verfolgung der Juden und Christen jüdischer Herkunft im "Dritten Reich"', in Büttner and Greschat, *Die verlassenen Kinder der Kirche*, pp. 43f.

43 'Kirchenkanzlei der Deutschen Evangelischen Kirchen (DEK) an die obersten Behörden der deutschen evangelischen Landeskirchen', signed by vice-president Dr Fürle, 22 December 1941, Evangelisches Zentralarchiv, Berlin. Wurm to DEK, 6 February 1941, response citing Galicians 3.28 and Romans 10.12 (he could also have cited John 14.6); Congregation of the Confessing Church, Potsdam, to DEK, 2 June 1943, Evangelisches Zentralarchiv, Berlin.

44 Richard C. Lukas, *The Forgotten Holocaust: The Poles under German Occupation, 1939–1944* (New York: Hippocrene, 1997), pp. 16–17. The Vatican tried to aid some Jews secretly in Rome and endeavoured to stop deportations from Hungary and Slovakia, but these efforts came too late.

45 Karol Jonca, 'Schlesiens Kirchen zur "Lösung der Judenfrage"', in *Das Unrechtsregime: Internationale Forschung über den Nationalsozialismus*, vol. 2: *Verfolgung – Exil – Belasteter Neubeginn*, ed. Ursula Büttner (Hamburg: Christians, 1986), pp. 123–48, here pp. 129–30.

46 Lutz-Eugen Reutter, *Katholische Kirche als Fluchthelfer im Dritten Reich: Die Betreuung von Auswanderern durch den St. Raphaels-Verein* (Hamburg: Paulus Verlag, 1971). On the attitude of the Catholic Church, Pius XII and the Jews, there is a large literature, including a balanced assessment with bibliography by Bernd Nellessen, 'Die schweigende Kirche: Katholiken und Judenverfolgung', in Büttner, ed., *Die Deutschen*

und die Judenverfolgung im Dritten Reich, pp. 305–19. More recent studies are: Klaus Kühlwein, *Warum der Papst schwieg: Pius XII. und der Holocaust* (Düsseldorf: Patmos, 2008); Kevin P. Spicer, *Hitler's Priests: Catholic Clergy and National Socialism* (DeKalb: Northern Illinois University Press, 2008); Hubert Wolf, *Papst & Teufel: Die Archive des Vatikan und das Dritte Reich* (Munich: Beck, 2008).

47 Report of Margarete Sommer, Berlin, 2 March 1943; Bertram to Frick, Muhs, Thierack, Lammers and RHSA, 2 March 1943, both documents in *Akten deutscher Bischöfe über die Lage der Kirche, 1933–1945*, vol. 6: *1943–1945*, ed. Ludwig Volk (Mainz: Matthias Grünewald, 1985), pp. 19–23. Heinrich Herzberg, *Dienst am höheren Gesetz: Dr. Margarete Sommer und das 'Hilfswerk beim Bischöflichen Ordinariat Berlin'* (Berlin: Servi, 2000), pp. 123f.

48 A Polish Jew to Bertram, from the General Government, 24 August 1943, *Akten deutscher Bischöfe*, vol. 6, pp. 210–15. I am not aware it has ever been quoted, which is not so surprising, as it has to be found among thousands of printed pages.

49 Bertram to Himmler, 17 November 1943, *Akten der deutscher Bischöfe*, vol. 6, pp. 281–2. For the meeting at Fulda a few weeks earlier in September, see ibid., pp. 197–205; Bernd Nellessen, 'Die schweigende Kirsche', 2nd ed., p. 305.

50 Dr Berthold Simonsohn, leader of the *Provinzreferat* of the Hamburg community from 1938 to 1942, in an interview with Schottelius after the war (21 April 1953, FZH, 6262), said that the lists were compiled mainly by the Jewish organisation; Plaut emphasised the opposite. What happened in Berlin may provide a clue. At the *Reichsvereinigung*, Martha Mosse was in charge of the accommodation office, which supplied information to the Gestapo from which the deportation lists were drawn up. In her post-war manuscript memoirs, written in 1963, she said the Gestapo would demand three or four thousand questionnaires filled in by individuals one or two weeks before a deportation transport was organised. The questionnaires were originally supposed to be for a housing register. Mosse was threatened by the Gestapo with concentration camp if she revealed their ulterior purpose. Martha Mosse, 'Erinnerungen', Leo Baeck Institute Archive, New York, Kreutzberger collection, AR 7183, Box 7.

51 Max Plaut, interview with Dr Schottelius, 25 January 1954, FZH, 12 Plaut.

52 Max Plaut to E. G. Loewenthal, 25 November 1968, Leo Baeck Institute Archive, New York, Kreutzberger collection, AR 7183.

53 *Bekanntmachungen*, FZH, 62631. Joseph Walk, *Das Sonderrecht für die Juden im NS-Staat: Eine Sammlung der gesetzlichen Maßnahmen und Richtlinien: Inhalt und Bedeutung* (Heidelberg and Karlsruhe: Müller, 1981). The laws and ordinances are printed in chronological order: pensions to civil servants, 19 July 1939; no individual actions against Jews, 7 September 1939; transport of containers, 16 July 1940.

54 Max Plaut, a collection of correspondence in St A H, 622-1 Familie Plaut.

55 Dr Hannes, married to an 'Aryan', was head of the Jewish hospital. Franz Rappolt, who had worked in the hospital, was deported on 11 July 1942 with his wife; neither survived.

56 The correspondence with tenants in the *Judenhäuser* was scattered in a cellar in the *Oberfinanzbehörde* (now St A H, 314-15 Oberfinanzpräsident (Devisenstelle und Vermögensverwertungsstelle)). Here were also compensation claims, sorted in files separately for each deportation.

57 I have reconstructed this account from one of the files in the Magdalenenstraße cellar. Anna's son served in the headquarters of the SS in Berlin, and, although he made a compensation claim for his stepfather jointly with his sister after the war, he transferred any compensation due to him to his sister. As a member of the SS he could not receive compensation for his Jewish stepfather. All the other accounts are reconstructions from the same source. I met the caretaker, who in 1945 was told to burn all the original files. Feeling they were of historic importance, he singlehandedly preserved them in the cellar. There this unique source of wartime Jewish life lay covered in dust until I secured the key from the current president of *Oberfinanzdirektion*, to whom I had written

enquiring whether they had any relevant records. How many more cellars are there to be discovered? The files have since been moved to the Hamburg State Archives: 314-15 Oberfinanzpräsident (Devisenstelle und Vermögensverwertungsstelle).

58 Dr Beate Meyer, of the *Institut für die Geschichte der deutschen Juden*, has researched divorces in Hamburg, where, between 1938 and 1945, 130 divorces were granted; to these would have to be added the divorces between 1933 and 1937. The divorce rate therefore exceeded the generally accepted 7 to 10 per cent to about one in seven, which nevertheless shows that at least six German partners out of seven refused to succumb to enormous pressure and persecution. Beate Meyer, *'Jüdische Mischlinge': Rassenpolitik und Verfolgungserfahrungen, 1933–1945* (Hamburg: Dölling & Galitz, 1999).

59 Beate Meyer, 'The Mixed Marriage: A Guarantee of Survival or a Reflection of German Society during the Nazi Regime?', in *Probing the Depths of German Antisemitism: German Society and the Persecution of the Jews, 1933–1941*, ed. David Bankier (Oxford: Berghahn, 1999), pp. 54–77. The researches by Dr Beate Meyer of divorces in Hamburg have uncovered some striking facts: the number of divorces had increased significantly as persecution radicalised in 1938 and during the principal deportation years from 1941 to 1943. What is also telling is that 103 men rid themselves of their inconvenient Jewish wives whereas only twenty-seven wives divorced their Jewish husbands, even though more Jewish wives had married gentile husbands than the other way around.

60 The reconstruction of life in the *Judenhäuser* is based on various folders in St A H, 314-15 Oberfinanzpräsident (Devisenstelle und Vermögensverwertungsstelle).

61 Auction sale lists showing where the goods came from, the name of the purchaser, the item, the price paid and the names of the auctioneers are in St A H, 314-15 Oberfinanzpräsident (Devisenstelle und Vermögensverwertungsstelle); there was no item too small – a handbag, a top hat – that it did not find a buyer at a bargain price. The more valuable items were spotted by keen *Volksgenossen*. Gerda D. to Heinz Horn, 13 July 1941, and Heinz Horn to Gerda D., 16 July 1941, ibid.

62 John A. S. Grenville, 'Juden, "Nichtarier" und "Deutsche Ärzte"': Die Anpassung der Ärzte im Dritten Reich', in Büttner, ed., *Die Deutschen und die Judenverfolgung im Dritten Reich*, pp. 191–206, 2nd ed., pp. 228–46.

63 On Schallert, see Plaut's account, St A H, 622-1 Familie Plaut, D39.

64 Grenville, 'Juden, "Nichtarier" und "Deutsche Ärzte"'. There is a file on the Unna Clinic in St A H, 352-10 Gesundheitsbehörde, Personalakten 43.

65 Compensation case, Michael Hauptmann, FZH, 18-1 Notgemeinschaft, 2.1, vol. 30. These valuable records of the *Notgemeinschaft der durch die Nürnberger Gesetze Betroffenen* (Emergency Association of those Aggrieved by the Nuremberg Laws) were saved almost by chance from destruction by the late Professor Werner Jochmann and Professor Ursula Büttner and brought to the *Forschungsstelle*, where they are now arranged alphabetically.

66 Max Plaut to E. G. Loewenthal, 14 June 1968, Leo Baeck Institute Archive, New York, Kreutzberger collection, AR 7183. 180 people left on that transport.

67 There is some correspondence between Dr Corten and Plaut in St A H, 622-1 Familie Plaut, but the most complete surviving records of a functionary, *Vertrauensmann*, of this successor organisation are those of the solicitor Berkowitz, married to an 'Aryan' in Hannover, kept in the Hannover City Archive.

68 Leo Lippmann, *Mein Leben und meine amtliche Tätigkeit: Erinnerungen und ein Beitrag zur Finanzgeschichte Hamburgs*, ed. Werner Jochmann (Hamburg: Christians, 1964), is sparse on the Nazi years. For the description of his life during the war and his suicide, Max Plaut to Arthur Lippmann, 16 August 1945, St A H, 622-1 Familie Plaut.

69 Dr Schottelius, interview with Plaut, 11 July 1953, FZH, 12 Plaut.

70 *Stimmungsberichte der Fürsorgestellen* in St A H, 351-10 I Sozialbehörde I, VG 30.70, especially 25 February 1943 (K. St 1a); 25 February and 24 June 1943 (K. St 2a); 24 February 1943 (K. St 2b); 26 February and 1 March 1943 (K. St 4a); 27 February 1943 (K. St 7); 28 June 1943 (K. St 8); 4 March 1943 (K. St 10). These reports are from seven areas covered by the welfare services in the poorer districts of Hamburg.

71 A graphic account based on documents and many eyewitnesses is Martin Middlebrook, *The Battle of Hamburg: Allied Bomber Forces against a German City in 1943* (Harmondsworth: Penguin, 1984).

72 Plaut to E. G. Loewenthal, 14 June 1960, Leo Baeck Institute Archive, New York, Kreutzberger collection, AR 7183.

73 *Reichsvereinigung der Juden in Deutschland,* Siegbert Israel Kleeman to *Oberfinanzpräsident* Berlin-Brandenburg, 18 August 1943; Ernst Israel Friedländer, on behalf of the *Reichsvereinigung, Kleiderkammer,* 20 August 1943, in *Reichsvereinigung,* Yad Vashem, Jerusalem.

74 Max Plaut, reply to Hamburg police questionnaire, 5 May 1967, St A H, 622-1 Familie Plaut, D39/6; Plaut to Loewenthal, 14 June 1968, Leo Baeck Institute Archive, New York, Kreutzberger collection, AR 7183. Plaut was not deported with the other members of the *Reichsvereinigung* in Hamburg and remained behind with his mother.

75 The account has been pieced together from a number of post-war interviews, all conducted by Dr Herbert Schottelius and now preserved in the Forschungstelle für Zeitgeschichte in Hamburg. They took place on 16 July 1954 with Martin Tobar, who acted as a nursing assistant; on 10 July 1954 with Dr Martin Corten, the last wartime head of the hospital; on 14 April 1953 with Dr Ernst Wolffson, Corten's predecessor; on 5 July 1954 with Felix Epstein, administrator of the hospital; and, finally, on 5 June 1954 with Dr Berthold Hannes, the post-war director of the hospital. FZH, 6262. For a general history, see Mary Lindemann, *140 Jahre Israelitisches Krankenhaus in Hamburg: Vorgeschichte und Entwicklung* (Hamburg: Israelitisches Krankenhaus, 1981), and, on the death marches, Martin Gilbert, *The Dent Atlas of the Holocaust* (London: Dent, 1993), and Martin Gilbert, *The Holocaust: Jewish Tragedy* (London: Collins, 1986), pp. 221–30.

76 Lorenz Treplin, documents in St A H: 221-11 Entnazifizierung, Military Government Fragebogen, M 634; 352-6 Gesundheitsbehörde, HV 39 V 25; 352-10 Gesundheitsverwaltung, Personalakte Treplin; 611-11 Israelitisches Krankenhaus, 29 Unterakte 2. Dr Hannes, oration, 2 September 1952 (Treplin died on 24 August 1952), St A H. Post-war witnesses: Schottelius's interview with Martin Tobar, 16 July 1954, and with Dr Hannes, 3 June 1954, FZH, 6262. Ina Lorenz, 'Das Leben der Hamburger Juden im Zeichen der Endlösung', in Arno Herzig and Ina Lorenz, *Verdrängung und Vernichtung der Juden unter dem Nationalsozialismus* (Hamburg: Christians, 1992), pp. 207–47.

77 Alice Kruse, 'Memoiren', Leo Baeck Institute Archive, New York.

78 *Geschlossener Arbeitseinsatz jüdischer Mischlinge,* 12 October 1944, referring to the Gestapo order by Kaltenbrunner of 6 October 1944; list of *Arbeitseinsatztransport,* 14 February 1945; *Schnellbrief* to *Reichsstatthalter, Einsatz jüdischer Mischlinge ersten Grades und jüdisch Versippter,* no date, but after 5 March 1945, and several later reports for compensation purposes, all in St A H, 131-5 Senatskanzlei-Verwaltungsbeschwerden, no. 237; report of one of the forced labourers: Harro Torneck, Vom kriegswichtigen Einsatz, manuscript, 15 June 1945, FZH, 6262.

79 Eberhard Kolb, *Bergen-Belsen* (Göttingen: Vandenhoeck & Ruprecht, 1985). The estimate of total deaths among all nationalities from 1943 to 1945 is 50,000, the majority Jews. The conversion of Bergen-Belsen to a concentration camp was completed in December 1944. The number of inmates increased from 22,000 on 1 February 1945 to approximately 60,000 on 15 April; approximately 34,000 perished between February 1945 and liberation on 15 April 1945, and 13,000 thereafter who could not be saved.

Werner Johe, *Neuengamme: Zur Geschichte der Konzentrationslager in Hamburg* (Hamburg: Landeszentrale für politische Bildung, 1981).

80 Fritz Bringmann, *Kindermord am Bullenhuserdamm: SS Verbrechen in Hamburg 1945* (Frankfurt: Röderberg, 1978).

81 *'Schließlich ist es meine Heimat ...': Harry Goldstein und die Jüdische Gemeinde in Hamburg in persönlichen Dokumenten und Fotos*, ed. Uwe Lohalm (Hamburg: Ergebnisse-Verlag, 2002). Ina Lorenz, 'Jüdischer Neubeginn im "Land der Mörder": Zur Entstehung der neuen Jüdischen Gemeinde in Hamburg 1945–1948', in *Leben im Land der Täter: Juden im Nachkriegsdeutschland (1945–1952)*, ed. Julius Schoeps (Berlin: Jüdische Verlagsanstalt, 2001), pp. 97–132. Ursula Büttner, 'Not nach der Befreiung: Die Situation der deutschen Juden in der britischen Besatzungszone 1945–1948', in *Das Unrechtsregime*, ed. Ursula Büttner, vol. 2, pp. 373–406. Struan Robertson, 'A History of the Jews in Hamburg', www1.uni-hamburg.de/rz3a035// jh_welcome.html; Ina Lorenz, 'To Leave or to Stay: The New Beginning of the Hamburg Jewish Community post 1945', www1.uni-hamburg.de/rz3a035// Lorenz.html.

82 For an account of the meetings of the senate from 3 to 8 May 1945 and Oskar Martini's quotation, see Uwe Bahnsen and Kerstin von Stürmer, 'Hamburg – besiegt, besetz, befreit', www.abendblatt.de/hamburg/article293372/Hamburg-besiegt-besetzt-befreit.html. For the last days of Nazi Hamburg and the post-war occupation, *Hamburg: Geschichte der Stadt und ihrer Bewohner*, ed. Werner Jochmann and Hans-Dieter Loose, vol. 2 (Hamburg: Hoffmann & Campe, 1986), contribution by Arnold Sywottek, pp. 377–466. Records found in the Magdalenenstraße cellar (now in St A H, 314-15 Oberfinanzpräsident (Devisenstelle und Vermögensverwertungsstelle)) show that Claus Göttsche, shortly before capitulation, had transferred the Gestapo funds into his bank account at the *Norddeutsche Bank*, a final example of corruption. See Frank Bajohr, *Parvenüs und Profiteure: Korruption in der NS-Zeit* (Frankfurt: Fischer, 2001).

SELECT BIBLIOGRAPHY

What to put in, what to leave out? It is hardly possible to do justice to all I have read and profited from over the last thirty years. Much too has been contributed by discussions with colleagues. The bibliography contains mainly the books and articles cited but not all those that informed this study. I can only apologise for omissions and lapses of memory.

I have divided the bibliography into two sections, 'General' and 'Hamburg', for a reason. It is intended to show how much can be contributed to the understanding of a country's general history from a regional study and to show the close interrelation of the two. Too often in the past, regional studies have been regarded as 'secondary', 'specific' and of limited antiquarian interest. This was particularly true in 1980 when I began my researches. Some of my colleagues were puzzled that a professional historian should so confine himself. The writing of social history, a field in which British historians have excelled, had already pioneered this approach. The same is true of medieval historians. But, even today, regional studies, while I concede they vary in scope and quality, are not always sufficiently valued. The research done in Hamburg has been and continues to be truly impressive, and my fortuitous choice of this city-state was fortunate indeed both personally and professionally.

General

Abel, Theodore, *Why Hitler Came to Power* (Cambridge, MA: Harvard University Press, 1986).

Adam, Uwe Dietrich, 'Wie Spontan war der Judenpogrom 1938', in Walter H. Pehle, *Der Judenpogrom 1938: Von der 'Reichskristallnacht' zum Völkermord* (Frankfurt: Fischer, 1988), pp. 74–93.

Adam, Uwe Dietrich, *Judenpolitik im Dritten Reich* (Düsseldorf: Droste, 1972, 3rd ed., 2003).

Adamovic, Aleksandr M., ed., *Eine Schuld die nicht erlischt: Dokumente über deutsche Kriegsverbrechen in der Sowjetunion* (Cologne: Pahl-Rugenstein, 1987).

Adler, Hans Günther, *Theresienstadt: Das Antlitz einer Zwangsgemeinschaft* (Tübingen: Mohr, 1955, 3rd ed., 2005).

Allen, Michael Thad, 'Not just a "Dating Game": Origins of the Holocaust at Auschwitz in the Light of Witness Testimony', *German History*, 25/2 (2007), pp. 162–91.

Aly, Götz, 'Endlösung': Völkerverschiebung und der Mord an den europäischen Juden (3rd ed., Frankfurt: Fischer Taschenbuch, 1995).

Amos, Elon, *The Pity of it All: A Portrait of German Jews, 1743–1933* (London: Allen Lane, 2002).

Angress, Werner T., 'The German Army's "Judenzählung" of 1916: Genesis – Consequences – Significance', *Leo Baeck Institute Year Book*, 23 (1978), pp. 117–38.

Aschheim, Steven E., *Brothers and Strangers: The East European Jew in German and German Jewish Consciousness, 1800–1923* (Madison: Wisconsin University Press, 1982).

Bankier, David, *The Germans and the Final Solution* (Oxford: Blackwell, 1992).

Bankier, David, ed., *Probing the Depths of German Antisemitism: German Society and the Persecution of the Jews, 1933–1941* (Oxford: Berghahn, 1999).

Barkai, Avraham, *From Boycott to Annihilation: The Economic Struggle of German Jews, 1933–1943*, trans. William Templer (London: University Press of New England, 1989).

Barkai, Avraham, 'German Interests in the *ha'avara* Transfer Agreement, 1933–1939', *Leo Baeck Institute Year Book*, 35 (1990), pp. 245–66.

Barkai, Avraham, Mendes-Flohr, Paul, and Lowenstein, Steven M., eds, *German-Jewish History in Modern Times* (New York: Columbia University Press, 1998).

Bartov, Omer, ed., *The Holocaust: Origins, Implementation, Aftermath* (London: Routledge, 2000).

Bauer, Yehuda, *The Holocaust in Historical Perspective* (London: Sheldon Press, 1978).

Benhar, Chenan, '107 Days on the SH-7: Experiences and Events of the Last Large Refugee Transport from the Reichsgebiet', *Leo Baeck Institute Year Book*, 46 (2001), pp. 305–32.

Benz, Wolfgang, ed., *Die Juden in Deutschland 1933–1945* (Munich: Beck, 1996).

Benz, Wolfgang, Paucker, Arnold and Pulzer, Peter, eds, *Jews in the Weimar Republic* (Tübingen: Mohr Siebeck, 1998).

Berenbaum, Michael, and Peck, Abraham J., eds, *The Holocaust and History: The Known, the Unknown, the Disputed and the Reexamined* (Bloomington: Indiana University Press, 1998).

Boas, Jacob, 'Germany or Diaspora? German Jewry's Shifting Perceptions in the Nazi Era (1933–1938)', *Leo Baeck Institute Year Book*, 27 (1982), pp. 109–26.

Boas, Jacob, 'The Shrinking World of German Jewry, 1933–1938', *Leo Baeck Institute Year Book*, 31 (1986), pp. 241–66.

Bracher, Karl Dietrich, *The German Dictatorship* (London: Weidenfeld & Nicolson, 1971).

Brakelmann, Günter, Greschat, Martin, and Jochmann, Werner, *Protestantismus und Politik: Werk und Wirkung Adolf Stoeckers* (Hamburg: Christians, 1982).

Breitmann, Richard, *The Architect of Genocide: Himmler and the Final Solution* (London: Bodley Head, 1991).

Browning, Christopher R., *Ordinary Men: Reserve Police Battalion 101 and the Final Solution in Poland* (London: HarperCollins, 1992).

Browning, Christopher R., *The Path to Genocide* (Cambridge: Cambridge University Press, 1998).

Bullock, Alan, *Hitler: A Study in Tyranny* (3rd ed., London: Hamlyn, 1973).

Bullock, Alan, *Hitler and Stalin: Parallel Lives* (2nd ed., London: Fontana, 1998).

Burleigh, Michael, *Death and Deliverance: 'Euthanasia' in Germany, c.1900–1945* (Cambridge: Cambridge University Press, 1994).

Burleigh, Michael, *The Third Reich: A New History* (London: Macmillan, 2000).

Burleigh, Michael, and Wippermann, Wolfgang, *The Racial State: Germany 1933–1945* (Cambridge: Cambridge University Press, 1991).

Büttner, Ursula, ed., *Das Unrechtsregime: Internationale Forschung über den Nationalsozialismus, vol. 1: Ideologie – Herrschaftssystem – Wirkung in Europa, vol. 2: Verfolgung – Exil – Belasteter Neubeginn* (Hamburg: Christians, 1986).

Büttner, Ursula, 'Not nach der Befreiung: Die Situation der deutschen Juden in der britischen Besatzungszone', in *Das Unrechtsregime: Internationale Forschung über den Nationalsozialismus, vol. 2: Verfolgung – Exil – Belasteter Neubeginn*, ed. Ursula, Büttner (Hamburg: Christians, 1986), pp. 373–406.

Büttner, Ursula, *Die Not der Juden teilen: Christlich-jüdische Familien im Dritten Reich: Beispiel und Zeugnis des Schriftstellers Robert Brendel* (Hamburg: Christians, 1988).

Büttner, Ursula, ed., *Die Deutschen und die Judenverfolgung* (Hamburg: Christians, 1992, 2nd ed., Frankfurt: Fischer, 2003).

Büttner, Ursula, *Weimar: Die überforderte Republik, 1918 –1933* (Stuttgart: Klett-Cotta, 2008).

Büttner, Ursula, and Greschat, Martin, *Die verlassenen Kinder der Kirche: Der Umgang mit Christen jüdischer Herkunft im 'Dritten Reich'* (Göttingen: Vanderhoeck & Ruprecht, 1998).

Cesarani, David, ed., *The Final Solution: Origins and Implementation* (London: Routledge, 1994).

Chamberlain, Houston Stewart, *The Foundations of the Nineteenth Century* (London: John Lane, 1911).

Clare, George, *Last Waltz in Vienna: The Destruction of a Family, 1842–1942* (London: Macmillan, 1982).

Cohn, Werner, 'Bearers of a Common Fate: The "Non-Aryan" Christian "Fate Comrades" of the Paulus-Bund, 1933–1939', *Leo Baeck Institute Year Book*, 33 (1988), pp. 327–66.

Conway, J. S., *The Nazi Persecution of the Churches 1933–45* (London: Weidenfeld & Nicolson, 1968).

Craig, Gordon A., *Germany 1866–1945* (Oxford: Oxford University Press, 1981).

Crane, Cynthia, *Divided Lives: The Untold Stories of Jewish-Christian Women in Nazi Germany* (New York: Palgrave Macmillan, 2003).

Dawidowicz, Lucy, *The War against the Jews, 1933–45* (London: Weidenfeld & Nicolson, 1975).

Deutsche jüdische Soldaten, 1914–1945, ed. Heinrich, Walle for Militärgeschichtliches Forschungsamt (Herford: Mittler, 1984, 3rd ed., 1987).

Diehl, Katrin, *Die jüdische Presse im Dritten Reich: Zwischen Selbstbehauptung und Fremdbestimmung* (Tübingen: Niemeyer, 1997).

Dobroszycki, Lucjan, ed., *The Chronicle of the Lodz Ghetto 1941–1944* (New Haven, CT: Yale University Press, 1984).

Dunker, Ulrich, *Der Reichsbund jüdischer Frontsoldaten, 1919–1938* (Düsseldorf: Droste, 1977).

Evans, Richard J., *The Coming of the Third Reich* (London: Allen Lane, 2003).

Evans, Richard J., *The Third Reich in Power, 1933–1939* (London: Allen Lane, 2005).

Evans, Richard J., *The Third Reich at War, 1939–1945* (London: Allen Lane, 2008).

Falter, Jürgen W., *Hitlers Wähler* (Munich: Beck, 1991).

Fest, Joachim, *The Face of the Third Reich* (London: Weidenfeld & Nicolson, 1970).

Fleming, Gerald, *Hitler and the Final Solution* (London: Hamish Hamilton, 1985).

Freeden, Herbert, *The Jewish Press in the Third Reich* (Oxford: Berg, 1993).

Freimark, Peter, *Juden in Preußen – Juden in Hamburg* (Hamburg: Christians, 1983).

Freimark, Peter, Jankowski, Alice, and Lorenz, Ina, eds, *Juden in Deutchland: Emanzipation, Integration, Verfolgung und Vernichtung* (Hamburg: Christians, 1991).

Friedlander, Henry, *The Origins of Nazi Genocide: From Euthanasia to the Final Solution* (Chapel Hill: North Carolina University Press, 1995).

Friedlander, Saul, *Wenn die Erinnerung kommt* (Frankfurt: Fischer, 1991).

Friedlander, Saul, *Years of Persecution, Years of Extermination* (London: Continuum, 2010).

Gailus, Manfred, ed., *Elisabeth Schmitz und ihre Denkschrift gegen die Judenverfolgung: Konturen einer vergessenen Biographie (1893–1977)* (Berlin: Wichern, 2008).

Gailus, Manfred, *Mir aber zerriss es das Herz: Der stille Widerstand der Elisabeth Schmitz* (Göttingen: Vandenhoeck & Ruprecht, 2010).

Gay, Peter, *My German Question: Growing up in Nazi Berlin* (New Haven, CT: Yale University Press, 1998).

Gay, Ruth, *The Jews of Germany* (New Haven, CT: Yale University Press, 1992).

Geisel, Eike, and Broder, Henryk M., *Premiere und Pogrom: Der Jüdische Kulturbund 1933–41* (Berlin: Siedler, 1992).

Gellately, Robert, *The Gestapo and German Society: Enforcing Racial Policy 1933–1945* (Oxford: Clarendon Press, 1990).

Gerlach, Wolfgang, *Als die Zeugen schwiegen: Bekennende Kirche und die Juden* (Berlin: Institut Kirche und Judentum, 1987).

Gilbert, Martin, *Auschwitz and the Allies* (London: Martin Joseph, 1981).

Gilbert, Martin, *The Holocaust: The Jewish Tragedy* (London: Collins, 1986).

Gilbert, Martin, *The Dent Atlas of the Holocaust* (London: Dent, 1993).

Gobineau, Arthur J. De, *Versuch über die Ungleichheit der Menschenrassen*, 4 vols (Stuttgart: Frommann, 1902–4).

Goebbels, Joseph, *Die Tagebücher von Joseph Goebbels*, ed. Elke Fröhlich, 32 vols (Munich: Saur, 1998–2008).

Goldhagen, Daniel, *Hitler's Willing Executioners: Ordinary Germans and the Holocaust* (New York: Alfred A. Knopf, 1996).

Gordon, Sarah, *Hitler, Germans and the Jewish Question* (Princeton, NJ: Princeton University Press, 1984).

Gotzmann, Andreas, Liedtke, Rainer, and Van Rahden, Till, eds, *Juden, Bürger, Deutsche: zuv Geschichte von Vielfalt und Differenz 1800–1933* (Tübingen: Mohr Siebeck, 2001).

Graml, Hermann, *Reichskristallnacht: Antisemitismus und Judenverfolgung im Dritten Reich* (3rd ed., Munich: Deutscher Taschenbuch-Verlag, 1988).

Graupe, Heinz Mosche, *The Rise of Modern Judaism: An Intellectual History of German Jewry, 1650–1942* (Huntington, NY: Krieger, 1978).

Greive, Hermann, *Geschichte des modernen Antisemitismus in Deutschland* (Darmstadt: Wissenschaftliche Buchgesellschaft, 1983).

Grenville, John A. S., 'Die "Endlösung" und die "Judenmischlinge" im Dritten Reich', in *Das Unrechtsregime: Internationale Forschung über den Nationalsozialismus, vol. 2: Verfolgung – Exil – Belasteter Neubeginn*, ed. Ursula, Büttner (Hamburg: Christians, 1986), pp. 91–121.

Grenville, John A. S., *The Collins History of the World in the Twentieth Century* (London: HarperCollins, 1994).

Grenville, John A. S., *Europe Reshaped, 1848–1878* (2nd ed, Oxford: Blackwell, 2000).

Grenville, John A. S., 'Juden, "Nichtarier" und "Deutsche Ärzte"', in *Die Deutschen und die Judenverfolgung im Dritten Reich*, ed. Ursula, Büttner (Hamburg: Christians, 1992; rev. ed., Frankfurt: Fischer Taschenbuch, 2003), pp. 228–46.

Grenville, John A. S., *A History of the World from the Twentieth to the Twenty-first Century* (London: Routledge, 2005).

Grenville, John A. S., and Wasserstein, Bernard, eds, *The Major International Treaties of the Twentieth Century: A History and Guide with Texts* (London: Routledge, 2001).

Gross, Raphael, *Carl Schmitt and the Jews: The 'Jewish Question', the Holocaust and German Legal Theory* (Madison: Wisconsin University Press, 2007).

Gross, Raphael, Lenarz, Michael, and Barkow, Ben, eds, *Novemberpogrom 1938: Die Augenzeugenberichte der Wiener Library, London* (Frankfurt: Jüdischer Verlag im Suhrkamp Verlag, 2008).

Gruchmann, Lothar, *Justiz im Dritten Reich 1933–1940: Anpassung und Unterwerfung in der Ära Gürtner* (3 rd ed., Munich: Oldenbourg, 2001).

Gruner, Wolf, *Der geschlossene Arbeitseinsatz deutscher Juden: Zwangsarbeit als Element der Verfolgung 1938–1943* (Berlin: Metropol, 1997).

Gruner, Wolf, *Öffentliche Wohlfahrt und Judenverfolgung: Wechselwirkungen lokaler und zentraler Politik im NS-Staat (1933–1942)* (Munich: Oldenbourg, 2002).

Gyssling, Walter, *Mein Leben in Deutschland vor und nach 1933* (Bremen: Donat Verlag, 2003) [includes *Der Anti-Nazi: Handbuch im Kampf gegen die NSDAP*].

Hahn, Susanne, 'Revolution der Heilkunst: Ausweg aus der Krise?', in *Der Wert des Menschen: Medizin in Deutschland 1918–1945*, ed. Christian Pross and Götz Aly (Berlin: Hentrich, 1989), pp. 71–99.

Hamel, Iris, *Völkischer Verband und nationale Gewerkschaft: Der Deutschnationale Handlungsgehilfen-Verband, 1893–1933* (Frankfurt: Europäische Verlagsanstalt, 1967).

Hart-Davis, Duff, *Hitler's Games: The 1936 Olympics* (London: Century, 1986).

Herbert, Ulrich, *Best: Biographische Studien über Radikalismus, Weltanschauung und Vernunft, 1903–1989* (Bonn: Dietz, 1996).

Hertz, Deborah, *Jewish High Society in Old Regime Berlin* (New Haven, CT: Yale University Press, 1988).

Herzberg, Heinrich, *Dienst am höheren Gesetz: Dr Margarete Sommer und das 'Hilfswerk beim Bischöflichen Ordinariat Berlin'* (Berlin: Servi, 2000).

Herzig, Arno, and Lorenz, Ina, *Verdrängung und Vernichtung der Juden unter dem Nationalsozialismus* (Hamburg: Christians, 1992).

Herzig, Arno, Horch, Otto, and Jütte, Robert, *Judentum und Aufklärung: jüdisches Selbstverständnis in der bürgerlichen Öffentlichkeit* (Göttingen: Vandenhoeck & Ruprecht, 2002).

Heuberger, Georg, and Backhaus, Fritz, eds, *Leo Baeck, 1873–1956: Aus dem Stamme von Rabbinern* (Frankfurt: Jüdischer Verlag im Suhrkamp Verlag, 2001).

Hilberg, Raul, *The Destruction of the European Jews* (London: W. H. Allen, 1961; enlarged ed., 3 vols, New York: Holmes & Meier, 1985).

Hilberg, Raul, *Perpetrators, Victims, Bystanders: The Jewish Catastrophe 1933–1945* (London: Lime Tree, 1993).

Hildesheimer, Esriel, *Jüdische Selbstverwaltung unter dem NS-Regime: Der Existenzkampf der Reichsvertretung und Reichsvereinigung der Juden in Deutschland* (Tübingen: Mohr, 1994).

Hitler, Adolf, *Monologe im Führer-Hauptquartier, 1941–1944*, ed. Werner Jochmann (Hamburg: A. Knaus, 1980).

Höhne, Heinz, *The Order of the Death's Head* (London: Pan, 1972).

Irving, David, *Hitler's War* (London: Hodder & Stoughton, 1977).

Jochmann, Werner, *Gesellschaftskrise und Judenfeindschaft in Deutschland, 1870–1945* (Hamburg: Christians, 1989).

Jochmann, Werner, and Jacobsen, Hans-Adolf, *Ausgewählte Dokumente zur Geschichte des Nationalsozialismus 1933–1945* (Bielefeld: Verlag Neue Gesellschaft, 1966).

Johnson, Eric A., *Nazi Terror: The Gestapo, Jews and Ordinary Germans* (London: John Murray, 2000).

Kaplan, Marion, *Between Dignity and Despair: Jewish Life in Nazi Germany* (Oxford: Oxford University Press 1988).

Katz, Jacob, *Aus dem Ghetto in die bürgerliche Gesellschaft: Jüdische Emanzipation 1770–1870* (Frankfurt: Jüdischer Verlag bei Athenäum, 1986).

Kauders, Anthony, *German Politics and the Jews: Düsseldorf and Nuremberg 1910–1933* (Oxford: Clarendon Press, 1996).

Kershaw, Ian, *Popular Opinion and Political Dissent in the Third Reich: Bavaria 1933–1945* (Oxford: Clarendon Press, 1983).

Kershaw, Ian, *The 'Hitler Myth': Image and Reality in the Third Reich* (Oxford: Clarendon Press, 1987).

Kershaw, Ian, *Hitler 1889–1936: Hubris* (Harmondsworth: Penguin, 1998).

Kershaw, Ian, *Hitler 1936–1945: Nemesis* (London: Allen Lane, 2000).

Kershaw, Ian, *Hitler, the Germans and the Final Solution* (New Haven, CT: Yale University Press, 2008).

Klee, Ernst, *'Euthanasie' im NS-Staat: Die 'Vernichtung lebensunwerten Lebens'* (11th ed., Frankfurt: Fischer, 2004).

Klemperer, Victor, *I Shall Bear Witness: The Diaries of Victor Klemperer 1933–1941* (London: Weidenfeld & Nicolson, 1998).

Klepper, Jochen, *Unter dem Schatten deiner Flügel: Aus den Tagebüchern der Jahre 1932–1942* (Munich: Europäischer Buchklub, 1976).

Konitzer, Werner, and Gross, Raphael, *Moralität des Bösen: Ethik und nationalsozialistische Verbrechen* (Frankfurt: Campus, 2009).

Krausnick, Helmut, and Broszat, Martin, *Anatomy of the SS State* (London: Collins, 1968).

Kulka, Otto Dov, ed., *Deutsches Judentum unter dem Nationalsozialismus, vol. 1: Dokumente zur Geschichte der Reichsvertretung der deutschen Juden, 1933–1939* (Tübingen: Mohr Siebeck, 1997).

Kulka, Otto Dov, and Jäckel, Eberhard, eds., *Die Juden in den geheimen NS-Stimmungsberichten: 1933–1945* (Düsseldorf: Droste, 2004).

Kwiet, Konrad, and Eschwege, Helmut, *Selbstbehauptung und Widerstand: Deutsche Juden im Kampf um Existenz und Menschenwürde 1933–1945* (Hamburg: Christians, 1984).

Lewy, Guenther, *The Nazi Persecution of the Gypsies* (Oxford: Oxford University Press, 2000).

Liebeschütz, Hans, and Paucker, Arnold, eds, *Das Judentum in der deutschen Umwelt, 1800–1850* (Tübingen: Mohr, 1977).

Liepach, Martin, *Das Wahlverhalten der jüdischen Bevölkerung* (Tübingen: Mohr, 1996).

Lifton, Robert J., *The Nazi Doctors: Medical Killing and the Psychology of Genocide* (London: Macmillan, 1986).

Lohalm, Uwe, *Völkischer Radikalismus: Die Geschichte des Deutschvölkischen Schutz- und Trutz-Bundes 1919–1923* (Hamburg: Leibniz, 1970).

Longerich, Peter, *Politik der Vernichtung: Eine Gesamtdarstellung der nationalsozialistischen Judenverfolgung* (Munich: Piper, 1998).

Longerich, Peter, *'Davon haben wir nichts gewusst!' Die Deutschen und Judenverfolgung, 1933–1945* (Munich: Siedler, 2006).

Longerich, Peter, *Heinrich Himmler: Biographie* (Munich: Siedler, 2006).

Longerich, Peter, *Holocaust: The Nazi Persecution and Murder of the Jews* (Oxford: Oxford University Press, 2010) [an updated ed. of the 1998 German ed. above, with additional documentary evidence; of especial value is new material from the Russian archives].

Lozowick, Yaacov, *Hitler's Bureaucrats: The Nazi Security Police and the Banality of Evil* (London: Continuum, 2002).

Majer, Diemut, *'Non-Germans' under the Third Reich* (Baltimore: Johns Hopkins University Press, 2003).

Marrus, Michael, *The Holocaust in History* (Harmondsworth: Penguin, 1989).

Marrus, Michael, ed., *The Nazi Holocaust: Historical Articles on the Destruction of the European Jews*, 9 vols (Westport, CT: Meckler, 1989).

Maurer, Trude, *Ostjuden in Deutschland 1918–1933* (Hamburg: Christians, 1986).

Meyer, Michael, *Response to Modernity: A History of the Reform Movement in Judaism* (Oxford: Oxford University Press, 1988).

Meyer, Michael, and Brenner, Michael, eds, *German-Jewish History in Modern Times*, 4 vols (New York: Columbia University Press, 1996) [leading scholars have collaborated to produce an authoritative history].

Mommsen, Hans, *The Rise and Fall of Weimar Democracy* (Chapel Hill: University of North Carolina Press, 1989).

Mosse, Werner, *Jews in the German Economy: The German-Jewish Economic Elite, 1820–1935* (Oxford: Clarendon Press, 1987).

Mosse, Werner, and Paucker, Arnold, eds, *Deutsches Judentum in Krieg und Revolution, 1916–1923* (Tübingen: Mohr, 1971).

Mosse, Werner, and Paucker, Arnold, eds, *Juden im Wilhelminischen Deutschland, 1890–1914* (Tübingen: Mohr, 1976).

Mosse, Werner, and Paucker, Arnold, *Entscheidungsjahr 1932: Zur Judenfrage in der Endphase der Weimarer Republik* (2nd ed., Tübingen: Mohr, 1986).

Mosse, Werner, Paucker, Arnold, and Rürup, Reinhard, eds, *Revolution und Evolution: 1848 in German-Jewish History* (Tübingen: Mohr, 1981).

Münch, Ingo von, and Brodersen, Uwe, *Gesetze des NS-Staates* (Paderborn: Schöningh, 1994).

Niewyck, Donald L., *Jews in Weimar Germany* (Baton Rouge: Louisiana State University Press, 1980).

Niewyck, Donald L., 'Solving the "Jewish Problem": Continuity and Change in German Antisemitism, 1871–1945', *Leo Baeck Institute Year Book*, 35 (1990), pp. 335–70.

Noakes, Jeremy, 'Wohin gehören die "Judenmischlinge"? Die Entstehung der ersten Durchführungsverordnungen zu den Nürnberger Gesetzen', in *Das Unrechtsregime: Internationale Forschung über den Nationalsozialismus, vol. 2: Verfolgung – Exil – Belasteter Neubeginn*, ed. Ursula Büttner (Hamburg: Christians, 1986), pp. 69–89.

Noakes, Jeremy, 'The Development of Nazi Policy towards the German-Jewish "Mischlinge", 1933–1945', *Leo Baeck Institute Year Book*, 34 (1989), pp. 291–354.

Noakes, Jeremy, and Pridham, Geoffrey, eds, *Nazism 1919–1945: A Documentary Reader*, 4 vols (Exeter: University of Exeter Press, 1983–98).

Padfield, Peter, *Himmler: Reichsführer SS* (London: Macmillan, 1990).

Pätzold, Kurt, and Schwarz, Erika, *Tagesordnung: Judenmord: Die Wannsee-Konferenz am 20. Januar 1942* (3rd ed., Berlin: Metropol, 1992).

Paucker, Arnold, *Der jüdische Abwehrkampf gegen Antisemitismus und Nationalsozialismus in den letzten Jahren der Weimarer Republik* (Hamburg: Leibniz, 1968).

Paucker, Arnold, *Jewish Resistance in Germany: The Facts and the Problems* (Berlin: Gedenkstätte Deutscher Widerstand, 1991).

Paucker, Arnold, *Standhalten und Widerstehen: Der Widerstand deutcher und österreichischer Juden gegen die nationalsozialistische Diktatur* (Essen: Klartext, 1995).

Paucker, Arnold, and Suchy, Barbara, *Deutsche Juden im Kampf um Recht und Freiheit* (Teetz: Hentrich & Hentrich, 2003).

Paucker, Arnold, Gilchrist, Sylvia, and Suchy, Barbara, eds, *Die Juden im nationalsozialistischen Deutschland 1933–1943* (Tübingen: Mohr, 1986).

Pehle, Walter H., ed., *Der Judenpogrom 1938: Von der 'Reichskristallnacht' zum Völkermord* (Frankfurt: Fischer, 1988).

Pulzer, Peter, *The Rise of Political Anti-Semitism in Germany & Austria* (rev. ed., London: Halban, 1988).

Pulzer, Peter, *Jews and the German State: The Political History of a Minority, 1848–1933* (Oxford: Blackwell, 1992).

Reichmann, Eva G., *Hostages of Civilisation: The Social Sources of National Socialist Anti-Semitism* (London: Gollancz, 1950).

Reichmann, Hans, *Deutscher Bürger und verfolgter Jude: Novemberpogrom und KZ Sachsenhausen 1937 bis 1939*, ed. Michael Wildt (Munich: Oldenbourg, 1998).

Reutter, Lutz Eugen, *Katholische Kirche als Fluchthelfer im Dritten Reich: Die Betreuung von Auswanderern durch den St. Raphaels-Verein* (Hamburg: Paulus Verlag, 1971).

Richarz, Monika, *Jüdisches Leben in Deutschland: Selbstzeugnisse zur Sozialgeschichte*, 3 vols (Stuttgart: Deutsche Verlagsanstalt, 1976–82) [1780–1945; vol 3: 1918–1945].

Röhm, Eberhard, and Thierfelder, Jörg, *Juden, Christen, Deutsche, 1933–1945*, 4 vols (Stuttgart: Calwer, 1990–2007).

Rürup, Reinhard, *Emanzipation und Antisemitismus: Studien zur Judenfrage der bürgerlichen Gesellschaft* (Göttingen: Vandenhoeck & Ruprecht, 1975).

Sauer, Paul, 'Otto Hirsch (1885–1941): Director of the Reichsvertretung', *Leo Baeck Institute Year Book*, 32 (1987), pp. 341–68.

Schmuhl, Hans-Walter, *The Kaiser Wilhelm Institute for Anthropology, Human Heredity, and Eugenics, 1927–1945* (Dordrecht: Springer: 2008).

Das Schwarzbuch: Tatsachen und Dokumente: Die Lage der Juden in Deutschland 1933 (orig. pubn, Paris: Comité des Delégations Juives, 1934; repr. Frankfurt: Ullstein, 1983)

Sherman, Ari Joshua, *Island Refuge: Britain and Refugees from the Third Reich, 1933–1939* (2nd ed., Ilford: Frank Cass, 1994).

Sorkin, David, *The Transformation of German Jewry, 1780–1840* (Oxford: Oxford University Press, 1987).

Steinweis, Alan E., 'Hans Hinkel and German Jewry', *Leo Baeck Institute Year Book*, 38 (1993), pp. 209–19.

Steinweis, Alan E., *Studying the Jew: Scholarly Antisemitism in Nazi Germany* (Cambridge, MA: Harvard University Press, 2006).

Stern, Fritz, *The Politics of Cultural Despair: A Study in the Rise of German Ideology* (Berkeley: University of California Press, 1961).

Steur, Claudia, *Theodor Dannecker: Ein Funktionär der 'Endlösung'* (Essen: Klartext, 1997).

Stoltzfus, Nathan, *Resistance of the Heart: Intermarriage and the Rosenstrasse Protest in Nazi Germany* (New York: W. W. Norton, 1996).

Stone, Dan, *Histories of the Holocaust* (Oxford: Oxford University Press, 2010).

Strauss, Herbert A., 'Jewish Emigration from Germany: Nazi Policies and Jewish Responses (I)', *Leo Baeck Institute Year Book*, 25 (1980), pp. 313–61.

Strauss, Herbert A., 'Jewish Emigration from Germany. Nazi Policies and Jewish Responses (II)', *Leo Baeck Institute Year Book*, 26 (1981), pp. 343–409.

Strauss, Herbert A., 'Jewish Autonomy within the limits of National Socialist Policy: The Communities and the Reichsvertretung', in *Die Juden im Nationalsozialistischen Deutschland 1933–1943*, ed. Arnold Paucker, Sylvia Gilchrist and Barbara Suchy (Tübingen: Mohr, 1986), pp. 125–52.

Suchy, Barbara, 'The Verein zur Abwehr des Antisemitismus (I): From its Beginnings to the First World War', *Leo Baeck Institute Year Book*, 28 (1983), pp. 205–39.

Tal, Uriel, *Christians and Jews in Germany: Religion, Politics and Ideology in the Second Reich* (Ithaca, NY: Cornell University Press, 1975).

Tannenbaum, Eugen, ed., *Kriegsbriefe deutscher und österreicher Juden* (Berlin: Neuer Verlag, 1915).

Toury, Jacob, *Soziale und politische Geschichte der Juden in Deutschland, 1847–1871: Zwichen Revolution, Reaktion und Emanzipation* (Düsseldorf: Droste, 1977).

Turner, Henry Ashby, *Hitler's Thirty Days to Power: January 1933* (Reading, MA: Addison-Wesley, 1996).

Vierhaus, Rudolf, and Brocke, Bernhard, *Forschung im Spannungsfeld von Politik und Gesellschaft: Geschichte und Struktur der Kaiser-Wilhelm/Max-Planck-Gesellschaft* (Stuttgart: Deutsche Verlags-Anstalt, 1990).

Volk, Ludwig, ed., *Akten Kardinal Michael von Faulhabers 1917–1945*, 2 vols (Mainz: Mattias Grünewald, 1975–8).

Volk, Ludwig, ed., *Akten deutscher Bischöfe über die Lage der Kirche, 1933–1945, vol. 6: 1943–1945* (Mainz: Matthias Grünewald, 1985).

Volkov, Schulamit, *Germans, Jews, and Antisemites: Trials in Emancipation* (Cambridge: Cambridge University Press, 2006).

Walk, Joseph, ed., *Das Sonderrecht für die Juden im NS-Staat: Eine Sammlung der gesetzlichen Maßnahmen und Richtlinien: Inhalt und Bedeutung* (Heidelberg: Müller, 1981).

Walk, Joseph, *Jüdische Schule und Erziehung im Dritten Reich* (Frankfurt: Hain, 1991).

Wendt, Bernd-Jürgen, *Deutschland 1933–1945: Das 'Dritte Reich': Handbuch zur Geschichte* (Hannover: Fackelträger, 1995).

Wildt, Michael, *Die Judenpolitik des SD 1935 bis 1938: Eine Dokumentation* (Munich: Oldenbourg, 1995).

Witte, Peter, Wildt, Michael, and Voigt, Martin, *Der Dienstkalender Heinrich Himmlers 1941/42* (Hamburg: Christians, 1999).

Yahil, Leni, *The Holocaust: The Fate of European Jewry, 1932–1945* (Oxford: Oxford University Press, 1990).

Zimmermann, Michael, *Rassenutopie und Genozid: Die nationalsozialistische 'Lösung der Zigeunerfrage'* (Hamburg: Christians, 1996).

Zimmermann, Moshe, *Wilhelm Marr: The Patriarch of Anti-Semitism* (Oxford: Oxford University Press, 1986).

Hamburg

Andrae, Matthias, *Die Vertreibung der jüdischen Ärzte aus dem Allgemeinen Krankenhaus Hamburg-St Georg*, thesis, Hamburg University (microfiche, 1997; Norderstedt: Books on Demand, 2003).

Apel, Linde, ed., *In den Tod geschickt: Die Deportationen von Juden, Roma und Sinti aus Hamburg 1940 bis 1945* (Berlin: Metropol, 2009) [with texts in German and English].

Bajohr, Frank, 'Hamburgs "Führer": Zur Person und Tätigkeit des Hamburger NSDAP-Gauleiters, Karl Kaufmann (1900–1969)', in *Hamburg in der NS-Zeit*, ed. Frank Bajohr and Joachim Szodrzynski (Hamburg: Ergebnisse-Verlag, 1995), pp. 59–91.

Bajohr, Frank, *'Aryanisation' in Hamburg: The Economic Exclusion of Jews and the Confiscation of their Property in Nazi Germany* (Oxford: Berghahn, 2001).

Bajohr, Frank, '"... Dann bitte keine Gefühlsduseleien": Die Hamburger und die Deportationen', in *Die Deportation der Hamburger Juden 1941–1945* (Hamburg: Forschungsstelle für Zeitgeschichte in Hamburg and Institut für die Geschichte der deutschen Juden, 2002), pp. 13–29.

Bästlein, Klaus, Grabitz, Helge, and Scheffler, Wolfgang, eds, *'Für Führer, Volk und Vaterland ...': Hamburger Justiz im Nationalsozialismus* (Hamburg: Ergebnisse-Verlag, 1992).

Baumbach, Sybille, *Rückblenden: Lebensgeschichtliche Interviews mit Verfolgten des NS-Regimes in Hamburg* (Hamburg: Ergebnisse-Verlag, 1999).

Bielfeldt, Hans, *Staat und Wirtschaft: Beiträge zur Geschichte der Handelskammer Hamburg* (Hamburg: Christians, 1980).

Böhme, Claus, and Lohalm, Uwe, eds, *Wege in den Tod: Hamburgs Anstalt Langenhorn und die Euthanasie in der Zeit des Nationalsozialismus* (Hamburg: Ergebnisse-Verlag, 1993).

Bottin, Angela, and Nicolaysen, Rainer, *Enge Zeit: Spuren Vertriebener und Verfolgter der Hamburger Universität* (Berlin and Hamburg: Reimer, 1991).

Brämer, Andreas, *Judentum und religiöse Reform: Der Hamburger Israelitische Tempel 1817–1938* (Hamburg: Dölling & Galitz, 2000).

Brämer, Andreas, *Joseph Carlebach* (Hamburg: Ellert & Richter, 2007).

Bringmann, Fritz, *Kindermord am Bullenhuserdamm: SS Verbrechen in Hamburg 1945* (Frankfurt: Röderberg, 1978).

Brücks, Andrea, Gross, Jan, Pfäfflin, Friedemann, and Rothmaler, Christiane, 'Sterilisation nach dem Gesetz zur Verhütung erbkranken Nachwuchses in Hamburg', in *1933 in Gesellschaft und Wissenschaft* (Hamburg: Hamburg University Press, 1984), vol. 2, pp. 157–84.

Buff, Reinhard, ed., *Stadthaus in Hamburg: Gestapo-Hauptquartier 1933 bis 1943* (Hamburg: Wartenberg, 1981).

Bussche, Hendrik van den, and Bottin, Angela, eds, *Medizinische Wissenschaft im 'Dritten Reich': Kontinuität, Anpassung und Opposition an der Hamburger Medizinischen Fakultät* (Berlin and Hamburg: Dietrich Reimer, 1987).

Büttner, Ursula, *Hamburg in der Staats- und Wirtschaftskrise 1928–1931* (Hamburg: Christians, 1982).

Büttner, Ursula, *Politische Gerechtigkeit und sozialer Geist: Hamburg zur Zeit der Weimarer Republik* (Hamburg: Christians, 1985).

Büttner, Ursula, and Jochmann, Werner, *Hamburg auf dem Weg ins Dritte Reich* (Hamburg: Landeszentrale für politische Bildung, 1983).

Büttner, Ursula, and Jochmann, Werner, eds., *Zwischen Demokratie und Diktatur: Nationalsozialistische Machtaneignung in Hamburg – Tendenzen und Reaktionen in Europa* (Hamburg: Christians, 1984).

Cecil, Lamar, *Albert Ballin: Business and Politics in Imperial Germany, 1888–1918* (Princeton, NJ: Princeton University Press, 1967).

Chernow, Ron, *The Warburgs: The Twentieth Century Odyssey of a Remarkable Jewish Family* (New York: Random House, 1993).

Ebbinghaus, Angelika, *Heilen und Vernichten im Mustergau Hamburg: Bevölkerungs- und Gesundheitspolitik im Dritten Reich* (Hamburg: Konkret-Literatur-Verlag, 1984).

Evans, Richard J., *Death in Hamburg: Society and Politics in the Cholera Years 1830–1910* (Oxford: Oxford University Press, 1987).

Fangmann, Helmut, Reifner, Udo, and Steinborn, Norbert, *Parteisoldaten: Die Hamburger Polizei im '3. Reich'* (Hamburg: VSA, 1987).

Freimark, Peter, and Herzig, Arno, *Die Hamburger Juden in der Emanzipationsphase (1780–1870)* (Hamburg: Christians, 1989).

Gillis-Carlebach, Miriam, *Jüdischer Alltag als humaner Widerstand: Dokumente des Hamburger Oberrabbiners Dr. Joseph Carlebach aus den Jahren 1939–1941* (Hamburg: Verein für Hamburgische Geschichte, 1990).

Gillis-Carlebach, Miriam, *Jedes Kind ist mein Einziges: Lotte Carlebach-Preuss: Antlitz einer Mutter und Rabbiner-Frau* (Hamburg: Dölling & Galitz, 1992).

Giordano, Ralph, *Die Bertinis* (Frankfurt: Fischer, 1982).

Giordano, Ralph, *Erinnerungen eines Davongekommenen* (Cologne: Kiepenheuer & Witsch, 2007).

Hamburg im 'Dritten Reich', ed. Forschungsstelle für Zeitgeschichte in Hamburg (Göttingen: Wallstein, 2005).

Hamburger jüdische Opfer des Nationalsozialismus: Gedenkbuch (Hamburg: Staatsarchiv, 1965; rev. ed., comp. Jürgen Sielemann and Paul Flamme, 1995).

Hecht, Ingeborg, *Als unsichtbare Mauern wuchsen: eine deutsche Familie unter den Nürnberger Rassengesetzen* (Hamburg: Dölling & Galitz, 1993).

Herzig, Arno and Rohde, Saskia, *Die Juden in Hamburg 1590 bis 1990*, 2 vols (Hamburg: Dölling & Galitz, 1991).

Herzig, Arno, Langewische, Dieter, and Sywottek, Arnold, *Arbeiter in Hamburg: Unterschichten, Arbeiter und Arbeiterbewegung seit dem ausgehenden 18. Jahrhundert* (Hamburg: Verlag Erziehung und Wissenschaft, 1983).

100 Jahre Beiersdorf: 1882–1982 (Hamburg: Beiersdorf, 1982).

Jenner, Harald, *150 Jahre Jerusalem-Arbeit in Hamburg* (Hamburg: Jerusalem Gemeinde, 2003).

Jochmann, Werner, *Im Kampf um die Macht: Hitlers Rede vor dem Nationalklub von 1919* (Frankfurt: Europäische Verlagsanstalt, 1960).

Jochmann, Werner, *Nationalsozialismus und Revolution: Ursprung und Geschichte der NSDAP in Hamburg, 1922–1933* (Frankfurt: Europäische Verlagsanstalt, 1983).

Jochmann, Werner, *Als Hamburg unter den Nazis lebte: 152 wiederendekte Fotos eines Zeitzeugen* (Hamburg: Rasch & Röhring, 1986).

Jochmann, Werner, and Loose, Hans-Dieter, eds, *Hamburg: Geschichte der Stadt und ihrer Bewohner*, 2 vols (Hamburg: Hoffmann & Campe, 1982–6).

Johe, Werner, *Die gleichgeschaltete Justiz: Organisation des Rechtswesens und Politisierung der Rechtsprechung 1933–1945, dargestellt am Beispiel des Oberlandesgerichtsbezirks Hamburg* (Frankfurt: Europäische Verlagsanstalt, 1967).

Johe, Werner, *Neuengamme: Zur Geschichte der Konzentrationslager in Hamburg* (Hamburg: Landeszentrale für politische Bildung, 1981).

Johe, Werner, *Hitler in Hamburg: Dokumente zu einem besonderen Verhältnis* (Hamburg: Ergebnisse-Verlag, 1996).

Kaum, Eckehard, *Oskar Troplowitz* (Hamburg: Wesche, 1982).

Kopitzsch, Wolfgang, 'Der Altonaer Blutsontag', in *Arbeiter in Hamburg*, ed. Arno Herzig, Dieter Langewiesche and Arnold Sywottek (Hamburg: Verlag Erziehung und Wissenschaft, 1983).

Krause, Eckart, Huber, Ludwig, and Fischer, Holger, *Hochschulalltag im 'Dritten Reich': Die Hamburger Universität 1933–1945*, 3 vols (Berlin and Hamburg: Reimer, 1991).

Krause, Thomas, *Hamburg wird braun: Der Aufstieg der NSDAP von 1921–1933* (Hamburg: Ergebnisse-Verlag, 1987).

Krebs, Albert, *The Infancy of Nazism: The Memoirs of Ex-Gauleiter Albert Krebs, 1923–1933*, ed. William Sheridan (London: New Viewpoints, 1976).

Krohn, Helga, *Die Juden in Hamburg 1800–1850: Ihre soziale, kulturelle und politische Entwicklung während der Emanzipationszeit* (Frankfurt: Europäische Verlagsanstalt, 1967).

Krohn, Helga, *Die Juden in Hamburg: Die politische, soziale und kulturelle Entwicklung einer jüdischen Großstadtgemeinde nach der Emanzipation, 1848–1918* (Hamburg: Christians, 1974).

Lindemann, Mary, *140 Jahre Israelitisches Krankenhaus in Hamburg: Vorgeschichte und Entwicklung* (Hamburg: Israelitisches Krankenhaus, 1981).

Lippmann, Leo, *Mein Leben und meine amtliche Tätigkeit: Erinnerungen und ein Beitrag zur Finanzgeschichte Hamburgs*, ed. Werner Jochmann (Hamburg: Christians, 1964).

Lippmann, Leo, '… daß ich wie ein guter Deutscher empfinde und handele': Zur Geschichte der Deutsch-Israelitischen Gemeinde in Hamburg in der Zeit vom Herbst 1935 bis zum Ende 1942*, ed. Ina Lorenz (Hamburg: Dölling & Galitz, 1993).

Lohalm Uwe, *Hamburgs nationalsozialistische Diktatur: Verfassung und Verwaltung 1933 bis 1945* (Hamburg: Landeszentrale für politische Bildung, 1997).

Lohalm, Uwe, *Fürsorge und Verfolgung: Öffentliche Wohlfahrtsverwaltung und national-sozialistische Judenpolitik in Hamburg 1933 bis 1942* (Hamburg: Ergebnisse-Verlag, 1998).

Lohalm, Uwe, *Die nationalsozialistische Judenverfolgung, 1933 bis 1945: Ein Überblick* (Hamburg: Landeszentrale für politische Bildung, 1999).

Lohalm, Uwe, '… anständig und aufopferungsbereit': Öffentlicher Dienst und Nationalsozialismus 1933 bis 1945* (Hamburg: Ergebnisse-Verlag, 2001).

Lohalm, Uwe, ed., 'Schließlich ist es meine Heimat …': Harry Goldstein und die Jüdische Gemeinde in Hamburg in persönlichen Dokumenten und Fotos* (Hamburg: Ergebnisse-Verlag, 2002).

Lohalm, Uwe, *Völkische Wohlfahrtsdiktatur: Öffentliche Wohlfahrtspolitik im nationalso-zialistischen Hamburg* (Munich: Dölling & Galitz, 2010).

Lorent, Hans-Peter de, 'Personalpolitik', in *'Die Fahne Hoch': Schulpolitik und Schulalltag in Hamburg unterm Hakenkreuz*, ed. Reiner Lehberger and Hans-Peter de Lorent (Hamburg: Ergebnisse-Verlag, 1986), pp. 203–12.

Lorenz, Ina, *Die Juden in Hamburg zur Zeit der Weimarer Republik*, 2 vols (Hamburg: Christians, 1987).

Lorenz, Ina, 'Seefahrt-Hachschara in Hamburg (1935–1938): Lucy Borchardt: Die einzige jüdische Reederin der Welt', *Zeitschrift des Vereins für Hamburgische Geschichte*, 83/1 (1997), pp. 445–72.

Matras, Yaron, *Roma und Cinti in Hamburg* (Hamburg: Hamburg Senate, 1994).

Meyer, Beate, *'Jüdische Mischlinge': Rassenpolitik und Verfolgungserfahrungen, 1933–1945* (Hamburg: Dölling & Galitz, 1999).

Meyer, Beate, ed., *Die Verfolgung und Ermordung der Hamburger Juden 1933–1945: Geschichte, Zeugnis, Erinnerung* (Göttingen: Wallstein, 2006).

Meyer, Gertrud, *Nacht über Hamburg: Berichte und Dokumente 1933–1945* (Frankfurt: Röderberg, 1983).

Milberg, Hildegard, *Schulpolitik in der pluralistischen Gesellschaft: Die politischen und sozialen Aspekte der Schulreform in Hamburg, 1890–1935* (Hamburg: Leibniz, 1970).

Morisse, Heiko, *Jüdische Rechtsanwälte in Hamburg: Ausgrenzung und Verfolgung im NS-Staat* (Hamburg: Christians, 2003).

Mosel, Wilhelm, *Wegweiser zu ehemaligen jüdischen Stätten in Hamburg*, 3 vols (Hamburg: Deutsch-Jüdische Gesellschaft, 1983–9).

Nellessen, Bernd, *Das mühsame Zeugnis: Die katholische Kirche in Hamburg im zwanzigsten Jahrhundert* (Hamburg: Christians, 1992).

Pritzlaff, Christiane, *Entrechtet – Ermordet – Vergessen: Jüdische Schüler in Hamburg* (Hamburg: Behörde für Schule, Jugend und Berufsbildung, Amt für Schule, 1996).

Randt, Ursula, *Carolinenstraße 35: Geschichte der Mädchenschule der Deutsch-Israelitischen Gemeinde in Hamburg* (Hamburg: Verein für Hamburgische Geschichte, 1984).

Randt, Ursula, '"Träume zerschellen an der Wirklichkeit": Die Situation jüdischer Schüler an jüdischen Schulen in Hamburg in der Frühphase der NS-Zeit', in *'Die Fahne Hoch': Schulpolitik und Schulalltag in Hamburg unterm Hakenkreuz*, ed. Reiner Lehberger and Hans-Peter de Lorent (Hamburg: Ergebnisse-Verlag, 1986), pp. 291–300.

Randt, Ursula, *Die Talmud-Tora-Schule in Hamburg, 1805 bis 1842* (Munich and Hamburg: Dölling & Galitz, 2005).

Robinsohn, Hans, *Justiz als politische Verfolgung: Die Rechtsprechung in 'Rassenschandefällen' beim Landgericht Hamburg, 1936–1943* (Stuttgart: Deutsche Verlags-Anstalt, 1973).

Rosenbaum, Eduard, and Sherman, Ari Joshua, *Das Bankhaus M. M. Warburg & Co., 1798–1938* (Hamburg: Christians, 1976), Eng. trans. as *M. M. Warburg & Co., 1798–1938, Merchant Bankers of Hamburg* (London: Hurst, 1979).

Schmidt, Uwe, *Hamburger Schulen im 'Dritten Reich'* (Hamburg: Hamburg University Press, 2010).

Schulz, Peter Rudolf, *Wilhelm-Gymnasium Hamburg, 1881–1981: Eine Dokumentation über 100 Jahre Wilhelm-Gymnasium* (Hamburg: Hower, 1981).

Schwarberg, Günther, *Der SS-Arzt und die Kinder vom Bullenhuser Damm* (Göttingen: Steidl, 1994).

Sielemann, Jürgen, 'Fragen und Antworten zur Reichskristallnacht in Hamburg', *Zeitschrift des Vereins für Hamburgische Geschichte*, 83 (1997), pp. 473–501.

Stein, Irmgard, *Jüdische Baudenkmäler in Hamburg* (Hamburg: Christians, 1984).

Timpke, Henning, *Dokumente zur Gleichschaltung des Landes Hamburg 1933* (Frankfurt: Europäische Verlagsanstalt, 1964).

Urias, Siegfried, *Die Hamburger Juden im Kriege 1914–1918: Eine statistische Abhandlung: Festschrift des Vaterländischen Bundes jüdischer Frontsoldaten in Hamburg aus Anlaß seines 10 jährigen Bestehens, 1919–1929* (2nd ed., Hamburg: Vaterländischer Bund Jüdischer Frontsoldaten, 1933).

Vieth, Harald, *Von der Hallerstraße 6/8 zum Isebek und Dammtor: Jüdische Schicksale und Alltägliches aus Harvestehude-Rotherbaum in Hamburg seit der Jahrhundertwende* (Hamburg: H. Vieth, 1991).

Villiez, Anna von, *Mit aller Kraft verdrängt: Entrechtung und Verfolgung 'nicht arischer' Ärzte in Hamburg 1933 bis 1945* (Munich and Hamburg: Dölling & Galitz, 2009).

Wamser, Ursula, and Weinke, Wilfried, eds, *Eine verschwundene Welt: Jüdisches Leben am Grindel* (Springe: Klampen, 2006).

Warburg, Erich, *Times and Tides* (privately printed, 1982).

Warburg, Max, *Aus meinen Aufzeichnungen* (New York: E. M. Warburg, 1952).

Weinke, Wilfried, 'The Persecution of Jewish Lawyers in Hamburg: A Case Study: Max Eichholz and Herbert Michaelis', *Leo Baeck Institute Year Book*, 42 (1997), pp. 221–37.

Wenzel-Burchard, Gertrud, *Granny: Gerta Warburg und die Ihren: Hamburger Schicksale* (Hamburg: Christians, 1970).

Wolfsburg-Aviad, Oscar, *Die Drei-Gemeinde: Aus der Geschichte der jüdischen Gemeinden Altona, Hamburg, Wandsbek* (Munich: NER-Tamid Verlag, 1960).

Wulff, Birgit, *Arbeitslosigkeit und Arbeitsbeschaffungsmaßnahmen in Hamburg 1933–1939: Eine Untersuchung zur nationalsozialistischen Wirtschafts- und Sozialpolitik* (Frankfurt and elsewhere: Lang, 1987).

Wünsche, Viviane, Lohalm Uwe, and Zimmermann, Michael, *Die nationalsozialistische Verfolgung Hamburger Roma und Sinti* (Hamburg: Landeszentrale für politische Bildung, 2002).

Index

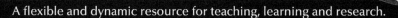